T0413299

INTERNATIONAL TRADE IN GOODS

Evidence from Transaction Data

Other Related Titles from World Scientific

International Trade, Capital Flows and Economic Development
  edited by Francisco L. Rivera-Batiz (Columbia University, USA) &
  Luis A. Rivera-Batiz (University of Puerto Rico, USA)

The Political Economy of International Trade
  edited by Edward D. Mansfield (University of Pennsylvania, USA)

International Trade: Theory, Evidence and Policy
  by Richard Pomfret (University of Adelaide, Australia
  & The Johns Hopkins University, Italy)

The Floating World: Issues in International Trade Theory
  by Wilfred J. Ethier (University of Pennsylvania, USA)

International Trade Policy Formation: Theory and Politics
  by Wolfgang Mayer (University of Cincinnati, USA)

INTERNATIONAL TRADE IN GOODS

Evidence from Transaction Data

Joachim Wagner

Leuphana University Lueneburg, Germany

 **World Scientific**

NEW JERSEY · LONDON · SINGAPORE · BEIJING · SHANGHAI · HONG KONG · TAIPEI · CHENNAI · TOKYO

Published by

World Scientific Publishing Co. Pte. Ltd.

5 Toh Tuck Link, Singapore 596224

USA office: 27 Warren Street, Suite 401-402, Hackensack, NJ 07601

UK office: 57 Shelton Street, Covent Garden, London WC2H 9HE

Library of Congress Cataloging-in-Publication Data
Names: Wagner, Joachim, 1954–   author.
Title: International trade in goods : evidence from transaction data /
     Joachim Wagner (Leuphana University Lueneburg, Germany).
Description: New Jersey : World Scientific, [2018]
Identifiers: LCCN 2018043880 | ISBN 9789813276970 (hc : alk. paper)
Subjects: LCSH: International trade. | Imports. | Exports.
Classification: LCC HF1379 .W339 2018 | DDC 382--dc23
LC record available at https://lccn.loc.gov/2018043880

British Library Cataloguing-in-Publication Data
A catalogue record for this book is available from the British Library.

For any available supplementary material, please visit
https://www.worldscientific.com/worldscibooks/10.1142/11175#t=suppl

Desk Editors: Anthony Alexander/Alisha Nguyen/Jiang Yulin

Typeset by Stallion Press
Email: enquiries@stallionpress.com

Printed in Singapore

About the Author

 **Joachim Wagner** (1954) studied economics at the University of Hannover (Germany) where he received his Diploma in 1979, his Doctoral degree in 1984, and his Habilitation in 1990. Since 1993 he is Professor of Economics at Leuphana University of Lüneburg (Germany). His main areas of research are international firm activities and applied microeconometrics. He is an editor of the *Journal of Economics and Statistics,* a co-editor of *Economics — The Open-Access Open-Assessment E-Journal* and the founding editor-in-chief of the *International Journal of Re-Views in Empirical Economics.* Joachim Wagner is a research fellow at IZA (Bonn, Germany) and CESIS (Stockholm, Sweden).

Acknowledgments

All chapters in this volume use data for export and import transactions of German firms that were prepared by the Federal Statistical Office of Germany (*Destatis*) and that are available in its Research Data Center. I thank Melanie Scheller from Destatis for preparing the data, for running a large number of Stata do-files for me over the years, and for checking the log-files with the results for any violation of privacy. Many papers included here combine transaction level data for exports and imports with data on firm characteristics from surveys conducted by the Statistical Offices of the German Federal States that are available in its Research Data Centers. I thank all staff members from the center in Berlin, and especially Ramona Voshage and Anja Malchin, for preparing the tailor-made data sets for me and for handling the many versions of my Stata do-files. Working with these highly confidential data by sending do-files to a Research Data Center and then waiting (often for long times) for output is no fun — but the chapters in this volume hopefully illustrate that it is well worth it.

Contents

Introduction: Transaction Level Data for Exports and Imports — A New Data Base for Microeconometric Studies on International Trade in Goods

When empirical trade economists realized that firms — not countries or industries — are the central actors in international trade, motivated by the pioneering study by Bernard and Jensen (1995) for the United States hundreds of studies looked at firm level data from countries all over the world to learn "Who trades?" and "Who trades how much?" The early papers in this literature focus on the questions "Who exports? What distinguishes exporters and non-exporters? How are exports linked to firm performance?" with a special view on the links between exports and productivity (see Wagner (2007) for a survey). Later on papers looked at "Who imports? What distinguishes importers and non-importers? How are imports linked to firm performance?" and the links between trade and other dimensions of firm performance besides productivity (including profitability, wages, and firm survival) were investigated (see Wager (2012a) for a survey).

In this literature the typical data set used is based on either census-type data collected regularly by official statistics or on large comprehensive surveys of firms from other sources. We learned a lot from these empirical studies, and this literature inspired a new branch of theory labeled *new new trade theory* with a focus on international activities of heterogeneous firms that was pioneered by Melitz (2003); see Melitz and Redding (2014) for a survey.

The next generation of empirical studies on foreign trade activities goes one step further by asking not only "Who trades how much?" but "Who trades how much of which goods (or services) with whom?" The data used are based on records of cross-border transaction regularly collected by the customs. The unit of observation in these data is a single transaction between economic agents located in two countries, e.g., the export of X tons of *good Y* with a value of Z Euro from country A to country B.

The record of the transaction usually includes a firm identifier (tax registration number) of the trading firm, and this allows the aggregation of transaction level information at the level of the trading firm to generate period-firm-product-value-weight-destination (or -origin) data. These data show who trades how much of which good with customers (or suppliers) from which country in a given period (a year, or a month). Products are distinguished according to very detailed classifications, and the recording of value and weight allows the easy calculation of unit values that act as proxy variables for prices or indicators of quality.

These transaction data can be linked over time to form longitudinal data. Furthermore, the data can be linked with data on firm characteristics (e.g., balance sheet data or data from surveys by statistical offices).

Compared with the census-type data used in the earlier literature these transaction-level based data allow the researcher to look not only at one extensive margin of trade (participation in exporting, or importing), but at two more extensive margins, the number of goods traded and the number of countries traded with. These margins, and their links with characteristics of the firm and dimensions of firm performance, are investigated in a new and rapidly emerging literature. Wagner (2016a) is a comprehensive survey of this literature; this paper is reprinted in this volume as Chapter 1.

Germany is number three among the exporters and importers in world merchandise trade (World Trade Organization, 2016, p. 94). International trade is important for the dynamics of the German economy as a whole, and in its regions and industries, in the short and in the long run. Reliable information on the causes and consequences of exports and imports, therefore, are important for analyses of the German economy. Over the last 25 years empirical studies on these issues were based more and more on firm level data. A typical paper in this literature used data collected in surveys by official statistics or others in local production units (establishments) or legal units (enterprises). This literature shed light on a number of important issues, including the characteristics of exporting and importing firms, the link between exports and wages, the role of international trade for profits of the firm, credit constraints and international trade, and trade and firm survival. Many of these papers are reprinted in Wagner (2016b).

For Germany transaction level data on exports and imports became available for researchers only recently. These data are collected by the customs (for trade with partners outside the European Union) or reported by the firms when trading with partners inside the EU (for the statistics on intra-EU trade). The data cover detailed information on the goods traded, its value, its weight, and the country of destination (for exports) or origin (for imports). Transaction level data that include information on the German firm involved in the transaction have been prepared by the Federal Statistical Office for the reporting years 2009 onwards.

Since 2012 these transaction data for German exports and imports of goods have been used in a number of empirical studies. This volume includes selected studies with these data that deal with nine topics: the extensive margins of trade in manufacturing firms (in Chapters 2 and 3); new evidence on the dynamics of trade in the short run (in Chapters 4 to 8); the links between productivity and the extensive margins of trade (in Chapters 9 to 12); the role of firm age for the extensive margins of trade (in Chapters 13 and 14); innovation activities (in Chapter 15); international trade and profits (in Chapters 16 to 18); distance and trade (in Chapters 19 to 22); and the lumpiness of international trade (in Chapters 23 and 24).[1]

References

Melitz, Marc (2003). The impact of trade on intra-industry reallocations and aggregate industry productivity. *Econometrica* 71 (6), 1695–1725.

Melitz, Marc and Stephen J. Redding (2014). Heterogeneous firms and trade. In: Gopinath, Elhanan Helpman, and Ken Rogoff (Eds.), *Handbook of International Economics.* Vol. 4, pp. 1–54. Gita. Amsterdam: Elsevier.

Raff, Horst and Joachim Wagner (2014). Foreign ownership and the extensive margins of exports: Evidence for manufacturing enterprises in Germany. *The World Economy* 37 (5), 579–591.

Wagner, Joachim (2007). Exports and productivity: A survey of the evidence from firm-level data. *The World Economy* 30 (1), 60–82.

Wagner, Joachim (2012a). International trade and firm performance: A survey of empirical studies since 2006. *Review of World Economics* 148 (2), 235–267.

Wagner, Joachim (2012b). German multiple-product, multiple destination exporters: Bernard-Redding-Schott under test. *Economics Bulletin* 32 (2), 1708–1714.

Wagner, Joachim (2015). Credit constraints and the extensive margins of exports: First evidence for German manufacturing. *Economics — The Open-Access, Open-Assessment E-Journal* 9 (2015–18), 1–17.

Wagner, Joachim (2016a). A survey of empirical studies using transaction level data on exports and imports. *Review of World Economics* 152 (1), 215–225.

Wagner, Joachim (2016b). Microeconometrics of international trade. *World Scientific Studies in International Economics 52.* Singapore *et al.*: World Scientific Publishing.

Wagner, Joachim (2017a). Intra-good trade in Germany: A first look at the evidence. *Applied Economics* 49 (57), 5753–5761.

Wagner, Joachim (2017b). Time zones and German exports: First evidence from firm-product level data. Mimeo.

---

[1] Studies with German transaction level data not reprinted in this volume include Raff and Wagner (2014) and Wagner (2012b; 2015; 2017a; 2017b; 2018a). For a comprehensive survey of papers that use transaction level data from Germany see Wagner (2018b).

Wagner, Joachim (2018a). Multiple import sourcing. First evidence for German enterprises from manufacturing industries. *Open Economies Review* 29 (1), 165–175.

Wagner, Joachim (2018b). Germany's trade in goods: A survey of the evidence from transaction data. *AStA Wirtschafts- und Sozialstatistisches Archiv* 12 (1), 69–82.

World Trade Organization (2016). World Trade Statistical Review 2016. Available at: https://www.wto.org/english/res_e/statis_e/wts2016_e/wts16_toc_e.htm.

Part 1
Literature Survey

Introduction

The introduction to this volume points out that in a new generation of microeconometric studies on foreign trade activities by firms transaction level data are used to investigate the extensive margins of exports and imports with respect to the number of goods traded and the number of countries traded with. A focus in this literature is on the links between these extensive margins, characteristics of the trading firms (like firm age and innovative activities) and various dimensions of firm performance (like productivity, profitability and firm survival).

These topics are investigated in a rapidly emerging literature. Chapter 1 (which was originally published in Wagner, 2016) is a survey of 147 empirical studies for 39 countries plus eight studies that cover multiple countries that use transaction level data on exports or imports of firms.[1] Important findings from these papers are summarized under seven topics that cover the role of "superstars" in trade; the average number of goods traded and countries traded with; the dynamics of trade in the short run; new insights on the links between firm characteristics and the extensive margins of trade; quality of traded goods and the number of goods and partner countries; evidence on hitherto undocumented

---

[1] See https://www.econstor.eu/bitstream/10419/126541/1/832102881.pdf, the working paper version of this paper, for a tabular survey of these empirical studies with details on countries covered, data used, topics dealt with, and a summary of important findings.

types of foreign trade activities; and econometric tests of implications of models of multi-product, multi-destination exporters.

Reference

Wagner, Joachim (2016). A survey of empirical studies using transaction level data on exports and imports. *Review of World Economics* 152 (1), 215–225.

Chapter 1

A Survey of Empirical Studies Using Transaction Level Data on Exports and Imports*

Abstract

This paper presents a tabular survey of 147 empirical studies for 39 countries, plus eight studies for multiple countries, that use transaction level data on exports or imports of firms. I hope this survey is useful for readers who want to get an impression of the huge number of different topics that have been investigated with transaction level data for a large number of countries already; who want to learn whether transaction level data have already been used for a particular (maybe, their own) country, by whom they have been used to investigate which topics, and what the important results found are; who have access to transaction level data and an idea how to use them, and who want to find out whether others pursued the same or a similar topic already; who want to compare results from their own study based on transaction level data to results from other (similar, neighbor) countries and who are looking for suitable studies; who have access to transaction level data and who are looking for studies based on data from other countries that they can replicate with their data to uncover and investigate differences across countries, or to contribute to the unraveling of stylized facts that hold across countries (and time).

Keywords: Transaction level data, exports, imports, literature survey.

*Originally Published in *Review of World Economics* (2016), 152 (1), 215–225.

1. Motivation

When economists discovered that trade is performed by firms, and not by countries or industries, following the pioneering empirical paper by Bernard and Jensen (1995) for the United States, hundreds of studies looked at firm level data from many different countries to investigate "Who trades?" and the closely related question "Who trades how much?" The focus of the early papers in this literature has been on "Who exports? What distinguishes exporters and non-exporters? How are exports linked to firm performance?" with a special view on the links between exports and productivity (see Wagner (2007) for a survey). Later the scope of studies on trade that use firm-level data widened to ask "Who imports? What distinguishes importers and non-importers? How are imports linked to firm performance?" and the links between trade and other dimensions of firm performance besides productivity (including profitability, wages, and firm survival) were investigated (see Wager (2012d) for a survey). In this literature a typical data set used is based on either census-type data collected regularly by official statistics or on large comprehensive surveys of firms from other sources. We learned a lot from these empirical studies, and this literature inspired a new branch of theory named the "new trade theory" with a focus on international activities of heterogeneous firms that was pioneered by Melitz (2003); see Melitz and Redding (2014) for a survey.

A new generation of empirical studies on foreign trade goes one step further by asking not only "Who trades how much?" but "Who trades how much of which goods (or services) with whom?" The data used in these studies are based on records of (legal) cross-border transaction regularly collected by the customs. The unit of observation in these data is a single transaction between economic agents located in two countries, e.g., the export of 15,234 tons of good A with a value of 124,756 Euro from Germany to China. The record of the transaction usually includes a firm identifier (tax registration number) of the exporting (or importing) firm. Using this identifier information at the transaction level can be aggregated at the level of the trading firm to generate period-firm-product-value-weight-destination (or -origin) data. These data show who trades how much of which good with customers (or suppliers) from which country in a given period (a year, or a month). Products are distinguished according to very detailed classifications, and the recording of value and weight allows the easy calculation of unit values that act as proxy variables for prices or indicators of quality. These transaction data can be linked over time to form panel data. Furthermore, the data can be linked to firm level data that has information on firm characteristics that is not included in the customs data, e.g., balance sheet data and data from regular surveys of the statistical offices.

Compared with the census-type data used in the earlier literature these transaction-level-based data allow the researcher to look not only at one extensive margin of trade (participation in exporting, or importing), but at two more extensive margins, the number of goods traded and the number of countries traded with. These margins, and their links with characteristics of the firm and dimensions of firm performance, are investigated in a new and rapidly emerging literature that is surveyed in this paper.

Findings of empirical studies are summarized under seven topics that cover the role of "superstars" in trade; the average number of goods traded and countries traded with; the dynamics of trade in the short run; new insights on the links between firm characteristics and the extensive margins of trade; quality of traded goods and the number of goods and partner countries; evidence on hitherto undocumented types of foreign trade activities; and econometric tests of implications of models of multi-product, multi-destination exporters.

I hope this survey is useful for readers who want to get an impression of the huge number of different topics that have been investigated with transaction level data for a large number of countries already; who want to learn whether transaction level data have already been used for a particular (maybe, their own) country, by whom they have been used to investigate which topics, and what the important results found are; who have access to transaction level data and an idea how to use them, and who want to find out whether others pursued the same or a similar topic already; who want to compare results from their own study based on transaction level data to results from other (similar, neighbor) countries and who are looking for suitable studies; who have access to transaction level data and who are looking for studies based on data from other countries that they can replicate with their data to uncover and investigate differences across countries, or to contribute to the unraveling of stylized facts that hold across countries (and time).

The rest of the paper is organized as follows. Section 2 presents a tabular synopsis of empirical studies by country, topic, and important findings. Section 3 comments on the lessons we learned from this new literature so far. Section 4 concludes with suggestions for future research.

2. Empirical Studies Using Transaction Level Data on Foreign Trade of Firms

The online-appendix to this paper includes a table with a tabular survey of 147 empirical studies for 39 countries plus eight studies that cover multiple countries, that use transaction level data on exports or imports of firms. This survey is limited in two ways. It covers only papers that are written in English, and that use data on cross-border transactions with detailed information on the products traded and the countries of destination or origin. While the first selection criterion is, hopefully, not too restrictive, the second might be considered to lead to an exclusion of important papers that look at *who trades, what, with whom* based on data from surveys of firms (like the papers by Lawless, 2009 or Iacovone and Javorcic, 2010) or on information derived from records of foreign trade activities that were matched to firm-level survey data (like in Castellani *et al.*, 2010). This focus of the survey, however, seems adequate given the now large number of papers that use "true" transaction level data from countries all over the world.

3. Lessons Learned

Empirical analyses that use transaction level data for exports and (to a much lesser extent) imports are available for a large number of countries from all over the world. While many papers deal with a singular, special topic, some cover common ground and uncover new results that can be considered as stylized facts that tend to hold over space and time. This section summarizes the findings of studies under seven topics that cover the role of "superstars" in trade; the average number of goods traded and countries traded with; the dynamics of trade in the short run; new insights on the links between firm characteristics and the extensive margins of trade; quality of traded goods and the number of goods and partner countries; evidence on hitherto undocumented types of foreign trade activities; and econometric tests of implications of models of multi-product, multi-destination exporters.

3.1. Exports and imports are dominated by "superstars" trading many goods with many countries

The top 1 percent of exporters — the so-called "export superstars" — tend to dominate exports, and to cover the lion's share of all exports. This fact is documented by Freund and Pierola (2012) for 32 countries based on data from the *World Bank Exporter Dynamics Database (EDD)*, and it is found in several other studies for countries not covered in the EDD (including Germany; see Wagner, 2012a). A similar high degree of concentration has been documented for importers in several countries, including Belgium (Muuls and Pisu, 2009), China (Manova and Zhang, 2009), Germany (Wagner, 2012a), Norway (Bernard *et al.*, 2014) and the United States (Bernard *et al.*, 2009a). These superstars trade many products with many countries of destination and origin.

3.2. Most firms trade a small number of goods with a small number of countries

While a few large firms trade a large number of goods with many countries, the bulk of firms export to and import from a small number of countries, and they trade a small number of goods only. This fact is documented for a number of countries, including Belgium (Muuls and Pisu, 2009), Denmark (Eriksson *et al.*, 2009), France (Eaton *et al.*, 2004), Germany (Wagner, 2012d), the United States (Bernard *et al.*, 2009a) and for Brazil, Chile, Denmark and Norway (Arkolakis and Muendler, 2013).

3.3. New evidence on the dynamics of trade in the short run

Transaction level data are used to document new facts on the dynamics of trade in the short run. Short-run dynamics of exports are dominated by the intensive margin; new exporters or firms that stop exporting are much less important for year-to-year changes in exports. Evidence on this is reported for Chile (Álvarez and Fuentes, 2011; Álvarez and Sáez, 2014), France (Bricogne *et al.*, 2010), Germany (Wagner, 2014f), Hungary (Muraközy, 2012), Portugal (Amador and Opromolla, 2010), Spain (De Lucio *et al.*, 2011), Turkey (Cebeci and Fernandes, 2015), United States (Bernard *et al.*, 2009b), and for 38 developing plus seven developed countries by Cebeci *et al.* (2012). Similar results for imports are available for several countries, including Argentina (Gopinath and Neiman, 2011), Germany (Wagner, 2013b) and Spain (De Lucio *et al.*, 2011).

Using data for Chile, Álvarez *et al.* (2010) report that an important fraction of firms start to export new products to new markets each year. Previous experience in exporting a certain product, or exporting to a certain market, increases the probability to export these products to new markets, or new products to the same markets. Again for Chile, Blum *et al.* (2013) find that one third of exporters enter into and exit from exporting multiple times, and that most continuing exporters enter and exit specific export destinations multiple times. Rahu (2015) report that in Estonia adding and dropping new products in exports is rife, about half of all firms change their export portfolio annually. Similarly, Buono and Fadinger (2012) find that export relationships are highly dynamic in France, where a large fraction is created and concluded each year. For Hungary, Békés and Muraközy (2012) report that about one third of firm-destination and about one half of firm-product-destination export spells are temporary only. Amador and Opromolla (2010) document frequent switching of products and destinations by firms. Similarly, Damijan *et al.* (2014) report that in Slovenia the average firm changes about one-quarter of imported and exported product-markets every year. For Spain, Esteve-Pérez *et al.* (2013) find that, while the firm export status is highly persistent, firms' destination portfolio is very dynamic with a median duration of firm-country exporting relationship of two years, but the risk of exiting sharply falls afterwards.

These findings based on transaction level data point to an enormous amount of heterogeneity in the short-run dynamics of exports that is hidden behind the veil of the more aggregate data used in earlier empirical investigations.

3.4. New insights on the links between firm characteristics and extensive margins of trade

Detailed information on the number of goods traded and the number of countries traded with reveal new insights on the links between firm characteristics and the extensive margins of trade. Cases in point include productivity, credit constraints, firm age, innovation, and profitability.

Productivity is not only positively related to export participation, but to the other extensive margins of exports (the number of goods exported, and the number of export destination countries), too. Evidence is reported in studies for a number of countries, including Belgium (Bernard *et al.*, 2014), Colombia (Casas *et al.*, 2015), Germany (Wagner, 2012c) and Sweden (Andersson *et al.*, 2008). Similar results are reported for imports to, among others, Belgium (Muuls and Pisu, 2009), Germany (Wagner, 2012c) and Sweden (Andersson *et al.*, 2008).

Note that although there is a strong positive link between productivity and the extensive margins of exports Wagner (2013a) reports that German low-productive exporters are not marginal exporters defined according to the number of goods exported or the number of countries exported to. These low-productive exporters are competitive because they export high-quality goods (Wagner, 2014e).

As regards credit constraints, it is well known that exporting firms are less financially constrained than non-exporting firms (see Wagner, 2014b) for a survey of the literature), and similar evidence is reported in the few studies that look at credit constraints and imports (see Wagner, 2015c). Using transaction level data for Belgium, Muuls (2015) reports that firms with lower credit constraints export more products and to a larger number of destinations, too, while this link shows up only for the number of products in imports. Manova *et al.* (2015) show that in China financial frictions restrict exporters' product scope, the number of export destinations, and the trade volume within each destination-product market. With German data Wagner (2015d) finds that credit constraints have a negative impact on both the number of goods exported and the number of export destination countries. In a companion paper Wagner (2014e) reports that a better credit rating score is positively related to the extensive margins of import;

firm with a better score import more goods and source from more countries of origin.

The positive link between firm age and participation in international trade has been documented before. Transaction level data shed new light on this issue. Bastos and Dias (2013) report that in Portugal the distribution of the number of export destinations and exported products shift progressively to the right with firm age. Similarly, Wagner (2015a; 2015b) shows that in Germany older firms export and import more different goods to and from more different countries.

It is well documented in the literature that innovative firms are more likely to export. Using transaction level data from Hungary Halpern and Muraközy (2012) show that innovative firms export more products to more countries, too. Wagner (2015e) reports comparable evidence for Germany.

The links between the extensive margins of trade and firm profitability have been investigated with transaction level data for German firms. Wagner (2014d) reports that profits tend to be larger in firms with less diversified export sales over goods and in firms with more diversified export sales over destination countries. As regards imports, profits are not higher in firms that import more goods and from more countries; the productivity advantages of importers with large extensive margins are eaten up by extra costs related to buying more goods in more countries.

3.5. Quality of traded goods and extensive margins of trade

Transaction level data usually have information on the value of a transaction and on the weight of the goods shipped. By dividing value and weight so-called unit values are computed. While unit values are not a perfect measure for the quality of traded goods, at least if the industry is controlled for at a detailed level of disaggregation, they serve as a suitable proxy variable. As Feenstra and Romalis (2014, p. 477) recently put it: "The unit values of internationally traded goods are heavily influenced by quality". These unit values have been used to investigate empirically the link between the quality of exported goods and the distance to destination countries. For Germany Wagner (2014a) finds that quality and distance to destination are not positively correlated. Wagner (2014g) reports that in Germany exporters of high-quality goods tend to use high-quality inputs, and they are more profitable (Wagner, 2014c).

As noted, unit values are only an indicator for the quality of the products traded. Two studies with data from France recently used the detailed information on the traded products from transaction level data to measure product quality more directly. Duvalaix-Treguer *et al.* (2015) look at firms that export cheese or cream. They merge the export transaction data with information from a list of firms and products concerned by protected designations of origin (PDO) to investigate the impact of the quality label on firms' export competitiveness in the cheese and cream industry. They find that PDO labeling has a positive impact on the number of destinations exported to. Martin and Mayneris (2015) merge transaction level data on exports with information from the Comité Colbert list of firms from the French luxury products sector to identify high-end variety exporters and to investigate the relation between quality and margins of exports. They report that high-end variety exporters do not export to more countries, but export to more distant destinations; in contrast to low-end exporters, distance has almost no effect on high-end variety export(er)s.

3.6. Evidence on the existence of hitherto undocumented types of trade activities

Transaction level data reveal the existence of types of trade activities that are hidden in the trade data collected in census-type firm level surveys. Bernard *et al.* (2010) document that a large majority of Belgian firms export products they do not produce — they are engaged in Carry-Along Trade (CAT). These CAT exports are concentrated in the largest and most productive firms. Empirical evidence for CAT is also reported by Abreha *et al.* (2013) for Denmark and by Lo Turco and Maggioni (2013) for Turkey. Damijan *et al.* (2013) find that in Slovenia on average 70 percent of all exporting firms engage in pass-on trade (POT), i.e., in simultaneous export and import of identical products. The use of POT is increasing in firm size, product diversification, multinational status, firm productivity and profitability.

3.7. Econometric tests of implications of models of multi-product, multi-destination exporters

While theoretical models of internationally trading firms usually consider firms that produce a single good that is exported or not, several models now investigate multi-product firms that may export many goods to many destinations. Bernard *et al.* (2011) develop a general equilibrium model of multi-product, multi-destination firms with heterogeneity in ability across firms and in product attributes within firms. They test core implications of this model with transaction level data from the United States. In line with the model they find that firms exporting many products also serve many export destinations and export more of a given product to a given destination. Wagner (2012a) takes this model to German transaction level data and, in line with the model, finds that the number of products exported and the number of export destinations are positively and statistically highly significantly related with total exports, exports of the largest product across all markets, and productivity.

This illustrates that transaction level data have the potential to serve as a data base for econometric tests of implications of multi-product models. Furthermore, stylized facts revealed by working with transaction level trade data can inspire theoreticians to build models that fit these newly revealed facts.

3.8. Final remarks

Results from several empirical studies that are summarized in this section demonstrate that transaction level data on exports and imports should be considered as a highly useful addition to the box of tools of trade economists. Many studies illustrate that the value of these data for research can be increased substantially when they are augmented by information on firm characteristics that are not recorded by the customs, including balance sheet data and data from regular surveys by the statistical offices.

4. Two Suggestions for Future Research

The empirical trade literature based on transaction level data grew exponentially over the recent years, and we learned a lot from these papers. However, there is plenty of scope for future research.

First and foremost, we do know much less about the extensive margins of imports, its determinants, and its role in the dynamics of trade, than about the respective margins of exports. Here, evidence for more countries is most welcome. It would be great if a project that is comparable to the *World Bank Exporter Dynamics Database* (Cebeci *et al.*, 2012) could be realized for imports, too.

Second, many results reported in the literature refer to a single country, or to a very small number of countries, only. This offers plenty of opportunities for replication studies, keeping in mind that "the credibility of a new finding that is based on carefully analyzing two data sets is far more than twice that of a result based only on one" (Hamermesh, 2000, p. 376). Hopefully, this survey is helpful to guide interested researchers here.

References

Abreha, Kaleb Girma, Valérie Smeets and Frédéric Warzynsky (2013). Coping with the crisis: Recent evolution in Danish firms' International trade involvement, 2000–2010. *Aarhus University Economics Working Papers*, No. 2013–15.

Álvarez, Roberto, Hasan Faruq and Ricardo A. López (2010). Is previous export experience important for new exports? *Central Bank of Chile Working Paper*, No. 599.

Álvarez, Roberto and J. Rodrigo Fuentes (2011). Entry into export markets and product qualtiy. *The World Economy* 34, 1237–1262.

Álvarez, Roberto and Camila Sáez (2014). Post financial crisis and exports expansion: Micro-evidence from Chilean exporters. *MPRA Munich Personal RePEc Archive Paper* 60637.

Amador, Joao and Luca David Opromolla (2010). The Margins of exports: Firms, products and destinations. *Economics Bulletin (Banco de Portugal)*, Spring, 103–119.

Andersson, Martin, Hans Lööf and Sara Johansson (2008). Productivity and international trade: Firm level evidence from a small open economy. *Review of World Economics/Weltwirtschaftliches Archiv* 144 (4), 776–801.

Arkolakis, Costas and Marc-Andreas Muendler (2013). Exporters and their products: A collection of empirical regularities. *CESifo Economic Studies* 59 (2), 223–248.

Bastos, Paulo and Daniel A. Dias (2013). The life cycle of exporting firms. *Mimeo.*

Békés, Gábor and Balázs Muraközy (2012): Temporary trade and heterogeneous firms. *Journal of International Economics* 87, 232–246.

Bernard, Andrew B. and Bradford Jensen (1995). Exporters, jobs, and wages in U.S. manufacturing: 1976–1987. *Brookings Papers on Economic Activity, Microeconomics* 1, 67–119.

Bernard, Andrew B. Bradford Jensen and Peter K. Schott (2009a). Importers, exporters, and multinationals. A portrait of firms in the U.S. that trade goods. In: Timothy Dunne, J. Bradford Jensen, and Mark J. Roberts (Eds.), *Producer Dynamics. New Evidence from Micro Data.* Chicago and London: University of Chicago Press, pp. 513–555.

Bernard, Andrew, Bradford Jensen, Stephen J. Redding and Peter K. Schott (2009b). The margins of U.S. trade. *American Economic Review Papers & Proceedings* 99 (2), 487–493.

Bernard, Andrew, Andreas Moxnes and Karen Helene Ulltveit-Moe (2014). Two-sided heterogeneity and trade. *National Bureau of Economic Research NBER Working Paper,* No. 20136.

Bernard, Andrew, Stephen Redding and Peter K. Schott (2011). Multiproduct firms and trade liberalization. *Quarterly Journal of Economics* 126 (3), 1271–1318.

Bernard, Andrew, Ilke Van Beveren and Hylke Vandenbussche (2010). Multiproduct exporters, carry-along trade and the margins of trade. *National Bank of Belgium NBB Working Paper Series,* No. 203.

Bernard, Andrew, Ilke Van Beveren and Hylke Vandenbussche (2014). Multiproduct exporters and the margins of trade. *Japanese Economic Review* 65 (2), 142–157.

Blum, Bernardo, Sebastian Claro and Ignatius J. Horstmann (2013). Occasional and perennial exporters. *Journal of International Economics* 90 (1), 65–74.

Bricogne, Jean-Charles, Lionel Fontagné, Guillaume Gaulier, Daria Taglioni and Vincent Vicard (2010). Exports and sectoral financial dependence. evidence on French firms during the Great Global Crisis. *European Central Bank Working Paper Series,* No. 1227.

Buono, Ines and Harald Fadinger (2012). The micro dynamics of exporting: Evidence from French firms. *Banca D'Italia Temi di Discussione* Number 880.

Casas, Camila, Federico J. Díez and Alejandra González (2015). Productivity and export market participation: Evidence from Colombia. *Banco de la Republica Colombia, Borradores de Economía* Núm 876.

Castellani, Davide, Francesco Serti and Chiara Tomasi (2010). Firms in international trade: Importers' and exporters' Heterogeneity in Italian manufacturing industry. *The World Economy* 33 (3), 424–457.

Cebeci, Tolga and Ana M. Fernandes (2015). Microdynamics of Turkey's export boom in the 2000s. *The World Economy* 38 (5), 825–855.

Cebeci, Tolga, Ana M. Fernandes, Caroline Freund and Matha Denisse Pierola (2012). Exporter dynamics database. *World Bank Policy Research Working Paper*, No. 6229.

Damijan, Joze, Jozef Konings and Saso Polanec (2013). Pass-on trade: Why do firms simultaneously engage in two-way trade in the same varieties? *Review of World Economics/Weltwirtschaftliches Archiv* 149 (1), 85–111.

Damijan, Joze, Jozef Konings and Saso Polanec (2014). Import churning and export performance of multi-product firms. *The World Economy* 37 (11), 1483–1506.

De Lucio, Juan, Raúl Minguez-Fuentes, Asier Minondo and Francisco Requena-Silvente (2011). The extensive and intensive margins of Spanish trade. *International Review of Applied Economics* 25 (5), 615–631.

Duvalaix-Treguer, Sabine, Charlotte Emlinger, Carl Gaigne and Karine Latouche (2015). Quality and export performance: Evidence from cheese industry. *Mimeo*

Eaton, Jonathan, Samuel Kortum and Francis Kramarz (2004). Dissecting Trade: firms, industries, and export destinations. *American Economic Review Papers & Proceedings* 94 (2), 150–154.

Eriksson, Tor, Valérie Smeets and Frédéric Warzynski (2009). Small open economy firms in international trade: Evidence from Danish transactions-level data. *Aarhus University Department of Economics Working Paper*, No. 09–7.

Esteve-Pérez, Silviano, Francisco Requena-Silvente and Vincente J. Pallardó-Lopez (2013). The duration of firm-destination export relationships: Evidence from Spain, 1997–2006. *Economic Inquiry* 51 (1), 159–180.

Feenstra, Robert and John Romalis (2014). International prices and endogenous quality. *Quarterly Journal of Economics* 129 (2), 477–527.

Freund, Caroline and Martha Denisse Pierola (2012). Export superstars. *The World Bank Policy Research Working Paper*, No. 6222.

Gopinath, Gita and Brent Neiman (2011). Trade adjustment and productivity in large crises. *National Bureau of Economic Research NBER Working Paper Series*, No. 16958.

Halpern, László and Balázs Muraközy (2012). Innovation, productivity and exports: The case of Hungary. *Economics of Innovation and New Technology* 21 (2), 151–173.

Hamermesh, Daniel (2000). The craft of labor metrics. *Industrial and Labor Relations Review* 53 (3), 363–380.

Iacovone, Leonardo and Beata S. Javorcik (2010). Multi-product exporter: Product churning, uncertainty and export discoveries. *Economic Journal* 120 (May), 481–499.

Lawless, Martina (2009). Firm export dynamics and the geography of trade. *Journal of International Economics* 77 (2), 245–254.

Lo Turco, Alessia and Daniela Maggioni (2013). CAT Exports in Turkish Manufacturing. Mimeo. Universitá Politecnica della Marche, Department of Economics and Social Sciences, Ancona.

Manova, Kalina, Shang-Jin Wei and Zhiwei Zhang (2015). Firm exports and multinational activity under credit constraints. *Review of Economics and Statistics* 97 (3), 574–588.

Manova, Kalina and Zhiwei Zhang (2009). China's exporters and importers: Firms, products and trade partners. *National Bureau of Economic Research NBER Working Paper Series*, No. 15249.

Martin, Julien and Florian Mayneris (2015). High-end variety exporters defying gravity: Micro facts and aggregate implications. *Journal of International Economics* 96 (1), 55–71.

Melitz, Marc (2003). The impact of trade on intra-industry reallocations and aggregate industry productivity. *Econometrica* 71 (6), 1695–1725.

Melitz, Marc and Stephen J. Redding (2014). Heterogeneous firms and trade. In: Gita Gopinath, Elhanan Helpman, and Ken Rogoff (Eds.), *Handbook of International Economics*, Vol. 4, pp. 1–54. Amsterdam: Elsevier.

Muraközy, Balázs (2012). Margins of Hungarian exports during crisis. *EFIGE Working Papers* 53.

Muuls, Mirabelle (2015). Exporters, importers and credit constraints. *Journal of International Economics* 95 (2), 333–343.

Muuls, Mirabelle and Mauro Pisu (2009). Imports and exports at the level of the firm: Evidence from Belgium. *The World Economy* 32 (5), 692–734.

Rahu, Siim (2015). The Role of uncertainty for export survival: Evidence from Estonia. *The University of Tartu FEBA Working Paper*.

Wagner, Joachim (2007). Exports and productivity: A survey of the evidence from firm-level data. *The World Economy* 30 (1), 60–82.

Wagner, Joachim (2012a). German multiple-product, multiple destination exporters: Bernard-Redding-Schott under test. *Economics Bulletin* 32 (2), 1708–1714.

Wagner, Joachim (2012b). International trade and firm performance: A survey of empirical studies since 2006. *Review of World Economics/Weltwirtschaftliches Archiv* 148 (2), 235–267.

Wagner, Joachim (2012c). Productivity and the extensive margins of trade in German manufacturing firms: Evidence from a non-parametric test. *Economics Bulletin* 32 (4), 3061–3070.

Wagner, Joachim (2012d). Trading many goods with many countries: Exporters and Importers from German manufacturing industries. *Review of Economics* 63 (2), 170–186.

Wagner, Joachim (2013a). Are low-productive exporters marginal exporters? Evidence from Germany. *Economics Bulletin* 33 (1), 467–481.

Wagner, Joachim (2013b). Extensive margins of imports in the great import recovery in Germany, 2009/2010. *Economics Bulletin* 33 (4), 2732–2743.

Wagner, Joachim (2014a). A note on quality of a firm's exports and distance to destination countries. First evidence from German. *Working Paper Series in Economics*, No. 302, University of Lüneburg.

Wagner, Joachim (2014b). Credit constraints and exports: A survey of empirical studies using firm-level data. *Industrial and Corporate Change* 23 (6), 1477–1492.

Wagner, Joachim (2014c). Exports and firm profitability: Quality matters! *Economics Bulletin* 34 (3), 1644–1652.

Wagner, Joachim (2014d). Is export diversification good for profitability? First evidence for manufacturing enterprises in Germany. *Applied Economics* 46 (33), 4083–4090.

Wagner, Joachim (2014e). Low-productive exporters are high-quality exporters. Evidence from Germany. *Economics Bulletin* 34 (2), 745–756.

Wagner, Joachim (2014f). The role of extensive margins of exports in The Great Export Recovery in Germany, 2009/2010. *Jahrbücher für Nationalökonomie und Statistik/Journal of Economics and Statistics* 234 (4), 518–526.

Wagner, Joachim (2014g). What makes a high-quality exporter? Evidence from Germany. *Economics Bulletin* 34 (2), 865–874.

Wagner, Joachim (2015a). A note on firm age and the margins of imports: First evidence from Germany. *Applied Economics Letters* 22 (9), 679–682.

Wagner, Joachim (2015b). A note on firm age and the margins of exports: First evidence from Germany. *The International Trade Journal* 29 (2), 93–102.

Wagner, Joachim (2015c). Credit constraints and margins of import: First evidence for German manufacturing enterprises. *Applied Economics* 47 (5), 415–430.

Wagner, Joachim (2015d). Credit constraints and the extensive margins of exports: First evidence for German manufacturing. *Working Paper Series in Economics*, No. 336, University of Lüneburg.

Wagner, Joachim (2015e). R&D activities and extensive margins of exports in manufacturing enterprises: First evidence for Germany. *Working Paper Series in Economics*, No. 343, University of Lüneburg.

Part 2

Extensive Margins
of Trade in
Manufacturing Firms

Introduction

Compared with the census-type data used in the earlier literature on the microeconometrics of international trade the newly available transaction-level data allow the researcher to look not only at one extensive margin of trade (participation in exporting, or importing), but at two more extensive margins, the number of goods traded and the number of countries traded with. These margins, and their links with characteristics of the firm and dimensions of firm performance, are investigated using data from a large number of countries in a new and rapidly emerging literature that is surveyed in Chapter 1.

The two papers in Part 2 of this volume report new facts on the extensive margins of trade in Germany, one of the leading actors on the international markets for goods. Chapter 2 (which was originally published in Wagner, 2018) uses data for more than 160 million export and import transactions by German firms from 2009 to 2012 to document the decisive role of multi-market traders that are active on many foreign markets, where a market is defined as a combination of a good traded and a country traded with. Using merged information from trade transactions and from surveys conducted by the statistical offices it shows that the number of foreign markets a firm is active on is higher in firms that are larger, older and foreign owned and that have higher labor productivity, human capital intensity and R&D intensity. These findings are in line with hypotheses that are derived from the literature on the links between firm characteristics and the extensive margins of foreign trade.

In Chapter 3 (which was originally published in Wagner, 2016) differences in extensive and intensive margins of exports in manufacturing firms from West Germany and from the former communist East Germany are investigated. Extensive margins do still differ in 2010, 20 years after the re-unification of Germany. West German firms outperform East German firms at all four margins of exports — they have a larger propensity to export, export a larger share of total sales, export more goods and export to a larger number of countries. All these differences are large from an economic point of view. A decomposition analysis shows that a large part of these differences can be explained by differences in firm characteristics.

References

Wagner, Joachim (2016). Still different after all these years. Extensive and intensive margins of exports in East and West German manufacturing enterprises. *Journal of Economics and Statistics* 236 (2), 297–322.

Wagner, Joachim (2018). Active on many foreign markets. A portrait of German multi-market exporters and importers from manufacturing industries. *Journal of Economics and Statistics* 238 (2), 157–182.

Chapter 2

Active on Many Foreign Markets: A Portrait of German Multi-market Exporters and Importers from Manufacturing Industries*

Abstract

This paper uses information on more than 160 million export and import transactions by German firms from 2009 to 2012 to document the decisive role of multi-market traders that are active on many foreign markets, where a market is defined as a combination of a good traded and a country traded with. Using merged information from trade transactions and from surveys conducted by the statistical offices it is shown that, controlling for detailed industry affiliation, the number of foreign markets a firm from manufacturing industries is active on as an exporter or importer is higher in firms that are larger, older and foreign owned and that have higher labor productivity, human capital intensity and R&D intensity. With the exception of labor productivity these results are valid

*Originally Published in *Journal of Economics and Statistics* (2018), 238 (2), 157–182. Keynote for AFiD-Workshop, Berlin, March 29–30, 2017. I thank two reviewers for helpful comments on an earlier version. All computations were done at the research data centers of the Federal Statistical Office in Wiesbaden and the Statistical Office Berlin-Brandenburg in Berlin. The transaction level data and firm level data used are strictly confidential but not exclusive, see www.forschungsdatenzentrum.de for access. To facilitate replication the Stata do-files used are available from the author on request.

ceteris paribus, too. All these results from a descriptive empirical investigation are in line with hypotheses that are derived from the literature on the links between firm characteristics and the extensive margins of foreign trade.

Keywords: Exports, Imports, Transaction level data, Germany.

1. Motivation

Germany is number three among the exporters and importers in world merchandise trade (World Trade Organization, 2016, p. 94). International trade is important for the dynamics of the German economy as a whole, and in its regions and industries, in the short and in the long run. Reliable information on the causes and consequences of exports and imports, therefore, are important for analyses of the German economy. Over the last 25 years empirical studies on these issues were based more and more on data from the actors on the world market for goods — the internationally trading firms. A typical paper in this literature uses data collected in surveys by official statistics or others in local production units (establishments) or legal units (enterprises). This literature is seriously limited in two ways:

The studies focus on exports (see Wagner, 2011a for a survey). Due to lack of information on imports in the surveys only a few papers deal with imports. Here, only the importer status of a firm is inferred from turnover tax data, and no information on the quantity of imports or any other details can be used (see Vogel and Wagner, 2010 and Wagner, 2012a, 2013).

The papers focus on which firms export how much. Due to missing information on other extensive margins of trade these studies do neither deal with the goods traded nor with the countries traded with. An exception is the distinction of exports to the Euro-zone vs. exports outside the Euro-zone in Wagner (2007a) and in Verardi and Wagner (2012).

Recently, new data on international trade in goods by German firms became available that overcome both limitations. These data are based on transaction level data collected by the customs (for trade with partners outside the European Union) or reported by the firms when trading with partners inside the EU (for the statistics on intra-EU trade). The data cover detailed information on the goods traded, its value, its weight, and the country of destination (for exports) or origin (for imports). In short, the data do not only show "who trades and how much", but also "who trades how much of which goods of which value and which weight with firms from which countries". Furthermore, this information is available not only for firms from manufacturing industries, but for firms from all parts of the economy.

Transaction level data that include information on the German firm involved in the transaction have been prepared by the Federal Statistical Office for the reporting years 2009 onwards. These data, however, do not contain any information on characteristics of these firms (e.g., its size, age, productivity, or innovative activities) that can be expected to be related to the margins of exports and imports.

A way out is to use the firm identifier that is included in the transaction level data to link these data with information from other sources, including surveys conducted by official statistics that use the same firm identifier. Merged data of this type have been used in a number of studies that shed light on various aspects of Germany's trade in goods for the first time.[1]

However, hitherto studies only looked at either the number of countries traded with or at the number of goods traded, one at a time. But exporting to, say, five countries the same good or exporting to five countries several different goods obviously makes a difference — in both cases, however, the extensive margin "number of countries exported to" is the same. The same reasoning applies to the extensive margin "number of goods exported" — it makes a difference whether five different goods are exported to one country only or whether some of them are exported to several countries.

This paper contributes to the literature by not looking at the number of countries traded with and the number of goods traded separately but by looking at the number of markets a trading firm is active on, where a market is defined as the combination of one traded good and one country traded with.

The rest of the paper is organized as follows. Section 2 introduces the transaction level data for German exports and imports of goods, reports

---

[1] See Wagner (2016) for a survey of the literature (including studies with data for Germany) that uses transaction level data on exports and imports of goods.

basic facts on the number of markets the exporting and importing firms are active on, and documents the decisive role of multi-market traders. Section 3 derives six empirical hypotheses on the links between firm characteristics and the number of foreign markets a firm is active on as an exporter or importer and reports results from an econometric investigation of these hypotheses. It should be pointed out that the empirical models used here cannot reveal any causal relationships, because the data at hand are not rich enough to estimate structural empirical models. Results, therefore, do only indicate correlations between the number of foreign markets a firm is active on and firm characteristics while controlling for industry affiliation. Section 4 concludes.

2. German Multi-market Exporters and Importers: Basic Facts

How important are firms that trade many goods on many foreign markets for German exports and imports as a whole? To the best of my knowledge, an answer to this basic question cannot be found in publications from official statistics (or elsewhere). The data that are needed to reveal it, however, are available, and these data are used here to document basic facts on the role of multi-market traders in Germany's foreign trade.

In Germany information on goods[2] traded across borders and on the countries traded with is available from the statistic on foreign trade (*Außenhandelsstatistik*). This statistic is based on two sources. One source is the reports by German firms on transactions with firms from countries that are members of the European Union (EU); these reports are used to compile the so-called *Intrahandelsstatistik* on intra-EU trade. The other source is transaction-level data collected by the customs on trade with countries outside the EU (the so-called *Extrahandelsstatistik*).[3] The raw

---

[2] Note that in Germany information on international trade in services is compiled by the German Central Bank (*Deutsche Bundesbank*) to build the balance of services trade (*Dienstleistungsbilanz*).

[3] Note that firms with a value of trade with EU-countries that did not exceed 400,000 Euro in the previous year or in the current year per direction of trade do not have to report to the statistic on intra-EU trade. For trade with firms from non-member countries all transactions

data that is used to build the statistic on foreign trade are transaction level data, i.e., they relate to one transaction of a German firm with a firm located outside Germany at a time. Published data from this statistic report exports and imports aggregated at the level of goods traded and by country of origin.

The data used in this section are based on the raw data at the transaction level. The unit of observation in these raw data is a single transaction between economic agents located in two countries, e.g., the import of X kilogram of *good A* with a value of Y Euro from China to Germany.[4] For a given year, the sum over all transactions is identical to the figures published by the Federal Statistical Office for total exports or imports of Germany.

The record of the transaction usually includes a firm identifier (tax registration number) of the trading German firm. Using this identifier information at the transaction level was aggregated at the level of the trading firm for the reporting years 2009–2012.[5] These data show which firm trades how much of which good with firms from which country. Products are distinguished according to very detailed classifications. In the data used for this paper, the Harmonized System at 6-digit level (HS6) is used as the product classification system.

In this paper, a *market* is defined as a combination of a HS6-good and a country of destination (for exports) or a country of origin (for imports).

For the reporting years 2009 to 2012 the transaction level data at the firm-product-country level were used to compute for each year the number of exporting or importing firms, the shares of the largest 3, 50 and 100 traders in total trade, the number of markets served by exporters and importers on average and at selected percentiles of the size distribution, and the share of traders with the 3, 50 and 100 largest numbers of markets in total trade.

---

that exceed 1,000 Euro (or have a weight that exceeds 1,000 kilogram) are registered. For details see Statistisches Bundesamt, Qualitätsbericht Außenhandel, January 2011.

[4] Transaction level data of this type have been used in numerous empirical studies on international trade for many countries in recent years; see Wagner (2016) for a survey.

[5] Note that the firm identifier is missing for 956,775 out of 117,746,292 export transactions and for 527,176 out of 44,496,776 import transactions for various reasons including traders that do not have a (German) tax identification number; further details were not revealed to me.

Table 1: Exporters in Germany, 2009–2012.

	2009	2010	2011	2012
No. of exporters	97,270	110,111	120,559	121,972
No. of markets served by exporters				
Mean	65.37	66.09	64.32	66.94
p1	1	1	1	1
p50	7	6	6	6
p99	1,036	1,074	1,054	1,096
Exporters with 3 largest no. of markets	30,502	31,453	32,544	23,802
Exporters with 50 largest no. of markets	7,857	8,574	8,292	8,749
Exporters with 100 largest no. of markets	5,840	5,925	6,269	6,444
Share of largest exporters in total exports				
Largest 3 exporters (%)	11.08	11.78	12.31	12.52
Largest 50 exporters (%)	34.09	34.02	33.97	34.46
Largest 100 exporters (%)	40.56	40.03	39.96	40.65
Share of exporters with largest number of markets in total exports				
Exporters with 3 largest no. of markets	8.32	8.58	8.67	8.90
Exporters with 50 largest no. of markets	21.15	22.65	23.11	23.46
Exporters with 100 largest no. of markets	29.93	28.47	29.47	29.18

Note: Exporters refer to exporters of goods. p1, p50 and p99 are the 1st, 50th and 99th percentile of the distribution of the number of markets, where a market is the combination of a HS6-good and a country of destination of exports. The minimum and maximum share/number of markets is confidential because these figures (may) refer to a single firm.

Results are reported in Table 1 for exports and in Table 2 for imports. To start with exports, we see that exports tend to be highly concentrated in the largest exporting firms. While there are 100,000 and more exporting firms, the largest three exporters cover more than ten percent of total

Table 2: Importers in Germany, 2009–2012.

	2009	2010	2011	2012
No. of importers	115,383	126,457	141,134	140,082
No. of markets served by importers				
Mean	25.84	25.54	24.72	25.68
p1	1	1	1	1
p50	6	6	5	5
p99	301	307	299	310
Importers with 3 largest no. of markets	2,497	2,513	2,596	2,736
Importers with 50 largest no. of markets	1,933	1,835	1,814	1,832
Importers with 100 largest no. of markets	1,322	1,257	1,380	1,396
Share of largest importers in total imports				
Largest 3 importers (%)	6.84	6.82	6.40	6.74
Largest 50 importers (%)	28.06	29.16	30.09	31.00
Largest 100 importers (%)	35.13	36.29	37.29	38.22
Share of importers with largest number of markets in total imports				
Importers with 3 largest no. of markets	0.10	0.13	0.10	0.13
Importers with 50 largest no. of markets	16.51	15.66	15.58	14.36
Importers with 100 largest no. of markets	19.85	18.04	18.14	17.52

Note: Importers refer to importers of goods. p1, p50 and p99 are the 1st, 50th and 99th percentile of the distribution of the number of markets, where a market is the combination of a HS6-good and a country of origin of imports. The minimum and maximum share/number of markets is confidential because these figures (may) refer to a single firm.

exports, the largest 50 exporters contribute more than a third of all exports, and the share of the largest 100 exporters is 40 percent. On average, the exporting firms serve more than 60 different markets. The bulk of firms is active on a much smaller number of export markets — the median value is six markets in 2010 to 2012. Some firms, however, export to a much larger number of markets. Firms from the top one percent of the distribution of the number of markets export to more than 1,000 different markets, where exporters with the very largest number of markets served cover many thousand export markets. Multi-market exporters play a decisive role for exports as a whole — the share of exporters with the 100 largest numbers of markets is 30 percent of total exports.

The big picture for imports documented in Table 2 is similar to the one for exports. Imports tend to be highly concentrated in the largest importing firms. While there are 115,000 to 140,000 importing firms, the largest three importers cover more than six percent of total imports, the largest 50 importers contribute more than a quarter of all imports, and the share of the largest 100 importers is more than a third. On average, the importing firms source from 25 different markets. The bulk of firms is active on a much smaller number of import markets — the median value is five or six markets in the years covered. Some firms, however, import from a much larger number of markets. Firms from the top one percent of the distribution of the number of markets import from more than 300 different markets, where importers with the very largest number of markets sourced cover 2,500 import markets. Multi-market importers play a decisive role for imports as a whole — the share of importers with the 100 largest numbers of markets is about one fifth of total imports.

The bottom line, then, is that in Germany the bulk of exporters and importers of goods is active on a small number of markets (defined as a combination of a HS6-good and a country of destination or origin) only, but that multi-market traders are responsible for the lion's share of foreign trade.

3. Characteristics of German Multi-market Traders

Using information on more than 160 million export and import transactions from 2009 to 2012 by German firms it was documented in Section 2 that the lion's share of foreign trade is due to firms that are active on many foreign markets (defined as a combination of a HS6-good and a foreign country). This section looks at the characteristics of these multi-market exporters and importers.

3.1. Data

The transaction level data on exports and imports does not include any information on the characteristics of the trading firms. However, the firm identifier that comes with this data can be used to merge the information on foreign trade activities at the firm level with information collected on these firms in other surveys. The empirical investigation here uses a tailor-made data set that combines information on the number of markets a firm exported to or imported from with information from high quality firm-level data from three other official sources.

The first source of firm level information is the regular survey of establishments from manufacturing industries by the Statistical Offices of the German federal states. The survey (known as the *Monatsbericht,* or monthly report) covers all establishments from manufacturing industries that employ at least twenty persons in the local production unit or in the company that owns the unit. Participation of firms in the survey is mandated in official statistics (see Malchin and Voshage, 2009 for details). For this study the monthly establishment data were aggregated to annual data and at the enterprise level to match the unit of observation in the other data sources (described below).[6] The use of the enterprise (the legal unit) instead of the establishment (the local production unit) as the unit of analysis is mandated by the use of the enterprise as the unit of observation in the other data sources used in this study. It seems appropriate here because decisions about export activities are taken at the enterprise level, taking the characteristics of all establishments in a multi-establishment enterprise into account.

The second source of data is the cost structure survey for enterprises in the manufacturing sector. This survey is carried out annually as a

---

[6] Note that beginning with reporting year 2007 firms with more than 20 but less than 50 persons no longer have to report to the *Monatsbericht.* However, these firms have to report information on total sales, exports, number of employees and the sum of wages and salaries paid in the so-called *Jahresbericht* (the annual report), and this information is added to the data set used here.

representative random sample survey in about 15,000 firms. The sample is stratified according to the number of employees and the industries; all firms with 500 and more employees are covered by the cost structure survey (see Fritsch *et al.*, 2004).[7]

The third source of data is the enterprise register system (*Unternehmensregister-System*) that is used to link information from the transaction level data on foreign trade with firm level data collected in the surveys by the statistical offices. With these linked data sets it is possible to investigate the role of firm characteristics for the number of foreign markets a firm is active on for firms from manufacturing industries (that are covered in the surveys).

3.2. Empirical hypotheses

Building on the literature on the links between firm characteristics and the extensive margins of foreign trade the empirical investigation tests for the correlation between the numbers of foreign markets that firms are active on in exporting or importing and the following firm characteristics.

Firm size: A positive link between firm size and margins of foreign trade qualifies as a stylized fact. This positive link is due to fixed costs of exporting and importing. Larger firms have efficiency advantages due to scale economies, advantages of specialization in management and better conditions on the markets for inputs. Large firms can be expected to have cost advantages on credit markets while small firms often face higher restrictions on the capital market leading to a higher risk of insolvency and illiquidity. Furthermore, there might be disadvantages of small firms in the competition for highly qualified employees. There are limits to the advantage of size, because coordination costs mount as the scale of operations increases, and at some point any further expansion might cease to be profitable. Therefore, a positive relationship between firm size and foreign trade, at least up to a point, is expected. For Germany empirical evidence in line with this is reported in a number of studies (see Wagner, 2011a for a survey). Firm size is measured here by the number of employees in a firm

---

[7]Data from the *monthly report*, the *annual report* and the *cost structure survey* are part of a combined data set known as the *AFiD Panel*; see Malchin and Voshage (2009) for details.

(also included in squares to take care of non-linearity). The source of information on the number of employees is the cost structure survey.

Labor productivity: The positive link between exports and productivity qualifies as a stylized fact that has been documented in hundreds of studies for countries from all over the world (see Wagner, 2007) for a survey). According to findings from this literature an important reason for the positive productivity differential between exporters and non-exporters is self-selection of more productive plants on export markets. Furthermore, there is evidence for a market driven selection process in which exporters that have low productivity fail as a successful exporter, while only those that are more productive continue to export. The reason for this is that there exist additional costs of selling goods in foreign countries. The range of extra costs include transportation costs, distribution or marketing costs, or production costs in modifying current domestic products for foreign consumption. This implies that firms that export to a larger number of foreign markets and a larger number of different goods have to be more productive, because at least some of the extra costs mentioned (e.g., preparing a user's manual in another language, or checking the relevant national laws) recur for each foreign market served and for each good exported. Vogel and Wagner (2010) show that similar arguments can be made with regard to imports and productivity. Empirical evidence for Germany reported in Wagner (2012b) is fully in line with this.

Labor productivity is measured here by value added per employee; the information on sales and costs used in the computation of this productivity variable are taken from the cost structure survey.[8]

Human capital intensity: Given that Germany is relatively rich in human capital, firms that use human capital intensively can be expected to have a comparative advantage on international markets. Empirical studies find that the qualification of the workforce is an important factor for the international competitiveness of German firms (Wagner, 2011b). Human capital intensity is measured here by the average wage per employee. Direct information on the qualification of the employees in a firm is not available in the

---

[8] Note that the data used has no information on the capital stock of the firms, so more elaborate measures of productivity like total factor productivity cannot be computed.

data used in this study, but Wagner (2012c) demonstrates that the average wage is indeed a good proxy variable for the qualification of the workforce in German manufacturing firms. The source for information on the amount of wages paid and the number of employees is the cost structure survey.

Innovation is measured by a firm's activities in Research and Development (R&D) that are closely related to product and process innovations. These activities are known to be positively linked to firms' participation in exports and to export intensity in German firms (see Wagner, 2011a; 2011b). That said, innovative firms cannot only be expected to outperform non-innovative firms with respect to export participation and the share of exports in total sales. More innovative firms can be expected to serve more foreign markets because their advantage compared to local producers of competing similar goods can be expected to be not limited to only one foreign market (or a small number of markets). Furthermore, they can be expected to export more different goods because innovation activities are often not concentrated on the development of one single good only, but spread over several lines of production. In line with this Wagner (2017) finds that more innovative firms outperform less innovative firms at both extensive margins of exports — they export more goods and they export to a larger number of countries.

R&D activity is measured here as the share of employees in R&D in all employees. Information on R&D activity is taken from the cost structure survey.

Firm age: Although some newly founded firms are "born globals" that export or import from the start, typically it takes years before firms eventually become active on one foreign market, and then enter further markets progressively. Firms gain expertise in entering new foreign markets from experience, and this lowers the fixed costs of entry to any further new market. A similar argument can be made with regard to the number of products traded. At any point in time, therefore, firm age and the margins of foreign can be expected to be closely linked. Germany is a case in point. Wagner (2015a; 2015b) shows that in Germany older firms are more often exporters and importers, and they export and import more different goods to and from more different countries compared to younger firms from the same industry.

Information on firm age is not available from the data used in this study. However, we know whether a firm was already active in 1995 (the first year data from the monthly report are available for) or not. Firms that reported to the monthly report in 1995, and that were founded before 1996 accordingly, are classified as old firms. Firms that started to report in the years between 1996 and 2002 are classified as medium-aged firms, and firms that started to report from 2003 onwards are classified as young firms.

Foreign owned firm: Firms that are subsidiaries of a multinational enterprise with headquarter in a foreign country are termed foreign owned firms. Foreign ownership is known to have a positive impact on the margins of exports, because these firms can use the international networks and trade contacts of their parent companies and are involved in international supply chains (see Raff and Wagner, 2014 for a discussion of the literature, a theoretical model, and empirical evidence for Germany). The same arguments hold for imports. A firm is considered to be foreign owned if more than 50 percent of the voting rights of the owners or more than 50 percent of the shares are controlled (directly or indirectly) by a firm or a person/institution located outside Germany. Information on foreign ownership status of an enterprise is taken from the enterprise register system.

Industry: Dummy variables for 4-digit industries are included in all empirical models to control for industry specific effects like competitive pressure, policy measures, demand shocks etc. Information on industry affiliation is taken from the cost structure survey.

This discussion of the links between firm characteristics and the activity of firms in exports and imports lead to the following six empirical hypotheses:

H1: The number of markets exported to and imported from increases with firm size.

H2: The number of markets exported to and imported from increases with labor productivity.

H3: The number of markets exported to and imported from increases with human capital intensity.

H4: The number of markets exported to and imported from increases with R&D intensity.

H5: The number of markets exported to and imported from increases with firm age.

H6: The number of markets exported to and imported is larger in foreign owned firms compared to domestically owned firms.

Note that all these hypotheses are expected to hold after controlling for detailed industry affiliation at the 4-digit level.

3.3. Econometric investigation

In the empirical investigation data for the years 2009 to 2012 for samples of enterprises from manufacturing industries are used. Firm characteristics are either constant (firm age) or they do not vary much over the four year period. Furthermore, in 2012 a new sample has been drawn for the cost structure survey that is the source of most of the variables. Therefore, the data are not used as a panel data set here.[9] Instead, all empirical models are estimated with cross-section data for each year separately.

Descriptive statistics for the samples of exporting and importing firms in 2012 are listed in the upper and lower panel of Table 3, respectively.[10] On average, the firms in the sample have about 150 employees, which is quite large compared to all manufacturing firms in Germany. However, by construction the data set used is limited to firms that are active in foreign trade, and these firms tend to be considerably larger on average than non-trading firms. About seven percent of all firms in the sample trade on a single foreign market only, while most trading firms are active on several foreign markets.

The number of foreign markets served in exports or sourced in imports varies widely across the trading firms. To test the six hypotheses H1 to H6 (detailed in Section 3.2) on the links between the number of

---

[9] See Wagner (2011b, Section 5) for a discussion of this issue.

[10] Results for the samples used for 2009–2011 are very similar and not reported here to economize on space.

Table 3: Descriptive statistics for samples of firms.

Exports, 2012	Mean	SD	p1	p50	p99
No. of markets	41.3	70.6	1	19	343
No. of employees	154.5	226.2	21	85	1,063
Labor productivity	64,641	75,784	8,998	55,801	198,055
Human capital intensity	36,257	11,544	13,566	35,447	67,093
R&D intensity	2.72	6.13	0.0	0.0	29.69
Medium aged firm (Dummy)	0.1790				
Young firm (Dummy)	0.2811				
Foreign owned firm (Dummy)	0.1422				
No. of observations	6,447				
No. of single-market exporters	463 (7.18%)				
Imports, 2012	Mean	SD	p1	p50	p99
No. of markets	139.4	409.4	1	30	1,889
No. of employees	151.75	224.5	21	83	1,054
Labor productivity	64,337	74,951	9,878	55,642	196,477
Human capital intensity	36,238	11,512	13,198	35,403	67,093
R&D intensity	2.71	6.09	0.0	0.0	29.69
Medium aged firm (Dummy)	0.1784				
Young firm (Dummy)	0.2752				
Foreign owned firm (Dummy)	0.1387				
No. of observations	6,490				
No. of single market importers	417 (6.43%)				

Note: For a definition of variables see text. The minimum and maximum values of variables are confidential because they (may) refer to a single firm.

foreign markets and firm characteristics empirical models are estimated with the number of markets (measured in logs) as the dependent variable and the firm characteristics listed above (i.e., firm size; labor productivity; human capital intensity; R&D intensity; firm age; and foreign ownership status) — either one at a time or taken together — plus detailed 4-digit industry controls as independent variables. The models are estimated by OLS for data for each year from 2009 to 2012 and for exports and imports separately.[11] These models cannot reveal any causal relationships, because the data at hand are not rich enough to estimate structural empirical models. Results, therefore, do only indicate correlations between the number of foreign markets a firm is active on and firm characteristics while controlling for industry affiliation.

Results for 2012 are reported in Table 4 for exports and in Table 5 for imports.[12] To start with results for the number of export markets, columns 1 to 6 of Table 4 report results for empirical tests of H1 and H6 (detailed above), one at a time. Results are fully in line with the theoretical hypotheses; all estimated regression coefficients are statistically highly significant and have the expected sign.[13] From column 7 we see that this is the case,

---

[11] Although the dependent variable in the empirical models is a count variable that can only take positive integer values equal to or larger than one (because by construction only firms that trade on at least one foreign market are included in the samples) all models are estimated by OLS. Both the number of export markets and the number of import markets are distributed over a broad range (see Table 3). This justifies the use of OLS in estimating the empirical models. As a robustness check all empirical models were estimated using a zero-truncated negative binomial model that is designed for instances like these, where observations are counts and where an outcome of zero exists (i.e., there are firms with no export or import markets at all) in the population but have been excluded from the sample (see Long and Freese, 2014, p. 518ff). The big picture from the signs and significance levels of the estimated coefficients is identical with the one from the OLS estimates reported here. Details are available on request.

[12] The big picture for the other years is very similar; detailed results are documented in Tables A.1 to A.6 in the Appendix.

[13] The estimated regression coefficients for the number of employees and the squared number of employees indicate a hump-shaped relation between firm size and the number of markets. The estimated maximum of this hump-shaped relation, however, is very large (2,735) compared to the distribution of the number of employees in the sample (see Table 3), and the estimated average marginal effect is positive (0.0043). Therefore,

Table 4: Firm characteristics and number of markets in exports, Germany, 2012.

Model		1	2	3	4	5	6	7
No. of employees	ß	0.005						0.004
	p	0.000						0.000
No. of employees (Squared)	ß	−9.14e−7						−7.58e−7
	p	0.000						0.000
Labor productivity	ß		2.21e−6					1.35e−7
	p		0.008					0.603
Human capital intensity	ß			0.000047				0.000025
	p			0.000				0.000
R&D intensity	ß				0.042			0.020
	p				0.000			0.000
Firm age: Medium aged firm (Dummy)	ß					−0.243		−0.075
	p					0.000		0.050
Firm age: Young firm (Dummy)	ß					−0.427		−0.160
	p					0.000		0.000
Foreign owned firm (Dummy)	ß						0.815	0.447
	p						0.000	0.000
Constant	ß	2.166	2.665	1.103	2.693	2.971	2.692	1.365
	p	0.000	0.000	0.000	0.000	0.000	0.000	0.000
Four-digit industry controls		[included in all models]						
R²		0.407	0.184	0.280	0.198	0.187	0.208	0.464
No. of observations		6,447	6,447	6,447	6,447	6,447	6,447	6,447

Note: All models were estimated by OLS with the log of the number of markets as the dependent variable, where a market is defined as a combination of a HS6-good and a country. For a definition of the independent variables see text. ß is the estimated regression coefficient and p is the prob-value (based on heteroscedasticity-consistent standard errors).

Table 5: Firm characteristics and number of markets in imports, Germany, 2012.

Model		1	2	3	4	5	6	7
No. of employees	ß	0.005						0.004
	p	0.000						0.000
No. of employees (Squared)	ß	−1.00e−6						−7.82e−7
	p	0.000						0.000
Labor productivity	ß		2.48e−6					−3.96e−7
	p		0.076					0.475
Human capital intensity	ß			0.000062				0.000042
	p			0.000				0.000
R&D intensity	ß				0.048			0.020
	p				0.000			0.000
Firm age: Medium aged firm (Dummy)	ß					−0.466		−0.233
	p					0.000		0.000
Firm age: Young firm (Dummy)	ß					−0.682		−0.362
	p					0.000		0.000
Foreign owned firm (Dummy)	ß						0.618	0.141
	p						0.000	0.008
Constant	ß	2.713	3.218	1.133	3.248	3.648	3.292	1.430
	p	0.000	0.000	0.000	0.000	0.000	0.000	0.000
Four-digit industry controls		[included in all models]						
R^2		0.366	0.211	0.324	0.223	0.228	0.215	0.436
No. of observations		6,490	6,490	6,490	6,490	6,490	6,490	6,490

Note. All models were estimated by OLS with the log of the number of markets as the dependent variable, where a market is defined as a combination of a HS6-good and a country. For a definition of the independent variables see text. ß is the estimated regression coefficient and p is the prob-value (based on heteroscedasticity-consistent standard errors).

too, when all variables are included in the empirical model, but with the exception of H2 (labor productivity). In Model 7 the estimated regression coefficient of labor productivity is no longer statistically significant. This is due to the fact that labor productivity is closely linked with human capital intensity.[14]

To put the estimation results for Model 7 into perspective we compute the size of the estimated effects of a change in the firm characteristics on the number of export markets. Remember that when the dependent variable is measured in logs (as is the case here) the estimated regression coefficient ß is the change in log (number of markets) when the respective independent variable is changed by one unit, and ß∗100 is the approximate percentage change in the number of markets. This is why ß∗100 is often labeled the semi-elasticity of the number of markets with respect to the respective independent variable. For dummy variables the percentage change due to a change of the value of the independent variable from zero to one is given by $(e^{ß}-1)*100$.[15]

That said, estimation results for Model 7 indicate that an increase in the number of employees by one standard deviation goes hand in hand with an increase in the number of export markets served by a firm of 81 percent.[16] For human capital intensity and R&D intensity the respective figures are 29 and 12 percent. Compared to old firms the number of markets served in exports is 7 percent smaller in medium aged firms and 15 percent smaller in young firms, while foreign owned firms export to 56 percent more markets than domestically owned firms. All these estimated effects can be considered to be of a relevant order of magnitude from an economic point of view.

---

the estimation results point to an increase of the number of markets with an increase in firm size at a decreasing rate.

[14] See Wagner (2011b, Section 6) for a discussion of the role of human capital intensity as a determinant of labor productivity in the context of empirical models for export activities of firms.

[15] For a discussion of the interpretation of estimated regression coefficients from models using a logarithmic functional form see e.g., Wooldridge (2006, p. 197ff).

[16] The estimated marginal effect for the number of employees in Model 7 is 0.0036 (see footnote 13); standard deviations of variables are reported in Table 3.

Turning to the number of import markets, columns 1 to 6 of Table 5 report results for empirical tests of H1 and H6. The big picture is rather similar to the results for the number of export markets. Again, all estimated regression coefficients have the expected sign.[17] From column 7 we see that this is the case, too, when all variables are included in the empirical model, but again with the exception of H2 (labor productivity). In Model 7 the estimated regression coefficient of labor productivity is no longer statistically significant at a conventional level. This is again due to the fact that labor productivity is closely linked with human capital intensity.[18]

An application of the same approach to interpret the estimation results for Model 7 that was used in the case of export markets above indicates that an increase in the number of employees by one standard deviation goes hand in hand with an increase in the number of import markets sourced by a firm of 81 percent.[19] For human capital intensity and R&D intensity the respective figures are 48 and 12 percent. Compared to old firms the number of markets sourced in imports is 21 percent smaller in medium aged firms and 30 percent smaller in young firms, while foreign owned firms import from 15 percent more markets than domestically owned firms. Like in the case of export markets all these estimated effects can be considered to be of a relevant order of magnitude from an economic point of view.

4. Concluding Remarks

This paper uses information on more than 160 million export and import transactions by German firms from 2009 to 2012 to document the decisive role of multi-market traders that are active on many foreign markets, where a market is defined as a combination of a good traded and a country traded with. It is shown that the bulk of exporters and

---

[17] Here the estimated average marginal effect for the number of employees is 0.0046.

[18] See Footnote 14.

[19] The estimated marginal effect for the number of employees in Model 7 is 0.0036 (see Footnote 13); standard deviations of variables are reported in Table 3.

importers of goods is active on a small number of markets only, but that multi-market traders are responsible for the lion's share of foreign trade.

Using merged information from trade transactions and from surveys conducted by the statistical offices it is shown that, controlling for detailed industry affiliation, the number of foreign markets a firm from manufacturing industries is active on as an exporter or importer is higher in firms that are larger, older and foreign owned and that have higher labor productivity, human capital intensity and R&D intensity. With the exception of labor productivity these results are valid ceteris paribus, too. All these empirical results are in line with hypotheses that are derived from the literature on the links between firm characteristics and the extensive margins of foreign trade.

In future research based on data for more years the role of self-selection of more productive firms into exporting to and importing from a larger number of markets should be investigated. Furthermore, the detailed information in the data should be used to investigate the reaction of firms that depend heavily on imports of certain goods (like rare earths) or exports to certain markets (like Russia) with regard to trade shocks like embargoes.

Table A.1: Firm characteristics and number of markets in exports, Germany, 2009.

Model		1	2	3	4	5	6	7
No. of employees	ß	0.004						0.004
	p	0.000						0.000
No. of employees (Squared)	ß	−5.95e−7						−5.15e−7
	p	0.000						0.000
Labor productivity	ß		1.66e−6					8.69e−8
	p		0.001					0.634
Human capital intensity	ß			0.000045				0.000025
	p			0.000				0.000
R&D intensity	ß				0.031			0.018
	p				0.000			0.000
Firm age: medium aged firm (Dummy)	ß					−0.219		−0.097
	p					0.000		0.011
Firm age: young firm (Dummy)	ß					−0.287		−0.149
	p					0.000		0.000
Foreign owned firm (Dummy)	ß						0.839	0.497
	p						0.000	0.000
Constant	ß	2.155	2.641	1.252	2.650	2.832	2.629	1.332
	p	0.000	0.000	0.000	0.000	0.000	0.000	0.000
Four-digit industry controls		[included in all models]						
R^2		0.382	0.165	0.248	0.172	0.165	0.194	0.439
No. of observations		6,120	6,120	6,120	6,120	6,120	6,120	6,120

Note: All models were estimated by OLS with the log of the number of markets as the dependent variable, where a market is defined as a combination of a HS6-good and a country. For a definition of the independent variables see text. ß is the estimated regression coefficient and p is the prob-value (based on heteroscedasticity-consistent standard errors).

Table A.2: Firm characteristics and number of markets in exports, Germany, 2010.

Model		1	2	3	4	5	6	7
No. of employees	ß	0.005						0.004
	p	0.000						0.000
No. of employees (Squared)	ß	−9.82e−7						−8.35e−7
	p	0.000						0.000
Labor productivity	ß		2.25e−6					1.66e−7
	p		0.002					0.493
Human capital intensity	ß			0.000048				0.000025
	p			0.000				0.000
R&D intensity	ß				0.039			0.020
	p				0.000			0.000
Firm age: medium aged firm (Dummy)	ß					−0.254		−0.090
	p					0.000		0.018
Firm age: young firm (Dummy)	ß					−0.273		−0.115
	p					0.000		0.003
Foreign owned firm (Dummy)	ß						0.859	0.489
	p						0.000	0.000
Constant	ß	2.128	2.635	1.137	2.668	2.879	2.663	1.271
	p	0.000	0.000	0.000	0.000	0.000	0.000	0.000
Four-digit industry controls		[included in all models]						
R^2		0.397	0.174	0.265	0.183	0.169	0.200	0.454
No. of observations		6,225	6,225	6,225	6,225	6,225	6,225	6,225

Note. All models were estimated by OLS with the log of the number of markets as the dependent variable, where a market is defined as a combination of a HS6-good and a country. For a definition of the independent variables see text. ß is the estimated regression coefficient and p is the prob-value (based on heteroscedasticity-consistent standard errors).

Table A.3: Firm characteristics and number of markets in exports, Germany, 2011.

Model		1	2	3	4	5	6	7
No. of employees	ß	0.005						0.004
	p	0.000						0.000
No. of employees (Squared)	ß	−9.42e−7						−8.08e−7
	p	0.000						0.000
Labor productivity	ß		2.20e−6					1.94e−7
	p		0.005					0.524
Human capital intensity	ß			0.000046				0.000023
	p			0.000				0.000
R&D intensity	ß				0.044			0.022
	p				0.000			0.000
Firm age: medium aged firm (Dummy)	ß					−0.220		−0.080
	p					0.000		0.030
Firm age: young firm (Dummy)	ß					−0.307		−0.151
	p					0.000		0.000
Foreign owned firm (Dummy)	ß						0.854	0.527
	p						0.000	0.000
Constant	ß	2.183	2.692	1.197	2.714	2.939	2.722	1.365
	p	0.000	0.000	0.000	0.000	0.000	0.000	0.000
Four-digit industry controls		[included in all models]						
R^2		0.409	0.177	0.263	0.193	0.173	0.204	0.466
No. of observations		6,330	6,330	6,330	6,330	6,330	6,330	6,330

Note: All models were estimated by OLS with the log of the number of markets as the dependent variable, where a market is defined as a combination of a HS6-good and a country. For a definition of the independent variables see text. ß is the estimated regression coefficient and p is the prob-value (based on heteroscedasticity-consistent standard errors).

Table A.4: Firm characteristics and number of markets in imports, Germany, 2009.

Model		1	2	3	4	5	6	7
No. of employees	ß	0.004						0.004
	p	0.000						0.000
No. of employees (Squared)	ß	−6.09e−7						−5.15e−7
	p	0.000						0.000
Labor productivity	ß		1.40e−6					−8.57e−7
	p		0.158					0.079
Human capital intensity	ß			0.000054				0.000039
	p			0.000				0.000
R&D intensity	ß				0.034			0.018
	p				0.000			0.000
Firm age: medium aged firm (Dummy)	ß					−0.412		−0.268
	p					0.000		0.000
Firm age: young firm (Dummy)	ß					−0.523		−0.360
	p					0.000		0.000
Foreign owned firm (Dummy)	ß						0.490	0.077
	p						0.000	0.172
Constant	ß	2.702	3.213	1.497	3.198	3.465	3.231	1.618
	p	0.000	0.000	0.000	0.000	0.000	0.000	0.000
Four-digit industry controls		[included in all models]						
R^2		0.346	0.194	0.278	0.202	0.207	0.199	0.401
No. of observations		6,196	6,196	6,196	6,196	6,196	6,196	6,196

Note: All models were estimated by OLS with the log of the number of markets as the dependent variable, where a market is defined as a combination of a HS6-good and a country. For a definition of the independent variables see text. ß is the estimated regression coefficient and p is the prob-value (based on heteroscedasticity-consistent standard errors).

Table A.5: Firm characteristics and number of markets in imports, Germany, 2010.

Model		1	2	3	4	5	6	7
No. of employees	ß	0.005						0.004
	p	0.000						0.000
No. of employees (Squared)	ß	$-1.06e^{-6}$						$-8.70e{-7}$
	p	0.000						0.000
Labor productivity	ß		$1.86e^{-6}$					$-8.65e{-7}$
	p		0.093					0.064
Human capital intensity	ß			0.000061				0.000043
	p			0.000				0.000
R&D intensity	ß				0.042			0.018
	p				0.000			0.000
Firm age: medium aged firm (Dummy)	ß					-0.448		-0.249
	p					0.000		0.000
Firm age: young firm (Dummy)	ß					-0.496		-0.293
	p					0.000		0.000
Foreign owned firm (Dummy)	ß						0.527	0.072
	p						0.000	0.189
Constant	ß	2.699	3.251	1.291	3.252	3.548	3.299	1.453
	p	0.000	0.000	0.000	0.000	0.000	0.000	0.000
Four-digit industry controls		[included in all models]						
R^2		0.374	0.213	0.317	0.224	0.223	0.217	0.436
No. of observations		6,265	6,265	6,265	6,265	6,265	6,265	6,265

Note. All models were estimated by OLS with the log of the number of markets as the dependent variable, where a market is defined as a combination of a HS6-good and a country. For a definition of the independent variables see text. ß is the estimated regression coefficient and p is the prob-value (based on heteroscedasticity-consistent standard errors).

Table A.6: Firm characteristics and number of markets in imports, Germany, 2011.

Model		1	2	3	4	5	6	7
No. of employees	ß	0.005						0.004
	p	0.000						0.000
No. of employees (Squared)	ß	-1.02e-6						-8.50e-7
	p	0.000						0.000
Labor productivity	ß		4.52e-6					5.54e-7
	p		0.000					0.094
Human capital intensity	ß			0.000060				0.000039
	p			0.000				0.000
R&D intensity	ß				0.044			0.018
	p				0.000			0.000
Firm age: medium aged firm (Dummy)	ß					-0.435		-0.248
	p					0.000		0.000
Firm age: young firm (Dummy)	ß					-0.470		-0.271
	p					0.000		0.000
Foreign owned firm (Dummy)	ß						0.520	0.093
	p						0.000	0.079
Four-digit industry controls		[included in all models]						
Constant	ß	2.772	3.147	1.298	3.315	3.612	3.371	1.501
	p	0.000	0.000	0.000	0.000	0.000	0.000	0.000
R²		0.391	0.244	0.332	0.244	0.240	0.235	0.451
No. of observations		6,303	6,303	6,303	6,303	6,303	6,303	6,303

Note: All models were estimated by OLS with the log of the number of markets as the dependent variable, where a market is defined as a combination of a HS6-good and a country. For a definition of the independent variables see text. ß is the estimated regression coefficient and p is the prob-value (based on heteroscedasticity-consistent standard errors).

References

Fritsch, Michael, Bernd Görzig, Ottmar Hennchen and Andreas Stephan (2004). Cost structure surveys for Germany. *Schmollers Jahrbuch/Journal of Applied Social Science Studies* 124 (4), 557–566.

Long, Scott and Jeremy Freese (2014). Regression Models for Categorical Dependent Variables Using Stata. Third Edition. College Station, TX: Stata Press.

Malchin, Anja and Ramona Voshage (2009). Official firm data for Germany. *Schmollers Jahrbuch/Journal of Applied Social Science Studies* 129 (3), 501–513.

Raff, Horst and Joachim Wagner (2014). Foreign ownership and the extensive margins of exports: Evidence for manufacturing enterprises in Germany. *The World Economy* 37 (5), 579–591.

Verardi, Vincenzo and Joachim Wagner (2012). Productivity premia for German manufacturing firms exporting to the euro-area and beyond: First evidence from robust fixed effects estimations. *The World Economy* 35 (6), 694–712.

Vogel, Alexander and Joachim Wagner (2010). Higher productivity in importing German manufacturing firms: Self-selection, learning from importing, or both? *Review of World Economics* 145 (4), 641–665.

Wagner, Joachim (2007a). Productivity and size of the export market. Evidence for West and East German plants, 2004. *Jahrbücher für Nationalökonomie und Statistik/Journal of Economics and Statistics* 227 (4), 403–408.

Wagner, Joachim (2007b). Exports and Productivity: A Survey of the Evidence from Firm-level Data. *The World Economy* 30 (1), 60–82.

Wagner, Joachim (2011a). Exports and firm characteristics in Germany: A survey of empirical studies (1991 to 2011). *Applied Economics Quarterly* 57 (2), 145–160.

Wagner, Joachim (2011b). Exports and firm characteristics in German manufacturing industries: New evidence from representative panel data. *Applied Economics Quarterly* 57 (2), 107–143.

Wagner, Joachim (2012a). Exports, imports and profitability: First evidence for manufacturing enterprises. *Open Economies Review* 23 (5), 747–765.

Wagner, Joachim (2012b). Trading many goods with many countries: Exporters and importers from German manufacturing industries. *Jahrbuch für Wirtschaftswissenschaften/Review of Economics* 63 (2), 170–186.

Wagner, Joachim (2012c). Average wage, qualification of the workforce and export performance in German enterprises: Evidence from *KombiFiD* data. *Journal of Labour Market Research* 45 (2), 161–170.

Wagner, Joachim (2013). Exports, imports and firm survival: First evidence for manufacturing enterprises in Germany. *Review of World Economics* 149 (1), 113–130.

Wagner, Joachim (2015a). A note on firm age and the margins of imports: First evidence from Germany. *Applied Economics Letters* 22 (9), 679–682.

Wagner, Joachim (2015b). A note on firm age and the margins of exports: First evidence from Germany. *The International Trade Journal* 29 (2), 93–102.

Wagner, Joachim (2016). A survey of empirical studies using transaction level data on exports and imports. *Review of World Economics* 152 (1), 215–225.

Wagner, Joachim (2017). R&D activities and extensive margins of exports in manufacturing enterprises: First evidence for Germany. *The International Trade Journal* 31 (3), 232–244.

Wooldridge, Jeffrey (2006). Introductory econometrics. A modern approach. Third Edition. Mason, OH, USA: Thomson South-Western.

World Trade Organization (2016). World Trade Statistical Review 2016. Available at: https://www.wto.org/english/res_e/statis_e/wts2016_e/wts16_toc_e.htm.

Chapter 3

Still Different After All These Years. Extensive and Intensive Margins of Exports in East and West German Manufacturing Enterprises*

Abstract

This paper uses a new tailor-made data set to investigate the differences in extensive and intensive margins of exports in manufacturing firms from East Germany and West Germany. It documents that these margins do still differ in 2010, 20 years after the re-unification of Germany. West German firms outperform East German firms at all four margins of exports — they have a larger propensity to export, export a larger share of total sales, export more goods and export to a

*Originally Published in *Journal of Economics and Statistics* (2016), 236 (2), 297–322.

All computations were done at the Research Data Centre of the Statistical Office of Berlin–Brandenburg in Berlin. The firm-level data used are strictly confidential but not exclusive; see http://www.forschungsdatenzentrum.de/datenzugang.asp for information on how to access the data. To facilitate replications the Stata do-file used is available from the author on request. I thank two anonymous referees and the editor, Werner Smolny, for comments on an earlier version that helped to improve the paper considerably. Many thanks to Paul Simon for his inspiration for the title of the paper (see: http://en.wikipedia.org/wiki/Still_Crazy_After_All_These_Years_%28song%29).

larger number of countries. All these differences are large from an economic point of view. A decomposition analysis shows that in 2010 between 59 and 78 percent of the difference in margins can be explained by differences in firm characteristics.

Keywords: Export margins, East Germany, West Germany, decomposition analysis.

1. Motivation

Germany is one of the leading actors on the world market for goods and services. Exports play a key role in shaping the development of the German economy over the short and the long run. Given this decisive role of exports for the dynamics of the German economy it comes as a surprise that exports do play only a minor role in the discussion of persisting differences and convergence processes in the two parts of Germany today, 25 years after the re-unification of East and West Germany. While differences in growth, earnings, unemployment or life satisfaction between the two parts of Germany make headlines, differences in exports do not. A case in point is the most recent comprehensive annual report of the federal government on the state of German unification where exports are mentioned only in passing by pointing to the still lower share of exports in total sales in the East German manufacturing industry compared to West Germany (Bundesminsterium für Wirtschaft und Energie (BMWI) 2014, p. 20f.) and to the importance of policy measures with a view to increase the internationalization of East German firms (*ibid.* p. 67).

While the difference in the share of exports in total sales (i.e., the difference in the intensive margin of exports) between East German and West German manufacturing industries is a widely known fact, information on the differences in the extensive margins of exports (i.e., the share of exporting firms in all firms, the number of different goods exported by exporting firms, and the number of destination countries exported to) is scarce. Furthermore, none of these studies investigate the reasons behind these differences in the four export margins empirically.[1]

---

[1] See Wagner (2011a) for a survey of empirical studies on the links between exports and firm characteristics in Germany that were published up to 2011. Wagner (2008) applies a decomposition analysis, but only for the propensity to export, and the method does not

This paper contributes to the literature by using a new tailor-made data set for manufacturing enterprises to document the differences in export margins between firms from both parts of Germany and to link these differences in margins to differences in firm characteristics. The paper has an explicit focus on descriptive analyses and does not claim to present results of causal analyses. To anticipate the most important results we find that West German firms outperform East German firms at all four margins of exports — they have a larger propensity to export, export a larger share of total sales, export more goods and export to a larger number of countries. All these differences are large from an economic point of view. A decomposition analysis shows that in 2010 between 59 and 78 percent of the difference in margins can be explained by differences in firm characteristics. However, the results of the decomposition analysis should not be considered to document stylized facts. These results are limited in a number of ways due to the use of data for one year only, limitations in the variables that are used to proxy the firm characteristics, and the large share of the difference in the export margins that remains unexplained in this empirical study.

The rest of the paper is organized as follows. Section 2 discusses the various data sets and the definition of variables that are used in the empirical investigations. Section 3 presents descriptive evidence for differences in the margins of exports in manufacturing enterprises in East and West Germany. Section 4 documents East/West differences in firm characteristics that are expected to be related to margins of exports. Section 5 reports results from an econometric investigation of the differences in the export margins between manufacturing firms from both parts of Germany. Section 6 concludes.

2. Data and Definition of Variables

The empirical investigation uses a tailor-made data set that combines high quality firm-level data from four official sources. The first source of firm

---

allow the kind of detailed decomposition applied here in this paper. Descriptive evidence on differences in the number of goods exported and the number of destination countries of exports in East and West German manufacturing firms is given in Wagner (2012a).

level information is the regular survey of establishments from manufacturing industries by the Statistical Offices of the German federal states. The survey (known as the *Monatsbericht,* or monthly report) covers all establishments from manufacturing industries that employ at least twenty persons in the local production unit or in the company that owns the unit. Participation of firms in the survey is mandated in official statistics (see Malchin and Voshage, 2009 for details). For this study the monthly establishment data were aggregated to annual data and at the enterprise level to match the unit of observation in the other data sources (described below).[2] Aggregation of establishment level information at the level of the enterprise implies that establishments located in in East Germany (West Germany) that are part of an enterprise with headquarter located in West Germany (East Germany) are included in the West German (East German) enterprise. The use of the enterprise (the legal unit) instead of the establishment (the local production unit) as the unit of analysis is mandated by the use of the enterprise as the unit of observation in the other data sources used in this study. It seems appropriate here because decisions about export activities are taken at the enterprise level, taking the characteristics of all establishments in a multi-establishment enterprise into account.

The second source of data is the cost structure survey for enterprises in the manufacturing sector. This survey is carried out annually as a representative random sample survey in about 15,000 firms. The sample is stratified according to the number of employees and the industries; all firms with 500 and more employees are covered by the cost structure survey (see Fritsch *et al.,* 2004).

Information on the goods traded internationally is available from the statistic on foreign trade (*Außenhandelsstatistik*). This statistic is based on two sources. One source is the reports by German firms on transactions with firms from countries that are members of the European Union (EU); these reports are used to compile the so-called *Intrahandelsstatistik* on

---

[2] Note that beginning with reporting year 2007 firms with more than 20 but less than 50 persons no longer have to report to the *Monatsbericht*. However, these firms have to report information on total sales, exports, number of employees and the sum of wages and salaries paid in the so-called *Jahresbericht* (the annual report), and this information is added to the data set used here.

intra-EU trade. The other source is transaction-level data collected by the customs on trade with countries outside the EU (the so-called *Extrahandelsstatistik*).[3] Data in the statistic of foreign trade are transaction-level data, i.e., they relate to one transaction of a German firm with a firm located outside Germany at a time. For the reporting year 2010 these transaction-level data have been aggregated at the level of the exporting firm (see Wagner, 2014a). This dataset is the third source of data used in this study.

These data were matched with the enterprise register system (*Unternehmensregister-System*) and with the enterprise level data from the two other sources discussed above. The enterprise register system is used as the fourth source of data.

With these linked four data sets it is possible to investigate the differences in the margins of exports in manufacturing firms from East Germany and West Germany. The definition of the variables used in the empirical investigation is discussed in detail below.

The study looks at four different margins of exports, one intensive margin and three extensive margins:

Exporter status: The first extensive margin measures the participation of a firm in exports (or not).

Share of exports in total sales: The intensive margin of export is the percentage share of all sales due to exports.

Information on the exporter status of a firm and on the share of exports in total sales of a firm is based on information on export sales and total turnover taken from the first data source (the monthly report). This information is available for each year starting in 1995 and for all firms from manufacturing industries with at least twenty employees.

Number of exported goods: The second extensive margin of exports is the number of different goods that a firm exported. A good is defined as an eight-digit number from the official nomenclature for the statistics of foreign trade.

---

[3] Note that firms with a value of imports from EU-countries that does not exceed 400,000 Euro do not have to report to the statistic on intra-EU trade. For trade with firms from non-member countries all transactions that exceed 1,000 Euro are registered. For details see Statistisches Bundesamt, Qualitätsbericht Außenhandel, January (2011).

Number of export destination countries: The third extensive margin is the number countries a firm exported to.

Information on the number of exported goods and the number of export destination countries is taken from the third source of data (the statistic on foreign trade). This information is available for each year starting in 2009; the most recent year the data were available when the computations for this paper were performed is 2010. Note that by construction this information is only available for exporting firms covered by the statistic on foreign trade, and for firms that were linked to the data from the monthly report (that are needed to distinguish between firms from East Germany and West Germany).

In the empirical investigation of the differences in the margins of exports between manufacturing firms from East and West Germany a number of firm characteristics are considered. The definition of the variables used in the empirical investigation is discussed in detail below.

Firm size: A positive link between firm size and margins of exports qualifies as a stylized fact. This positive link is due to fixed costs of exporting and efficiency advantages of larger firms due to scale economies, advantages of specialization in management and better conditions on the markets for inputs. Large firms can be expected to have cost advantages on credit markets while small firms often face higher restrictions on the capital market leading to a higher risk of insolvency and illiquidity. Furthermore, there might be disadvantages of small firms in the competition for highly qualified employees. There are limits to the advantage of size, because coordination costs mount as the scale of operations increases, and at some point any further expansion might cease to be profitable. Therefore, a positive relationship between firm size and exports, at least up to a point, is expected. For Germany empirical evidence in line with this is reported in a number of studies (see Wagner, 2011a for a survey). Firm size is measured here by the number of employees in a firm (also included in squares to take care of non-linearity). The source is the first data set (the monthly report).

Human capital intensity: Given that Germany is relatively rich in human capital, firms that use human capital intensively can be expected to have a comparative advantage on international markets. Empirical studies find that the qualification of the workforce is an important factor for the international competitiveness of German firms (Wagner, 2011b). Human capital intensity is measured here by the average wage per employee. Direct information on the qualification of the employees in a firm is not available in the data used in this study, but Wagner (2012b) demonstrates that the average wage is indeed a good proxy variable for the qualification of the workforce in German manufacturing firms. However, while this is the case for the link between the average wage per employee in an enterprise and the qualification of the workforce of this enterprise, it is problematic to use the average wage per employee as a proxy variable in a comparison of enterprises from West Germany and East Germany. The reason is that the level of wages in the manufacturing sector is known to be considerably lower in East Germany than in West Germany (see Bundesministerium für Wirtschaft und Energie, BMWI, 2014, p. 87) and that this difference is not only due to differences in the qualification of the workforce between the two parts of Germany. While the exact amount of the wage gap for identically qualified employees between East Germany and West Germany is unknown we have empirical evidence from econometric studies that point to an order of magnitude of about twenty to thirty percent (Gühne and Markwardt, 2014). The difference in the average wage per employee between an enterprise in East Germany and an enterprise in West Germany, therefore, cannot be considered as an unbiased measure for the difference in human capital used in both firms. This shortcoming has to be kept in mind when interpreting the results of the empirical study. The source is for information on the amount of wages paid and the number of employees is the first data set (the monthly report).

R&D intensity: Activities in research and development that are closely related to product and process innovations are known to be positively linked to success in exports in German firms (see Wagner (2011a; 2011b)). R&D intensity is measured here by the share of employees that are active in R&D in all employees in a firm. This intensity measure is based on information on R&D employees and total employees taken from the second data source (the cost structure survey).

Capital intensity: The amount of capital used per employee is traditionally expected to be positively liked to exports in a relatively capital-abundant country like Germany. In the data used in this study, however, there is no direct information on the capital stock of the firms. Therefore, the amount of depreciation per employee is used as a proxy variable that can be expected to be (more or less) proportional to the amount of capital per head. Information on the amount of depreciation and the number of employees is taken from the second data source (the cost structure survey).

Firm age: Although some newly founded firms are "born globals" that export from the start, typically it takes years before firms eventually export to one foreign market, and then enter further markets progressively. Firms gain expertise in entering new foreign markets from experience, and this lowers the fixed costs of entry to any further new market. A similar argument can be made with regard to the number of products exported. At any point in time, therefore, firm age and the margins of exports can be expected to be closely linked. Germany is a case in point. Wagner (2015) reports that older firms are more often exporters, export more and more different goods to more different destination countries. Information on firm age is not available from the data used in this study. However, we know whether a firm was already active in 1995 (the first year data from the monthly report are available for). Firms that were active in 1995, and that were founded before 1996 accordingly, are classified as old firms (based on this information from the first data source, the monthly report).

Foreign owned firm: Firms that are subsidies of a multinational enterprise that has its headquarter in a foreign country are termed foreign owned firms. Foreign ownership is known to have a positive impact on the margins of exports, because these firms can use the international networks and trade contacts of their parent companies and are involved in international supply chains (see Raff and Wagner, 2014) for a discussion of the literature, a theoretical model, and empirical evidence for Germany). A firm is considered to be foreign owned if more than 50 percent of the voting rights of the owners or more than 50 percent of the shares are controlled (directly or indirectly) by a firm or a person/institution located outside Germany. Information on foreign ownership status of an enterprise is taken from the fourth source of data, the enterprise register system.

Industry: Dummy variables for 2-digit-industries are included in the empirical models to control for industry specific effects like competitive pressure, policy measures, demand shocks etc. The source is the first data set (the monthly report).

3. Descriptive Evidence on Differences in the Margins of Exports

The empirical investigation of differences in the margins of export between enterprises from manufacturing industries in East and West Germany starts with showing that these differences do exist. Using information from the first source of data (the monthly report) Table 1 reports the share of exporters and the average share of exports in total sales among exporters in East and West Germany in four years, namely 1995 (the first year information is available for), 2001, 2006 and 2010 (the most recent year the information was available for when the computations for this study were performed).

The difference in the share of exporters (the first extensive margin investigated here) between East and West German firms was rather large in 1995 (some 25 percentage points). This difference declined over time, but it can still be considered to be large from an economic point of view in 2010 when it was nearly 14 percentage points. Note that this decline in the gap between both parts of Germany is not due a shrinking export participation in West Germany; the share of exporters grew in both parts, but the growth was more pronounced in East Germany.

The difference in the average share of exports in total sales among the exporters is remarkably stable (about five percentage points) over the years, and it is in favor of the West German firms. This difference is statistically highly significant not only at the mean (according to *t*-test) but over the whole distribution of the export/sales ratio (according to a Kolmogorov–Smirnov-test for first-order stochastic dominance). Given that the average share of exports in total sales is 30 percent and 25 percent in West and East Germany in 2010, the size of the difference between firms from both parts of Germany can be considered to be large from an economic point of view. Note that the average share of exports in total sales increased considerably in both groups of firms.

Differences in exporting between East and West German firms are not limited to the propensity to export and to the export/sales ratio. Using information from the third source of data (the statistic on foreign trade)

Table 1: Margins of exports in enterprises from manufacturing industries in West and East Germany, Part I: Share of exporters and share of exports in total sales, 1995, 2001, 2006 and 2010.

		1995	2001	2006	2010
Number of firms	West Germany	33,865	34,007	31,482	27,992
	East Germany	6,478	7,056	6,894	6,141
Share of exporters (percent)	West Germany	64.36	64.39	69.47	73.95
	East Germany	39.13	44.35	52.61	60.14
Difference (percentage points)		25.23	20.04	16.86	13.81
Average share of exports in total sales among exporters (percent)	West Germany	21.94	26.46	29.91	30.05
	East Germany	16.92	20.96	24.69	24.81
Difference (percentage points)		5.02	5.50	5.22	5.24
t-Test for H_0: Difference = 0 (prob-value)		0.000	0.000	0.000	0.000
Kolmogorov–Smirnov-tests (prob-values)					
H_0: Distributions do not differ between West and East		0.000	0.000	0.000	0.000
H_0: Larger values in East compared to West		0.000	0.000	0.000	0.000
H_0: Larger values in West compared to East		0.998	0.980	0.936	0.946

Table 2: Margins of exports in enterprises from manufacturing industries in West and East Germany, Part II: Number of exported goods and number of destination countries, 2010.

Number of firms	West Germany		11,972
	East Germany		1,924
Average number of exported goods	West Germany		29.25
	East Germany		14.85
Difference (number of exported goods)		14.40	
t-Test for H_0: Difference = 0 (prob-value)			0.000
Kolmogorov–Smirnov-tests (*prob-values*)			
H_0: Distributions do not differ between West and East			0.000
H_0: Larger values in East compared to West			0.000
H_0: Larger values in West compared to East			1.000
Number of firms	West Germany		11,455
	East Germany		1,928
Average number of export destination countries	West Germany		21.68
	East Germany		14.16
Difference (number of destination countries)		7.52	
t-Test for H_0: Difference = 0 (prob-value)			0.000
Kolmogorov–Smirnov-tests (*prob-values*)			
H_0: Distributions do not differ between West and East			0.000
H_0: Larger values in East compared to West			0.000
H_0: Larger values in West compared to East			0.999

Table 2 reports that in 2010 both the number of exported goods (the second extensive margin of exports considered in this study) and the number of export destination countries (the third extensive margin) is considerably larger in West German firms than in East German firms. These differences are statistically highly significant not only at the mean (according to *t*-test) but over the whole distribution of the number of exported goods and the number of destination countries of exports (according to a Kolmogorov–Smirnov test for first-order stochastic dominance). Given that the average number of exported goods is 30 in West Germany and 15 in East Germany, the size of the difference between firms from both parts of Germany is large from an economic point of view. The same holds for the difference in the number of destination countries that is 7.5 countries with an average number of destination countries of 21.7 in West Germany and 14.2 in East Germany.[4]

The bottom line, then, is that West German firms outperform East German firms at all four margins of exports — they have a larger propensity to export, export more, more goods and to a larger number of countries. All these differences are large from an economic point of view.

4. Differences in Firm Characteristics between East and West Germany

The next step in the empirical investigation of differences in the margins of exports between East and West German manufacturing firms consists in reporting differences in firm characteristics that are expected to be related to margins of exports. Here we consider the following characteristics: Firm size, human capital intensity, R&D intensity, capital intensity, firm age and foreign ownership.[5]

Two of these characteristics (R&D intensity and capital intensity) are based on information taken from the second data source, the cost structure survey. As said, this is a stratified sample of firms that covers some 15,000 manufacturing enterprises. All of these firms are covered in the monthly report, too, that is the source for information on three other firm characteristics, namely firm size, human capital intensity, and whether or not a firm is an old firm that existed in 1995 already. Furthermore, all these firms are in the enterprise register system that is the source of information on the foreign ownership status of the firm. The 14,716 firms with information from these three sources are in the estimation sample that is used to empirically investigate the differences

---

[4] Data from the statistics on foreign trade are available at the enterprise level for reporting years from 2009 onwards only. Therefore, changes over time in these extensive margins and in the differences between East and West Germany cannot be documented here.

[5] For a detailed definition of each characteristic, its measurement, and a discussion of the relation with exports see Section 2.

in one extensive margin, the participation in exports, and in the intensive margin of exports (the share of exports in total sales).

Information on the two other extensive margins of exports, the number of goods exported and the number of countries exported to, is available only for an exporting firms. Matching firms with information on these extensive margins and information on the firm characteristics considered here reduces the sample of firms to 7,225.[6]

This leads to two different samples to be used in this descriptive part of the study, *Sample A* (that covers 14,716 firms, 2,594 of which are from East Germany and 12,122 of which are from West Germany) and *Sample B* (made of 7,225 firms, where 1,042 are from East Germany and 6,183 are form West Germany). Information on the average value of the firm characteristics for firms in each part of Germany is reported in Table 3 (for *Sample A*) and Table 4 (for *Sample B*).

From Table 3 we see that in *Sample A* firms in West Germany are considerably larger, have a higher intensity of human capital and lower capital intensity than East German firms. Furthermore, the proportion of old firms is larger in West Germany than in East Germany, while the share of foreign firms and the R&D intensity is about the same in both parts of Germany. The picture is similar for firms from *Sample B* (see Table 4) except that the difference in R&D intensity and in the share of foreign owned firms is in favor of East German firms here. Note that *Sample B* does by construction include exporting firms only. Therefore, due to this selection this sample cannot be considered to be representative for all firms in East and West Germany. On average, exporters tend to be larger, have higher human capital intensity, higher R&D intensity, and higher capital intensity, and they are more often older firms and foreign owned firms. This is shown by a comparison of the figures reported in Tables 3 and 4.

5. Econometric Investigation of Differences in East/West Export Margins

The descriptive evidence reported so far documents that there are large differences in both the margins of exports and in firm characteristics

---

[6] 7,225 is the number of firms with information on the number of goods exported. Information on the number of destination countries is available for 7,213 firms only.

Table 3: Difference in characteristics in enterprises from manufacturing industries in East and West Germany 2010: Sample A.

	East		West
Number of enterprises	2,594		12,122
Firm size (no. of employees)	178.11		277.51
t-Test for H_0: Difference in means = 0 (prob-value)		0.001	
Kolmogorov–Smirnov-tests (prob-value)			
H_0: Distributions do not differ		0.000	
H_0: Larger values in East Germany		0.000	
H_0: Larger values in West Germany		1.000	
Human capital intensity (wage per employee; €)	25,454		34,975
t-Test for H_0: Difference in means = 0 (prob-value)		0.000	
Kolmogorov–Smirnov-tests (prob-value)			
H_0: Distributions do not differ		0.000	
H_0: Larger values in East Germany		0.000	
H_0: Larger values in West Germany		0.999	
R&D intensity (share of R&D employees; percent)	2.66		2.47
t-Test for H_0: Difference in means = 0 (prob-value)		0.190	
Kolmogorov–Smirnov-tests (prob-value)			
H_0: Distributions do not differ		0.001	
H_0: Larger values in East Germany		0.001	
H_0: Larger values in West Germany		0.433	
Capital intensity (depreciations per employees; €)	7,791		5,362
t-Test for H_0: Difference in means = 0 (prob-value)		0.000	
Kolmogorov–Smirnov-tests (prob-value)			
H_0: Distributions do not differ		0.000	
H_0: Larger values in East Germany		1.000	
H_0: Larger values in West Germany		0.000	
Share of firms founded before 1996 (percent)	38.74		55.81
Share of foreign owned firms (percent)	13.11		13.93

Note: Entries for firm characteristics are average values for firms in the sample.

Table 4: Difference in characteristics in enterprises from manufacturing industries in East and West Germany 2010: Sample B.

	East		West
Number of enterprises	1,042		6,183
Firm size (no. of employees)	248.41		315.65
t-Test for H_0: Difference in means = 0 (prob-value)		0.324	
Kolmogorov–Smirnov-tests (prob-value)			
H_0: Distributions do not differ		0.000	
H_0: Larger values in East Germany		0.000	
H_0: Larger values in West Germany		0.987	
Human capital intensity (wage per employee; €)	27,780		36,491
t-Test for H_0: Difference in means = 0 (prob-value)		0.000	
Kolmogorov–Smirnov-tests (prob-value)			
H_0: Distributions do not differ		0.000	
H_0: Larger values in East Germany		0.000	
H_0: Larger values in West Germany		0.998	
R&D intensity (share of R&D employees; percent)	3.83		2.94
t-Test for H_0: Difference in means = 0 (prob-value)		0.000	
Kolmogorov–Smirnov-tests (prob-value)			
H_0: Distributions do not differ		0.015	
H_0: Larger values in East Germany		1.000	
H_0: Larger values in West Germany		0.007	
Capital intensity (depreciations per employees; €)	9,262		5,748
t-Test for H_0: Difference in means = 0 (prob-value)		0.000	
Kolmogorov–Smirnov-tests (prob-value)			
H_0: Distributions do not differ		0.000	
H_0: Larger values in East Germany		1.000	
H_0: Larger values in West Germany		0.000	
Share of firms founded before 1996 (percent)	42.99		61.07
Share of foreign owned firms (percent)	18.14		15.67

Note: Entries for firm characteristics are average values for firms in the sample.

related to exports between manufacturing firms from East and West Germany. To investigate the role of firm characteristics in shaping the differences in export margins the econometric study[7] proceeds in two steps.

Step one analyses whether differences in the export margins can still be observed after controlling for differences in the firm characteristics considered here. Results reported in Tables 5 and 6 reveal that this is indeed the case. Empirical models for each of the export margins that include the complete set of firm characteristics plus a dummy variable indicating whether a firm is from West Germany or not show a positive and statistically highly significant coefficient for being located in West Germany after controlling for firm characteristics. This holds for all four export margins, and for different estimation methods in the empirical model for export participation and the share of exports in total sales.[8]

Step two looks at the role of differences in characteristics between East and West German firms for the explanation of differences in the margins of exports. The approach applied here is a so-called decomposition technique. This type of empirical analysis that looks at differences in an outcome (e.g., the number of goods exported) between members of two groups (e.g., firms from East and West Germany) and that decomposes the difference into a part that is explained by differences in (observed) characteristics between members of the groups (e.g., by the different share of old firms in East and West German firms) and into a part that is due to differences in the coefficients that link firm characteristics to the outcome in a

---

[7] The econometric study is limited to the reporting year 2010. While information on export participation and on the share of exports in total sales is available for earlier years (see Table 1), information on important variables used in the econometric investigation is not: data on R&D is available from reporting year 1999 onwards only, information on foreign ownership starts in 2007, and the dummy-variable for old firms does not make (much) sense for 1995 and 2001. Furthermore, the sample used in the cost structure survey changed several times between 1995 and 2010, so that any comparison over time might be influenced by changes in the composition of the sample.

[8] Here the empirical models serve as a tool to demonstrate that East/West differences in export margins are present after controlling for firm characteristics only. Therefore, we do not go into any detail to discuss the estimation results. See Wagner (2011b) for a study with a focus on this topic.

Table 5: Empirical models for the margins of exports in enterprises from manufacturing industries in Germany 2010: Export participation and share of exports in total sales.

		Export participation		Share of exports in total sales	
		OLS	Probit	OLS	Fractional logit
West Germany	ß	0.041	0.140	0.021	0.142
(Dummy; 1 = yes)	p	0.000	0.000	0.000	0.000
Firm size	ß	5.37e–6	0.00041	0.000021	0.00011
(No. of employees)	p	0.023	0.005	0.000	0.000
Firm size (Squared)	ß	−5.70e–11	−3.22e–9	−1.78e–10	−8.68e–10
	p	0.018	0.004	0.000	0.000
Human capital	ß	5.75e–6	0.000026	6.11e–11	0.000034
(Wage per employee)	p	0.000	0.000	0.000	0.000
R&D intensity	ß	0.429	4.702	0.544	2.369
(Share of employees)	p	0.000	0.000	0.000	0.000
Capital intensity	ß	6.91e–7	−3.55e–7	5.99e–7	4.21e–6
(Depreciation/Empl.)	p	0.088	0.861	0.070	0.019
Old firm (Dummy)	ß	0.067	0.244	0.018	0.130
(1 = founded < 1996)	p	0.000	0.000	0.000	0.000
Foreign owned firm	ß	0.062	0.361	0.117	0.550
(Dummy; 1 = yes)	p	0.000	0.000	0.000	0.000
Industry controls		yes	yes	yes	yes
Number of firms		14,716	14,716	14,716	14,716

Note: ß is the estimated regression coefficient and p is the prob-value. All models include a constant; standard errors are based on robust estimates.

regression model between the two groups is widely used in in the social sciences. Some 40 years ago regression decomposition has been introduced into the economics literature by Blinder (1973) and Oaxaca (1973), and it has been widely used ever since on a broad number of topics.

Recently, Powers *et al.* (2011) published a Stata command, *mvdcmp*, for carrying out multivariate decomposition for different types of models. A discussion of the details of the decomposition techniques used by this command is far beyond the scope of this applied paper. Suffice it to say here that one novel feature of *mvdcmp* that will be used here is that it

Table 6: Empirical models for the margins of exports in enterprises from manufacturing industries in Germany 2010: Number of destination countries and number of goods exported.

		Number of destination countries	Number of goods exported
		OLS	OLS
West Germany	ß	3.811	9.144
(Dummy; 1 = yes)	p	0.000	0.000
Firm size	ß	0.0076	0.0477
(No. of employees)	p	0.000	0.000
Firm size (squared)	ß	$-5.76\mathrm{e}{-8}$	$-2.90\mathrm{e}{-7}$
	p	0.000	0.000
Human capital	ß	0.00053	0.00086
(Wage per employee)	p	0.000	0.000
R&D intensity	ß	30.527	114.29
(Share of employees)	p	0.000	0.000
Capital intensity	ß	-0.000058	-0.00022
(Depreciation/Empl.)	p	0.066	0.129
Old firm (Dummy)	ß	3.415	1.362
(1 = founded < 1996)	p	0.000	0.351
Foreign owned firm	ß	2.341	-0.547
(Dummy; 1 = yes)	p	0.001	0.819
Industry controls		yes	yes
Number of firms		7,225	7,213

Note: ß is the estimated regression coefficient and p is the prob-value. All models include a constant; standard errors are based on robust estimates.

provides a detailed decomposition (and standard errors) for the part of the difference of the outcome between the two groups of firms that is explained by differences in firm characteristics. To state it differently, *mvdcmp* reports the share of the difference in a margin of exports between East German an West German firms that can be explained by differences in the observed characteristics of the firms that are included in the empirical model for the margin, and it reports the share that each of these characteristics contributes to the explanation of the difference (plus the estimated standard error of this contribution).[9]

5.1. Export participation

At first, we look at the first extensive margin of exports, the decision to export or not. The empirical models for the participation in exports are estimated separately for East German and West German firms. The dependent variable in these models is a dummy variable that takes on the value of one for an exporting firm and that is zero for a non-exporting firm. Two variants of these models are considered here. The first is estimated by OLS, applying a LPM, the second is estimated using Probit. While the critique of an application of LPM is well known from introductory textbooks on econometrics, it should be pointed out that "it often does a very good job" (Wooldridge, 2010, p. 563). Note that the standard errors are based on estimates that are robust against heteroscedasticity. The use of the LPM is attractive here because this will be the basis for the decomposition analysis.[10]

Results for the empirical models are reported in Table 7. As expected, human capital intensity, R&D intensity, firm age and foreign ownership status are positively related to export participation in both parts of Germany, while capital intensity is not and the link between firm size and export participation is only statistically significant at a usual level for West German firms.

Results for the decomposition of the difference in export participation between East and West German firms (that amounts to 11.61 percentage points in favor of West German firms in the sample used in the estimation)

---

[9] Note that *mvdcmp* computes the same information for the part of the difference in a margin that is related to differences in the estimated coefficients. We focus here on the part that is due to observed firm characteristics and consider the part related to differences in the estimated coefficients as an unexplained part. Wagner (2008) is an earlier attempt to investigate the difference in one extensive margin, the propensity to export, for firms from East and West Germany in 2004. In that paper, that uses a less rich data set, a different decomposition method is applied that does not provide a detailed decomposition.

[10] For a "defense" of the use of the LPM (with heterosecedasticity-robust standard errors) see Wooldridge (2010, p. 562f.).

Table 7: Determinants of margins of exports in enterprises from manufacturing industries in East and West Germany 2010: Export participation.

		Linear probability model		Probit (Average marginal effects)	
		East	West	East	West
Firm size	ß	0.232e–4	6.51e–6		
(No. of employees)	p	0.194	0.011	0.00012[a]	0.878e–4[a]
Firm size (Squared)	ß	−3.72e–10	−6.45e–11	0.080	0.011
	p	0.187	0.009		
Human capital	ß	4.96e–06	6.04e–6	5.93e–6	5.74e–6
(Wage per employee)	p	0.000	0.000	0.000	0.000
R&D intensity	ß	0.862	0.293	1.586	0.917
(Share of employees)	p	0.000	0.000	0.000	0.000
Capital intensity	ß	1.18e–6	4.49e–7	8.44e–7	−3.57e–7
(Depreciation/Empl.)	p	0.075	0.382	0.346	0.514
Old firm (Dummy)	ß	0.040	0.071	0.030	0.061
(1 = founded < 1996)	p	0.019	0.000	0.078	0.000
Foreign owned firm	ß	0.114	0.052	0.120	0.064
(Dummy; 1 = yes)	p	0.000	0.000	0.000	0.000
Industry controls		yes	yes	yes	yes
Number of firms		2,594	12,122	2,594	12,122

[a]The average marginal effect for firm size takes into account that firm size is included in the model in squares, too.

Note: All models include a constant; standard errors are based on robust estimates.

are reported in Table 8.[11] More than two third of this difference is explained by differences in firm characteristics. Results for the detailed decomposition show that by far the most important characteristic is the average wage per employee that is used as a proxy variable for human capital intensity. It should be kept in mind, however, that (as discussed in Section 2)

---

[11] Note that these results are based on the LPM estimates reported in Table 7. Due to numerically problems the *mvdcmp* program could not compute results from a decomposition based on the Probit estimates.

Table 8: Decomposition of difference in the margins of exports in enterprises from manufacturing industries in East and West Germany 2010: Export participation.

	East	West
Number of enterprises	2,594	12,122
Share of exporters (percent)	70.32	81.93
Difference (percentage points)	11.61	
Decomposition results: Linear probability model		
	Share	*p*-value
Share of difference (percent) in export participation due to		
Differences in enterprise characteristics	68.47	0.000
Differences in coefficients of characteristics	31.53	0.000
Share of difference (percent) in export participation due to differences in		
Firm size	0.56	0.118
Firm size (squared)	−0.08	0.127
Human capital intensity	49.55	0.000
R&D intensity	−0.46	0.000
Capital intensity	−0.94	0.292
Old fim	10.50	0.000
Foreign owned firm	0.37	0.000
Two-digit industries	(not reported in detail)	

Note: The decomposition is based on the estimates reported in Table 7.

differences in the average wage per employee between East and West German firms do not only reflect differences in human capital but differences in the wage structure, too. The higher share of old firms that were founded before 1996 in West Germany explains 10.5 percent of the difference in the export propensity. All other characteristics do not matter.

5.2. Share of exports in total sales

Next, we look at the intensive margins of exports, the share of exports in total sales. The empirical models for the export/sales ratio are estimated separately for East German and West German firms. The dependent variable in these models is a percentage variable with a probability mass at zero due to many firms that do not export at all. An appropriate method to estimate an empirical model with this type of dependent variable is to use a fractional logit model (see Wagner, 2001 for a discussion with a view to the export/sales ratio). However, given that OLS estimates often lead to the same conclusions, and with a view on the decomposition analysis, the empirical model is estimated by OLS, too.

Results for the empirical models are reported in Table 9. Firm size, human capital intensity, R&D intensity and foreign ownership status are positively linked to export intensity as expected in firms from both parts

Table 9: Determinants of margins of exports in enterprises from manufacturing industries in East and West Germany 2010: Share of exports in sales.

		OLS		Fractional logit (Average marginal effects)	
		East	West	East	West
Firm size	ß	0.55e–4	0.21e–4		
(No. of employees)	p	0.000	0.000	0.000033[a]	0.000019[a]
Firm size (Squared)	ß	−7.74e–10	−1.70e–10	0.000	0.000
	p	0.000	0.000		
Human capital	ß	5.47e–6	6.14e–6	4.84e–6	6.00e–6
(Wage per employee)	p	0.000	0.000	0.000	0.000
R&D intensity	ß	0.465	0.584	0.330	0.433
(Share of employees)	p	0.000	0.000	0.000	0.000
Capital intensity	ß	1.19e–6	1.97e–7	9.81e–7	−3.60e–7
(Depreciation/Empl.)	p	0.005	0.641	0.009	0.353
Old firm (Dummy)	ß	−0.006	0.022	−0.001	0.026
(1 = founded < 1996)	p	0.497	0.000	0.868	0.000
Foreign owned firm	ß	0.152	0.111	0.134	0.096
(Dummy; 1 = yes)	p	0.000	0.000	0.000	0.000
Industry controls		yes	yes	yes	yes
Number of firms		2,594	12,122	2,594	12,122

[a]The average marginal effect for firm size takes into account that firm size is included in the model in squares, too.

Note: All models include a constant; standard errors are based on robust estimates.

Table 10: Decomposition of difference in the margins of exports in enterprises from manufacturing industries in East and West Germany 2010: Share of exports in sales.

	East	West
Number of enterprises	2,594	12,122
Share of exports in sales (for exporters, percent)	27.22	34.02
Difference (percentage points)	6.80	
Decomposition results: OLS estimates		
	Share	*p*-value
Share of difference (percent) in share of exports in sales due to		
Differences in enterprise characteristics	75.51	0.000
Differences in coefficients of characteristics	21.49	0.000
Share of difference (percent) in share of exports in sales due to differences in		
Firm size	2.39	0.000
Firm size (squared)	−0.29	0.000
Human capital intensity	67.01	0.000
R&D intensity	−1.22	0.000
Capital intensity	−0.55	0.464
Old fim	4.34	0.000
Foreign owned firm	1.05	0.000
Two-digit industries	(not reported in detail)	

Note: The decomposition is based on the estimates reported in Table 9.

of Germany. Firm age is only statistically significant among West German firms, while the same holds for capital intensity among East German firms only. These links are both positive as expected. Note that the coefficient estimates from the OLS models and the comparable average marginal effects based on the estimated coefficients from the fractional logit models tend to be rather similar.

Results for the decomposition of the difference in export intensity between firms from both parts of Germany are reported in Table 10.[12] More than three fourth of the difference of 6.8 percentage points (that is

---

[12] Note that these results are based on the OLS estimates reported in Table 9, because the *mvdcmp* program cannot compute the decomposition based on the fractional logit estimates.

in favor of West German firms) is explained by differences in firm characteristics. Results for the detailed decomposition show that, like in the case of export participation, the lion's share of this is due to the higher human capital intensity of West German firms that explains more than two thirds of the difference in the average export/sales ratio. However, the caveat that was mentioned above with regard to an interpretation of the difference in the average wage as a difference in human capital endowment between firms should be pointed out here, too. The contribution of the higher share of old firms in West Germany to the explanation of the difference in export intensity is about 4 percent. The other characteristics do not matter much.

5.3. Number of destination countries of exports

The third margin to look at is the number of destination countries of exports. Results for the empirical models for firms from East Germany and West Germany are reported in Table 11.[13] The estimated coefficients point to positive links between all firm characteristics and the number of countries exported to with the exception of the (insignificant) coefficients of capital intensity.

Results for the decomposition of the difference in the number of destination countries between East and West German firms (that amounts to 9.5 countries in favor of West German firms in the sample used in the estimation) are reported in Table 12. About two thirds of this difference is explained by differences in firm characteristics. Results for the detailed decomposition show that one half of the difference in the number of destination countries is explained by higher human capital intensity in West Germany. Again, the caveat with regard to an interpretation of the

---

[13] Although the dependent variable in the empirical models is a count variable that can only take positive integer values equal to or larger than one (because by construction only firms that export to at least one country are included in the sample) with a view on the decomposition analysis the models are estimated by OLS and not by using a count data model. The number of countries of destination is distributed over a rather broad range — the 99th percentile of the distribution is 90 for West German firms and 71 for East German firms (the maximum number of countries is confidential because it refers to a single firm). This justifies the use of OLS in estimating the empirical models.

Table 11: Determinants of margins of exports in enterprises from manufacturing industries in East and West Germany 2010: Number of destination countries.

		OLS	
		East	West
Firm size	ß	0.016	0.008
(No. of employees)	p	0.000	0.000
Firm size	ß	−2.20e−7	−6.01e−8
(Squared)	p	0.000	0.000
Human capital	ß	0.00027	0.00055
(Wage per employee)	p	0.007	0.000
R&D intensity	ß	5.873	37.796
(Share of employees)	p	0.408	0.000
Capital intensity	ß	−0.00006	−0.00008
(Depreciation/Empl.)	p	0.140	0.092
Old firm (Dummy)	ß	3.189	3.433
(1 = founded < 1996)	p	0.001	0.000
Foreign owned firm	ß	4.070	1.876
(Dummy; 1 = yes)	p	0.007	0.015
Industry controls		yes	yes
Number of firms		1,042	6,183

Note: All models include a constant; standard errors are based on robust estimates.

difference in the average wage as a difference in human capital endowment between firms should be kept in mind here. The second largest impact is due to the higher share of old firms that were founded before 1996 in West Germany which explains 6.5 percent of the difference in the number of export countries.

5.4. Number of goods exported

The last margin of exports to be investigated is the number of goods exported. Results for the empirical models for East German and West

Table 12: Decomposition of difference in the margins of exports in enterprises from manufacturing industries in East and West Germany 2010: Number of destination countries.

	East	West
Number of enterprises	1,042	6,183
Number of destination countries	16.38	25.89
Difference (number of countries)	9.51	
Decomposition results: OLS estimates		
	Share	*p*-value
Share of difference (percent) in number of destination countries due to		
Differences in enterprise characteristics	63.60	0.000
Differences in coefficients of characteristics	36.40	0.000
Share of difference (percent) in number of destination countries due to differences in		
Firm size	5.67	0.000
Firm size (squared)	−0.85	0.000
Human capital intensity	50.64	0.000
R&D intensity	−3.53	0.000
Capital intensity	2.94	0.020
Old fim	6.53	0.000
Foreign owned firm	−0.49	0.008
Two-digit industries	(not reported in detail)	

Note: The decomposition is based on the estimates reported in Table 11.

German firms are reported in Table 13.[14] The estimated coefficients point to positive links between the number of goods and firm size and human capital intensity in both parts of Germany, while R&D intensity only

---

[14] Although the dependent variable in the empirical models is a count variable that can only take positive integer values equal to or larger than one (because by construction only firms that export at least one good are included in the sample) with a view on the decomposition analysis the models are estimated by OLS and not by using a count data model. The number of exported goods is distributed over a rather broad range — the 99th percentile of the distribution is 311 for West German firms and 186 for East German firms (the maximum number of goods is confidential because it refers to a single firm). This justifies the use of OLS in estimating the empirical models.

Table 13: Determinants of margins of exports in enterprises from manufacturing industries in East and West Germany 2010: Number of exported goods.

		OLS	
		East	West
Firm size	ß	0.055	0.051
(No. of employees)	p	0.000	0.000
Firm size (Squared)	ß	−5.61e–7	−3.15e–7
	p	0.000	0.000
Human capital	ß	0.00052	0.0009
(Wage per employee)	p	0.016	0.000
R&D intensity	ß	20.78	140.14
(Share of employees)	p	0.472	0.000
Capital intensity	ß	−0.00017	−0.00024
(Depreciation/Empl.)	p	0.006	0.286
Old firm (Dummy)	ß	0.521	1.405
(1 = founded < 1996)	p	0.822	0.397
Foreign owned firm	ß	5.315	−2.354
(Dummy; 1 = yes)	p	0.154	0.392
Industry controls		yes	yes
Number of firms		1,040	6,173

Note: All models include a constant; standard errors are based on robust estimates.

matters for West Germany and capital intensity only matters (negatively) for East Germany. Firm age and foreign ownership status is not linked to this extensive export margin.

Results for the decomposition of the difference in in the number of exported goods between firms from East Germany and West German (that amounts to 21.3 goods in favor of West German firms in the sample used in the estimation) are reported in Table 14. About 60 percent of this difference is explained by differences in firm characteristics. According to the results for the detailed decomposition the difference in human capital intensity (measured by the average wage as a proxy variable) is again the by far most important factor to explain the difference. Here firm size matters, too, while other characteristics do not matter much (or not at all).

Table 14: Decomposition of difference in the margins of exports in enterprises from manufacturing industries in East and West Germany 2010: Number of exported goods.

	East		West
Number of enterprises	1,040		6,173
Number of destination countries	17.98		39.26
Difference (number of goods)		21.28	
Decomposition results: OLS estimates			
	Share		*p*-value
Share of difference (percent) in number of exported goods due to			
Differences in enterprise characteristics	59.14		0.000
Differences in coefficients of characteristics	40.86		0.000
Share of difference (percent) in number of exported goods due to differences in			
Firm size	16.17		0.000
Firm size (squared)	−1.99		0.000
Human capital intensity	37.02		0.000
R&D intensity	−5.87		0.000
Capital intensity	3.96		0.067
Old firm	1.19		0.404
Foreign owned firm	0.28		0.317
Two-digit industries	(not reported in detail)		

Note: The decomposition is based on the estimates reported in Table 13.

6. Discussion

This paper uses a new tailor-made data set to investigate the differences in extensive and intensive margins of exports in manufacturing firms from East Germany and West Germany. It documents that these margins do still differ in 2010, 20 years after the re-unification of Germany. West German firms outperform East German firms at all four margins of exports — they have a larger propensity to export, export a larger share of total sales, export more goods and export to a larger number of countries. All these differences are large from an economic point of view. A decomposition analysis shows that in 2010 between 59 percent and 78 percent of the difference in margins can be explained by differences in firm characteristics. Most important here is the average wage per employee that serves as a proxy-variable for human capital intensity (but that reflects difference in the wage structure between both parts of Germany, too) and the larger share of old firms in West Germany compared to East Germany.

Should these findings considered to be stylized facts that can be used as a firm foundation to discuss any policy measures with a view to close the gap in the margins of exports between East and West Germany? I doubt. One reason is that (as discussed in Section 2) differences in the average wage per employee between East and West German firms do not only reflect differences in human capital intensity but differences in the wage structure, too, and that the degree to which this is the case is not known exactly; empirical evidence from econometric studies points to an order of magnitude of the wage gap of about twenty to thirty percent (Gühne and Markwardt, 2014). Another reason is that the difference in the extensive margins related to the number of goods exported and the number of countries traded with is only documented for one year. This is due to the availability of data on these margins at the enterprise level (see Section 2). There is no information about the size of these differences in the past or in more recent years. Furthermore, 2010 might well be considered as a "non-typical" year, because it is the year of the *Great Export Recovery* that followed the *Great Export Recession* during the world-wide great financial crisis in 2008/2009 (see Wagner, 2013a; 2013b; 2014b) for empirical analyses of the export dynamics in Germany in both periods that use firm-level data). And it should be kept in mind that according to the decomposition analysis a considerable part of the difference in the export margins between manufacturing firms from East Germany and West Germany cannot be explained by differences in the observable firm characteristics that are considered in the empirical models.

With a view on these caveats the bottom line of this empirical investigation can be stated as follows. There are sizeable differences in all margins of exports between manufacturing firms in East Germany and West Germany that are only rarely recognized in comparisons of the economy in both parts of Germany. These differences can only be documented and analyzed with combined firm level data from various sources from official statistics. These firm level data should be amended for more recent reporting years and be used to closely monitor the dynamics of export margins. This will contribute to a better understanding of the causes of differences in export margins and to a firm foundation for the discussion of any policy measures that aim to reduce these differences in margins.

References

Blinder, Alan S. (1973). Wage discrimination: Reduced form and structural estimates. *Journal of Human Resources* 8 (4), 436–455.

Bundesminsterium für Wirtschaft und Energie (BMWI) (2014). *Jahresbericht der Bundesregierung zum Stand der Deutschen Einheit 2014.* Berlin: BMWI.

Fritsch, Michael, Bernd Görzig, Ottmar Hennchen and Andreas Stephan (2004). Cost structure surveys for Germany. *Schmollers Jahrbuch/Journal of Applied Social Science Studies* 124 (4), 557–566.

Gühne, Michael and Gunther Markwardt (2014). *Lohnunterschiede zwischen Ost- und Westdeutschland: Neue Einsichten. ifo Dresden berichtet* 3/2014, 37–44.

Malchin, Anja and Ramona Voshage (2009). Official firm data for Germany. *Schmollers Jahrbuch/Journal of Applied Social Science Studies* 129 (3), 501–513.

Oaxaca, Ronald (1073). Male-female wage differentials in urban labor markets. *International Economic Review* 14 (3), 693–709.

Powers, Daniel A., Hirotoshi Yoshioka and Myeong-Su Yun (2011). mvdcomp: Multivariate decomposition for nonlinear response models. *The Stata Journal* 11 (4), 556–576.

Raff, Horst and Joachim Wagner (2014). Foreign ownership and the extensive margins of exports: Evidence for manufacturing enterprises in Germany. *The World Economy* 37 (5), 579–591.

Wagner, Joachim (2001). A note on the firm size — Export relationship. *Small Business Economics* 17 (4), 229–237.

Wagner, Joachim (2008). A note on why more West than East German firms export. *International Economics and Economic Policy* 5 (4), 363–370.

Wagner, Joachim (2011a). Exports and firm characteristics in Germany: A survey of empirical studies (1991 to 2011). *Applied Economics Quarterly* 57 (2), 145–160.

Wagner, Joachim (2011b). Exports and firm characteristics in German manufacturing industries: New evidence from Representative Panel Data. *Applied Economics Quarterly* 57 (2), 107–143.

Wagner, Joachim (2012a). Trading many goods with many countries: Exporters and importers from German manufacturing industries. *Review of Economics* 63 (2), 170–186.

Wagner, Joachim (2012b). Average wage, qualification of the workforce and export performance in German enterprises: Evidence from *KombiFiD* data. *Journal of Labour Market Research* 45 (2), 161–170.

Wagner, Joachim (2013a). The granular nature of the great export collapse in German manufacturing industries, 2008/2009. *Economics — The Open-Access, Open-Assessment E-Journal* 7 (5), 1–21.

Wagner, Joachim (2013b). The great export recovery in German manufacturing industries, 2009/2010. *Review of Economics* 64 (3), 325–339.

Wagner, Joachim (2014a). New data from official statistics for imports and exports of goods by German enterprises. *Schmollers Jahrbuch/Journal of Applied Social Science Studies* 134 (3), 371–378.

Wagner, Joachim (2014b). The role of extensive margins of exports in The Great Export Recovery in Germany, 2009/2010. *Jahrbücher für Nationalökonomie und Statistik/Journal of Economics and Statistics* 234 (4), 518–526.

Wagner, Joachim (2015). A note on firm age and the margins of exports: First evidence from Germany. *The International Trade Journal* 29 (2), 93–102.

Wooldridge, Jeffrey M. (2010). Econometric analysis of cross section and panel data. Second Edition. Cambridge, Massachusetts, and London, England: The MIT Press.

Part 3

New Evidence on the Dynamics of Trade in the Short Run

Introduction

Transaction level data reveal new facts on the dynamics of trade in the short run. For the years 2009 to 2012 detailed information on the exporter and importer entry and exit by firms, on product and country entry and exit rates, and on many other indicators of the dynamics of international trade in goods is available in the *Exporter and Importer Dynamics Database for Germany* that is based on transaction level data and that is described in detail in Chapter 4 (that was originally published in Wagner, 2016).[1] In Chapter 5 (that was originally published in Wagner, 2017) information from this database is used to look at the links between measures of trade dynamics (entry, exit and survival rates, and share of entrants, in exports and imports) and characteristics of destination countries and countries of origin (distance to Germany, difficulty of foreign trade, market size).

Chapter 6 (that was originally published in Wagner, 2014a) documents the contribution of adding and dropping goods and destination countries in the sharp increase in exports of goods in Germany during the *Great Export Recovery* in 2009/2010. Firms that exported in both 2009 and 2010 are much more important for export dynamics than export starters and export stoppers. Firms that increased their exports — the drivers of the export boom — exported on average more goods and to more

---

[1] Information on exports is part of the World Bank's *Exporter Dynamics Database* that has strictly comparable information for 70 countries; see http://econ.worldbank.org/exporter-dynamics-database.

destination countries in 2009 than firms that decreased their exports. On average these firms increased both extensive margins of exports, while firms with decreased exports reduced both the number of goods exported and the number of countries exported to. Results for the dynamics of German imports in 2009/2010 that are reported in Chapter 7 (originally published as Wagner, 2013) show an identical pattern.

In Chapter 8 (that was originally published in Wagner, 2014b) an approach suggested by Gabaix (2011) is applied to investigate for the first time the role of idiosyncratic shocks to the largest firms from manufacturing industries in the dynamics of German imports. Imports are power-law distributed and that the distribution of imports in the industries can be characterized as fat-tailed. Results show that idiosyncratic shocks to very large firms are important for the import dynamics in 2010/2011 but not in 2009/2010.

References

Gabaix, Xavier (2011). The granular origins of aggregate fluctuations. *Econometrica* 79 (3), 733–772.

Wagner, Joachim (2013). Extensive margins of imports in the great import recovery in Germany, 2009/2010. *Economics Bulletin* 33 (4), 2732–2743.

Wagner, Joachim (2014a). The role of extensive margins of exports in the great export recovery in Germany, 2009/2010. *Journal of Economics and Statistics* 234 (4), 518–526.

Wagner, Joachim (2014b). A note on the granular nature of imports in German manufacturing industries. *Review of Economics* 65 (3), 241–252.

Wagner, Joachim (2016). Exporter and importer dynamics database for Germany. *Journal of Economics and Statistics* 236 (3), 411–420.

Wagner, Joachim (2017). Trade dynamics, Trade costs and market size: First evidence from the exporter and importer dynamics database for Germany. *Review of Economics* 63 (2), 137–159.

Chapter 4

Exporter and Importer Dynamics Database for Germany*

1. Introduction

Researchers from the Word Bank recently released version 2.0 of the Exporter Dynamics Database (EDD).[1] This database includes exporter characteristics and measures of exporter growth based on firm-level customs information from 70 countries, primarily for the period between 2005 and 2012. The measures are available at the country-year, country-year-product, and country-year-destination level. One shortcoming of the earlier version 1.0 of the Exporter Dynamics Database was the absence of information on several of the most important countries in world exports, including Germany, the third largest exporter (and importer) of goods.

* Originally Published in *Journal of Economics and Statistics* (2016), 236 (3), 411–420.
The data used in this paper and the Stata do-file that extracts the information reported are available from the data archive of the journal. The readme-file included there gives further information on the data. I thank Melanie Scheller from Destatis for preparing the data base, running the Stata do-files and checking the results for violation of privacy. Furthermore, I thank Ana M. Fernandes and Aldo Pazzini Bortoluzzi from the World Bank for providing the Stata do-files that are used to compute the statistics included in the data base.

[1] See http://econ.worldbank.org/exporter-dynamics-database.

This note contributes to the project by providing the evidence for exports of Germany for the years 2009 to 2012 that is now part of the World Bank's EDD. Furthermore, it provides for the first time strictly comparable statistics for imports, thereby introducing the *Importer Dynamics Database* for Germany. The note provides details regarding the EDD and IDD for Germany, and it documents selected results for goods trade as a whole, and for trade with three of the most important partner countries (France, USA, and China).

2. Transaction Level Data on German Exports and Imports of Goods

In Germany information on the goods traded internationally and on the countries with which these goods are traded[2] is available from the statistic on foreign trade (*Außenhandelsstatistik*). This statistic is based on two sources. One source is the reports by German firms on transactions with firms from countries that are members of the European Union (EU); these reports are used to compile the so-called *Intrahandelsstatistik* on intra-EU trade. The other source is transaction-level data collected by the customs on trade with countries outside the EU (the so-called *Extrahandelsstatistik*).[3] The raw data that are used to build the statistic on foreign trade are transaction level data, i.e., they relate to one transaction of a German firm with a firm located outside Germany at a time. Published data from this statistic report exports or imports aggregated at the level of goods traded and by country of destination or origin.

This paper uses the raw data at the transaction level. The unit of observation in these data is a single transaction between economic agents located in two countries, e.g., the export of X kilogram of *Good A* with a

---

[2] Note that in Germany information on international trade in services is compiled by the German Central Bank (*Deutsche Bundesbank*) to build the balance of services trade (*Dienstleistungsbilanz*).

[3] Note that firms with a value of exports to and imports from EU-countries that did not exceed 400,000 Euro in the previous year or in the current year do not have to report to the statistic on intra-EU trade. For trade with firms from non-member countries all transactions that exceed 1,000 Euro (or have a weight that exceeds 1,000 kilogram) are registered. For details see Statistisches Bundesamt, Qualitätsbericht Außenhandel, January 2011.

value of Y Euro from Germany to the USA. For a given year, the sum over all export or import transactions is identical to the figures published by the Federal Statistical Office for total exports or imports of Germany.[4]

The record of the transaction usually[5] includes a firm identifier (tax registration number) of the exporting (or importing) firm. Using this identifier information at the transaction level can be aggregated at the level of the trading firm to generate year-firm-product-value-weight-destination (or -origin) data. The Federal Statistical Office prepared this type of data for the reporting year 2009 for the first time; the latest data available at the time of writing this note are for 2012. These data show who trades how much of which good with customers (or suppliers) from which country in a given year.

Products are distinguished according to very detailed classifications. In the data used for this paper, the Harmonized System at 6-digit level (HS6) is used as the product classification system. Although transactions are recorded at a higher level of disaggregation, HS6 is used since this is the most detailed level comparable internationally (see Cebeci *et al.*, 2012, p. 9). Note that due to privacy protection any published results refer to the more aggregate HS2 level.

Following the procedure applied by the World Bank team in preparing the Exporter Dynamics Database transaction that cover goods from HS Chapter 27 (hydrocarbons such as oil, petroleum, natural gas, and coal etc.) were eliminated from the raw data set (see Cebeci *et al.*, 2012, p. 11).

3. Exporter and Importer Dynamics Database for Germany: A First Look

Using the year-firm-product-value-weight-destination (or -origin) data that were linked over the four years from 2009 to 2012 and the original Stata do-files that were used to compute the statistics in the World Bank's

---

[4] This has been confirmed by Melanie Scheller from the Federal Statistical Office in a mail sent on May 20, 2015.

[5] Note that this identifier is missing for several transactions for various reasons including traders that do not have a (German) tax identification number; further details were not revealed to me.

Exporter Dynamics Database a series of measures was computed that cover for German exports and imports information on basic characteristics, concentration/diversification, firm dynamics, product dynamics, destination/origin dynamics, and unit prices. For Germany all measures are available for exports and imports at different disaggregation levels, i.e., by year, by year-product (HS2) and by year-destination (or year-origin); furthermore, information for exports and imports are available by year-3-digit-ISIC-category. The database has information for 98 measures by year, 113 measures for year-product (and year-3-digit-ISIC-category) and 74 measures for year-destination (or year-origin). Cebeci *et al.* (2012, p. 14ff.) give the exact definition of all measures and report in a table which measures are available at which level of disaggregation.

To give an impression on the content of the Exporter and Importer Dynamics Database for Germany Table 1 reports results for selected measures and the reporting years 2010 and 2011. The two years were chosen because some measures refer to changes over time, and information has to be available for the year before (i.e., for 2009 in 2010) and for the following year (i.e., for 2012 in 2011).

In Table 1, *trade* refers to either export or import. *Traders* are firms that trade in year t. *Entrants* are firms that do not trade in year $t - 1$ but trade in year t. *Exiters* trade in t but not in $t + 1$. *Incumbents* trade both in $t - 1$ and t. *Survivors* do not trade in $t - 1$ but trade in both t and $t + 1$. *Product Entry Rate of Incumbents* is defined as the number of HS6 products not traded in $t - 1$ but traded in t by a specific incumbent over the number of all HS6 products traded by the same incumbent in t. The *Share of New Products in Total Trade Value of Incumbents* is defined as the trade value of new HS6 products traded by a specific incumbent over the total trade value of the same incumbent. *Product Exit Rate of Incumbents* is defined as the number of HS6 products traded by a specific incumbent in t but not in $t + 1$ over the number of all HS6 products traded by the same incumbent. *Country Entry and Exit Rate* and *Share of New Countries in Total Trade Value of Incumbents* are defined analogously, where a country is either a country of destination (exports) or a country of origin (imports).

The big picture tends to be rather similar over time (although the overall dynamics of trade were rather different in 2009/2010 compared to

Table 1: Exporter and importer dynamics in Germany: All goods and all countries.

	2010		2011	
	Export	Import	Export	Import
Number of traders	108,136	124,196	118,473	138,656
Number of incumbents	81,252	94,884	90,392	103,732
Share of top five percent of traders	0.85	0.84	0.86	0.85
Share of top 10 largest traders	0.22	0.14	0.22	0.13
Firm entry rate (Number entrants/ Number traders)	0.25	0.24	0.24	0.25
Firm exit rate (Number exiters/ Number traders)	0.15	0.16	0.16	0.16
Firm survival rate (Number survivors/ Number entrants)	0.70	0.71	0.63	0.63
Share of entrants in trade (Total trade value of entrants/Total trade value in that year)	0.05	0.08	0.05	0.06
Number of HS6 products per trader (Median)	3	4	3	4
Product entry rate of incumbents (Median)	0.29	0.41	0.25	0.43
Share of new products in total trade value of incumbents (Median)	0.006	0.029	0.005	0.031
Product exit rate of incumbents (Median)	0.17	0.36	0.21	0.37
Number of countries per trader (Median)	3	2	3	2
Country entry rate of incumbents (Median)	0.21	0.17	0.17	0.17
Share of new countries in total trade value of incumbents (Median)	0.016	0.0007	0.009	0.0007
Country exit rate of incumbents (Median)	0.093	0.083	0.13	0.083

Note: Trade refers to either export or import. Traders are firms that trade in year t. Entrants are firms that do not trade in year $t-1$ but trade in year t. Exiters trade in t but not in $t+1$. Incumbents trade both in $t-1$ and t. Survivors do not trade in $t-1$ but trade in both t and $t+1$. Product Entry Rate of Incumbents is defined as the number of HS6 products not traded in $t-1$ but traded in t by a specific incumbent over the number of all HS6 products traded by the same incumbent in t. The Share of New Products in Total Trade Value of Incumbents is defined as the trade value of new HS6 products traded by a specific incumbent over the total trade value of the same incumbent. Product Exit Rate of Incumbents is defined as the number of HS6 products traded by a specific incumbent in t but not in $t+1$ over the number of all HS6 products traded by the same incumbent. Country Entry and Exit Rate and Share of New Countries in Total Trade Value of Incumbents are defined analogously, where a country is either a country of destination (exports) or a country of origin (imports).

2010/2011 — total exports grew by 18.5 percent and total imports grew by 19.9 percent in 2009/2010, while the respective growth rates were 11.4 percent and 13.2 percent in 2011/2012). Furthermore, many measures are highly similar for exports and imports (including the share of top five percent of traders, the measures of dynamics in trade participation, and the number of products and countries trades with per trader), while others differ considerably (the share of top 10 largest traders is much larger in exports than in imports; both the product entry rate and the product exit rate of incumbents is much smaller in exports than in imports).

The firm entry and exit rate is quite large for both exports and imports; the share of new traders in total trade, however, is small. The same holds for product entry and exit rates and the share of new products in total trade value of incumbents, and for the corresponding measures for countries trades with. This illustrates that the dynamics of both exports and imports are dominated by the intensive margin (the change in trade by incumbents) and that the extensive margins (firm entry/exit, product entry/exit, country entry/exit) play a minor role only.[6]

Given that strictly comparable figures for all statistics related to exports (but not to imports) are available from the World Bank's Exporter Dynamics Database for many countries, the figures reported in Table 1 for Germany can be used as a benchmark for any comparison with other countries from the EDD to see how different (or similar) Germany is compared to its trading partners.

Evidence in the Exporter and Importer Dynamics Database for Germany is not limited to trade in all goods with all countries. The measures included in Table 1 (and the other measures from the World Bank's Exporter Dynamics Database) are available for trade in all goods with each country, and for trade with all countries in each HS2 product (or product from each 3-digit-ISIC category). To illustrate the usefulness of this more disaggregate information Tables 2–4 report the measures for the trade with the three most important partner countries, France (that was

---

[6] Evidence on the minor role of firm entry and exit for the dynamics of trade in the short run is in line with results reported for the manufacturing sector of Germany in Wagner (2013; 2014).

Table 2: Exporter and importer dynamics in Germany: Trade with France (all goods).

	2010		2011	
	Export	Import	Export	Import
Number of traders	29,633	22,643	30,550	22,981
Number of incumbents	24,048	17,040	24,815	17,386
Share of top five percent of traders	0.80	0.85	0.81	0.85
Share of top 10 largest traders	0.28	0.35	0.29	0.32
Firm entry rate (Number entrants/ Number traders)	0.19	0.25	0.19	0.24
Firm exit rate (Number exiters/ Number traders)	0.18	0.23	0.16	0.23
Firm survival rate (Number survivors/Number entrants)	0.70	0.59	0.67	0.61
Share of entrants in trade (Total trade value of entrants/Total trade value in that year)	0.05	0.05	0.05	0.05
Number of HS6 products per trader (Median)	2	2	2	2
Product entry rate of incumbents (Median)	0	0.2	0	0.2
Share of new products in total trade value of incumbents (Median)	0	0.004	0	0.003
Product exit rate of incumbents (Median)	0	0.2	0	0.2

Note: Trade refers to either export or import. Traders are firms that trade in year t. Entrants are firms that do not trade in year $t-1$ but trade in year t. Exiters trade in t but not in $t+1$. Incumbents trade both in $t-1$ and t. Survivors do not trade in $t-1$ but trade in both t and $t+1$. Product Entry Rate of Incumbents is defined as the number of HS6 products not traded in $t-1$ but traded in t by a specific incumbent over the number of all HS6 products traded by the same incumbent in t. The Share of New Products in Total Trade Value of Incumbents is defined as the trade value of new HS6 products traded by a specific incumbent over the total trade value of the same incumbent. Product Exit Rate of Incumbents is defined as the number of HS6 products traded by a specific incumbent in t but not in $t+1$ over the number of all HS6 products traded by the same incumbent.

Table 3: Exporter and importer dynamics in Germany: Trade with USA (all goods).

	2010		2011	
	Export	Import	Export	Import
Number of traders	26,755	40,574	28,229	48,048
Number of incumbents	17,671	26,748	20,356	30,442
Share of top five percent of traders	0.88	0.93	0.88	0.94
Share of top 10 largest traders	0.39	0.31	0.38	0.31
Firm entry rate (Number entrants/Number traders)	0.34	0.34	0.28	0.37
Firm exit rate (Number exiters/Number traders)	0.19	0.25	0.24	0.25
Firm survival rate (Number survivors/Number entrants)	0.55	0.57	0.50	0.47
Share of entrants in trade (Total trade value of entrants/Total trade value in that year)	0.03	0.07	0.04	0.05
Number of HS6 products per trader (Median)	2	2	2	2
Product entry rate of incumbents (Median)	0.25	0.5	0.17	0.53
Share of new products in total trade value of incumbents (Median)	0.002	0.14	0.0005	0.16
Product exit rate of incumbents (Median)	0	0.5	0.08	0.5

Note: Trade refers to either export or import. Traders are firms that trade in year t. Entrants are firms that do not trade in year $t - 1$ but trade in year t. Exiters trade in t but not in $t + 1$. Incumbents trade both in $t - 1$ and t. Survivors do not trade in $t - 1$ but trade in both t and $t + 1$. Product Entry Rate of Incumbents is defined as the number of HS6 products not traded in $t - 1$ but traded in t by a specific incumbent over the number of all HS6 products traded by the same incumbent in t. The Share of New Products in Total Trade Value of Incumbents is defined as the trade value of new HS6 products traded by a specific incumbent over the total trade value of the same incumbent. Product Exit Rate of Incumbents is defined as the number of HS6 products traded by a specific incumbent in t but not in $t + 1$ over the number of all HS6 products traded by the same incumbent.

Table 4: Exporter and importer dynamics in Germany: Trade with China (all goods).

	2010		2011	
	Export	Import	Export	Import
Number of traders	18,889	49,079	20,334	57,461
Number of incumbents	11,628	32,593	13,866	37,652
Share of top five percent of traders	0.88	0.86	0.88	0.87
Share of top 10 largest traders	0.41	0.16	0.41	0.13
Firm entry rate (Number entrants/ Number traders)	0.38	0.34	0.32	0.34
Firm exit rate (Number exiters/ Number traders)	0.21	0.22	0.27	0.23
Firm survival rate (Number survivors/Number entrants)	0.54	0.61	0.50	0.54
Share of entrants in trade (Total trade value of entrants/Total trade value in that year)	0.05	0.08	0.04	0.08
Number of HS6 products per trader (Median)	2	3	2	3
Product entry rate of incumbents (Median)	0.29	0.5	0.24	0.5
Share of new products in total trade value of incumbents (Median)	0.004	0.09	0.002	0.10
Product exit rate of incumbents (Median)	0	0.48	0.14	0.5

Note: Trade refers to either export or import. Traders are firms that trade in year t. Entrants are firms that do not trade in year $t-1$ but trade in year t. Exiters trade in t but not in $t+1$. Incumbents trade both in $t-1$ and t. Survivors do not trade in $t-1$ but trade in both t and $t+1$. Product Entry Rate of Incumbents is defined as the number of HS6 products not traded in $t-1$ but traded in t by a specific incumbent over the number of all HS6 products traded by the same incumbent in t. The Share of New Products in Total Trade Value of Incumbents is defined as the trade value of new HS6 products traded by a specific incumbent over the total trade value of the same incumbent. Product Exit Rate of Incumbents is defined as the number of HS6 products traded by a specific incumbent in t but not in $t+1$ over the number of all HS6 products traded by the same incumbent.

number 1 in exports and number 3 in imports in 2011), USA (numbers 2 and 4) and China (numbers 4 and 2).

The top five percent of traders play a dominant role in exports and imports with all three trade partners. Firm entry and exit tends to be more pronounced in trade with the more distant partners USA and China compared to the neighbor country France. However, the share of new traders in total trade is small in all three countries, and the same holds for product entry and exit rates and the share of new products in total trade value of incumbents. Identical to the case of trade with all countries (documented in Table 1) the dynamics of both exports and imports are dominated by the intensive margin (the change in trade by incumbents) and the extensive margins (firm entry/exit, product entry/exit) play a minor role only.

Information at the level of partner countries in trade (or at the level of goods traded) can be used to search for systematic patterns in the links between measures of exports or imports dynamics on the one hand and characteristics of trade partners (like distance to Germany, GDP as a measure of market size, or indicators of the ease of doing business with a country) or of traded goods (like consumer goods vs. investment goods), and for tests of theoretical hypotheses on these links.

4. Selected Applications of the World Bank Exporter Dynamics Database

Data from the World Bank Exporter Dynamics Database have been used in recent papers to document some stylized facts that hold for a large number of countries and to investigate more specific topics of interest.

Freund and Pierola (2012) use data for 32 countries to investigate the role of the largest exporters for shaping trade patterns. They report that the top one percent of exporters — which they call "export superstars" — dominate exports and cover about half of all exports on average in the 32 countries (while the top 10 percent cover 90 percent).

Cebeci *et al.* (2012) use data for 38 developing and seven developed countries to document a number of stylized facts, including the following: Larger or more developed economies have more exporters, larger and more diversified exporters, and lower entry and exit rates into exporting;

export expansion along intensive margin (size of exporters) is more important for export growth than entry of new exporters (the extensive margin); export exit and entry rates are highly and strongly positively correlated; there is a high importance of a small number of large multi-product firms that export to many destinations; bilateral exports increase with the size of the destination market and decrease with distance and with bilateral tariffs.

Fernandes *et al.* (2013) investigate the extent of "export entrepreneurship" (i.e., the advent of new exporting firms, new export products, and new export market destinations) with data from 11 Latin American and Caribbean countries. They report that countries from this region appear to be no less entrepreneurial in terms of the extensive margins of exports than comparator countries.

Jaud *et al.* (2015) look at data from 34 developing countries to investigate the implications of financial vulnerability for export diversification. They find a negative and economically large effect.

Fernandes *et al.* (2015) use data for 42 developing countries across different regions of the world to estimate the effect of pesticide standards on firms' export decisions. The analysis shows that product standards significantly affect foreign market access.

5. Concluding Remarks

The papers summarized in Section 5 illustrate that the Exporter Dynamics Database (EDD) makes a very useful addition to the box of tools available for empirical trade economists. Data are open access, and it is easy to use the information to investigate a broad range of topics, including the discovery and documentation of new stylized facts. Furthermore, the data can be used in empirical investigations of hypotheses derived in theoretical models. Here, the great advantage of the EDD data is that they are strictly comparable over a large number of countries, which adds tremendous value to every empirical exercise performed with these data, because "the credibility of a new finding that is based on carefully analyzing two data sets is far more twice that of a result based only on one". (Hamermesh, 2000, p. 376)

Although the empirical trade literature based on transaction level data (surveyed in Wagner, 2016) grew exponentially over the recent years, and we learned a lot from these papers, there is plenty of scope for future research. First and foremost, we do know much less about imports, its margins, and its role in the dynamics of trade, than about exports. The Importer Dynamics Database for Germany introduced in this note is a first step to fill this gap. Here, evidence for more countries is most welcome. It would be great if a project that is comparable to the World Bank Exporter Dynamics Database could be realized for imports, too.

References

Fernandes, Ana M. Daniel Lederman and Mario Gutierrez-Rocha (2013). Export entrepreneurship and trade structure in Latin America during good and bad times. *Policy Research Paper*, No. 6413 (Washington, DC: World Bank).

Fernandes, Ana M. Esteban Ferro and John S. Wilson (2015). Product standards and firms' export decisions. *Policy Research Paper*, No. 7315 (Washington, DC: World Bank).

Cebeci, Tolga, Ana M. Fernandes, Caroline Freund and Martha Denisse Pierola (2012). Exporter dynamics database. *Policy Research Working Paper*, No. 6229 (Washington, DC: World Bank).

Freund, Caroline and Martha Denisse Pierola (2012). Export superstars. *Policy Research Working Paper*, No. 6222 (Washington, DC: World Bank).

Hamermesh, Daniel S. (2000). The craft of labormetrics. *Industrial and Labor Relations Review* 53 (3), 363380.

Jaud, Mélise, Youssouf Kiendrebeogo and Marie-Ange Veganzones-Varoudakis (2015). Financial vulnerability and export dynamics. Mimeo.

Wagner, Joachim (2013). The granular nature of the great export collapse in German manufacturing industries, 2008/2009. *Economics: The Open-Access, Open-Assessment E-Journal* 7 (20135), 121.

Wagner, Joachim (2014). The role of extensive margins of exports in *The Great Export Recovery* in Germany, 2009/2010. *Jahrbücher für Nationalökonomie und Statistik/Journal of Economics and Statistics* 234 (4), 518526.

Wagner, Joachim (2016). A survey of empirical studies using transaction level data on exports and imports. *Review of World Economics* 152 (1), 215–225.

Chapter 5

Trade Dynamics, Trade Costs and Market Size: First Evidence from the Exporter and Importer Dynamics Database for Germany*

Abstract

This note uses the newly available Exporter and Importer Dynamics Database for Germany to investigate the links between trade dynamics, trade costs and market

* Originally Published in *Review of Economics* (2017), 63 (2), 137–159.
I thank two anonymous referees for comments that helped to improve an earlier version. The transaction level data on German exports and imports used to prepare the Exporter and Importer Dynamics Database for Germany are strictly confidential and can only be used inside the research data center of the German Federal Statistical Office. I thank Melanie Scheller for preparing the data base and checking the results for violation of privacy. The data from the exporter and importer dynamics data base for Germany are available from the web; see the data archive entry for Wagner (2016b) available at http://www.degruyter.com/view/j/jbnst.2016.236.issue-3/jbnst-2015-1015/jbnst-2015-1015.xml?format=INT#supplementaryMaterialBlock. To facilitate replication the Stata do-files used to compute the results reported in this paper are available from the author on request.

size. It shows results for the dynamics of Germany's goods trade as a whole, and for trade with two of the most important partner countries, namely France and China. Furthermore, it reports results from the first empirical study that searches for links between measures of trade dynamics (entry, exit and survival rates, and share of entrants in total exports and imports) in destination countries of exports and countries of origin of imports on the one hand and characteristics of these countries (distance to Germany, difficulty of foreign trade, and market size) on the other hand.

Keywords: Exports, imports, transaction level data, Germany.

1. Motivation

Over the past 20 years researchers from all over the world used either census-type firm level data collected by the statistical offices or other large surveys of firms to investigate which firms trade (how much) and how trade is related to various dimensions of firm performance.[1] More recently, empirical trade economists went one step further and investigated which firms trade how much of which goods with customers or suppliers from which countries. The data used in these studies are based on records of (legal) cross-border transaction regularly collected by the customs (or other institutions). The unit of observation in these data is a single transaction between economic agents located in two countries, e.g., the export of X kilogram of *good A* with a value of Y Euro from Germany to China. The record of the transaction usually includes a firm identifier (tax registration number) of the exporting or importing firm. Using this identifier information at the transaction level can be aggregated at the level of the trading firm to generate year-firm-product-value-weight-destination (or -origin) data. Wagner (2016a) provides a survey of 147 empirical studies for 39 countries, plus eight studies for multiple countries, that use such transaction level data on exports or imports.

---

[1] This literature was started by Bernard and Jensen (1995) and grew exponentially over time; for surveys, see Wagner (2007; 2012).

To facilitate research based on internationally comparable data of this type researchers from the Word Bank's Trade and Integration Team, Development Research Group, prepared the *Exporter Dynamics Database* (Cebeci *et al.*, 2012). This database includes measures of exporter dynamics based on firm-level customs information from 38 developing and seven developed countries, primarily for the period between 2003 and 2010. The measures are available at the country-year, country-year-product, and country-year-destination level. They can be downloaded free of charge from http://econ.worldbank.org/exporter-dynamics-database. Cebeci *et al.* (2012) use these data to document several new stylized facts about exporter behavior across countries.

One shortcoming of the Exporter Dynamics Database in the version described in Cebeci *et al.* (2012) is the absence of information on several of the most important countries in world exports, including Germany, the third largest exporter (and importer) of goods (World Trade Organization, 2012, p. 30). To overcome this shortcoming Wagner (2016b) prepared this information for Germany for the years 2009 to 2012. This information is now part of version 2.0 of the World Bank's Exporter Dynamic Database. Furthermore, Wagner (2016b) provides for the first time strictly comparable statistics for imports.[2]

This note intends to demonstrate the usefulness of this newly available Exporter and Importer Dynamics Database for Germany for empirical studies in the dynamics of trade relations. It documents facts on selected measures of export and import dynamics for Germany and investigates the links between these measures and characteristics of trade partner countries that measure trade costs and market size.

The paper looks at four measures of trade dynamics[3] that are defined as follows: *Traders* are firms that trade in year *t*. *Entrants* are firms that do

---

[2] The data from the Exporter and Importer Dynamics Data Base for Germany are available from the web; see the data archive entry for Wagner (2016b) available at http://www.degruyter.com/view/j/jbnst.2016.236.issue-3/jbnst-2015-1015/jbnst-2015-1015.xml?format=INT#supplementaryMaterialBlock.

[3] For a complete list of all indicators included in the Exporter and Importer Dynamics Data Base for Germany see the online Appendix for Wagner (2016b) that is available at the link given in footnote 2.

not trade in year $t - 1$ but trade in year t. *Exiters* trade in t but not in $t + 1$. *Incumbents* trade both in $t - 1$ and t. *Survivors* do not trade in $t - 1$ but trade in both t and $t + 1$. The paper looks at four measures of trade dynamics: The *Firm Entry Rate* is computed as the number of entrants divided by the number of traders. The *Firm Exit Rate* is defined by the number of exiters divided by the number of traders. The *Firm Survival Rate* is equal to the number of survivors divided by the number of entrants. The *Share of Entrants in Trade* is given by the total trade value of entrants divided by the total trade value in that year.

As is documented in Section 3 below (and in more detail in the Appendix) these indicators of trade dynamics vary widely across countries of export destination and across countries of origin of imports. Given that export and import dynamics are important for the development of the German economy in the short and in the long run it is important to understand how trade dynamics is related to characteristics of the trade partner countries. This paper contributes to the literature by looking at the links between the selected indicators of trade dynamics defined above and three characteristics of partner countries, namely two indicators of trade costs and an indicator of market size.

Trade costs are measured by the geographical distance of Germany to the country of destination of exports or the country of origin of imports as a proxy variable for transportation costs, and by an index that proxies the ease of trading across borders in the destination/origin countries by measuring the time and cost associated with exporting and importing a standardized cargo of goods by sea transport. Market size is measured by the Gross Domestic Product of a partner country (for details see Section 4.1).

The rest of the paper is organized as follows. Section 2 provides details regarding the transaction level data for German exports and imports of goods used to prepare the data base. Section 3 documents selected results from the *Exporter and Importer Dynamics Database for Germany* for the dynamics of goods trade as a whole, and for trade with two of the most important partner countries, namely France and China. Section 4 reports results from an econometric investigation of the links between trade dynamics and trade costs. Section 5 concludes.

2. Transaction Level Data on German Exports and Imports of Goods[4]

In Germany information on the goods traded internationally and on the countries with which these goods are traded is available from the statistic on foreign trade (*Außenhandelsstatistik*). The raw data that are used to build the statistic on foreign trade are transaction level data, i.e., they relate to one transaction of a German firm with a firm located outside Germany at a time. Published data from this statistic report exports or imports aggregated at the level of goods traded and by country of destination or origin.

The data used in this paper are based on the raw data at the transaction level. The unit of observation in these data is a single transaction between economic agents located in two countries, e.g., the export of X kilogram of *good A* with a value of Y Euro from Germany to China. For a given year, the sum over all export or import transactions is identical to the figures published by the Federal Statistical Office for total exports or imports of Germany.

The record of the transaction usually includes a firm identifier (tax registration number) of the exporting (or importing) firm. Using this identifier information at the transaction level can be aggregated at the level of the trading firm to generate year-firm-product-value-weight-destination (or -origin) data. The Federal Statistical Office prepared this type of data for the reporting year 2009 for the first time; the latest data available at the time of writing this note are for 2012. These data show who trades how much of which good with customers (or suppliers) from which country in a given year.

Following the procedure applied by the World Bank team in preparing the Exporter Dynamics Database transaction that cover goods from HS Chapter 27 (hydrocarbons such as oil, petroleum, natural gas, and coal etc.) were eliminated from the raw data set (see Cebeci *et al.*, 2012, p. 11). Goods from all other sectors are included.

---

[4] For a more detailed description of the data see Wagner (2016b).

3. Exporter and Importer Dynamics in Germany: A First Glance at the Evidence

Using the year-firm-product-value-weight-destination (or -origin) data that were linked over the four years from 2009 to 2012 and the original Stata do-files that were used to compute the statistics in the World Bank's Exporter Dynamics Database a series of measures was computed that cover for German exports and imports information on basic characteristics, concentration/diversification, firm dynamics, product dynamics, destination/origin dynamics, and unit prices. For Germany all measures are available for exports and imports at different disaggregation levels, i.e., by year, by year-product (HS2) and by year-destination (or year-origin); furthermore, information for exports and imports are available by year-3-digit-ISIC-category. Cebeci *et al.* (2012, p. 14ff) give the exact definition of all measures and report in a table which measures are available at which level of disaggregation.

Table 1 reports results for selected measures and the reporting year 2010. This year was chosen because for all but the first measure (the number of trading firms in a year t) information has to be available for the year $t - 1$ and/or for the year $t + 1$, too.[5]

In the table *trade* refers to either export or import. *Traders* are firms that trade in year t. *Entrants* are firms that do not trade in year $t - 1$ but trade in year t. *Exiters* trade in t but not in $t + 1$. *Incumbents* trade both in $t - 1$ and t. *Survivors* do not trade in $t - 1$ but trade in both t and $t + 1$. The *Firm Entry Rate* is computed as the number of entrants divided by the number of traders. The *Firm Exit Rate* is defined by the number of exiters divided by the number of traders. The *Firm Survival Rate* is equal to the number of survivors divided by the number of entrants. The *Share of Entrants in Trade* is given by the total trade value of entrants divided by the total trade value in that year.

For Germany's trade with all countries the firm entry and exit rate is quite large for both exports and imports; the share of new traders in total trade, however, is small. This is in line with evidence reported for exports for Chile by Álvarez and Fuentes (2011), for Hungary by Békés and Muraközy (2012), for Turkey by Cebeci and Fernandes (2015), and for

---

[5] Comparable results for 2011 can be easily computed from the raw data.

Table 1: **Exporter and importer dynamics, Germany, 2010.**

	2010	
	Export	Import
Trade with all countries		
Firm Entry Rate (Number Entrants/Number Traders) (percent)	24.86	23.60
Firm Exit Rate (Number Exiters/Number Traders) (percent)	14.88	16.28
Firm Survival Rate (Number Survivors/Number Entrants) (percent)	69.78	71.11
Share of Entrants in Trade (Total Trade Value of Entrants/Total Trade Value in that Year) (percent)	5.44	7.91
Trade with France		
Firm Entry Rate (Number Entrants/Number Traders) (percent)	18.85	24.74
Firm Exit Rate (Number Exiters/Number Traders) (percent)	17.53	22.94
Firm Survival Rate (Number Survivors/Number Entrants) (percent)	69.97	58.75
Share of Entrants in Trade (Total Trade Value of Entrants/Total Trade Value in that Year) (percent)	5.24	5.37
Trade with China		
Firm Entry Rate (Number Entrants/Number Traders) (percent)	38.44	33.59
Firm Exit Rate (Number Exiters/Number Traders) (percent)	21.21	22.46
Firm Survival Rate (Number Survivors/Number Entrants) (percent)	54.15	61.26
Share of Entrants in Trade (Total Trade Value of Entrants/Total Trade Value in that Year) (percent)	4.57	8.43

Note: Trade refers to either export or import. Traders are firms that trade in year t. Entrants are firms that do not trade in year $t-1$ but trade in year t. Exiters trade in t but not in $t+1$. Survivors do not trade in $t-1$ but trade in both t and $t+1$. Incumbents trade both in $t-1$ and t.

exports and imports in Slovenia by Damijan *et al.* (2014). Furthermore, entry/exit/survival rates are highly similar for exports and imports.

Given that strictly comparable figures for all statistics related to exports (but not to imports) are available from the World Bank's Exporter

Dynamics Database for many countries, the figures reported in Table 1 for Germany can be used as a benchmark for any comparison with other countries from the EDD to see how different (or similar) Germany is compared to its trading partners.

Evidence in the Exporter and Importer Dynamics Database for Germany is not limited to trade in all goods with all countries. The measures reported in Table 1 for Germany's total trade (and all other measures from the World Bank's Exporter Dynamics Database) are available for trade in all goods with each country, and for trade with all countries in each HS2 product (or product from each 3-digit-ISIC category). To illustrate the usefulness of this more disaggregate information Table 1 reports the respective figures for the trade with two of the most important partner countries, France (that was number 1 in exports and number 3 in imports in 2011), and China (that was numbers 4 and 2, respectively). Here, firm entry and exit tends to be more pronounced in trade with the more distant partner China compared to the neighbor country France.

Information at the level of partner countries in trade (or at the level of goods traded) can be used to search for systematic patterns in the links between measures of exports or imports dynamics on the one hand and characteristics of trade partners (like distance to Germany, GDP as a measure of market size, or indicators of the ease of doing business with a country) or of traded goods (like consumer goods vs. investment goods), and for tests of theoretical hypotheses on these links.

4. Trade Dynamics and Trade Costs in German Exports and Imports

The evidence on the dynamics of exports and imports reported in Table 1 already revealed that there are differences in these dynamics when different countries of destination or origin are compared. In this section we will search for systematic patterns in the links between the four measures of exports or imports dynamics introduced in Table 1 on the one hand and characteristics of trade partner countries (to be discussed below).

Here, two groups of trade partner countries are distinguished, namely countries that are members of the European Union (EU) and Non-EU countries, because tariffs and non-tariff barriers to trade play a much smaller role in intra-EU trade.[6]

All computations are performed for the years 2010 and 2011 separately. These years were chosen because for all but the first measure (the number of trading firms in a year t) information has to be available for the year $t - 1$ and/or for the year $t + 1$, too, and the transaction level information for Germany is available for the reporting years 2009 to 2012 only. Looking at these two years serves as a robustness check of the results, because the overall dynamics of trade were rather different in 2009/2010 (the time of the great trade recovery following the great trade collapse of the great recession in 2008/2009) compared to 2010/2011 — total exports grew by 18.5 percent and total imports grew by 19.9 percent in 2009/2010, while the respective growth rates were 11.4 percent and 13.2 percent, and therefore much smaller, in 2010/2011 (see Statistisches Bundesamt, 2012, p. 414).

4.1. Data on trade partner characteristics

In our search for systematic patterns in the links between the four measures of exports or imports dynamics introduced in Table 1 on the one hand and characteristics of trade partner countries on the other hand we will focus on trade costs and market size.

Variable trade costs are either due to tariffs and non-tariff barriers or due to the costs of transporting goods across space. While tariffs and non-tariff barriers are product-specific and, therefore, cannot be measured adequately for trade with a country as a whole, transportation costs are proxied by geographic distance (following the large gravity literature). Data on distance between Germany and the destination countries of exports or the countries of origin of imports are taken from the CEPII's

---

[6] However, there still is a role for trade barriers in intra-EU trade. While intra-EU market access is free of duty, tariff advantages over competitors vary from market to market, impacting bilateral trade. Non-tariff measures are not entirely eliminated inside the Single Market. Remaining barriers may be due to lack of implementation and inconsistent enforcement of rules, adding national rules to European law, excessive fees and inspection charges, complex VAT regimes, as well as tax deals between large firms and national administrations. (I thank a reviewer for pointing this out to me.)

GeoDist database (Mayer and Zignago 2011). The "distw" — measure is used that calculates the distance between two countries based on bilateral distances between the biggest cities of those two countries, those inter-city distances being weighted by the share of the city in the overall country's population (see Mayer and Zignango, 2011, p. 11 for details and the download-link).

Ease of trading across borders in a country is proxied by an index that is taken from the World Bank's *Doing Business* project. It measures the time and cost (excluding tariffs) associated with exporting and importing a standardized cargo of goods by sea transport (including document preparation, customs clearance and inspections). The index measures the distance of a country to a best-practice frontier on a scale from 0 to 100, where 0 represents the lowest performance and 100 the frontier. The data used can be downloaded free of charge at http://www.doingbusiness.org/data/exploretopics/trading-across-borders/frontier.

Market size is proxied by the Gross Domestic Product of the country of destination or origin, measured in millions of US Dollar in current prices. Information is taken from the World Bank World Development Indicators database (see http://data.worldbank.org/indicator/NY.GDP.MKTP.CD).

Descriptive statistics and correlations for the three country characteristics are reported for the various sub-samples (EU and non-EU countries in 2010 and 2011 by destination countries of exports and countries of origin for imports) in the Appendix.[7] Note that for all sub-samples of countries the correlation tends to be low between any two country characteristics with values never exceeding 0.28.

4.2. Trade dynamics and trade costs in German exports and imports: Regression results

To search for systematic patterns in the links between the four measures of exports or imports dynamics introduced in Table 1 on the one hand and the three characteristics of the trade partner countries (distance to Germany,

---

[7] To economize on space this Appendix is available from the author on request.

ease of trading with a country, and size of partner country) discussed in the last section regression models are estimated for each measure of trade dynamics as the dependent variable and the three country characteristics (plus a constant) as the independent variables.

Given that the rules of trading goods do differ considerably between countries that are members of the EU on the one hand and non-EU member countries on the other hand the empirical models include a Dummy-variable that takes the value one for EU-members (and zero otherwise). Furthermore, interaction terms of the three country characteristics and the EU-dummy are included, too. All country characteristics are included in logs in the empirical model.

The empirical models are estimated separately for exports and imports, for the four measures of trade dynamics, and for the two years 2010 and 2011. Results for the 16 regressions are reported in Table 2.[8]

Results reported in Table 2 can help to shed light on a number of hypotheses on the links between these measures of trade dynamics and the country characteristics included in the empirical models.

A fist set of hypotheses is related to differences in the dynamics of German exports and imports with EU-members on the one hand and with non-member states on the other hand. Given that trade relations with member states tend to be older and more stable on average we expect entry and exit rates for exports and imports to be smaller compared to non-member states. As shown by the estimated average marginal effect of EU-membership (that takes care of the EU-dummy variable and the interaction terms included in the empirical model) the empirical results are in line with this expectation (although the negative coefficient is not statistically significant at a conventional level for the firm entry rate for importers). Similarly, we expect new trade relationships with EU-members to be more stable, and this is the case according to the results reported. And a smaller entry rate on EU-markets can be expected to go hand in

---

[8] Note that not all country characteristics are available for all trade partner countries. Furthermore, results from the Exporter and Importer Dynamics Database for Germany are confidential for some combinations of measures and countries. Therefore, the sample size differs between regressions.

Table 2: Trade dynamics and trade costs in Germany — regression results.

Trade dynamics indicator		Export		Import	
		2010	2011	2010	2011
Firm Entry Rate (Number Entrants/Number Traders)					
log Distance to Germany (km)	ß	0.0013	−0.0004	−0.0181	−0.0029
	p	0.861	0.966	0.213	0.852
log Trading Across Borders (index)	ß	−0.0304	−0.0402	−0.0221	−0.0107
	p	0.001	0.000	0.198	0.602
log Gross Domestic Product (Millions of US Dollar)	ß	−0.0332	−0.0340	−0.0247	−0.0247
	p	0.000	0.000	0.001	0.001
EU-Member (Dummy, 1 = yes)	ß	−0.8560	−0.9664	−1.0006	−0.4327
	p	0.000	0.000	0.010	0.194
EU-Member * log Distance to Germany	ß	0.0389	0.0333	0.0781	0.0553
	p	0.000	0.003	0.000	0.002
EU-Member * log Trading Across Borders	ß	0.0845	0.1246	0.1084	0.0074
	p	0.078	0.013	0.195	0.922
EU-Member * log Gross Domestic Product	ß	0.0027	0.0035	−0.0129	−0.0103
	p	0.490	0.378	0.113	0.230
Constant	ß	0.9688	0.9923	1.0128	0.8551
	p	0.000	0.000	0.000	0.000
R-Squared		0.835	0.788	0.389	0.356

		170	166	163	162
No. of cases					
Average marginal effect of EU-Membership	β	-0.1580	-0.1443	-0.0423	-0.0479
	p	0.000	0.000	0.192	0.099
Firm Exit Rate (Number Exiters/Number Traders)					
log Distance to Germany (km)	β	0.0233	0.0245	-0.0017	-0.0179
	p	0.006	0.008	0.919	0.371
log Trading Across Borders (index)	β	-0.024	-0.0395	-0.0205	-0.0417
	p	0.002	0.000	0.330	0.038
log Gross Domestic Product (Millions of US Dollar)	β	-0.0507	-0.0485	-0.0587	-0.0316
	p	0.000	0.000	0.000	0.000
EU-Member (Dummy, 1 = yes)	β	-0.6552	-0.9125	-1.7894	-1.5498
	p	0.004	0.001	0.000	0.000
EU-Member * log Distance to Germany	β	0.0155	0.0213	0.0745	0.0817
	p	0.151	0.083	0.001	0.001
EU-Member * log Trading Across Borders	β	0.0390	0.0790	0.2347	0.1942
	p	0.422	0.188	0.010	0.026
EU-Member * log Gross Domestic Product	β	0.0284	0.0271	0.0094	-0.0035
	p	0.000	0.000	0.230	0.707
Constant	β	0.8234	0.9091	1.2775	1.1749
	p	0.000	0.000	0.000	0.000
R-squared		0.830	0.824	0.645	0.449

(*Continued*)

Table 2: (*Continued*)

Trade dynamics indicator		Export		Import	
		2010	2011	2010	2011
No. of cases		170	170	166	160
Average marginal effect of EU-Membership	ß	−0.0702	−0.1286	−0.1151	−0.1159
	p	0.001	0.000	0.003	0.002
Firm Survival Rate (Number Survivors/Number Entrants)					
log Distance to Germany (km)	ß	−0.0222	−0.0010	0.0198	0.0097
	p	0.014	0.920	0.268	0.470
log Trading Across Borders (index)	ß	0.0204	0.0170	0.0004	0.0167
	p	0.041	0.109	0.983	0.443
log Gross Domestic Product (Millions of US Dollar)	ß	0.0405	0.0242	0.0314	0.0259
	p	0.000	0.000	0.000	0.000
EU-Member (Dummy, 1 = yes)	ß	0.9307	0.6984	1.1445	1.1545
	p	0.004	0.053	0.003	0.000
EU-Member * log Distance to Germany	ß	−0.0312	−0.0480	−0.0922	−0.0592
	p	0.039	0.001	0.000	0.002
EU-Member * log Trading Across Borders	ß	−0.0971	−0.0474	−0.0734	−0.1486
	p	0.221	0.557	0.407	0.038
EU-Member * log Gross Domestic Product	ß	−0.0152	0.0004	−0.0010	0.0068
	p	0.003	0.940	0.911	0.345

Constant	ß	0.0783	0.0659	-0.1665	-0.1016
	p	0.371	0.411	0.277	0.466
R-squared		0.791	0.686	0.449	0.477
No. of cases		164	166	155	147
Average marginal effect of EU-Membership	ß	0.1168	0.1077	0.0641	0.1190
	p	0.003	0.000	0.067	0.000
Share of Entrants in Trade (Total Trade Value of Entrants/Total Trade Value in that Year)					
log Distance to Germany (km)	ß	0.0303	0.0414	0.0299	0.0335
	p	0.039	0.025	0.155	0.146
log Trading Across Borders (index)	ß	-0.0314	-0.0130	0.0366	-0.0790
	p	0.147	0.370	0.297	0.093
log Gross Domestic Product (Millions of US Dollar)	ß	-0.0647	-0.0509	-0.0543	-0.0395
	p	0.000	0.000	0.000	0.001
EU-Member (Dummy, 1 = yes)	ß	-0.4915	-0.7507	-2.0940	-1.1132
	p	0.082	0.005	0.164	0.035
EU-Member * log Distance to Germany	ß	-0.0385	-0.0222	-0.0099	-0.0178
	p	0.111	0.245	0.781	0.474
EU-Member * log Trading Across Borders	ß	0.0386	0.1312	-0.4050	0.2126
	p	0.479	0.008	0.223	0.079
EU-Member * log Gross Domestic Product	ß	0.0503	0.0301	0.0340	0.0235
	p	0.000	0.000	0.011	0.055

(*Continued*)

Table 2: (*Continued*)

Trade dynamics indicator		Export		Import	
		2010	2011	2010	2011
Constant	ß	0.7875	0.4454	0.3808	0.7019
	p	0.000	0.004	0.067	0.005
R-squared		0.583	0.462	0.266	0.226
No. of cases		170	166	162	161
Average marginal effect of EU-Membership	ß	−0.1384	−0.0862	−0.1807	−0.1482
	p	0.000	0.000	0.085	0.001

Note: For a definition of the *Trade Dynamics Indicators* see Table 1. The table reports results from OLS regressions; ß is the estimated regression coefficient; p is the prob-value (based on heteroscedasticity-consistent standard errors). *Distance* is the distance of the country of destination (for exports) or country of origin (for imports) to Germany; *Trading Across Borders* is an index for the time and cost (excluding tariffs) associated with trading, where a larger value indicates lower costs; *Gross Domestic Product* refers to the country of destination (for exports) or country of origin (for imports); for details, see text. The estimated average marginal effect of EU-Membership takes care of the EU-Membership dummy variable and of the interaction terms; the *p*-value is based on estimated standard errors that are computed by the Delta-method.

hand with a smaller share of entrants in total trade, as revealed by the estimated negative average marginal effect of EU-membership in the last models reported in Table 2.

A second set of hypotheses is related to the links between trade dynamics and country characteristic in non-EU countries. To start with distance between Germany and the partner countries, we expect that the entry rate is smaller in more distant countries because the larger distance can be expected to go hand with higher trade costs. This, however, is not the case. According to the results reported in the first panel of Table 2, distance and the export or import entry rate are not related significantly. The same holds for the link between distance and all other measures of import dynamics considered here. For exports, we find a higher exit rate in more distant markets (that goes along with a lower survival rate) and a larger share of new exporters in total trade with partners that are more far away from Germany. Frankly, these results are puzzling.

Next, we look at the link between the ease of trading across borders in the partner countries and the four measures of trade dynamics. Note that, by definition, the higher the value of the *Trading Across Borders* index is, the easier it is to trade with this country. Firm entry might be expected to be higher, therefore, in countries with a larger value of this index. However, if it easy to enter a market today it can be expected that it was easier in the past, too, and one would not expect a higher entry rate today. Results reported in the first panel of Table 2 are in accordance with this, and the same holds for the missing evidence for any relation between the ease of trading and the share of new entrants in total trade (see the last panel of Table 2). Market exit, on the other hand, can be expected to be negatively related to the index because firms will tend to stay in markets where exporting and importing is easy. Results reported in the second panel of Table 2 are in line with this hypothesis. Empirical evidence for a higher survival rate of entrants in markets with a higher value of the index, however, is weak only according to results in third panel of Table 2.

The last country characteristic that has to be discussed with a view to its link to trade dynamics is market size, proxied by the Gross Domestic Product of the partner country. The entry rate is expected to be smaller for larger partners because more firms will be active already in these countries, and, therefore, a smaller share of new firms in trade with larger partners is expected, too. Exit rates can be expected to be smaller in larger markets because it might be more attractive to serve these markets and it might be easier to survive in these markets; the last arguments points to a higher survival rate of firms that enter a larger market, too. Results reported in Table 2 are fully in line with these hypotheses.

To the best of my knowledge, and based on the comprehensive survey of the literature that uses transaction-level data to investigate export and import activities in Wagner (2016a), this is the first empirical study that searches for links between measures of trade dynamics (entry, exit and survival rates, and share of entrants, in total exports and imports) in destination countries of exports and countries of origin of imports on the one hand and characteristics of these countries (distance to Germany, difficulty of foreign trade, and market size) on the other hand. Therefore, further empirical investigations that replicate the approach applied here are needed to learn whether the findings reported for Germany here qualify as stylized facts that hold over space.

5. Concluding Remarks

The findings reported in several papers based on the Word Bank's Exporter Dynamics Database (EDD) that are summarized in Wagner (2016b) illustrate that this data base makes a very useful addition to the box of tools available for empirical trade economists. Data are open access, and it is easy to use the information to investigate a broad range of topics, including the discovery and documentation of new facts like those reported for exporter and importer dynamics in Germany in Section 4 in this paper. Furthermore, the data can be used in empirical investigations of hypotheses derived in theoretical models. Here, the great advantage of the EDD data is that they are strictly comparable over a large number of countries, which adds tremendous value to every empirical exercise performed with these data, because "the credibility of a new finding that is based on carefully analyzing two data sets is far more twice that of a result based only on one". (Hamermesh, 2000, p. 376)

That said, although the empirical trade literature based on transaction level data (surveyed in Wagner, 2016a) grew exponentially over the recent years, and we learned a lot from these papers, there is plenty of scope for future research. First and foremost, we do know much less about imports, its margins, and its role in the dynamics of trade, than about exports. Information on the importer dynamics for Germany introduced in this note is a first step to fill this gap. Here, evidence for more countries is most welcome. It would be great if a project that is comparable to the *World Bank Exporter Dynamics Database* (Cebeci *et al.*, 2012) could be realized for imports, too.

Appendix

The Appendix Tables use the original variable names from the World Bank's *Exporter Dynamics Database*:

C1 Firm Entry Rate (Number Entrants/Number Traders)
C2 Firm Exit Rate (Number Exiters/Number Traders)
C3 Firm Survival Rate (Number Survivors/Number Entrants)
C4 Share of Entrants in Trade (Total Trade Value of Entrants/ Total Trade Value in that Year)

Country characteristics are listed in the Appendix Tables with the following names:

distance	Distance to country of destination (exports) or origin (imports); kilometers
db2010, db2011	*Trading Across Borders* index for trade costs (excluding tariffs)
gdp2010, gdp2011	Gross Domestic Product of country of destination or origin; Millions of US Dollar

Appendix Tables

Table A.1a: Exporter Dynamics 2010 — EU: Part 1: Descriptive statistics
Table A.1b: Exporter Dynamics 2010 — EU: Part 2: Correlation matrix
Table A.2a: Exporter Dynamics 2010 — Non-EU: Part 1: Descriptive statistics
Table A.2b: Exporter Dynamics 2010 — Non-EU: Part 2: Correlation matrix

Table A.1a: Exporter Dynamics 2010 — EU: Part 1: Descriptive statistics.

stats	C1	C2	C3	C4
N	25	25	25	25
Mean	.2521946	.2279854	.6152155	.095438
SD	.0563276	.0449896	.0572284	.0403259
Min	.176476	.1670355	.4870317	.0524169
Max	.3740837	.3346321	.7076446	.240425

stats	distance	db2010	gdp2010
N	25	25	25
Mean	1054.04	83.4084	538311.4
SD	557.3542	6.197964	767777.6
Min	378	73.6	19482
Max	2621	93.16	2646995

Table A.1b: Exporter Dynamics 2010 — EU: Part 2: Correlation matrix.

	C1	C2	C3	C4	distance	db2010	gdp2010
C1	1.0000						
C2	0.9514	1.0000					
C3	−0.8452	−0.9471	1.0000				
C4	0.4774	0.4393	−0.3804	1.0000			
distance	0.5539	0.6485	−0.6734	0.0762	1.0000		
db2010	−0.1493	−0.1798	0.0854	−0.1279	−0.0323	1.0000	
gdp2010	−0.5580	−0.5561	0.5338	−0.4380	−0.1492	0.2444	1.0000

Table A.2a: Exporter Dynamics 2010 — Non-EU: Part 1: Descriptive statistics.

stats	C1	C2	C3	C4
N	145	145	139	145
Mean	.5265142	.4222814	.379018	.278019
SD	.1025305	.1427041	.1187875	.2191201
Min	.3223041	.16675	0	.0324653
Max	1	1	.6254731	1

stats	distance	db2010	gdp2010
N	145	145	145
Mean	7041.021	60.60972	328179.6
SD	3575.986	21.77732	1431225
Min	543	2.83	150
Max	18220	96.62	1.50e + 07

Table A.2b: Exporter Dynamics 2010 — Non-EU: Part 2: Correlation matrix.

	C1	C2	C3	C4	distance	db2010	gdp2010
C1	1.0000						
C2	0.8983	1.0000					
C3	−0.8199	−0.8953	1.0000				
C4	0.7352	0.7625	−0.7027	1.0000			
distance	0.0785	0.2237	−0.1152	0.1671	1.0000		
db2010	−0.3595	−0.2541	0.2990	−0.1835	0.2474	1.0000	
gdp2010	−0.3326	−0.3186	0.3008	−0.2244	0.0396	0.1835	1.0000

Table A.3a: Importer Dynamics 2010 — EU: Part 1: Descriptive statistics.

stats	C1	C2	C3	C4
N	25	25	25	25
Mean	.3422472	.3273362	.5310423	.1266966
SD	.0729952	.094072	.0710372	.0938297
Min	.2200046	.2056837	.3695652	.0536903
Max	.4825175	.5647059	.6572257	.5073377

stats	distance	db2010	gdp2010
N	25	25	25
Mean	1054.04	83.4084	538311.4
SD	557.3542	6.197964	767777.6
Min	378	73.6	19482
Max	2621	93.16	2646995

Table A.3b: Importer Dynamics 2010 — EU: Part 2: Correlation matrix.

	C1	C2	C3	C4	distance	db2010	gdp2010
C1	1.0000						
C2	0.9177	1.0000					
C3	−0.9232	−0.9133	1.0000				
C4	0.4408	0.3429	−0.3277	1.0000			
distance	0.6085	0.6021	−0.7123	0.0813	1.0000		
db2010	−0.1221	−0.0470	0.1040	0.2764	−0.0323	1.0000	
gdp2010	−0.6523	−0.5642	0.5364	−0.2375	−0.1492	0.2444	1.0000

Table A.4a: Importer Dynamics 2010 — Non-EU: Part 1: Descriptive statistics.

stats	C1	C2	C3	C4
N	138	135	125	137
Mean	.5166182	.5709252	.3388243	.2302015
SD	.1334405	.1749992	.1311639	.2490652
Min	0	.2246039	0	.0113716
Max	1	1	.6666667	1

stats	distance	db2010	gdp2010
N	138	138	138
Mean	6866.174	60.27413	344789.9
SD	3402.646	22.13204	1465371
Min	543	2.83	150
Max	18220	96.62	$1.50e + 07$

Table A.4b: Importer Dynamics 2010 — Non-EU: Part 2: Correlation matrix.

	C1	C2	C3	C4	distance	db2010	gdp2010
C1	1.0000						
C2	0.7484	1.0000					
C3	−0.5448	−0.7657	1.0000				
C4	0.5855	0.5511	−0.3961	1.0000			
distance	−0.1072	−0.0996	0.1874	0.1309	1.0000		
db2010	−0.1582	−0.2686	0.1282	0.0572	0.2387	1.0000	
gdp2010	−0.2210	−0.3311	0.2922	−0.1244	0.0549	0.1890	1.0000

Table A.5a: **Exporter Dynamics 2011 — EU: Part 1: Descriptive statistics.**

stats	C1	C2	C3	C4
N	25	25	25	25
Mean	.2476066	.2189444	.5989827	.0922916
SD	.0537259	.0466937	.0541157	.0356225
Min	.1791841	.1538695	.4769327	.0513148
Max	.3579631	.3417421	.6956736	.1757306

stats	distance	db2011	gdp2011
N	25	25	25
Mean	1054.04	83.9444	579463.4
SD	557.3542	5.774906	824457.7
Min	378	74.78	22802
Max	2621	92.89	2862502

Table A.5b: **Exporter Dynamics 2011 — EU: Part 2: Correlation matrix.**

	C1	C2	C3	C4	distance	db2011	gdp2011
C1	1.0000						
C2	0.9003	1.0000					
C3	−0.8098	−0.9363	1.0000				
C4	0.9322	0.8401	−0.7108	1.0000			
distance	0.4984	0.7112	−0.6708	0.4928	1.0000		
db2011	−0.1298	−0.1465	0.1615	−0.0150	−0.0576	1.0000	
gdp2011	−0.5629	−0.5293	0.5666	−0.5677	−0.1565	0.2765	1.0000

Table A.6a: Exporter Dynamics 2011 — Non-EU: Part 1: Descriptive statistics.

stats	C1	C2	C3	C4
N	141	141	139	141
Mean	.479808	.4614725	.3782156	.2299754
SD	.1063682	.130487	.0813079	.1907085
Min	.2788976	.2009487	0	.0381533
Max	.8333333	.9333333	.5833333	.9985951

stats	distance	db2011	gdp2011
N	141	141	141
Mean	6852.071	60.8505	377575.7
SD	3427.823	22.01139	1554688
Min	543	4.17	173
Max	18220	96.69	1.55e + 07

Table A.6b: Exporter Dynamics 2011 — Non-EU: Part 2: Correlation matrix.

	C1	C2	C3	C4	distance	db2011	gdp2011
C1	1.0000						
C2	0.8648	1.0000					
C3	−0.6576	−0.6940	1.0000				
C4	0.7039	0.6862	−0.4819	1.0000			
distance	−0.0326	0.0748	0.1125	0.1754	1.0000		
db2011	−0.4090	−0.3788	0.3142	−0.1619	0.2372	1.0000	
gdp2011	−0.3561	−0.3449	0.2956	−0.2140	0.0563	0.1825	1.0000

Table A.7a: Importer Dynamics 2011 — EU: Part 1: Descriptive statistics.

stats	C1	C2	C3	C4
N	25	25	25	25
Mean	.3333433	.300889	.5308367	.0906181
SD	.0675661	.0714131	.0627217	.0366376
Min	.2283289	.1964327	.3956835	.0402354
Max	.4760274	.465035	.6460081	.1947787

stats	distance	db2011	gdp2011
N	25	25	25
Mean	1054.04	83.9444	579463.4
SD	557.3542	5.774906	824457.7
Min	378	74.78	22802
Max	2621	92.89	2862502

Table A.7b: Importer Dynamics 2011 — EU: Part 2: Correlation matrix.

	C1	C2	C3	C4	distance	db2011	gdp2011
C1	1.0000						
C2	0.9666	1.0000					
C3	−0.9142	−0.9528	1.0000				
C4	0.6179	0.5893	−0.5291	1.0000			
distance	0.6024	0.6650	−0.6208	0.3714	1.0000		
db2011	−0.2247	−0.0674	0.0752	0.0683	−0.0576	1.0000	
gdp2011	−0.6469	−0.5789	0.6241	−0.4239	−0.1565	0.2765	1.0000

Table A.8a: Importer Dynamics 2011 — Non-EU: Part 1: Descriptive statistics.

stats	C1	C2	C3	C4
N	137	130	117	136
Mean	.5322914	.5204858	.3383829	.268357
SD	.147	.1435482	.109821	.2668722
Min	0	.2328287	0	.0079831
Max	1	1	.6111111	1

stats	distance	db2011	gdp2011
N	137	137	137
Mean	6959.642	61.06752	388448.2
SD	3558.124	22.01865	1576054
Min	543	4.17	173
Max	18220	96.69	1.55e + 07

Table A.8b: Importer Dynamics 2011 — Non-EU: Part 2: Correlation matrix

	C1	C2	C3	C4	distance	db2011	gdp2011
C1	1.0000						
C2	0.8154	1.0000					
C3	−0.2824	−0.5506	1.0000				
C4	0.6753	0.5765	−0.1272	1.0000			
distance	0.0252	−0.1453	0.1856	0.0846	1.0000		
db2011	−0.0862	−0.2634	0.2080	−0.1966	0.2438	1.0000	
gdp2011	−0.2052	−0.3315	0.2318	−0.1441	0.0475	0.1829	1.0000

References

Álvarez, Roberto and J. Rodrigo Fuentes (2011). Entry into export markets and product quality. *The World Economy* 34 (8), 1237–1262.

Békés, Gábor and Balázs Muraközy (2012). Temporary trade and heterogeneous firms. *Journal of International Economics* 87 (2), 232–246.

Bernard, Andrew B. and J. Bradford Jensen (1995). Exporters, jobs, and wages in U.S. Manufacturing: 1976–1987. *Brookings Papers on Economic Activity, Microeconomics*, 1, 67–119.

Cebeci, Tolga and Ana M. Fernandes (2015). Microdynamics of Turkey's export boom in the 2000s. *The World Economy* 38 (5), 825–855.

Cebeci, Tolga, Ana M. Fernandes, Caroline Freund and Martha Denisse Pierola (2012). Exporter dynamics database. *Policy Research Working Paper* 6229 (Washington, DC: World Bank).

Damijan, Joze P., Jozef Konings and Saso Polanec (2014). Import churning and export performance of mulit-product firms. *The World Economy* 37 (11), 1483–1506.

Hamermesh, Daniel S. (2000). The craft of labormetrics. *Industrial and Labor Relations Review* 53 (3), 363–380.

Mayer, Thierry and Soledad Zignago (2011). Notes on CEPII's distance measures: The GeoDist database. *CEPII Document de Travail No* 2011–25.

Statistisches Bundesamt (2012), Statistisches Jahrbuch Deutschland (2012). Wiesbaden: Statistisches Bundesamt.

Wagner, Joachim (2007). Exports and productivity: A survey of the evidence from firm-level data. *The World Economy* 30 (1), 60–82.

Wagner, Joachim (2012). International trade and firm performance: A survey of empirical studies since 2006. *Review of World Economics* 148 (2), 235–267.

Wagner, Joachim (2016a). A survey of empirical studies using transaction level data on exports and imports. *Review of World Economics* 152 (1), 215–225.

Wagner, Joachim (2016b). Exporter and importer dynamics database for Germany. *Jahrbücher für Nationalökonomie und StatistikJournal of Economics and Statistics* 236 (3), 411–420.

World Trade Organization (2012). World Trade Report (2012): (Geneva: WTO Publications).

Chapter 6

The Role of Extensive Margins of Exports in The Great Export Recovery in Germany, 2009/2010*

Abstract

This paper contributes to the literature by documenting for the first time the contribution of adding (and dropping) goods and destination countries to the sharp increase in exports of goods in the German economy as a whole during the Great Export Recovery in 2009/2010. The empirical investigation finds that firms that exported in both 2009 and 2010 are much more important for the export dynamics than export starters and export stoppers. Firms that increased their exports (and that were the drivers of the export boom) exported on average more goods and to more destination countries in 2009 than firms that decreased their exports, and they increased both extensive margins of exports on average while firms with

* Originally Published in *Journal of Economics and Statistics* (2014), 234 (4), 518–526.
I thank three anonymous referees and the editor-in-chief for helpful comments that guided me in revising an earlier version of the paper. All computations were done at the Research Data Centre of the German Statistical Office. I thank Rafael Beier for preparing the data, running my Stata do-files and checking the results for any violation of privacy. The enterprise level data used are confidential but not exclusive; see http://www. forschungsdatenzentrum.de/nutzungsbedingungen.asp for any details regarding the access to the data. To facilitate replication the Stata do-file used is available on request.

decreased exports reduced both the number of goods exported and the number of countries exported to.

Keywords: Extensive margins of exports, The Great Export Recovery, Germany.

1. Motivation

After the severe collapse of exports during the Great Recession in 2009 global trade flows rebounded strongly in 2010. According to the WTO's World Trade Report 2011 the rise in the volume in goods exports in 2010 was the largest on record, enabling world trade to return to its pre-crisis level (World Trade Organization, 2011, p. 19). German exports of goods are a case in point. In 2009 the value of total exports declined by 18.4 percent compared to 2008. This was followed by an increase in exports by 18.5 percent in 2010 (Statistisches Bundesamt, 2012, p. 414).

While a number of studies analyze the Great Trade Collapse of 2008/2009 from a macroeconomic point of view, some studies take a microeconomic perspective and try to understand what was going on under the veil of the macroeconomic developments by looking at firm level data.[1] Behrens *et al.* (2013) match firm-level data for firm-country-product exports with balance sheet data for Belgium and decompose the trade collapse along the extensive and the intensive margins, where the extensive margin is defined as changes in exports due to firms that stop or start to export and the intensive margin refers to (negative or positive) changes in exports by firms that continue to export. They find that firm exit and the dropping of products and markets played only a small role during the trade collapse — changes in trade volumes were essentially driven by reduced quantities and unit prices. The intensive margin was much more important than the extensive margin. Similarly, based on analyses of firm-level data for France Fontagné and Gaulier (2009) report that the number of exporters has been only slightly reduced by the crisis, while the bulk of the observed decline in exports happened at the intensive margin and, more precisely, was due to the drop in the value exported by

---

[1] An in-depth analysis of the great trade collapse can be found in Bems, Johnson and Yi (2012).

the top 1 percent of exporters (see also Bricongne *et al.*, 2010; 2011). Using data for imports by Brazil, the European Union, Indonesia and the United States Haddad *et al.* (2011) decompose the fall in international trade during 2008–2009 into product entry and exit, price changes, and quantity changes. The evidence reported suggests that the intensive rather than the extensive margin matter the most. Wagner (2013) shows that a very large share of the decline in exports from manufacturing firms in Germany in 2009 was due to negative changes of exports in enterprises that continued to export (i.e., at the intensive margin) while the decrease of exports due to export stoppers (at the extensive margin) was tiny. The bottom line, then, is that studies based on micro-level data show that changes at the intensive margin were much more important than changes at the extensive margin during the great trade crisis of 2008–2009.

There is, to the best of my knowledge, only one investigation of the Great Export Recovery of 2009/2010 that is based on firm-level data.[2] Wagner (2012) uses data for firms from manufacturing industries in Germany and finds that a very large share of the increase in exports in 2010 was due to positive changes of exports in enterprises that continued to export while the increase of exports due to export starters was tiny.[3] Due to the data used this study is limited in two ways. First, only firms from manufacturing industries are considered. Second, no information on the number of goods exported and the number of countries exported to is available in the data, and, therefore, the role of these extensive margins of exports are not analyzed.

This paper contributes to the literature by documenting for the first time the contribution of adding (and dropping) goods and destination countries to the sharp increase in exports of goods in the German economy as a whole during the Great Export Recovery in 2009/2010. Given

---

[2] For studies using macroeconomic data see World Trade Organization (2011) with evidence for many countries and Loschky (2011) for detailed evidence on Germany.

[3] In West Germany, exports from manufacturing firms increased by 16.01 percent from 2009 to 2010. The increase of exports due to export starters was 0.1 percent and the increase due to firms with increased exports was 21.68 percent; the decrease of exports due to firms with decreased exports was −5.39 percent and the decrease due to export stoppers was −0.39 percent. Results for East Germany are of a similar order of magnitude; see Wagner (2012) for details.

that Germany is one of the leading actors on the world market for goods, the findings reported are interesting *per se*. Furthermore, the empirical approach used can easily be applied for other countries with suitable data, and the results could be used to learn more about the micro-structure of the recent export boom from a cross-country perspective.

To anticipate the most important results, we find that firms that exported in both 2009 and 2010 are much more important for the export dynamics than export starters and export stoppers. A more detailed classification of firms with increased (decreased) exports reveals that some of these firms decreased (increased) the number of goods exported and/or the number of countries exported to. However, the most important subgroups are firm with increased exports that export more goods to more countries and firms with decreased exports that export a smaller number of goods to a smaller number of countries.

The rest of the paper is organized as follows. Section 2 introduces the data used and the empirical approach applied. Section 3 reports the results from the empirical investigation. Section 4 concludes.

2. Data and Empirical Method

The empirical investigation uses a newly constructed data set that is based on customs' records about goods exported to countries outside the EU and on information delivered by firms about goods exported to EU-member countries (that exceed a reporting threshold of 400,000 Euro). These transaction-level data were aggregated at the level of the exporting enterprise by the German Statistical Office for the first time for the reporting year 2009 and are now available for the reporting year 2010, too. The data have information at the firm level about the value of all exports, the number of different goods exported (measured at the 8-digit level of classification) and the number of destination countries. These firm-level data are the basis for the aggregate figures of goods exported reported by the Statistical Office. The amount of exports in the firm-level data sum up to 794,780 million Euro in 2009 and 943,987 Euro in 2010, and the growth rate is 18.7 percent. These figures are very close to the amounts published in the Statistical Yearbook (803,312 and 951,959 million Euro and a growth rate of 18.5 percent; see Statistisches Bundesamt, 2012, p. 414); the differences are due to estimates added by the Statistical Office to cover exports below the reporting threshold and to take care of non-reporting by some firms.

The data for 2009 and 2010 can be used to compare firms between both years. Firms that did not export in both years are ignored here. Each of the other firms belongs to one of five types:

(1) *Export starters* (firms that did not report exports in 2009 but in 2010).
(2) *Enterprises with increased exports* between 2009 and 2010.
(3) *Enterprises with constant exports* in both years.
(4) *Enterprises with decreased exports* between 2009 and 2010.
(5) *Export stoppers* (firms that did report exports in 2009 but not in 2010).

Note that the group of export starters includes plants which exported in 2009 to countries inside the EU only but which had not to report because the amount of exports was below the reporting threshold of 400,000 Euro. A similar point applies to firms classified as export stoppers that continued to export to EU-member countries only in 2010, but which had not to report any longer because the sum of exports was below the threshold value.

The net change in total exports between the two years is the sum of the positive gross changes by the first two types and the negative gross changes by the last two types of firms. The percentage rate of change in total exports can be decomposed accordingly to show the relative contribution of each of these types of firms to total export dynamics (see Wagner, 2013). Furthermore, the change in the number of goods exported and in the number of countries exported to can be documented for the types of firms to learn about the role of these extensive margins of exports in export dynamics.

3. Results from the Empirical Investigation

Results for the decomposition of export dynamics for the types of firms defined above are reported in Table 1. Note that there are no firms with constant exports. This is due to the use of a deflator when transforming nominal export values reported by the enterprises into real export values (measured in constant 2005 prices) used in the calculations here.

Table 1: Decomposition of export dynamics in Germany, 2009/2010.

	[1] Total exports in 2009 (Million Euro; 2005 prices)	[2] Total exports in 2010 (Million Euro; 2005 prices)	[3] Rate of change of exports (percent)	[4] Increase of exports due to export starters (percent of [1])	[5] Increase of exports due to firms with increased exports (percent of [1])	[6] Decrease of exports due to firms with decreased exports (percent of [1])	[7] Decrease of exports due to export stoppers (percent of [1])
All enterprises	775,590.2	890,553.6	14.82	5.36	27.78	-14.55	-3.76
No. of firms	75,493	85,176		19,657	43,918	21,601	9,974
Share in all firms (percent)				20.66	46.16	22.70	10.48
Share in total exports in 2009 (percent)				—	67.05	29.19	3.76
Share in total exports in 2010 (percent)				4.66	82,59	12.75	—

Source: Research Data Center of the German Statistical Office, Foreign Trade Statistics 2009/2010, own calculations.

From the first row of Table 1 it can be seen that exports from manufacturing enterprises rose dramatically by 14.8 percent in real terms from 2009 to 2010 during the Great Export Recovery. Most of this increase is due to positive changes of exports in enterprises that exported in both years; these firms form the largest group. The increase of exports due to the 20,000 export starters is small. Surprisingly (at least for readers not familiar with earlier studies on export dynamics based on firm level panel data) even in this period of an extreme export increase there were more than 20,000 enterprises with decreased exports — more than one fifth of all firms fall into this group (see third row of Table 1). The decrease of exports due to these firms is about the same size as the overall increase of exports. Firms that stop to export form the smallest group of firms, and their contribution to the dynamic of exports is small.

Note that the group of firms that increased their exports from 2009 to 2010 are the drivers of the export-boom. The share of these firms in total exports increased from 67 percent in 2009 to more than 82 percent in 2010.

Information on the extensive margins of exports — the number of destination countries and the number of goods exported — in the four types of firms in both years are reported in Table 2. Both export starters and export stoppers are on average less engaged in exports at both extensive margins than firms that continue to export. Firms with increased exports exported more goods to more countries in 2009 than firms that decreased their exports, and firms with increased exports increased both extensive margins from 2009 to 2010, while firms with decreased exports exported a smaller number of goods to a smaller number of countries. This is a new fact that has not been reported before, and it reveals that a change at the intensive margin (the amount of exports) goes hand in hand with a change in the same direction at both extensive margins (number of goods exported, number of destination countries).

In the last step of the empirical investigation we look at firms with increased exports and decreased exports separately and classify firms of each type in nine groups according to both the change in the number of destination countries (increased/constant/decreased) and the change in the number of goods exported (increased/constant/decreased).

Table 2: Extensive margins in types of exporters in Germany, 2009/2010.

	Export starters	Firms with increased exports	Firms with decreased exports	Export stoppers
No. of destination countries 2009	0	12.61	9.14	5.29
SD	(0)	(16.24)	(11.63)	(9.86)
No. of destination countries 2010	4.13	14.79	8.70	0
SD	(7.70)	(17.73)	(11.72)	(0)
No. of goods exported 2009	0	22.22	18.29	9.08
SD	(0)	(71.85)	(79.76)	(32.31)
No. of goods exported 2010	8.36	26.53	17.26	0
SD	(35.40)	(78.17)	(74.52)	(0.0)

Source: Research Data Center of the German Statistical Office, Foreign Trade Statistics 2009/2010, own calculations.

Table 3 reports results for firms with increased exports. The most important group according to both the number of firms and the share in exports in both years is made of firms with an increase in both extensive margins. These firms increased both the number of goods exported and the number of countries exported to considerably, and their share in total exports expanded by some 10 percentage points. All other groups are far less important.

Results for firms with decreased exports are reported in Table 4. Here, the most important group according to both the number of firms and the share in exports in both years is made of firms with a decrease in both extensive margins. These firms decreased both the number of goods exported and the number of countries exported to considerably, and their share in total exports decreased by more than twelve percentage points. Again, all other groups are far less important.

The results of this paper may appear to suggest that exports became more concentrated in terms of exporters because firms that increased their exports account for a higher share of exports in 2010 compared to 2009. However, this is not the case. Table 5 reports the share of the largest firms in terms of number of products exported and destination markets in total

Table 3: Change in extensive margins in firms with increased exports in Germany, 2009/2010.

	Number of countries		
	Increased	Constant	Decreased
Number of goods			
Increased	[1]	[2]	[3]
No. of firms	16,537	4,978	2,822
(Share; percent)	(37.65)	(11.33)	(6.43)
Share in exports 2009 (percent)	33.33	2.96	12.48
Share in exports 2010 (percent)	42.93	3.51	14,56
No. of goods 2009	29.14	14.27	41.92
No. of goods 2010	39.86	19.99	49.83
No. of countries 2009	15.28	11.02	19.11
No. of countries 2010	20.11	11.02	17.03
Constant	[4]	[5]	[6]
No. of firms	4,664	4,458	1,504
(Share; percent)	(10.62)	(10.15)	(3,42)
Share in exports 2009 (percent)	1.86	0.76	0.83
Share in exports 2010 (percent)	2.41	1.06	0.94
No. of goods 2009	6.37	2.61	6.87
No. of goods 2010	6.37	2.61	6.87
No. of countries 2009	10.54	3.19	11.22
No. of countries 2010	13.46	3.19	9.43
Decreased	[7]	[8]	[9]
No. of firms	4,420	2,220	2,315
(Share; percent)	(10.06)	(5.05)	(5.27)
Share in exports 2009 (percent)	7.17	1.69	5.98
Share in exports 2010 (percent)	8.33	2.17	6.67
No. of goods 2009	32.68	16.30	31.16
No. of goods 2010	28.26	12.94	26.18
No. of countries 2009	18.94	7.30	15.53
No. of countries 2010	22.53	7.30	13.20

Note: Share is the percentage share of firms from the type in all firms with increased exports. No. of goods is the average number of different goods exported by firms from the type, no. of countries is the average number of destination countries of exports by firms from the type.

Source: Research Data Center of the German Statistical Office, Foreign Trade Statistics 2009/2010, own calculations.

Table 4: Change in extensive margins in firms with decreased exports in Germany, 2009/2010.

	Number of countries		
	Increased	Constant	Decreased
Number of goods			
Increased	[1]	[2]	[3]
No. of firms	2,974	1,687	1,589
(Share; percent)	(13.77)	(7.81)	(7.36)
Share in exports 2009 (percent)	4.16	0.95	2.26
Share in exports 2010 (percent)	2.96	0.61	1.64
No. of goods 2009	28.50	14.73	19.56
No. of goods 2010	36.63	19.38	25.28
No. of countries 2009	13.12	6.23	15.09
No. of countries 2010	16.14	6.23	12.34
Constant	[4]	[5]	[6]
No. of firms	1,338	3,023	1,878
(Share; percent)	(6.19)	(13.99)	(8.69)
Share in exports 2009 (percent)	0.61	0.53	0.56
Share in exports 2010 (percent)	0.43	0.32	0.31
No. of goods 2009	6.28	2.41	4.54
No. of goods 2010	6.28	2.41	4.54
No. of countries 2009	8.99	2.75	8.80
No. of countries 2010	11.10	2.75	6.44
Decreased	[7]	[8]	[9]
No. of firms	1,952	2,601	4,559
(Share; percent)	(9.04)	(12.04)	(21.11)
Share in exports 2009 (percent)	2.87	0.70	16.55
Share in exports 2010 (percent)	1.78	0.42	4.29
No. of goods 2009	35.86	16.15	25.92
No. of goods 2010	29.53	11.49	17.41
No. of countries 2009	12.84	4.26	11.19
No. of countries 2010	15.32	4.26	7.38

Note: Share is the percentage share of firms from the type in all firms with decreased exports. No. of goods is the average number of different goods exported by firms from the type, no. of countries is the average number of destination countries of exports by firms from the type.

Source: Research Data Center of the German Statistical Office, Foreign Trade Statistics 2009/2010, own calculations.

Table 5: Share of largest firms in terms of number of products exported and destination markets in total exports, Germany, 2009/2010.

Largest firms in terms of	Share in total exports (percent) in year	
	2009	2010
Number of products exported		
Top 1 (percent)	48.01	42.19
Top 5 (percent)	63.18	59.61
Top 10 (percent)	72.47	69.78
Number of destination markets		
Top 1 (percent)	52.24	46.91
Top 5 (percent)	67.34	63.85
Top 10 (percent)	75.50	73.62

Source: Research Data Center of the German Statistical Office, Foreign Trade Statistics 2009/2010, own calculations.

exports in both years. While the share of the top 1, 5 and 10 percent of all exporters are high in both years (showing once again that exports are highly concentrated in the largest firms) the degree of concentration declined from 2009 to 2010. Table 6 shows why this is the case. The rate of growth of exports among the very large exporters (in terms of total exports) was negative on average while it was positive for overall exporters (see Table 1). Note that the number of destination countries and the number of goods exported was by and large the same in both years among the top exporters. To state it differently, export dynamics were not shaped by the largest exporters.[4]

---

[4] I thank an anonymous referee for suggesting to look at these groups of largest exporters. Note that it is not possible to prepare a decomposition of export dynamics and the other computations reported in Tables 1–4 for the largest firms due to confidentiality restrictions.

Table 6: On the role of the largest exporters for export dynamics in Germany, 2009/2010.

	Largest 10 exporters in 2009	Largest 50 exporters in 2009	Largest 100 exporters in 2009
Share in total exports in 2009 (percent)	30.73	42.20	48.06
Share in total exports in 2010 (percent)	22.31	34.40	40.10
Rate of change of exports 2009/2010 (percent)	−16.64	−6.39	−4.19
Average number of destination countries 2009	158.50	104.68	95.20
Average number of destination countries 2010	155.50	104.93	93.90
Average number of goods exported 2009	2022.3	733.88	601.57
Average number of goods exported in 2010	2011.4	767.53	617.33

Note: The 10 (50, 100) largest exporters are the 10 (50, 100) enterprises with the largest amount of exports in 2009.

Source: Research Data Center of the German Statistical Office, Foreign Trade Statistics 2009/2010, own calculations.

4. Concluding Remarks

The empirical investigation finds that firms that exported in both 2009 and 2010 are much more important for the export dynamics than export starters and export stoppers. Firms that increased their exports (and that were the drivers of the export boom) exported on average more goods and to more destination countries in 2009 than firms that decreased their exports, and they increased both extensive margins of exports on average while firms with decreased exports reduced both the number of goods exported and the number of countries exported to. A more detailed classification of firms with increased (decreased) exports reveals that some of these firms decreased (increased) one or both extensive margins. However, the most important sub-groups are firm with increased exports that export more goods to more countries and firms with decreased exports that export a smaller number of goods to a smaller number of countries.

The overall result reported here — changes at the intensive margin were much more important than changes at the extensive margin during the great trade recovery in 2009–2010 — is well in line with the big picture found in studies that analyze the great trade collapse of 2008–2009 using micro level data for Germany and for other countries.

References

Behrens, Kristian, Gregory Corcos and Giordano Mion (2013) Trade crisis? What trade crisis? *Review of Economics and Statistics* 95 (2), 702–709.

Bems, Rudolfs, Robert C. Johnson and Kei-Mu Yi (2012). The great trade collape. *NBER Working Paper* 18632, December.

Bricongne, Jean-Charles, Lionel Fontagné, Guillaume Gaulier and Vincent Vicard (2011). An analysis of the dynamics of French firms' exports from 2000 to 2009: Lessons for the recovery. In: Filippo di Mauro and Benjamin R. Mandel (Ed.), *Recovery and Beyond. Lessons for Trade Adjustment and Competitiveness.* Frankfurt/Main: European Central Bank.

Bricongne, Jean-Charles, Lionel Fontagné, Guillaume Gaulier, Daria Taglioni and Vincent Vicard (2010). Exports and sectoral financial dependence. Evidence on French firms during the great global crisis. *European Central Bank Working Paper Series,* No. 1227, July.

Fontagné, Lionel and Guillaume Gaulier (2009). French exporters in the global crisis. In: Richard Baldwin (Ed.), *The Great Trade Collapse: Causes, Consequences and Prospects.* London: Centre for Economic Policy Research (CEPR), pp. 143–150.

Haddad, Mona, Ann Harrison and Catherine Hausman (2011). Decomposing the great trade collapse. Products, prices and quantities in the 2008–2009 crisis. *World Band Policy Research Working Paper,* No. 5749, August.

Loschky, Alexander (2011): *Außenhandel 2010 — eine Geschichte von Gewinnern und Verlierern. Wirtschaft und Statstik,* pp. 353–362, April.

Statistisches Bundesamt (2012). *Statistisches Jahrbuch (2012): Wiesbaden: Statistisches Bundesamt.*

Wagner, Joachim (2012). The Great Export Recovery in German manufacturing industries, 2009/2010. *Working Paper Series in Economics,* No. 253, University of Luneburg November.

Wagner, Joachim (2013). The granular nature of the great export collapse in German manufacturing industries, 2008/2009. *Economics: The Open-Access, Open-Assessment E-Journal*, Vol. 7, 1–21.

World Trade Organization (2011). World Trade Report (2011): (Geneva: World Trade Organization).

Chapter 7

Extensive Margins of Imports in The Great Import Recovery in Germany, 2009/2010*

Abstract

This chapter contributes to the literature by documenting for the first time the contribution of adding (and dropping) goods and countries of origin to the sharp increase in imports of goods in the German economy as a whole during The Great Import Recovery in 2009/2010. The empirical investigation finds that firms that imported in both 2009 and 2010 are much more important for the import dynamics than import starters and import stoppers. Firms that increased their imports (and that were the drivers of the import boom) imported on average more goods and from more countries of origin in 2009 than firms that decreased their imports, and they increased both extensive margins of imports on average while firms with decreased imports reduced both the number of goods exported and the number of countries of origin.

Keywords: Extensive margins of imports, The Great Import Recovery, Germany.

* Originally Published in *Economics Bulletin* (2013), 33 (4), 2732–2743.
All computations were done at the Research Data Centre of the German Statistical Office. I thank Rafael Beier for preparing the data, running my Stata do-files and checking the results for any violation of privacy. The enterprise level data used are confidential but not exclusive; see http://www.forschungsdatenzentrum.de/nutzungsbedingungen.asp for any details regarding the access to the data. To facilitate replication the Stata do-file used is available on request.

1. Motivation

After the severe collapse of international trade during the Great Recession in 2009 global trade flows rebounded strongly in 2010. According to the WTO's World Trade Report 2011 world exports of merchandise dropped by 22 percent from 2008 to 2009 and increased by 22 percent from 2009 to 2010, enabling world trade to return to its pre-crisis level (World Trade Organization, 2011, p. 24). Germany, one of the leading actors on the world market for goods,[1] is a case in point. Measured in current prices the value of total exports (imports) declined by 18.4 (17.5) percent from 2008 to 2009. This was followed by an increase in exports (imports) by 18.5 (19.9) percent in 2010 (Statistisches Bundesamt, 2012, p. 414).

The dynamics of exports over this period have been investigated for several countries. While a number of studies analyze the Great Trade Collapse of 2008/2009 from a macroeconomic point of view, some studies take a microeconomic perspective and try to understand what was going on under the veil of the macroeconomic developments by looking at firm level data.[2] Behrens *et al.* (2013) match firm-level data for firm-country-product exports with balance sheet data for Belgium and decompose the trade collapse along the extensive and the intensive margins, where the extensive margin is defined as changes in exports due to firms that stop or start to export and the intensive margin refers to (negative or positive) changes in exports by firms that continue to export. They find that firm exit and the dropping of products and markets played only a small role during the trade collapse — changes in trade volumes were essentially driven by reduced quantities and unit prices. The intensive margin was much more important than the extensive margin. Similarly, based on analyses of firm-level data for France Fontagné and Gaulier (2009) report that the number of exporters has been only slightly reduced by the crisis, while the bulk of the observed decline in exports happened at the intensive margin and, more precisely, was due to the

---

[1] In 2010, Germany was the third-largest exporter and importer of goods, see World Trade Organization (2011, p. 33).

[2] An in-depth analysis of the great trade collapse can be found in Bems *et al.* (2012).

drop in the value exported by the top 1 percent of exporters (see also Bricongne *et al.*, 2010; 2011). Using data for imports by Brazil, the EU, Indonesia and the United States Haddad *et al.* (2011) decompose the fall in international trade during 2008–2009 into product entry and exit, price changes, and quantity changes. The evidence reported suggests that the intensive rather than the extensive margin matter the most. Wagner (2013a) shows that a very large share of the decline in exports from manufacturing firms in Germany in 2009 was due to negative changes of exports in enterprises that continued to export (i.e., at the intensive margin) while the decrease of exports due to export stoppers (at the extensive margin) was tiny. The bottom line, then, is that studies based on micro-level data show that changes at the intensive margin were much more important than changes at the extensive margin during the great trade crisis of 2008–2009.

In contrast to the Great Export Collapse of 2008/2009 the Great Export Recovery of 2009/2010 has (at least, to the best of my knowledge) been investigated with firm-level data for Germany only.[3] Wagner (2013b) finds that firms that exported in both 2009 and 2010 are much more important for the export dynamics than export starters and export stoppers. Firms that increased their exports (and that were the drivers of the export boom) exported on average more goods and to more destination countries in 2009 than firms that decreased their exports, and they increased both extensive margins of exports on average while firms with decreased exports reduced both the number of goods exported and the number of countries exported to.

This chapter contributes to the literature by looking for the first time at the dynamics of imports (instead of exports) during The Great Import Recovery in 2009/2010.[4] It uses newly available comprehensive enterprise level data for Germany and documents the contribution of adding (and dropping) goods and countries of origin to the sharp increase in imports

---

[3] For studies using macroeconomic data see World Trade Organization (2011) with evidence for many countries and Loschky (2011) for detailed evidence on Germany.

[4] Unfortunately, the data used here (that are described in detail in Section 2) are available from reporting year 2009 onwards only, so the Great Trade Collapse cannot be investigated with these data.

of goods in the German economy as a whole. Given that Germany is one of the leading actors on the world market for goods, the findings reported are interesting *per se*. Furthermore, the empirical approach used can easily be applied for other countries with suitable data, and the results could be used to learn more about the micro-structure of the recent import boom from a cross-country perspective.

To anticipate the most important results, we find that firms that imported in both 2009 and 2010 are much more important for the import dynamics than import starters and import stoppers. A more detailed classification of firms with increased (decreased) imports reveals that some of these firms decreased (increased) the number of goods imported and/or the number of countries imported from. However, the most important sub-groups are firm with increased imports that import more goods from more countries and firms with decreased imports that import a smaller number of goods from a smaller number of countries.

The rest of the chapter is organized as follows. Section 2 introduces the data used and the empirical approach applied. Section 3 reports the results from the empirical investigation. Section 4 concludes.

2. Data and Empirical Method

The empirical investigation uses a newly constructed data set that is based on customs' records about goods imported from countries outside the EU and on information delivered by firms about goods imported from EU-member countries (that exceed a reporting threshold of 400,000 Euro). These transaction-level data were aggregated at the level of the importing enterprise by the German Statistical Office for the first time for the reporting year 2009 and are now available for the reporting year 2010 too. The data have information at the firm level about the value of all imports, the number of different goods imported (measured at the 8-digit level of classification) and the number of countries of origin. These firm-level data are the basis for the aggregate figures of goods imported reported by the Statistical Office.

The data for 2009 and 2010 can be used to compare firms between both years. Firms that did not import in both years are ignored here. Each of the other firms belongs to one among the following five types:

(1) Import starters (firms that did not report imports in 2009 but in 2010).
(2) Enterprises with increased imports between 2009 and 2010.
(3) Enterprises with constant imports in both years.
(4) Enterprises with decreased imports between 2009 and 2010.
(5) Import stoppers (firms that did report imports in 2009 but not in 2010).

Note that the group of import starters includes plants which imported in 2009 from countries inside the EU only but which had not to report because the amount of imports was below the reporting threshold of 400,000 Euro. A similar point applies to firms classified as import stoppers that continued to import from EU-member countries only in 2010, but which had not to report any longer because the sum of imports was below the threshold value.

The net change in total imports between the two years is the sum of the positive gross changes by the first two types and the negative gross changes by the last two types of firms. The percentage rate of change in total imports can be decomposed accordingly to show the relative contribution of each of these types of firms to total import dynamics (see Wagner, 2013b). Furthermore, the change in the number of goods imported and in the number of countries imported from can be documented for the types of firms to learn about the role of these extensive margins of imports in export dynamics.

3. Results from the Empirical Investigation

Results for the decomposition of import dynamics for the types of firms defined above are reported in Table 1. Note that there are no firms with constant imports. This is due to the use of a deflator when transforming nominal import values reported by the enterprises into real import values (measured in constant 2005 prices) used in the calculations here.

Table 1: Decomposition of import dynamics in Germany, 2009/2010.

	[1] Total imports in 2009 (Million Euro; 2005 prices)	[2] Total imports in 2010 (Million Euro; 2005 prices)	[3] Rate of change of imports (percent)	[4] Increase of imports due to import starters (percent of [1])	[5] Increase of imports due to firms with increased imports (percent of [1])	[6] Decrease of imports due to firms with decreased imports (percent of [1])	[7] Decrease of imports due to import stoppers (percent of [1])
All enterprises	662,933.2	739,456.4	11.54	6.49	23.73	−14.69	−3.99
No. of firms				20,622	41,044	35,261	12,493
Share in all firms (percent)				18.85	37.51	32.23	11.42
Share in total imports in 2009 (percent)				0.0	53.42	42.59	3.99
Share in total imports in 2010 (percent)				5.82	69.17	25.02	0.0

Source: Research Data Center of the German Statistical Office, Foreign Trade Statistics 2009/2010, own calculations.

From the first row of Table 1 it can be seen that imports from manu-facturing enterprises rose dramatically by 11.54 percent in real terms from 2009 to 2010 during The Great Import Recovery. Most of this increase is due to positive changes of imports in enterprises that imported in both years; these firms form the largest group. The increase of imports due to the 20,000 import starters is considerably smaller. Surprisingly (at least for readers not familiar with the studies on export dynamics based on firm level panel data) even in this period of an extreme import increase there were more than 35,000 enterprises with decreased imports — about one third of all firms fall into this group (see third row of Table 1). The decrease of imports due to these firms is larger than the overall increase of imports. Firms that stop importing form the smallest group of firms, and their contribution to the dynamic of imports is small, too.

Note that the group of firms that increased their imports from 2009 to 2010 are the drivers of the import-boom. The share of these firms in total imports increased from 53.42 percent in 2009 to 69.17 percent in 2010.

Information on the extensive margins of imports — the number of countries of origin and the number of goods imported — in the four types of firms in both years are reported in Table 2. Both import starters and import stoppers are on average less engaged in imports at both extensive margins than firms that continue to import. Firms with increased imports imported more goods from more countries in 2009 than firms that

Table 2: Extensive margins in types of importers in Germany, 2009/2010.

	Import starters	Firms with increased imports	Firms with decreased imports	Import stoppers
No. of countries of origin 2009 (SD)	0 (0)	6.77 (8.53)	5.63 (7.09)	3.15 (5.14)
No. of countries of origin 2010 (SD)	2.96 (4.31)	7.54 (8.77)	5.30 (6.84)	0 (0)
No. of goods imported 2009 (SD)	0 (0)	24.46 (67.97)	20.37 (66.69)	9.12 (27.62)
No. of goods imported 2010 (SD)	9.17 (28.69)	28.30 (71.63)	19.00 (63.77)	0 (0)

Source: Research Data Center of the German Statistical Office, Foreign Trade Statistics 2009/2010, own calculations.

decreased their imports, and firms with increased imports increased both extensive margins from 2009 to 2010, while firms with decreased imports imported a smaller number of goods from a smaller number of countries. This is a new fact that has not been reported before, and it reveals that a change at the intensive margin (the amount of imports) goes hand in hand with a change in the same direction at both extensive margins (number of goods imported, number of countries of origin).

In the last step of the empirical investigation we look at firms with increased imports and decreased imports separately and classify firms of each type in nine groups according to both the change in the number of countries of origin (increased/constant/decreased) and the change in the number of goods imported (increased/constant/decreased).

Table 3 reports results for firms with increased imports. The most important group according to both the number of firms and the share in

Table 3: Change in extensive margins in firms with increased imports in Germany, 2009/2010.

	Number of countries of origin		
	Increased	Constant	Decreased
Number of goods			
Increased	[1]	[2]	[3]
No. of firms	13,755	6,071	3,929
(Share; percent)	(33.51)	(14.79)	(9.57)
Share in imports 2009 (percent)	19.53	3.35	16.71
Share in imports 2010 (percent)	27.79	4.11	19.08
No. of goods 2009	27.05	16.17	50.12
No. of goods 2010	37.43	21.01	58.42
No. of countries 2009	7.30	4.57	13.05
No. of countries 2010	10.28	4.57	11.00
Constant	[4]	[5]	[6]
No. of firms	1,712	4,445	1,143
(Share; percent)	(4,17)	(10.83)	(2.78)
Share in imports 2009 (percent)	0.85	1.27	0.68

(Continued)

Table 3:   (*Continued*)

	Number of countries of origin		
	Increased	Constant	Decreased
Share in imports 2010 (percent)	1.19	1.64	0.88
No. of goods 2009	10.29	1.84	10.41
No. of goods 2010	10.29	1.84	10.41
No. of countries 2009	4.46	3.27	6.34
No. of countries 2010	6.16	3.27	4.74
Decreased	[7]	[8]	[9]
No. of firms	2,803	3,298	3,888
(Share; percent)	(6.83)	(8.04)	(9.47)
Share in imports 2009 (percent)	3.49	1.48	6.05
Share in imports 2010 (percent)	4.79	1.82	7.86
No. of goods 2009	33.99	17.12	36.26
No. of goods 2010	29.30	13.99	30.19
No. of countries 2009	8.18	4.16	10.00
No. of countries 2010	10.27	4.16	7.84

Note: Share is the percentage share of firms from the type in all firms with increased imports. Number of goods is the average number of different goods imported by firms from the type, number of countries is the average number of countries of origin of imports by firms from the type.
Source: Research Data Center of the German Statistical Office, Foreign Trade Statistics 2009/2010, own calculations.

imports in both years is made of firms with an increase at both extensive margins. These firms increased both the number of goods imported and the number of countries imported from considerably, and their share in total imports expanded by more than eight percentage points. All other groups (with the exception of firms that simultaneously increased the number of goods imported and decreased the number of countries of origin) are far less important.

Results for firms with decreased imports are reported in Table 4. Here, the most important group according to both the number of firms and the share in imports in both years is made of firms with a decrease at both extensive margins. These firms decreased both the number of goods imported and the number of countries imported from considerably, and their share in total imports decreased by more than 10 percentage points. Again, all other groups are far less important.

The results reported here may appear to suggest that imports became more concentrated in terms of importers because firms that increased their imports account for a higher share of imports in 2010 compared to 2009. This, however, is not the case. Table 5 reports the share of the largest firms

Table 4: Change in extensive margins in firms with decreased imports in Germany, 2009/2010.

	Number of countries of origin		
	Increased	Constant	Decreased
Number of goods			
Increased	[1]	[2]	[3]
No. of firms	4,916	3,414	2,582
(Share; percent)	(13.94)	(9.68)	(7.32)
Share in imports 2009 (percent)	6.06	1.88	5.44
Share in imports 2010 (percent)	4.34	1.38	3.53
No. of goods 2009	25.62	14.10	34.37
No. of goods 2010	32.57	17.80	40.49
No. of countries 2009	6.86	4.13	11.15
No. of countries 2010	9.15	4.13	9.06
Constant	[4]	[5]	[6]
No. of firms	1,210	4,758	1,517
(Share; percent)	(3.43)	(13.49)	(4.30)
Share in imports 2009 (percent)	0.63	1.13	0.83
Share in imports 2010 (percent)	0.44	0.74	0.51
No. of goods 2009	9.29	3.18	7.81
No. of goods 2010	9.29	3.18	7.81
No. of countries 2009	4.18	1.69	5.62
No. of countries 2010	5.70	1.69	3.90

(*Continued*)

Table 4:   (*Continued*)

	Number of countries of origin		
	Increased	Constant	Decreased
Decreased	[7]	[8]	[9]
No. of firms	2,804	5,828	8,232
(Share; percent)	(7.95)	(16.53)	(23.35)
Share in imports 2009 (percent)	3.45	2.37	20.82
Share in imports 2010 (percent)	2.38	1.59	10.11
No. of goods 2009	35.45	14.79	28.14
No. of goods 2010	29.63	10.67	19.57
No. of countries 2009	6.81	2.96	7.75
No. of countries 2010	8.63	2.96	5.13

Note: Share is the percentage share of firms from the type in all firms with decreased imports. Number of goods is the average number of different goods imported by firms from the type, number of countries is the average number of countries of origin of imports by firms from the type.
Source: Research Data Center of the German Statistical Office, Foreign Trade Statistics 2009/2010, own calculations.

Table 5: Share of largest firms in terms of number of products imported and countries of origin in total exports, Germany, 2009/2010.

	Share in total imports (percent) in year	
	2009	2010
Largest firms in terms of		
Number of products imported		
Top 1 percent	45.78	41.45
Top 5 percent	64.32	61.42
Top 10 percent	72.11	70.28
Number of countries of origin		
Top 1 percent	47.89	43.08
Top 5 percent	64.92	63.63
Top 10 percent	72.86	72.99

Source: Research Data Center of the German Statistical Office, Foreign Trade Statistics 2009/2010, own calculations.

Table 6: On the role of the largest importers for import dynamics in Germany, 2009/2010.

	Largest 10 importers in 2009	Largest 50 importers in 2009	Largest 100 importers in 2009
Share in total imports in 2009 (percent)	25.36	38.24	44.66
Share in total imports in 2010 (percent)	18.14	30.67	37.97
Rate of change of imports 2009/2010 (percent)	−20.22	−10.55	−5.18
Average number of countries of origin 2009	103.3	64.7	51.3
Average number of countries of origin 2010	99.0	64.1	50.8
Average number of goods imported 2009	1678.6	776.2	525.7
Average number of goods imported in 2010	1690.9	786.6	538.2

Note: The 10 (50, 100) largest importers are the 10 (50, 100) enterprises with the largest amount of imports in 2009.

Source: Research Data Center of the German Statistical Office, Foreign Trade Statistics 2009/2010, own calculations.

in terms of number of products imported and of countries of origin in total imports in both years. While the share of the top 1, 5 and 10 percent of all importers are high in both years (showing once again that imports are highly concentrated in the largest firms) the degree of concentration declined from 2009 to 2010. Table 6 shows why this is the case. The rate of growth of imports among the very large importers (in terms of total imports) was negative on average while it was positive for overall importers (see Table 1). Note that the average number of countries of origin and the average number of goods imported was by and large the same in both years among the top importers. To state it differently, import dynamics were not shaped by the largest importers.[5]

---

[5] Note that it is not possible to prepare a decomposition of import dynamics and the other computations reported in Tables 1–4 for the largest firms due to confidentiality restrictions.

4. Concluding Remarks

The empirical investigation finds that firms that imported in both 2009 and 2010 are much more important for the import dynamics than import starters and import stoppers. Firms that increased their imports (and that were the drivers of the import boom) imported on average more goods and from more countries of origin in 2009 than firms that decreased their imports, and they increased both extensive margins of imports on average while firms with decreased imports reduced both the number of goods imported and the number of countries imported from. A more detailed classification of firms with increased (decreased) imports reveals that some of these firms decreased (increased) one or both extensive margins. However, the most important sub-groups are firms with increased imports that import more goods from more countries and firms with decreased imports that import a smaller number of goods from a smaller number of countries.

The overall result reported here — changes at the intensive margin were much more important than changes at the extensive margin during the import recovery in 2009–2010 — is well in line with the big picture found in studies that use firm level data for Germany and for other countries to analyze the great export collapse of 2008–2009 and the great export recovery of 2009–2010. Given that this is (at least, to the best of my knowledge) the first analysis of the extensive and intensive margins of imports, further evidence from other countries would contribute to our knowledge and would help to decide whether the patterns found for Germany qualify as a stylized fact.

References

Behrens, Kristian, Gregory Corcos and Giordano Mion (2013). Trade crisis? What trade crisis? *Review of Economics and Statistics* 95 (2), 702–709.

Bems, Rudolfs, Robert C. Johnson and Kei-Mu Yi (2012). The Great Trade Collapse. *NBER Working Paper*, No. 18632, December.

Bricongne, Jean-Charles, Lionel Fontagné, Guillaume Gaulier, Daria Taglioni and Vincent Vicard (2010). Exports and sectoral financial dependence: Evidence on French firms during the great global crisis. *Working Paper Series*, No. 1227, European Central Bank, July.

Bricongne, Jean-Charles, Lionel Fontagné, Guillaume Gaulier and Vincent Vicard (2011). An analysis of the dynamics of French firms' exports from 2000 to

2009: Lessons for the recovery. In: Filippo Di Mauro and Benjamin R. Mandel (Eds.), *Recovery and Beyond: Lessons for Trade Adjustment and Competitiveness.* Frankfurt/Main: European Central Bank.

Fontagné, Lionel and Guillaume Gaulier (2009). French exporters in the global crisis. In: Richard Baldwin (Ed.), *The Great Trade Collapse: Causes, Consequences and Prospects.* London: Centre for Economic Policy Research (CEPR), pp. 143–150.

Haddad, Mona, Ann Harrison and Catherine Hausman (2011). Decomposing the great trade collapse. Products, prices and quantities in the 2008–2009 crisis. *World Band Policy Research Working Paper,* No. 5749, August.

Loschky, Alexander (2011). *Außenhandel 2010 — eine Geschichte von Gewinnern und Verlierern. Wirtschaft und Statstik,* April, 353–362.

Statistisches Bundesamt (2012). *Statistisches Jahrbuch 2012.* Wiesbaden: Statistisches Bundesamt.

Wagner, Joachim (2013a). The granular nature of the great export collapse in German manufacturing industries, 2008/2009. *Economics: The Open-Access, Open-Assessment E-Journal,* 7, 2013–2015.

Wagner, Joachim (2013b). The role of extensive margins of exports in The Great Export Recovery in Germany, 2009/2010. *Working Paper Series in Economics,* No. 266, University of Luneburg, March.

World Trade Organization (2011). World Trade Report (2011): (Geneva: World Trade Organization).

Chapter 8

A Note on the Granular Nature of Imports in German Manufacturing Industries*

Abstract

This paper uses an approach recently suggested by Gabaix (Econometrica, 2011) to investigate for the first time the role of idiosyncratic shocks to the largest firms in the dynamics of imports by firms from manufacturing industries. For Germany we find evidence that imports are power-law distributed and that the distribution of imports in the industries can be characterized as fat-tailed. Results show that idiosyncratic shocks to very large firms are important for the import dynamics in 2010/2011 but not in 2009/2010.

Keywords: Imports, power law, granular residual, Germany.

* Originally Published in *Review of Economics* (2014), 65 (3), 241–252.
All computations were done inside the Research Data Centre of the Statistical Office of Berlin-Brandenburg. The data used are confidential but not exclusive; see www.forschungsdatenzentrum.de for information how to access the data. To facilitate replication the Stata do-files used are available from the author on request.

1. Motivation

Exports and imports tend to be highly concentrated. There is empirical evidence for a number of countries that a small share of firms are responsible for the lion's share of international trade (see World Trade Organization (2008, p. 54)). Bernard *et al.* (2011, p. 10) call this one of the striking features of international trade data. Germany, one of the leading actors on the world market for goods and services, is a case in point. More than half of total exports and imports in Germany stem from the largest 50 trading firms (see Wagner, 2012a for details).

Detailed analyses that use firm-level data to decompose the overall change in exports in Germany during the "Great Export Collapse" in 2008/09 and during the "Great Export Recovery" in 2009/2010 reveal that a small fraction of firms from the largest size class is responsible for shaping the big picture that is familiar from published aggregate figures. This illustrates that a macroeconomic development — the change in total exports from year to year — can be driven by a small number of large firms (see Wagner, 2013a; 2013b).

This finding of a decisive role of a small number of large firms is in line with a view recently presented by Gabiax (2011) who argues that many economic fluctuations are attributable to the incompressible "grains" of economic activity, the large firms. Therefore, he names this view the "granular" hypothesis. We have empirical evidence that supports this granular view for the German manufacturing sector, where idiosyncratic shocks in the largest firms are important for an understanding of aggregate volatility (see Wagner, 2012b), and similar evidence for manufacturing exports from Germany (see Wagner, 2013a, 2013b).

This paper contributes to the literature by investigating the granular nature of imports for the first time, not only for Germany but for any country. The case of Germany is especially interesting here because Germany is the third largest importer of goods on the world market (World Trade Organization, 2014, p. 34), and a better understanding of the dynamics of German imports is, therefore, important for a better understanding of the dynamics of imports *per se.* To investigate the role of large firms in shaping the dynamics of imports, and to test for a granular nature of imports, longitudinal data at the firm level are necessary that make it possible to look behind the veil of the aggregate figures published by the statistical offices and to track the volume of imports of each firm over time. This analysis uses newly available data for imports at the firm level that are based on transaction-level data. These data have been aggregated at the level of the firm for the first time for the reporting year 2009, and as of today they are available for the period 2009 to 2011. These years are investigated in this study.

To anticipate the most important findings, we find evidence for a granular nature of imports in manufacturing industries in Germany for 2010/2011 but not for 2009/2010.

The rest of the paper is organized as follows: Section 2 introduces the enterprise level data used in this study. Section 3 presents the empirical approach applied to investigate the role of idiosyncratic shocks to the largest firms for the overall change in imports and discusses the results for Germany. Section 4 concludes.

2. Data

Information on imports is available from the statistic on foreign trade (*Außenhandelsstatistik*). This statistic is based on two sources. One source is the reports by German firms on transactions with firms from countries that are members of the European Union (EU); these reports are used to compile the so-called *Intrahandelsstatistik* on intra-EU trade. The other source is transaction-level data collected by the customs on trade with countries outside the EU (the so-called *Extrahandelsstatistik*).[1] Data in the statistic of foreign trade are transaction-level data, i.e., they relate to one transaction of a German firm with a firm located outside Germany at a time. Published data from this statistic report imports aggregated at the level of goods imported and by country of origin.

For the reporting years 2009 to 2011 these transaction-level data have been aggregated at the level of the importing firm for the first time.

---

[1] Note that firms with a value of imports from EU-countries that does not exceed 400,000 Euro in 2009 do not have to report to the statistic on intra-EU trade. For trade with firms from non-member countries all transactions that exceed 1,000 Euro are registered. For details see Statistisches Bundesamt, Qualitätsbericht Außenhandel, January 2011.

For each importing firm that reported either to the statistic on intra-EU trade, or to the statistic on trade with countries outside the EU, we know from these data the value of imports.

Using the firms' registration number for turnover tax statistics these data were matched with the enterprise register system (*Unternehmensregister-System*). For enterprises from manufacturing industries this matching made it possible to add information (that is taken from a regular survey of manufacturing firms) on industry affiliation.

These newly available data on import activities of firms from German manufacturing industries are used in this paper to look at the role of idiosyncratic shocks to large firms in shaping the dynamics of imports from 2009 to 2010, and from 2010 to 2011, respectively.

3. Empirical Investigation

Standard macroeconomic reasoning usually discards the possibility that idiosyncratic microeconomic shocks to firms may lead to large aggregate fluctuations by referring to a diversification argument.[2] A classical case in point is the argument put forward by Lucas (1977) that such microeconomic shocks would average out and, therefore, should only have negligible aggregate effects. In a recent Econometrica paper Gabaix (2011) proposes that, contrary to this traditional view, idiosyncratic firm-level shocks can indeed explain an important part of aggregate economic movements and provide a micro-foundation for aggregate shocks. He shows that the "averaging out" argument breaks down if the size distribution of firms is fat-tailed and very large firms play an important role in an economy. This is the case in the United States, where, according to the findings of Gabaix (2011), the idiosyncratic movements of the largest 100 firms appear to explain about one-third of variations in output growth. Wagner (2012b; 2013a; 2013b) reports similar evidence for the manufacturing sector in Germany and for German exports of goods. He finds that idiosyncratic shocks in the largest firms are important for an understanding of aggregate volatility in German manufacturing industries and its exports.

---

[2] This section builds on the investigation of the granular nature of exports from the German manufacturing sector in Wagner (2013b).

Gabaix (2011) argues that many economic fluctuations are attributable to the incompressible "grains" of economic activity, the large firms. Therefore, he names this view the "granular" hypothesis. The granular view does not neglect the role of aggregate shocks like changes in monetary, fiscal, and exchange rate policy as important drivers of macroeconomic activity. It only argues that such aggregate shocks are not the only important drivers, and that firm specific idiosyncratic shocks, too, are an important, and possibly the major, part of the origin of business-cycle fluctuations (Gabaix, 2011, p. 764).

As said the "averaging out" argument of standard macroeconomic reasoning breaks down if the size distribution of firms is fat-tailed and very large firms play an important role in an economy. From the percentage shares of the largest enterprises in total imports in manufacturing industries in West Germany[3] in 2010 and 2011 that are documented in Table 1 it is evident that the imports of manufacturing enterprises are highly concentrated. The very large firms, therefore, represent a large part of the import activity in the manufacturing sector.

In Tables 2 and 3 the estimated power law exponents for imports are reported for all firms and for firms from 24 manufacturing industries.[4] A power law is a relation of the type $Y = k * X^{\beta}$, where Y and X are variables

Table 1: Concentration of imports in enterprises from German manufacturing industries, 2010 and 2011.

	Share of largest importers in total imports (%)			
	10	50	100	Number of importers
2010	39.05	59.22	65.82	10,870
2011	41.92	58.87	65.23	11,064

---

[3] This study looks at West Germany only. A separate analysis of the imports from the East German manufacturing sector is not possible because the number of firms in many industries is far too small.

[4] The industries are at the 2-digit level. For a definition of industries see the Table A.1.

Table 2: Estimated power law exponents for imports in manufacturing industries, West Germany, 2010.

Industry	ß	*t*-value	R²	Number of enterprises
All	−0.308	−73.72	0.706	10,870
10	−0.446	−18.80	0.801	707
11	−0.312	−7.55	0.818	114
12	−0.393	−1.41	0.878	8
13	−0.256	−12.14	0.688	295
14	−0.394	−9.08	0.713	165
15	−0.364	−5.61	0.766	63
16	−0.245	−11.14	0.700	248
17	−0.313	−13.17	0.699	347
18	−0.188	−10.48	0.689	220
19	−0.653	−3.32	0.888	22
20	−0.383	−16.49	0.756	544
21	−0.373	−7.14	0.685	102
22	−0.283	−21.49	0.718	924
23	−0.297	−14.09	0.701	397
24	−0.377	−13.40	0.733	359
25	−0.235	−27.96	0.692	1,564
26	−0.342	−18.73	0.730	702
27	−0.322	−19.57	0.720	766
28	−0.264	−31.75	0.690	2,016
29	−0.435	−12.94	0.736	335
30	−0.415	−6.60	0.767	87
31	−0.262	−12.10	0.734	293
32	−0.284	−13.78	0.711	380
33	−0.284	−10.30	0.652	212

Note: For a definition of the industries see the Table A.1. The power law exponent ß and its standard error are estimated by the method suggested in Gabaix and Ibragimov (2011); see text.

Table 3: Estimated power law exponents for imports in manufacturing industries, West Germany, 2010.

Industry	ß	t-value	R^2	Number of enterprises
All	−0.230	−74.38	0.697	11,064
10	−0.425	−18.69	0.774	699
11	−0.254	−7.42	0.623	110
12	−0.384	−1.87	0.884	7
13	−0.272	−11.96	0.721	286
14	−0.464	−9.11	0.810	166
15	−0.441	−5.24	0.814	55
16	−0.241	−11.20	0.724	251
17	−0.299	−13.19	0.685	348
18	−0.168	−10.86	0.691	236
19	−0.564	−3.00	0.808	18
20	−0.353	−16.43	0.720	540
21	−0.462	−7.25	0.776	105
22	−0.276	−22.12	0.717	979
23	−0.286	−14.21	0.707	404
24	−0.403	−13.27	0.743	352
25	−0.227	−28.55	0.688	1,630
26	−0.337	−18.55	0.773	688
27	0.304	19.84	0.707	787
28	−0.265	−31.98	0.678	2,046
29	−0.409	−13.21	0.725	349
30	−0.459	−6.67	0.817	89
31	−0.249	−12.23	0.715	299
32	−0.297	−13.58	0.729	369
33	−0.268	−11.20	0.621	251

Note: For a definition of the industries see the Table A.1. The power law exponent ß and its standard error are estimated by the method suggested in Gabaix and Ibragimov (2011); see text.

of interest, ß is the power law exponent, and k is a constant.[5] A popular way to estimate the power law exponent ß for the firm size distribution (where firm size is measured by exports here) is to compute the rank of each firm in the size distribution and to run an OLS regression of log(rank) on a constant and log(size). The estimated regression coefficient of log(size) is an estimate for ß. Gabaix and Ibragimov (2011) show that this procedure leads to strongly biased estimates in small samples. They provide a simple practical remedy for this bias by suggesting to use rank −½ instead of rank and then run log(rank −½) = k−ß∗log(size). They show that the shift of ½ is optimal and reduces the bias to a leading order. Note that the standard error of ß is not the OLS standard error reported by the computer program, but is asymptotically given by $(2/n)^{\frac{1}{2}}$ ∗ |b| (where n is the number of firms used in the estimation).

The estimated power-law coefficient for exports is statistically significantly different from zero at an error level of less than one percent for all imports and for imports in every industry (except industry 12, where the number of importing firms is tiny). According to the R^2-value the fit is rather tight. These results indicate that imports are power-law distributed in all industries. Descriptive results, therefore, indicate that the distribution of imports from the German manufacturing sector as a whole and from the various industries that are part of it can be characterized as fat-tailed.

To test for the granular nature of imports from German manufacturing industries the data for enterprises from 22 of the 24 manufacturing industries that are described above are used and the role of the 10 largest firms in each industry is considered.[6] The empirical approach closely follows Gabaix (2011, p. 750ff.). The idiosyncratic firm-level sales shock is measured by the "granular residual" that is computed as follows. g_{it} is the growth rate of imports for firm i and year t, computed as log(imports$_{it}$) − log(imports$_{it-1}$). $g10_t$ is the average of the growth rates of the 10 largest

---

[5] Gabaix (2009) is a comprehensive survey of power laws and applications in economics and finance.

[6] Industry 12 (manufacture of tobacco products) and industry 19 (manufacture of coke and refined petroleum products) were dropped due to the small number of firms from these industries.

firms (according to imports in year $t-1$) in an industry. The granular residual is a weighted sum of the 10 largest firm's growth rate minus $g10_t$, where the weights are the shares of the firms in total imports of all firms in an industry in year $t-1$. Here, t refers to 2010 (2011) and $t-1$ refers to 2009 (2010).

The growth rate of total imports in an industry, defined as log(total imports in t) minus log(total imports in $t-1$), is regressed on the granular residual from the industry using Ordinary Least Squares (OLS). Results are reported in the first column of Table 4. For 2009/2010 these results are not supportive of the granular hypothesis. The estimated coefficient for the granular residual is not statistically significant. If only aggregate shocks were important for the growth rate of total imports in an industry, then the R^2 of the regressions in Table 4 would be zero. It is. Idiosyncratic movements of the top 10 firms in an industry cannot explain a large fraction of import fluctuations. Results for 2010/2011 differ considerably. The estimated coefficient for the granular residual is statistically significant, and the R^2 is different from zero. Here, we have empirical evidence that idiosyncratic movements of the top 10 firms in an industry can explain a fraction of import fluctuations.

However, it is well known that results estimated by OLS can be highly sensitive to a small fraction of observations that lay far away from the majority of observations in the sample. As a robustness check, therefore, we investigate whether the results reported depend on extreme observations, or outliers. Rousseeuw and Leroy (1987) distinguish three types of outliers that influence the OLS estimator: vertical outliers, bad leverage points, and good leverage points. Verardi and Croux (2009, p. 440) illustrate this terminology in a simple linear regression framework that is used here (the generalization to higher dimensions is straightforward) as follows: "Vertical outliers are those observations that have outlying values for the corresponding error term (the y dimension) but are not outlying in the space of explanatory variables (the x dimension). Their presence affects the OLS estimation and, in particular, the estimated intercept. Good leverage points are observations that are outlying in the space of explanatory variables but that are located close to the regression line. Their presence does not affect the OLS estimation, but it affects statistical inference because they do deflate the estimated standard errors. Finally, bad leverage

Table 4: **Explanatory power of the granular residual for import growth in manufacturing industries, West Germany, 2009/2010 and 2010/2011.**

Dependent variable: import growth 2009/2010 (%)			
Estimation method:		OLS	S-estimator
Granular residual 2009/2010	ß	−0.0015	0.0014
	p	0.667	0.854
Constant	ß	17.240	19.211
	P	0.000	0.000
Number of industries		22	18
R^2		0.010	0.0022

Dependent variable: import growth 2010/2011 (%)			
Estimation method:		OLS	S-estimator
Granular residual 2010/2011	ß	−0.0062	−0.0444
	p	0.008	0.004
Constant	ß	15.189	13.943
	p	0.000	0.000
Number of industries		22	17
R^2		0.215	0.431

Note: ß is the estimated regression coefficient, p is the prob-value. For a definition of the industries see the Table A.1. For a definition of the granular residual see text.

points are observations that are both outlying in the space of explanatory variables and located far from the true regression line. Their presence significantly affects the OLS estimation of both the intercept and the slope".

Using this terminology one can state that the popular median regression estimator (also known as Least Absolute Deviations or LAD) protects against vertical outliers but not against bad leverage points (Verardi and Croux, 2009, p. 441). Full robustness can be achieved by using the so-called S-estimator that can resist contamination of the data set of up to 50 percent of outliers (i.e., that has a breakdown point[7] of 50 percent compared to

---

[7] The breakdown point of an estimator is the highest fraction of outliers that an estimator can withstand, and it is a popular measure of robustness.

zero percent for OLS). A discussion of any details of this estimator is beyond the scope of this paper (see Verardi and McCathie, 2012 for this estimator and for Stata commands to compute it).

Results computed by the S-estimator are reported in the second column of Table 4. For 2009/2010 the robust estimator identifies four outliers. These outliers are the observations from the industries 11 (beverages), 21 (basic pharmaceutical products), 22 (rubber and plastic products) and 30 (other transport equipments). Dropping these outliers from the estimation sample does not change the big picture at all. Idiosyncratic movements of the top 10 firms in an industry cannot explain a large fraction of import fluctuations in 2009/2010.

For 2010/2011 the robust estimator identifies five outliers. These outliers are the observations from the industries 10 (food products), 21 (basic pharmaceutical products), 30 (other transport equipments), 31 (furniture) and 32 (other manufacturing). Again, dropping these outliers from the estimation sample does not change the big picture from the OLS regression, but this big picture is different from the one found for 2009/2010. Idiosyncratic movements of the top 10 firms in an industry can explain a fraction of import fluctuations in 2010/2011, and according to the R^2-value this fraction is considerably larger if the outliers are dropped from the estimation sample.

4. Discussion

The bottom line, then, is that we find evidence for a granular nature of imports in manufacturing industries in Germany for 2010/2011 but not for 2009/2010. The reasons for this difference between the two periods under investigation are not at all obvious. According to the results reported in Tables 2 and 3 imports are power-law distributed in all industries both in 2010 and 1011, and the distribution of imports in the industries can be characterized as fat-tailed. This seems to be a structural characteristic of the German manufacturing sector that does not vary (at least not in the short run). The different results with regard to the role of idiosyncratic shocks to the largest firms for the two period might be due to the fact that imports of the firms included in the sample used here increased by 32.4 percent during the "Great Import Recovery" in 2009/2010 (that followed after the large drop in imports during the Great Recession of 2008/2009), but grew only more moderately by 16.9 percent during 2010/2011. Maybe, the huge import increase in 2009/2010 was so large that even large shocks to large firms had no decisive influence on import dynamics as a whole. Given that data for imports at the firm-level are available in Germany for 2009 to 2011 as yet, future research using data for later years with smaller overall growth rates of imports might shed more light on this.

The different findings for the two periods investigated in this paper illustrate that empirical results based on data for one period cannot be a sound basis for any conclusions regarding the validity of theoretical reasoning. Stylized facts that can guide economic theory and policy should be based on empirical investigations that replicate results for different data sets from many different years. Therefore, the jury is still out with respect to a decision on the granular nature of imports in German manufacturing industries. That said, the granular approach recently introduced by Gabaix (2011) offers a highly useful tool for the analysis of import dynamics, too. Policy makers (and their advisors) should be aware of the decisive role of a small number of very large firms for the dynamics of imports. To better understand and forecast changes in imports these "big players" should be closely monitored. And in any discussion of policy measures that affect imports special emphasis should be put on its potential effects on these firms.

Table A.1: Definition of Manufacturing Industries.

No.	Industry
10	Manufacture of food products
11	Manufacture of beverages
12	Manufacture of tobacco products
13	Manufacture of textiles
14	Manufacture of wearing apparel
15	Manufacture of leather and related products
16	Manufacture of wood and products of wood, except furniture
17	Manufacture of paper and paper products
18	Printing and reproduction of recorded media

(Continued)

Table A.1: (*Continued*)

No.	Industry
19	Manufacture of coke and refined petroleum products
20	Manufacture of chemicals and chemical products
21	Manufacture of basic pharmaceutical products and pharmaceutical preparations
22	Manufacture of rubber and plastic products
23	Manufacture of other non-metallic mineral products
24	Manufacture of basic metals
25	Manufacture of fabricated metal products, except machinery and equipment
26	Manufacture of computer, electronic and optical products
27	Manufacture of electrical equipment
28	Manufacture of machinery and equipment n.e.c.
29	Manufacture of motor vehicles, trailers and semi-trailers
30	Manufacture of other transport equipment
31	Manufacture of furniture
32	Other manufacturing
33	Repair and installation of machinery and equipment

Note: The 2-digit-industries are defined according to the German classification WZ 2008.

References

Bernard, Andrew B., J. Bradford Jensen, Steven J. Redding and Peter K. Schott (2011). The empirics of firm heterogeneity and international trade. *National Bureau of Economic Research NBER Working Paper*, No. 17672.

Gabaix, Xavier (2009). Power laws in economics and finance. *Annual Review of Economics* 1, 255–293.

Gabaix, Xavier (2011). The granular origins of aggregate fluctuations. *Econometrica* 79, 733–772.

Gabaix, Xaxier and Rustam Ibragimov (2011). Rank -1/2: A simple way to improve the OLS estimation of tail exponents. *Journal of Economics and Business Statistics* 29, 24–39.

Lucas, Robert E. (1977). Understanding business cycles. *Carnegie-Rochester Conference Series on Public Policy* 5, 7–29.

Rousseeuw, Peter J. and Annick M. Leroy (1987). Robust regression and outlier detection. (New York: John Wiley and Sons).

Verardi, Vincenzo and Christophe Croux (2009). Robust regression in Stata. *The Stata Journal* 9, 439–453.

Verardi, Vincenzo and Alice McCathie (2012). The S-estimator of multivariate location and scatter in Stata. *The Stata Journal* 12, 299–307.

Wagner, Joachim (2012a). Trading many goods with many countries: Exporters and importers from German manufacturing industries. *Review of Economics* 63, 170–186.

Wagner, Joachim (2012b). The German manufacturing sector is a granular economy. *Applied Economics Letters* 19, 1663–1665.

Wagner, Joachim (2013a). The granular nature of the great export collapse in German manufacturing industries, 2008/2009. *Economics: The Open-Access, Open-Assessment E-Journal*, Vol. 7, 2013–2015.

Wagner, Joachim (2013b). The great export recovery in German manufacturing industries, 2009/2010. *Review of Economics* 64, 325–340.

World Trade Organization (2008). World Trade Report 2008. Trade in a Globalizing World. (Geneva: WTO Publications).

World Trade Organization (2014). World Trade Report 2014. Trade and development: Recent trends and the role of the WTO. (Geneva: WTO Publications).

Part 4

Productivity and the Extensive Margins of Trade

Introduction

Detailed information on the number of goods traded and the number of countries traded with reveal new insights on the links between firm characteristics and the extensive margins of trade. Productivity of firms is a case in point.

The positive relationship between productivity and participation in exports qualifies as a stylized fact (see Wagner, 2007 for a survey of the literature), and the same holds for imports. Empirical investigations reveal that productivity is positively related to the other extensive margins of foreign trade, too. Chapter 9 (originally published in Wagner, 2012) reports that in Germany firms that trade many goods or that trade with many countries are more productive than firms that trade some goods or trade with some countries only; this regularity not only holds on average but over the whole productivity distribution.

Note that although there is a strong positive link between productivity and the extensive margins of exports Chapter 10 (originally published in Wagner, 2013) reports that German low-productive exporters are not marginal exporters defined according to the number of goods exported or the number of countries exported to. Chapter 11 (originally published in Wagner, 2014a) shows that these low-productive exporters are competitive because they export high-quality goods. According to results reported in Chapter 12 (originally published in Wagner, 2014b) these exporters of high-quality goods tend to use high-quality inputs.

References

Wagner, Joachim (2007). Exports and productivity: A survey of the evidence from firm-level data. *The World Economy* 30 (1), 60–82.

Wagner, Joachim (2012). Productivity and the extensive margins of trade in German Manufacturing firms: Evidence from a non-parametric test. *Economics Bulletin* 32 (4), 3061–3070.

Wagner, Joachim (2013). Are low-productive exporters marginal exporters? Evidence from Germany. *Economics Bulletin* 33 (1), 467–481.

Wagner, Joachim (2014a). Low-productive exporters are high-quality exporters: Evidence from Germany. *Economics Bulletin* 34 (2), 745–756.

Wagner, Joachim (2014b). What makes a high-quality exporter? Evidence from Germany. *Economics Bulletin* 34 (2), 865–874.

Chapter 9

Productivity and the Extensive Margins of Trade in German Manufacturing Firms: Evidence from a Non-parametric Test*

Abstract

This paper contributes to the literature by comparing the productivity distribution for firms with various numbers of goods traded and various numbers of countries traded with from Germany, one of the leading actors on the world market for goods. It applies a non-parametric test for first-order stochastic dominance of one productivity distribution over another. We find that the larger the number of goods exported or imported, and the larger the number of countries exported

* Originally Published in *Economics Bulletin* (2012), 32 (4), 3061–3070.
All computations were done at the Research Data Centre of the German Statistical Office. I thank Christopher Gürke for preparing the data, running my Stata do-files and checking the results for any violation of privacy. The enterprise level data used are confidential but not exclusive; see http://www.forschungsdatenzentrum.de/nutzungsbedingungen.asp for any details regarding the access to the data. I thank the editor Rod Falvey and an anonymous referee for helpful comments on an earlier version.

to or imported from, the higher is the productivity of the firms — not only on average, but over the whole productivity distribution. This is in line with implications of recent theoretical models of multi-product multi-country trading firms.

Keywords: Exports, imports, number of goods, number of countries, Germany.

1. Motivation

Firms that are engaged in international trade are more productive than firms that do not export or import. This stylized fact has been documented over the past 15 years in a large number of micro-econometric studies that use firm-level data from countries all over the world (see Wagner, 2007; 2012a for surveys). The theoretical rational behind this empirical regularity is that there are extra cost of exporting and importing (including the cost of market studies and finding reliable trading partners, of adapting products for a market in a country they are not produced in, and of familiarization with customs procedures). Most of these extra costs are fixed costs and sunk costs. Only the more productive firms can cover these extra costs of trade and produce profitably (see Melitz, 2003 for exports and Castellani *et al.*, 2010 for imports).

While this positive relationship between participation in international trade and productivity has been documented for a long time, only recently researchers used transaction level data that report not only the sum of exports or imports for a firm but that have information on the goods traded and on the countries of the trading partners, too, to look at two extensive margins of trade, namely the number of goods traded and the number of countries traded with. With these data new stylized facts have been uncovered. It is shown that international trade is dominated by a small number of firms that trade many goods with many countries (see Bernard *et al.*, 2007 for the United States and Wagner, 2012b for Germany). Furthermore, there is a positive link between firm productivity and both the number of goods traded and the number of countries traded with. The theoretical rational for this link is similar to the one discussed above for exporting and importing *per se*: Many costs associated with exports or imports recur when a new country is added as a destination of exports or source of imports of a firm, and many costs recur when a new product is added to the portfolio of products a firm exports or imports. Bernard *et al.* (2011) present a theoretical model of this link between productivity and both the number of goods exported and of export destinations. In their empirical investigation they find that, on average, productivity of firms from the United States increases with the number of exported goods and destination countries. Wagner (2012c) reports a strikingly similar result for Germany; similar findings from empirical studies for firms from other countries are surveyed in Wagner (2012a).

However, it is well known that firms are highly heterogeneous. Results that point to productivity differences at the (unconditional or conditional) mean might not tell the whole story. As Buchinsky (1994, p. 453) put it: "'On the average' has never been a satisfactory statement with which to conclude a study of heterogeneous populations". An empirical study of heterogeneous firms should look at differences in the whole distribution of the variable under investigation between groups of firms, not only at differences at the mean.

This paper contributes to the literature by comparing the productivity distribution for firms with various numbers of goods traded and numbers of countries traded with from Germany, one of the leading actors on the world market for goods. It applies a non-parametric test for first-order stochastic dominance of one productivity distribution over another. To anticipate the most important result, the larger the number of goods exported or imported, and the larger the number of countries exported to or imported from, the higher is the productivity of the firms — not only on average, but over the whole productivity distribution.

2. Data and Descriptive Evidence

The empirical investigation uses a newly constructed data set that is based on customs' records about goods traded by German firms with countries outside the EU and on information delivered by firms about goods traded with EU-member countries.[1] These transaction-level data were aggregated at the level of the exporting enterprise by the German Statistical Office for

---

[1] Note that firms with a value of exports to and imports from EU-countries that does not exceed 400,000 Euro in 2009 do not have to report to the statistic on intra-EU trade. Small exporters and importers that trade with EU-countries only are therefore underrepresented in the sample. For trade with firms from non-member countries all transactions that exceed 1,000 Euro are registered. For details see Statistisches Bundesamt, Qualitätsbericht Außenhandel, January 2011.

the first time for the reporting year 2009; data for more recent years are not yet available. The data have, among others, information at the firm level about the number of different goods traded[2] and the number of countries traded with. These firm level data on transactions in foreign trade were linked to the enterprise register system. By linking the aggregated transaction-level data to the enterprise register system it was possible to match these data with information on the number of employees in the firm and total turnover of the firm taken from the regular survey of manufacturing firms.

Productivity is measured as labor productivity (defined as total turnover per employee) because information on the capital stock of a firm is not available, so more elaborate measures of total factor productivity cannot be used in this study. Bartelsman and Doms (2000, p. 575) point to the fact that heterogeneity in labor productivity has been found to be accompanied by similar heterogeneity in total factor productivity in the reviewed research where both concepts are measured. In a recent comprehensive survey Syverson (2011) argues that high-productivity producers will tend to look efficient regardless of the specific way that their productivity is measured. Furthermore, Foster *et al.* (2008) show that productivity measures that use sales (i.e., quantities multiplied by prices) and measures that use quantities only are highly positively correlated. Therefore, we argue that labor productivity is a suitable measure for productivity at the firm level. Furthermore, to control for differences in capital intensity between firms productivity is measured in percentage of the 5-digit-industry mean value.

In the empirical investigation four groups of firms are distinguished according to either the number of goods exported or imported and according to either the number of countries exported from or imported to, namely firms with only one good traded or country traded with, firms with two to five goods traded or countries traded with, firms with six to nine goods traded or countries traded with, and firms with 10 or more goods traded or countries traded with. The sample has information on 13,004 firms from West Germany and 2,273 firms from East Germany that traded internationally in 2009.[3] Table 1 reports the number of firms by number of

---

[2] A good is an 8-digit number from the official nomenclature for the statistics of foreign trade.
[3] The economy still differs considerably between West Germany and the former communist East Germany even many years after the unification in 1990, and this is especially true with

Table 1: Number of firms by number of goods traded and number of countries traded with. German manufacturing firms, 2009.

	Number of goods traded				Number of countries traded with			
	Exports		Imports		Exports		Imports	
	No. of firms	Share (%)	No. of firms	Share (%)	No. of firms	Share (%)	No. of firms	Share (%)
West Germany								
1	1,698	14.14	903	7.91	975	8.22	1,223	10.93
2–5	3,426	28.54	2,301	20.15	1,830	15.42	3,152	28.18
6–9	1,595	13.29	1,524	13.35	1,332	11.23	2,289	20.46
10 and more	5,287	44.04	6,689	58.59	7,727	65.13	4,522	40.43
East Germany								
1	384	19.55	242	12.43	250	12.94	283	14.93
2–5	707	36.00	434	22.29	479	24.79	571	30.13
6–9	297	15.12	281	14.43	257	13.30	444	23.43
10 and more	576	29.33	990	50.85	946	48.96	597	31.50

Source: Research Data Center of the German Statistical Office, Foreign Trade Statistics 2009, own calculations.

goods traded and by number of countries traded with and the share of each group of firms in all firms by trade activity. While there are many firms that trade only some goods with some countries, many firms trade 10 or more goods and with 10 or more countries.

3. Productivity Distribution and the Extensive Margins of Foreign Trade

Table 2 reports means and selected percentiles of the productivity distribution of the firms in our sample by the number of goods traded and by the number of countries traded with. With a few exceptions that are mainly found at 99th percentile the big picture is in line with the theoretical hypothesis that there is a positive link between firm productivity and both the number of goods traded and the number of countries traded with. The empirical strategy used here to test this hypothesis applies a non-parametric test for First order stochastic dominance of one distribution over another that was introduced into the empirical literature on exports by Delgado *et al.* (2002).[4] Let *F* and *G* denote the cumulative distribution functions of productivity for two groups of firms (say, firms that export one good and firms that export — two to five goods). First order stochastic dominance of *F* relative to *G* is given if $F(z) - G(z)$ is less or equal zero for all z with strict inequality for some z. Given two independent random samples of plants from each group, the hypothesis that *F* is to the right of *G* can be tested by the Kolmogorov–Smirnov-test based on the empirical distribution functions for *F* and *G* in the samples (for details, see Conover, 1999, p. 456ff.). Note that this tests not only for differences in the mean productivity of both groups but for differences in all moments of the distribution.

Results for the 48 tests that compare the productivity distributions of two groups of firms each are reported in Table 3. Results for West

---

regard to international trade and productivity (see Wagner, 2008). Therefore, the analysis is carried out separately for both parts of Germany.

[4] Results of *t*-tests for differences in means of productivity between the groups of firms by the number of products traded and by the number of countries traded with are available on request.

Table 2: Labor productivity by number of goods traded and number of countries traded with.

	West Germany							East Germany						
	Mean	SD	p1	p10	p50	p90	p99	Mean	SD	p1	p10	p50	p90	p99
Number of goods exported														
1	86.2	56.8	18.7	38.2	73.9	144.5	286.4	86.2	48.0	12.1	35.7	74.4	155.5	233.6
2–5	93.8	69.0	21.2	41.3	79.3	157.6	320.1	96.8	59.6	19.1	42.7	86.1	156.2	341.9
6–9	97.2	63.3	22.0	44.0	83.4	157.1	371.0	100.6	71.3	13.3	40.9	87.1	168.6	394.9
10 and more	111.8	85.5	26.3	50.8	95.6	182.5	372.0	115.9	74.8	20.3	51.5	100.0	198.3	364.1
Number of goods imported														
1	82.6	81.7	17.1	37.5	68.8	130.5	298.6	87.9	75.7	19.1	37.0	75.4	138.5	289.2
2–5	90.4	73.5	18.2	39.5	74.4	152.1	361.4	91.3	53.9	19.7	42.0	80.2	144.4	293.0
6–9	96.7	59.9	18.8	43.1	82.9	158.1	315.8	101.7	64.6	15.5	40.2	91.4	167.4	353.7
10 and more	111.8	83.2	24.4	51.0	95.6	184.2	373.8	113.1	71.9	18.1	48.1	100.0	190.4	339.0

(*Continued*)

Table 2: (*Continued*)

	West Germany							East Germany						
	Mean	SD	p1	p10	p50	p90	p99	Mean	SD	p1	p10	p50	p90	p99
Number of countries exported to														
1	79.1	47.5	18.0	36.7	69.5	129.4	254.4	82.5	49.1	13.9	33.6	70.8	143.2	243.1
2–5	92.4	101.2	15.4	37.4	75.5	151.5	362.9	93.6	67.3	16.3	36.6	79.8	163.4	291.0
6–9	98.8	74.2	22.8	40.7	82.0	166.5	407.3	99.9	74.9	17.8	42.0	86.5	154.8	468.5
10 and more	106.7	70.6	26.5	49.2	91.7	177.0	349.8	110.5	64.0	21.8	49.4	100.0	183.2	334.2
Number of countries imported from														
1	78.5	71.4	18.0	37.0	66.8	124.2	272.8	78.3	40.9	20.1	36.8	73.1	126.9	228.6
2–5	92.6	70.5	19.5	40.7	77.4	154.3	344.1	96.9	59.3	16.3	41.1	86.3	158.3	353.7
6–9	105.2	69.9	19.5	47.5	88.7	178.7	350.7	104.7	55.8	12.6	42.3	98.9	176.3	288.6
10 and more	117.8	89.0	29.1	54.9	100.0	190.3	418.9	121.5	81.3	21.8	52.3	100.5	208.7	409.1

Note: Labor productivity is calculated as total sales per employee and is in percentage of the 5-digit-industry mean value.
Source: Research Data Center of the German Statistical Office, Foreign Trade Statistics 2009, own calculations.

Table 3: Test for difference in distribution of labor productivity by number of products traded and number of countries traded with. (p-value of Kolmogorov–Smirnov-test).

	Number of goods exported			Number of goods imported			Number of countries exported to			Number of countries imported from		
	H1	H2	H3	H1	H2	H3	H1	H2	H3	H1	H2	H3
West Germany												
1 vs. 2–5	0.000	0.981	0.030	0.001	0.998	0.000	0.000	0.963	0.000	0.000	0.998	0.000
1 vs. 6–9	0.000	0.995	0.030	0.000	0.989	0.000	0.000	0.997	0.000	0.000	0.999	0.000
1 vs. 10 and more	0.000	0.999	0.030	0.000	0.999	0.000	0.000	1.000	0.000	0.000	0.999	0.000
2–5 vs. 6–9	0.004	0.970	0.022	0.000	0.940	0.000	0.000	0.996	0.000	0.000	0.995	0.000
2–5 vs. 10 and more	0.000	1.000	0.000	0.000	0.999	0.000	0.000	0.997	0.000	0.000	0.999	0.000
6–9 vs. 10 and more	0.000	1.000	0.000	0.000	1.000	0.000	0.000	0.959	0.000	0.000	0.999	0.000
East Germany												
1 vs. 2–5	0.006	0.999	0.003	0.041	0.916	0.020	0.056	0.964	0.028	0.000	0.848	0.000
1 vs. 6–9	0.011	1.000	0.005	0.000	0.894	0.000	0.001	1.000	0.001	0.000	0.930	0.000
1 vs. 10 and more	0.000	0.999	0.000	0.000	0.986	0.000	0.000	1.000	0.000	0.000	0.997	0.000
2–5 vs. 6–9	0.700	0.511	0.368	0.006	0.879	0.003	0.167	0.747	0.084	0.001	0.830	0.001
2–5 vs. 10 and more	0.000	0.992	0.000	0.000	0.986	0.000	0.000	0.997	0.000	0.000	0.999	0.000
6–9 vs. 10 and more	0.001	0.996	0.000	0.026	0.993	0.013	0.000	0.894	0.000	0.029	1.000	0.014

Note: Labor productivity is calculated as total sales per employee and is in percentage of the 5-digit-industry mean value. The hypotheses tested are:

H1: The productivity distributions of the two groups of firms do not differ.

H2: The productivity distribution of the first group is first-order stochastically dominated by the productivity distribution of the second group.

H3: The productivity distribution of the second group is first-order stochastically dominated by the productivity distribution of the first group.

Source: Research Data Center of the German Statistical Office, Foreign Trade Statistics 2009, own calculations.

Table 4: Labor productivity by number of goods traded and number of countries traded with. Robustness check.

	West Germany							East Germany						
	Mean	SD	p1	p10	p50	p90	p99	Mean	SD	p1	p10	p50	p90	p99
Number of goods exported														
First quartile of distribution	89.67	66.35	19.51	39.26	76.15	149.74	310.94	89.52	49.88	15.50	38.45	78.91	155.48	250.09
Second quartile of distribution	96.86	62.08	24.14	44.03	82.67	163.87	327.39	97.61	64.09	18.53	44.11	85.86	151.08	353.67
Third quartile of distribution	102.80	86.15	22.50	46.26	86.21	165.18	400.08	100.03	65.29	15.72	42.33	88.57	164.65	341.87
Fourth quartile of distribution	117.29	80.09	28.00	55.07	100.00	188.95	366.46	118.94	78.47	21.63	51.48	100.00	207.78	369.43
Number of goods imported														
First quartile of distribution	88.24	76.00	17.39	38.78	72.75	147.98	347.83	87.56	66.55	18.53	36.85	75.49	139.36	355.55
Second quartile of distribution	98.74	66.25	19.63	44.19	84.01	162.79	324.72	99.96	58.53	16.57	43.66	90.21	160.15	304.36
Third quartile of distribution	107.60	91.15	24.40	48.76	90.22	177.64	351.66	107.38	72.60	13.34	46.31	94.24	179.06	369.43
Fourth quartile of distribution	119.99	77.21	27.84	57.22	102.66	193.17	418.92	120.12	72.56	21.63	48.90	102.70	209.98	338.98

Number of countries exported to

First quartile of distribution	88.33	84.05	15.98	37.02	73.62	146.82	339.04	85.41	49.70	16.30	35.76	73.52	147.76	250.09
Second quartile of distribution	99.50	71.88	22.93	44.05	82.73	165.59	349.85	100.65	79.61	16.57	41.44	85.29	167.13	409.08
Third quartile of distribution	105.66	72.70	26.09	49.02	89.81	173.68	336.85	105.16	63.61	21.83	47.78	95.25	174.46	293.01
Fourth quartile of distribution	113.42	69.46	31.76	54.71	98.39	184.42	372.03	115.84	63.94	20.33	51.48	100.66	194.90	338.98

Number of countries imported from

First quartile of distribution	83.79	63.80	17.39	38.38	71.94	137.59	286.40	84.21	47.16	18.12	37.08	75.47	137.70	257.11
Second quartile of distribution	100.17	73.85	20.42	43.45	83.90	167.39	346.94	103.99	62.75	15.50	42.45	93.68	166.14	355.55
Third quartile of distribution	110.26	80.36	23.76	50.64	92.93	184.31	371.01	109.85	59.97	17.53	48.17	100.00	183.36	324.71
Fourth quartile of distribution	123.06	94.06	31.28	59.39	104.06	196.71	436.22	122.87	85.64	20.96	51.89	100.00	217.36	390.33

Note: Labor productivity is calculated as total sales per employee and is in percentage of the 5-digit-industry mean value.
Source: Research Data Center of the German Statistical Office, Foreign Trade Statistics 2009, own calculations.

Table 5: Test for difference in distribution of labor productivity by number of products traded and number of countries traded with. (*p*-value of Kolmogorov–Smirnov-test). Robustness check.

	Number of goods exported			Number of goods imported			Number of countries exported to			Number of countries imported from		
	H1	H2	H3	H1	H2	H3	H1	H2	H3	H1	H2	H3
West Germany												
Q1 vs. Q2	0.000	0.997	0.000	0.000	0.986	0.000	0.000	0.999	0.000	0.000	0.999	0.000
Q1 vs.Q3	0.000	1.000	0.000	0.000	1.000	0.000	0.000	0.997	0.000	0.000	0.999	0.000
Q1 vs.Q4	0.000	1.000	0.000	0.000	0.999	0.000	0.000	0.998	0.000	0.000	1.000	0.000
Q2 vs. Q3	0.006	0.966	0.003	0.000	1.000	0.000	0.000	0.983	0.000	0.000	0.995	0.000
Q2 vs. Q4	0.000	0.991	0.000	0.000	0.999	0.000	0.000	0.982	0.000	0.000	0.997	0.000
Q3 vs. Q4	0.000	0.989	0.000	0.000	0.991	0.000	0.000	0.916	0.000	0.000	0.985	0.000
East Germany												
Q1 vs. Q2	0.114	0.915	0.057	0.000	0.974	0.000	0.003	1.000	0.001	0.000	0.975	0.000
Q1 vs.Q3	0.006	0.998	0.003	0.000	0.963	0.000	0.000	1.000	0.000	0.000	0.976	0.000
Q1 vs.Q4	0.000	0.998	0.000	0.000	0.992	0.000	0.000	1.000	0.000	0.000	0.996	0.000
Q2 vs. Q3	0.494	0.835	0.251	0.233	0.916	0.117	0.001	0.740	0.000	0.270	0.974	0.135
Q2 vs. Q4	0.000	0.998	0.000	0.000	0.965	0.000	0.000	0.944	0.000	0.006	0.999	0.003
Q3 vs. Q4	0.000	0.998	0.000	0.000	0.981	0.000	0.012	0.907	0.006	0.350	0.977	0.176

Note: Q1 (Q2, Q3, Q4) indicates the first (second, third, fourth) quartile of the distribution of the number of goods or the number of countries, respectively. Labor productivity is calculated as total sales per employee and is in percentage of the 5-digit-industry mean value. The hypotheses tested are:

H1: The productivity distributions of the two groups of firms do not differ.

H2: The productivity distribution of the first group is first-order stochastically dominated by the productivity distribution of the second group.

H3: The productivity distribution of the second group is first-order stochastically dominated by the productivity distribution of the first group.

Source: Research Data Center of the German Statistical Office, Foreign Trade Statistics 2009, own calculations.

Germany are fully in line with the theoretical hypothesis. The hypothesis that the two distributions do not differ is rejected at an error level of less than one percent, and the results clearly indicate that the productivity distribution of firms with a smaller number of goods traded or with a smaller number of trading partners is dominated by the productivity distribution of firms with a larger number of products traded or with a larger number of trading partners in all 24 cases investigated. The big picture for East Germany is the same, although the hypothesis of no difference in the productivity distribution cannot be rejected at an error level of five percent in three out of 24 cases (two to five vs. six to nine goods exported; one vs. two to five and two to five vs. six to nine ountries exported to).

The division of firms into four groups by the number of goods traded and the number of countries traded with used here is in a sense arbitrary. Furthermore, in some of the performed comparisons, the last group concentrates more than 50 percent of the whole distribution of firms. As a robustness check, the investigation was performed for groups of firms defined by the four quartiles of the distribution of firms by the number of goods traded and the number of countries traded with.[5] Results are reported in Tables 4 and 5. These results confirm the results reported in Tables 2 and 3.

The bottom line, then, is that there are statistically significant differences in the productivity distribution as a whole — and not only at the mean — between firms by their extensive margins of trade. The more goods firms trade, and the more countries firms trade with, the higher is the productivity of the firms. This is in line with implications of recent theoretical models of multi-product multi-country traders.

References

Bartelsman, Eric J. and Mark Doms (2000). Understanding productivity: Lessons from longitudinal micro data. *Journal of Economic Literature* 38, 569–594.

Bernard, Andrew B., J. Bradford Jensen, Steven J. Redding and Peter K. Schott (2007). Firms in international trade. *Journal of Economic Perspectives* 21(3), 105–130.

---

[5] I thank an anonymous referee for suggesting this robustness check.

Bernard, Andrew B., Steven J. Redding and Peter K. Schott (2011). Multiproduct firms and trade liberalization. *Quarterly Journal of Economics* 126, 1271–1318.

Buchinsky, Moshe (1994). Changes in the U.S. wage structure 1963–1987: Application of quantile regression. *Econometrica* 62, 405–458.

Castellani, Davide, Francesco Serti and Chiara Tomasi (2010). Firms in international trade: Importers' and exporters' heterogeneity in the Italian manufacturing industry. *The World Economy* 33, 424–457.

Conover, William. J. (1999). *Practical Nonparametric Statistics.* Third edition. (New York: John Wiley).

Delgado, Miguel A., Jose C. Farinas and Sonia Ruano (2002). Firm productivity and export markets: A non-parametric approach. *Journal on International Economics* 57, 397–422.

Foster, Lucia, John Haltiwanger and Chad Syverson (2008). Reallocation, firm turnover, and efficiency: Selection on productivity or profitability? *American Economic Review* 98, 394–425.

Melitz, Marc J. (2003). The impact of trade on intra-industry reallocations and aggregate industry productivity. *Econometrica* 71, 1695–1725.

Syverson, Chad (2011). What determines productivity? *Journal of Economic Literature* 49, 326–365.

Wagner, Joachim (2007). Exports and productivity: A survey of the evidence from firm-level data. *The World Economy* 30, 60–82.

Wagner, Joachim (2008). A note why more West than East German firms export. *International Economics and Economic Policy* 5, 363–370.

Wagner, Joachim (2012a). International trade and firm performance: A survey of empirical studies since 2006. *Review of World Economics/Weltwirtschaftliches Archiv* 148, 235–267.

Wagner, Joachim (2012b). Trading many goods with many countries: Exporters and importers from German manufacturing industries. *Jahrbuch für Wirtschaftswissenschaften* 63, 170–186.

Wagner, Joachim (2012c). German multiple-product, multiple-destination exporters: Bernard-Redding-Schott under test. *Economics Bulletin* 32, 1708–1714.

Chapter 10

Are Low-productive Exporters Marginal Exporters? Evidence from Germany*

Abstract

A stylized fact from the emerging literature on the micro-econometrics of international trade and a central implication of the heterogeneous firm models from the new trade theory is that exporters are more productive than non-exporters. It is argued that this exporter-productivity premium is due to extra cost of exporting that can be covered profitably by more productive firms only. Germany is a case in point — exporting firms from manufacturing industries are more productive than non-exporting firms from the same 4-digit-industry both on average and over the whole productivity distribution. However, many firms from the lower end of this distribution are exporters. This paper report that these low-productivity exporters are not marginal exporters defined according to the share of exports in total sales, or export participation over time, or the number of goods exported, or the number of countries exported to.

Keywords: Exports, productivity, low-productive exporters.

* Originally Published in *Economics Bulletin* (2013), 33 (1), 467–481.

All computations were done at the Research Data Centres of the Federal Statistical Office in Wiesbaden and of the Statistical Office of Berlin-Brandenburg in Berlin. The firm-level data used are strictly confidential but not exclusive; see http://www.forschungsdatenzentrum.de/datenzugang.asp for information on how to access the data.

1. Motivation

Ever since Bernard and Jensen (1995) started the literature on what is now labeled the Micro-econometrics of International Firm Activities some twenty years ago empirical studies that compare exporting and non-exporting firms report that exporters are more productive than non-exporters of the same size and from the same narrowly defined industry. This positive exporter productivity premium has been found in hundreds of studies for countries from all over the world, and it is considered as a stylized fact today (see the surveys by Greenaway and Kneller (2007), Bernard *et al.* (2012) and Wagner (2007a; 2012a)). Germany, one of the leading actors on the world market for goods and services, is a case in point (see Bernard and Wagner (1997) for manufacturing firms from one federal state, Lower Saxony, and Wagner (2007b) for German manufacturing as a whole).

The empirical finding of a positive exporter productivity premium motivated Melitz (2003) to develop a dynamic industry model with heterogeneous firms in which a firm that exports has to have a productivity value that lies beyond some threshold, while firms with a lower productivity serve the home market only (and the least productive firms exit the market). The reason for this productivity threshold that divides exporters from non-exporters is that exporters have to cover extra-costs to serve a foreign market (including cost for finding foreign customers, transportation costs, distribution or marketing costs, costs for personnel with skill to manage foreign networks, or costs to modify products for foreign customers), and only the more productive firms can cover these export-related costs while still being profitable.

The Melitz (2003) model has become the workhorse model of a large and growing theoretical literature labeled the *New Trade Theory* (reviewed in Helpman, 2006; 2011, Redding, 2011 and Melitz and Redding, 2014). Recently, the core ideas made its way into undergraduate classes on International Economics (see Krugman *et al.*, 2012, Chapter 8). A graph showing productivity thresholds that divide firms into three groups — exits, non-exporters and exporters — like Figure 5.1 in Helpman (2011, p. 103) or Figure 2 in Melitz and Redding (2014, p. 18) will soon be as familiar to students of international trade all over the world as a graph showing the consequences of a tariff on production and consumption in a small open economy.

That said, there is empirical evidence that does not fit well into the picture sketched so far: There are exporting firms which are located at the lower end of the productivity distribution and high-productive non-exporting firms. Powell and Wagner (2011) document that in Germany exporters and non-exporters are highly heterogeneous with regard to productivity. Neither low-productivity exporters nor high-productivity non-exporters are a rare species. Hallak and Sivadasan (2010) document similar evidence for India, the US, Chile, and Columbia. There is no such thing as a single cut-off point in the productivity distribution that separates non-exporters and exporters.

This paper discusses whether this evidence for low-productive exporters casts doubts on the validity of the stylized fact that exporters tend to be more productive than non-exporters and on the usefulness of theoretical models of the Melitz (2003) type that assume a productivity threshold that exporters have to cross. To do so it uses firm-level data from German manufacturing industries to look at the characteristics of these low-productive exporters for the first time. To anticipate the contribution of this paper to the literature we find that low-productivity exporters are not marginal exporters defined according to the share of exports in total sales, or export participation over time, or the number of goods exported, or the number of countries exported to. The hypothesis that the lack of an observed productivity threshold between exporters and non-exporters in German manufacturing industries is due to the fact that low-productive exporters are marginal exporters for which the extra costs of exporting compared to selling on the home market might be considered as negligible, therefore, is not supported by the data.

2. Low-productive Exporters in German Manufacturing Industries

2.1. Data and measurement issues

The empirical investigation uses data from two sources. The first source is the regular survey of establishments from manufacturing industries by the

Statistical Offices of the German federal states. The survey covers all establishments from manufacturing industries that employ at least twenty persons in the local production unit or in the company that owns the unit. Participation of firms in the survey is mandated in official statistics (see Malchin and Voshage (2009) for details). For this study establishment data were aggregated to the enterprise level to match the unit of observation in the second data source (described below). The survey has information on the number of employees in the firm, total turnover, total exports and detailed industry affiliation.

These data do not cover any information about the goods exported and the countries of destination of the goods. In other words, we know from these data *who* trades *how much*, but not *what* and *with whom*. Information on the goods traded internationally and on the countries with which these goods are traded is available from the statistic on foreign trade (*Außenhandelsstatistik*). This statistic is based on two sources. One source is the reports by German firms on transactions with firms from countries that are members of the European Union (EU); these reports are used to compile the so-called *Intrahandelsstatistik* on intra-EU trade. The other source is transaction-level data collected by the customs on trade with countries outside the EU (the so-called *Extrahandelsstatistik*).[1] Data in the statistic of foreign trade are transaction-level data, i.e., they relate to one transaction of a German firm with a firm located outside Germany at a time.

For the reporting year 2009 these transaction-level data have been aggregated at the level of the exporting firm for the first time. For each exporting firm that reported either to the statistic on intra-EU trade, or to the statistic on trade with countries outside the EU, we know from these data, among others, the number of goods exported and the number of countries exported to.[2] Using the firms' registration number for turnover

---

[1] Note that firms with a value of exports to and imports from EU-countries that does not exceed 400,000 Euro in 2009 do not have to report to the statistic on intra-EU trade. For trade with firms from non-member countries all transactions that exceed 1,000 Euro are registered. For details see Statistisches Bundesamt, Qualitätsbericht Außenhandel, January 2011.

[2] Note that information for firms with a value of exports to and imports from EU-countries that does not exceed 400,000 Euro in 2009 is not covered in the data (see footnote 1).

tax statistics these data were matched with the enterprise register system (*Unternehmensregister-System*). For enterprises from manufacturing industries this matching made it possible to add information (that is taken from the regular survey of manufacturing firms discussed above) on industry affiliation, total turnover and the number of employees (see Wagner, 2012b). These newly available data are the second source of data used in this paper. With these data it is possible to investigate the relationship between productivity on the one hand and the number of goods exported and the number of countries traded with on the other hand.

In this section of the paper cross-section data for 2009 are used. The reason is that as of today the newly available firm level data that are based on transaction level data are only available for this year. Given that the East German economy still differs in many respects from the West German economy, especially with regard to exporting (see Wagner, 2008), this study looks at West German and East German manufacturing enterprises separately.

Productivity is measured as labor productivity because information on the capital stock of a firm is not available, so more elaborate measures of total factor productivity cannot be used in this study. However, Bartelsman and Doms (2000, p. 575) point to the fact that heterogeneity in labor productivity has been found to be accompanied by similar heterogeneity in total factor productivity in the reviewed research where both concepts are measured. In a recent comprehensive survey Syverson (2011) argues that high-productivity producers will tend to look efficient regardless of the specific way that their productivity is measured. Furthermore, Foster *et al.* (2008) show that productivity measures that use sales (i.e., quantities multiplied by prices) and measures that use quantities only are highly positively correlated. Labor productivity is expressed in percentage of the mean value of labor productivity in the 4-digit-industry to take care of productivity differences across industries due to differences in capital intensity, demand conditions, regulation and trade barriers, among others.

Small exporters and importers that trade with EU-countries only are therefore underrepresented in the sample. Presumably, many of these are firms that trade only one good (or a very small number of goods) with one country (or a very small number of countries).

2.2. Empirical findings

The empirical investigation starts with reproducing one empirical finding that has been reported for Germany (and for many other countries) in numerous studies before: Exporters are more productive than non-exporters

Table 1 documents this finding for enterprises from manufacturing industries in both parts of Germany in 2009. Controlling for 4-digit level industries productivity is much higher in exporting firms compared to non-exporting firms both at the mean and at any other point of the productivity distribution. Statistical tests (*t*-tests for comparison of mean values and Kolmogorov–Smirnov-tests for comparison of distributions) reject the null-hypothesis of equality and point to higher productivity of exporting compared to non-exporting firms (with p-values reported to be $p = 0.000$).

Furthermore, Table 1 indicates that both exporters and non-exporters are highly heterogeneous — low-productive and high-productive exporters and low-productive and high-productive non-exporters coexist. Table 2

Table 1: Productivity distribution of exporters and non-exporters in manufacturing industries in Germany, 2009.

	Mean (SD)	p1	p25	p50	p75	p99
West Germany						
Exporters	105.60	19.25	61.48	87.23	126.01	384.58
($N = 22,286$)	(85.13)					
Non-exporters	86.45	7.09	44.98	66.13	101.35	353.04
($N = 8,380$)	(105.70)					
East Germany						
Exporters	109.76	14.54	59.41	88.06	131.02	454.71
($N = 3,974$)	(113.55)					
Non-exporters	87.56	10.34	49.27	69.60	104.77	341.91
($N = 2,893$)	(82.67)					

Note: Productivity is total sales/employees, measured as a percentage of the average value of the 4-digit level industry. Columns labeled p1–p99 refer to percentiles of the productivity distribution.

Table 2: Share of exporters and non-exporters in the deciles of the productivity distribution in manufacturing enterprises in Germany, 2009.

	West Germany		East Germany	
	Exporters (%)	Non-exporters (%)	Exporters (%)	Non-exporters (%)
Deciles				
1	49.85	50.15	48.79	51.21
2	59.94	40.06	46.01	53.99
3	67.71	32.29	48.12	51.88
4	70.86	29.14	49.78	50.22
5	76.90	23.10	56.81	43.19
6	78.49	21.51	61.10	38.90
7	81.35	18.65	63.62	36.38
8	81.25	18.75	62.99	37.01
9	80.86	19.14	69.42	30.58
10	78.68	21.32	71.70	28.30

Note: Productivity is total sales/employees, measured as a percentage of the average value of the 4-digit level industry.

reports the share of exporters and non-exporters in the deciles of the productivity distribution in manufacturing enterprises in Germany in 2009. While the share of exporting firms in all firms increases over the deciles, there are high shares of exporters at the lower end of the productivity distribution (and many non-exporting firms at the upper end). This is the second finding: Low-productive exporters abound.

This finding is at odds with a core implication of the dynamic industry model with heterogeneous firms by Melitz (2003) in which a firm that exports has to have a productivity value that lies beyond some threshold, while firms with a lower productivity serve the home market only (and the least productive firms exit the market). There is no productivity threshold that divides non-exporters and exporters in German manufacturing industries. This lack of a productivity threshold between exporters and non-exporters has been pointed out before by Hallak and Sivadasan (2010) for India, the US, Chile, and Columbia, and by Powell and Wagner (2011) for German manufacturing industries based on firm-level data for earlier years.

The literature on heterogeneous firms and exports argues that the reason for a productivity threshold that divides exporters from non-exporters is that exporters have to cover extra-costs to serve a foreign market (including cost for finding foreign customers, transportation costs, distribution or marketing costs, costs for personnel with skill to manage foreign networks, or costs to modify products for foreign customers), and only the more productive firms can cover these export-related costs while still being profitable. How can this be reconciled with the finding reported here?

An explanation for the lack of a productivity threshold between exporters and non-exporters observed in the data here might be that the extra-costs to serve a foreign market are (close to) zero for some exporters. This could be the case if low-productive exporters are marginal exporters. When talking to owners or managers of firms about the way they (started to) export one often hears answers like "There was this guy from Denmark I met at the trade fair, and he ordered some units of our *good X*", or "I received a mail from *company Y* in Switzerland in which they asked for one of our new machines". In situations like this, or in similar situations where firms export only a tiny share of their total product, export only one single good, or export to one single foreign country only, the extra costs of exporting compared to selling on the home market mentioned above might well be negligible. To see whether this is the case in Germany we will next take a closer look at the low-productive exporters.

One way to test whether low-productive exporters are marginal exporters, and whether high-productive exporters are not, is to look at the share of exports in total sales for exporting manufacturing enterprises in the deciles of the productivity distribution. Table 3 reports empirical evidence for Germany in 2009. On average, the share of exports in total sales is higher at the top than at the bottom of the productivity distribution, but marginal exporters are found in each decile (and firms with very large shares of exports to total sales, too), and the average value of the exports to sales ratio is far from small at the bottom end of the productivity distribution. This is the third empirical finding: Low-productive exporters are not marginal exporters with a low share of exports in total sales.

A second way to define a marginal exporter is to consider firms that export occasionally only (presumably when they receive an unsolicited

Table 3: Share of exports in total sales for exporting manufacturing enterprises in the deciles of the productivity distribution in Germany, 2009.

	West Germany			East Germany		
	Mean	p1	p99	Mean	p1	p99
Deciles						
1	23.22	0.04	97.77	24.35	0.02	100.0
2	23.47	0.06	90.83	19.47	0.02	87.27
3	24.66	0.05	92.37	18.76	0.03	92.00
4	25.47	0.06	88.42	20.31	0.06	95.74
5	26.74	0.04	91.83	20.58	0.07	80.96
6	28.53	0.07	91.28	22.11	0.02	93.53
7	30.69	0.07	94.52	22.88	0.03	93.01
8	32.72	0.06	94.04	23.87	0.03	89.11
9	35.73	0.13	94.19	28.56	0.03	99.42
10	38.37	0.06	98.65	34.41	0.01	99.99

Note: Productivity is total sales/employees, measured as a percentage of the average value of the 4-digit level industry. Columns labeled p1 and p99 refer to percentiles of the distribution of the share of exports in total sales.

export order) as marginally engaged in exporting, and firms that export continuously as non-marginal exporters. In general, participation in exporting tends to be highly persistent among firms from manufacturing industries in Germany. Among firms from manufacturing industries that exported in at least one year over the period from 2008 to 2010 in West Germany 90.2 percent exported in each year; the corresponding figure for East Germany is 86.3 percent. Table 4 reports the share of continuous exporters over the period 2008–2010 in all exporting firms in the deciles of the productivity distribution. While this share increases along the pro-ductivity distribution, it is only slightly below average at the lower end. This is the fourth empirical finding: Low-productive exporters are not marginal exporters that export only occasionally.

Another way to define a marginal exporter is to consider the number of different goods exported or the number of countries traded with (or both). We know that in Germany productivity increases with both the number of goods traded and the number of countries traded with

Table 4: Share of continuous exporters over the period 2008–2010 in all exporting firms in the deciles of the productivity distribution in manufacturing industries in Germany.

	West Germany	East Germany
Deciles (% of firms)		
1	79.89	79.44
2	84.96	80.14
3	88.55	84.12
4	90.66	86.67
5	91.83	87.03
6	90.56	86.51
7	92.34	86.84
8	92.26	88.12
9	92.24	88.84
10	92.73	90.43

Note: Productivity is total sales/employees in 2009, measured as a percentage of the average value of the 4-digit level industry. The entries in the table are the percentage shares of firms that exported in each year between 2008 and 2010 in all firms that exported in at least one year between 2008 and 2010.

(see Wagner, 2012b; 2012c). Table 5 reports the number of goods exported by manufacturing enterprises in the deciles of the productivity distribution.[3] The share of firms that exported only one good (or a small number of goods) declines over the productivity distribution, but the fraction of firms which export only few goods is not extremely large at the lower end of this distribution, and many firms with a low-productivity export many goods. This is the fifth empirical finding: Low-productive exporters are not marginal exporters that export only one good or few different goods.

---

[3] A good is an 8-digit number from the official nomenclature for the statistics of foreign trade. Note that the results reported in Tables 5–8 are based on the figures reported in the statistic on foreign trade (discussed in detail in the introductory section), so exports to EU-countries with a value of up to 400,000 Euro are not included (see footnotes 1 and 2). Firms that export only to the EU with an export value of less than 400,000 Euro are, therefore, not included in the sample analysed here.

Table 5: Number of goods exported by manufacturing enterprises in the deciles of the productivity distribution in Germany, 2009.

No. of goods	West Germany				East Germany			
	1	2–5	6–9	>= 10	1	2–5	6–9	>= 10
Deciles (Share of firms; %)								
1	22.4	34.6	14.5	28.5	27.1	35.4	16.7	20.8
2	17.7	35.3	14.0	33.0	27.1	39.1	17.7	16.1
3	16.1	31.9	13.6	38.4	21.7	39.1	15.9	23.3
4	14.4	30.5	13.9	41.2	21.8	39.9	14.5	23.8
5	12.5	29.0	14.2	44.3	16.5	35.6	13.8	34.0
6	12.8	26.1	14.8	46.2	11.3	40.2	16.5	32.0
7	11.1	25.1	13.1	50.7	19.2	36.3	15.5	29.0
8	11.0	24.7	13.0	51.2	13.4	39.7	11.9	35.0
9	9.9	22.7	12.1	55.4	16.1	30.0	16.6	37.3
10	8.1	23.6	10.9	57.5	11.5	26.6	14.6	47.4

Note: Productivity is total sales/employees, measured as a percentage of the average value of the 4-digit level industry. The entries in the table are the shares of firms from a decile of the productivity distribution with the number of products exported listed in the column header.

Table 6 reports a similar finding for the number of countries exported to. The share of firms that exported to one country (or to a small number of countries) only declines over the productivity distribution, but many firms with a low-productivity export to many countries. This is the sixth empirical finding: Low-productive exporters are not marginal exporters that export only to one country or to a few countries.

Firms that export one good only might be non-marginal exporters because they export this good to a large number of countries (which might cause high extra cost for, inter alia, doing market research, finding trading partners and adapt the good to special requirements in each country). Similarly, firms that export to one country only might be non-marginal exporters because they export many goods to this country (which might cause high extra costs for, inter alia, adapt each good to special requirements in that country). A different way to define a marginal exporter, therefore, is to consider firms that export one good to one country only,

Table 6: Number of countries exported to by manufacturing enterprises in the deciles of the productivity distribution in Germany, 2009.

	West Germany				East Germany			
No. of countries	1	2–5	6–9	≥10	1	2–5	6–9	≥10
Deciles (Share of firms; %)								
1	16.1	24.4	14.4	45.1	19.3	32.8	12.5	35.4
2	12.6	21.4	12.0	54.0	20.3	30.7	16.7	32.3
3	9.9	16.4	13.6	60.1	16.9	28.0	15.3	39.7
4	9.3	15.2	10.4	65.1	15.0	28.0	12.4	44.6
5	7.8	14.6	11.0	66.6	12.2	29.1	15.3	43.4
6	7.4	14.6	8.9	69.1	8.8	19.1	13.9	58.3
7	5.0	12.5	11.1	71.5	11.4	22.3	13.0	53.4
8	6.2	12.3	9.5	72.1	9.8	19.6	11.9	58.8
9	3.9	11.9	10.4	73.9	7.3	18.1	13.0	61.7
10	3.2	10.5	11.1	75.2	6.3	20.3	9.9	63.5

Note: Productivity is total sales/employees, measured as a percentage of the average value of the 4-digit level industry. The entries in the table are the shares of firms from a decile of the productivity distribution with the number of countries exported to listed in the column header.

maybe dealing only with one customer who placed an order with the German company. Table 7 reports the share of exporting manufacturing enterprises of this "one-good-one-target-country-only" — type in the deciles of the productivity distribution. The share of these marginal exporters declines over the productivity distribution, but by far not all exporters from the lower end of the distribution are marginal exporters of this type. This is the seventh empirical finding: Low-productive exporters are not marginal exporters that export only one good to one country.

3. Concluding Remarks

The bottom line, then, is that low-productivity exporters are not marginal exporters defined according to the share of exports in total sales, or export participation over time, or the number of goods exported, or the number of countries exported to. The hypothesis that the lack of an observed

Table 7: Share of exporting manufacturing enterprises with one good exported to one country in the deciles of the productivity distribution in Germany, 2009.

	West Germany	East Germany
Deciles (% of firms)		
1	10.85	15.63
2	7.51	14.58
3	5.60	12.70
4	5.99	9.33
5	4.43	7.41
6	4.49	5.15
7	2.95	6.74
8	4.23	5.15
9	2.28	4.15
10	1.76	3.65

Note: Productivity is total sales/employees, measured as a percentage of the average value of the 4-digit level industry. The entries in the table are the shares of firms in all exporting firms from a decile of the productivity distribution that export one good to one country only.

productivity threshold between exporters and non-exporters in German manufacturing industries is due to the fact that low-productive exporters are marginal exporters for which the extra costs of exporting compared to selling on the home market might be considered as negligible, therefore, is not supported by the data.

To put these findings into perspective, it seems appropriate to quote at some length from a recent paper[4] by two of the most important theoreticians in this area, Melitz and Redding (2012, p. 5): "Naturally, the model is an abstraction and does not capture all of the features of the data. … (M)uch of our analysis concentrates on heterogeneity in productivity …, and hence does not capture the rich range of dimensions along which trading and non-trading firms can differ. Additionally, the baseline version of the

[4]This paper is forthcoming in Vol. 4 of the highly prestigious *Handbook of International Economics*.

model yields sharp predictions such as a single productivity threshold above which all firms export ... Although these sharp predictions are unlikely to be literally satisfied in the data, they capture systematic relationships or average tendencies in the data, as the higher average productivity of exporters ....."

We demonstrate that, indeed, the sharp prediction from the baseline version of the Melitz (2003) model, namely that there is a single productivity threshold above which all firms export, is at odds with the data from German manufacturing enterprises. While this does not at all devaluate the Melitz (2003) model as a tool for theoretical analyses, it points to the need for a closer look at "the rich range of dimensions along which trading and non-trading firms can differ" mentioned by Melitz and Redding (2012, p. 20). Unfortunately, however, the data used here are not rich enough to proceed in this direction.

References

Bartelsman, Erik and Mark Doms (2000). Understanding productivity: Lessons from longitudinal micro data. *Journal of Economic Literature* 38 (3), 569–594.

Bernard, Andrew and Bradford Jensen (1995). Exporters, jobs and wages in U.S. manufacturing: 1976–1987. *Brookings Papers on Economic Activity, Microeconomcis* 1, 67–119.

Bernard, Andrew B. and Joachim Wagner (1997). Exports and success in German manufacturing. *Review of World Economics* 133 (1), 134–157.

Bernard, Andrew, Bradford Jensen, Stephen J. Redding and Peter K. Schott (2012). The empirics of firm heterogeneity and international trade. *Annual Review of Economics* 4 (1), 283–313.

Foster, Lucia, John Haltiwanger and Chad Syverson (2008). Reallocation, firm turnover, and efficiency: Selection on productivity or profitability? *American Economic Review* 98 (1), 394–425.

Greenaway, David and Richard Kneller (2007). Firm heterogeneity, exporting and foreign direct investment. *Economic Journal* 117 (517), F134–F161.

Hallak, Juan Carlos and Jagadeesh Sivadasan (2010). Firms' exporting behavior under quality constraints. *Working Paper*, No. 99, Universidad de San Andres, Departomento de Economia.

Helpman, Elhanan (2006). Trade, FDI, and the organization of firms. *Journal of Economic Literature* 44 (3), 589–630.

Helpman, Elhanan (2011). Understanding global trade. Cambridge, MA and London, England: Harvard University Press.

Krugman, Paul R., Maurice Obstfeld and Marc J. Melitz (2012). International economics, theory and policy. Ninth Edition. Boston: Pearson.

Malchin, Anja and Ramona Voshage (2009). Official firm data for Germany. *Schmollers Jahrbuch/Journal of Applied Social Science Studies* 129 (3), 501–513.

Melitz, Marc J. (2003). The impact of trade on intra-industry reallocations and aggregate industry productivity. *Econometrica* 71 (6), 1695–1725.

Melitz, Marc J. and Stephen J. Redding (2014). Heterogeneous firms and trade. In: Gita Gopinath, Elhanan Helpman and Kenneth Rogoff (Eds.) *Handbook of International Economics*. Amsterdam: Elsevier, Vol. 4, pp. 1–54.

Powell, David and Joachim Wagner (2011). The exporter productivity premium along the productivity distribution. Evidence from unconditional quantile regression with firm fixed effects. *RAND Working Paper*, No. WR-837.

Redding, Stephen J. (2011). Theories of heterogeneous firms and trade. *Annual Review of Economics* 3 (1), 77–105.

Syverson, Chad (2011). What determines productivity? *Journal of Economic Literature* 49 (2), 326–365.

Wagner, Joachim (2007a). Exports and productivity: A survey of the evidence from firm level data. *The World Economy* 30 (1), 60–82.

Wagner, Joachim (2007b). Exports and productivity in Germany. *Applied Economics Quarterly* 53 (4), 354–373.

Wagner, Joachim (2008). A note why more West than East German firms export. *International Economics and Economic Policy* 5 (4), 363–370.

Wagner, Joachim (2012a). International trade and firm performance: A survey of empirical studies since 2006. *Review of World Economics* 148 (2), 235–267.

Wagner, Joachim (2012b). Trading many goods with many countries: Exporters and importers from German manufacturing industries. *Jahrbuch für Wirtschaftswissenschaft/Review of Economics* 63 (2), 170–186.

Wagner, Joachim (2012c). Productivity and the extensive margins of trade in German manufacturing firms: Evidence from a non-parametric test. *Economics Bulletin* 32 (4), 3061–3070.

Chapter 11

Low-productive Exporters are High-quality Exporters — Evidence from Germany*

Abstract

A stylized fact from the emerging literature on the micro-econometrics of international trade and a central implication of the heterogeneous firm models from the new trade theory is that exporters are more productive than non-exporters. However, many firms from the lower end of the productivity distribution are exporters. Germany is a case in point. A recent study reports that these low-productivity exporters are not marginal exporters defined according to the share of exports in total sales, or export participation over time, or the number of goods exported, or the number of countries exported to. This paper documents that low-productive exporters are competitive because they export high-quality goods. The quality of exports is much higher among exporters from the lower end of the productivity distribution than among highly productive exporters.

Keywords: Exports, productivity, low-productive exporters, export quality.

* Originally Published in *Economics Bulletin* (2014), 34 (2), 745–756.
All computations were done at the Research Data Centre of the Statistical Office of Berlin-Brandenburg in Berlin. The firm-level data used are strictly confidential but not exclusive; see http://www.forschungsdatenzentrum.de/datenzugang.asp for information on how to access the data. To facilitate replications the Stata do-file used is available from the author on request.

1. Motivation

Hundreds of empirical studies from countries all over the world that use firm-level data to compare exporting and non-exporting firms report that exporters are more productive than non-exporters of the same size and from the same narrowly defined industry. This positive exporter productivity premium is considered as a stylized fact today (see the surveys by Greenaway and Kneller, 2007, Bernard *et al.*, 2012 and Wagner, 2007; 2012). The empirical finding of a positive exporter productivity premium motivated Melitz (2003) to develop a dynamic industry model with heterogeneous firms in which a firm that exports has to have a productivity value that lies beyond some threshold, while firms with a lower productivity serve the home market only (and the least productive firms exit the market). The reason for this productivity threshold that divides exporters from non-exporters is that exporters have to cover extra-costs to serve a foreign market (including cost for finding foreign customers, transportation costs, distribution or marketing costs, costs for personnel with skill to manage foreign networks, or costs to modify products for foreign customers), and only the more productive firms can cover these export-related costs while still being profitable. The Melitz (2003) model has become the workhorse model of a large and growing theoretical literature.

That said, there is empirical evidence that does not fit well into the picture sketched so far: There are exporting firms which are located at the lower end of the productivity distribution and high-productive non-exporting firms. Wagner (2013) documents that in Germany exporters and non-exporters are highly heterogeneous with regard to productivity. Neither low-productive exporters nor high-productive non-exporters are a rare species. Hallak and Sivadasan (2013) document similar evidence for India, the US, Chile, and Columbia. There is no such thing as a single cut-off point in the productivity distribution that separates non-exporters and exporters.

For Germany, Wagner (2013) shows that low-productive exporters are not marginal exporters defined according to the share of exports in total sales, or export participation over time, or the number of goods exported, or the number of countries exported to. The hypothesis that the lack of an observed productivity threshold between exporters and non-exporters in German manufacturing industries is due to the fact that low-productive exporters are marginal exporters for which the extra costs of exporting compared to selling on the home market might be considered as negligible, therefore, is not supported by the data.

This points to the need for a closer look at "the rich range of dimensions along which trading and non-trading firms can differ" pointed to in a recent paper by Melitz and Redding (2014), two of the most important theoreticians in this area. One of these dimensions is product quality. High product quality is often regarded as a decisive characteristic of goods exported by German manufacturing firms. In a recent annual report on the economic status published by the German Ministry of Economics and Technology it is argued that 40 percent of German exports are investment goods, and that for many of these goods, quality is the most important factor, while demand is comparably price-inelastic (see Bundesministerium für Wirtschaft und Technologie, 2011, p. 16). High-quality investment goods that are highly attractive for customers in foreign countries are sold for a high price. This means that comparably low productive firms can make a profit from serving a foreign market after paying the extra costs of exporting if they produce high-quality goods.

This paper contributes to the literature by testing for the first time for the existence of a negative relationship between productivity and export quality. To anticipate the most important finding, in the line with the reasoning outlined above the paper demonstrates that low-productive exporters can compete because they export high-quality goods. The quality of exports is much higher among exporters from the lower end of the productivity distribution than among highly productive exporters.

2. Low-productive Exporters and High-quality Exporters in German Manufacturing Industries

2.1. Data and measurement issues

The empirical investigation uses data from two sources. The first source is the regular survey of establishments from manufacturing industries by the Statistical Offices of the German federal states. The survey covers all establishments from manufacturing industries that employ at least 20 persons in the local production unit or in the company that owns the unit. Participation of firms in the survey is mandated in official statistics (see Malchin and Voshage, 2009 for details). For this study establishment data were aggregated to the enterprise level to match the unit of observation in the second data source (described below). The survey has information on the number of employees in the firm, total turnover, total exports and detailed industry affiliation.

These data do not cover any information about the goods exported. In other words, we know from these data *who* trades *how much*, but not *what*. Information on the goods traded internationally is available from the statistic on foreign trade (*Außenhandelsstatistik*). This statistic is based on two sources. One source is the reports by German firms on transactions with firms from countries that are members of the European Union (EU); these reports are used to compile the so-called *Intrahandelsstatistik* on intra-EU trade. The other source is transaction-level data collected by the customs on trade with countries outside the EU (the so-called *Extrahandelsstatistik*).[1] Data in the statistic of foreign trade are transaction-level data, i.e., they relate to one transaction of a German firm with a firm located outside Germany at a time.

For the reporting years 2009 and 2010 these transaction-level data have been aggregated at the level of the exporting firm for the first time. For each exporting firm that reported either to the statistic on intra-EU trade, or to the statistic on trade with countries outside the EU, we know from these data the value and the volume of exports for the 10 most important exported goods. Using the firms' registration number for turnover tax statistics these data were matched with the enterprise register system (*Unternehmensregister-System*). For enterprises from manufacturing industries this matching made it possible to add information (that is taken from the regular survey of manufacturing firms discussed above) on industry affiliation, total turnover and the number of employees. These newly available data are the second source of data used in this paper.

With these data it is possible to investigate the relationship between productivity on the one hand and the quality of goods exported:

Productivity is measured as labor productivity because information on the capital stock of a firm is not available, so more elaborate measures

---

[1] Note that firms with a value of exports to EU-countries that does not exceed 400,000 Euro in 2009 do not have to report to the statistic on intra-EU trade. For trade with firms from non-member countries all transactions that exceed 1,000 Euro are registered. For details see Statistisches Bundesamt, Qualitätsbericht Außenhandel, January 2011.

of total factor productivity cannot be used in this study. However, Bartelsman and Doms (2000, p. 575) point to the fact that heterogeneity in labor productivity has been found to be accompanied by similar heterogeneity in total factor productivity in the reviewed rescarch where both concepts are measured. In a recent comprehensive survey Syverson (2011) argues that high-productivity producers will tend to look efficient regardless of the specific way that their productivity is measured. Furthermore, Foster *et al.* (2008) show that productivity measures that use sales (i.e., quantities multiplied by prices) and measures that use quantities only are highly positively correlated. Labor productivity is expressed in percentage of the mean value of labor productivity in the 4-digit industry to take care of productivity differences across industries due to differences in capital intensity, demand conditions, regulation and trade barriers, among others.

Export quality is not directly observed. Therefore, a proxy variable is used that is defined as the unit value of exports and computed as value of exports (measured in Euro) over quantity of exports (measured in tons). In the data set used here we have information on the value of exports and the quantity of exports for the 10 most important products (measured by the value of exports) exported by a firm. For firms that exported more than one good the unit value of exports is the weighted sum of the unit values of the (up to 10) different goods exported, and the weights are the shares of the value of exports of a good in the total exports of the firm of these (up to 10) goods. The unit value of exports is expressed in percentage of the mean value of unit values in the 4-digit industry to take care of differences across industries due to the nature of the products (e.g., mobile phones and cement). Furthermore, inside a narrowly defined industry we can expect that a higher unit value is a valid proxy variable for product quality. Under competitive conditions a manufacturer of a specific good can charge a higher price than another firm that produces a very similar good (that is of the same weight) only if the quality of the good he produces is higher.

Given that the East German economy still differs in many respects from the West German economy, especially with regard to exporting (see Wagner, 2008), this study looks at West German and East German manufacturing enterprises separately. All computations are performed for two years, 2009 and 2010. In 2009, the value of German exports of goods declined by 18.4 percent compared to 2008. This was followed by an increase in exports by 18.5 percent in 2010 (Statistisches Bundesamt, 2012, p. 414). Therefore, a look at these two very different years can be considered as a robustness check to make sure that the results reported are not specific for a crises or recovery period.

2.2. Empirical findings

The empirical investigation of the relationship between productivity and export quality starts with a description of the distribution of export quality in the deciles of the productivity distribution of West German manufacturing firms. Tables 1 and 2 report figures for the mean of export

Table 1: **Export quality in the deciles of the productivity distribution, West German manufacturing enterprises, 2009.**

	Export quality				
	Mean	Std. Dev.	p1	p50	p99
Decile of productivity distribution					
1	151.27	435.74	0.71	57.53	1397.09
2	121.24	234.26	0.62	54.20	1233.80
3	131.96	336.37	0.39	52.27	1674.37
4	102.22	262.25	0.59	45.51	900.49
5	113.43	428.51	0.40	49.11	940.94
6	84.37	197.41	0.38	42.78	710.74
7	93.62	230.40	0.24	40.54	1151.21
8	89.77	466.28	0.28	37.32	637.57
9	82.87	377.01	0.27	33.79	675.62
10	74.66	190.20	0.27	31.18	1020.73

Note: Export quality is defined as the unit value of exports (computed as value of exports over quantity of exports) and measured as a percentage of the average value of the 4-digit-level industry; see text for details. Productivity is defined as total sales over employees and measured as a percentage of the average value of the 4-digit-level industry. Columns labeled p1–p99 refer to percentiles of the export quality distribution.

Table 2: Export quality in the deciles of the productivity distribution, West German manufacturing enterprises, 2010.

	Export quality				
	Mean	Std. Dev.	p1	p50	p99
Decile of productivity distribution					
1	140.59	272.17	0.80	66.99	1610.60
2	137.24	360.26	0.81	56.44	1765.81
3	118.73	399.87	1.07	50.18	960.95
4	114.73	364.57	0.69	50.81	1229.01
5	118.14	448.55	0.77	49.14	1179.93
6	95.73	214.43	0.90	49.16	816.31
7	85.31	194.71	0.70	40.51	797.56
8	91.29	275.74	0.62	39.62	848.18
9	74.33	204.09	0.81	36.27	630.69
10	69.79	177.77	0.51	32.73	572.87

Note: Export quality is defined as the unit value of exports (computed as value of exports over quantity of exports) and measured as a percentage of the average value of the 4-digit-level industry; see text for details. Productivity is defined as total sales over employees and measured as a percentage of the average value of the 4-digit-level industry. Columns labeled p1–p99 refer to percentiles of the export quality distribution.

quality and the respective values for the first, 50th and 99th percentile of the export quality distribution in the firms in the deciles of the productivity distribution. In both years the mean and median values of export quality tend to decline (though not always monotonically) over the deciles of the productivity distribution from the lower to the higher end of the distribution. Export quality is much larger on average and at the median in low-productive exporting firms (defined as firms from the first to the third decile of the productivity distribution) than in high-productive exporting firms (that are located in the three top deciles of the productivity distribution).

In a second step of the empirical investigation the statistical significance of the difference in means of the export quality between firms from the deciles of the productivity distribution is tested. Tables 3 and 4 report results of a two-sample *t* test with unequal variances of H_0: Difference in

Table 3: Test of equality of means of the export quality between the deciles of the productivity distribution, West German manufacturing enterprises, 2009.

Decile of productivity distribution	2	3	4	5	6
1	0.059	0.172	0.005	0.039	0.0001
2		0.785	0.049	0.302	0.0001
3			0.014	0.133	0.0000
4				0.772	0.034
5					0.018

	7	8	9	10
1	0.001	0.002	0.0003	0.0000
2	0.004	0.018	0.002	0.0000
3	0.001	0.006	0.0005	0.0000
4	0.201	0.202	0.068	0.002
5	0.081	0.092	0.030	0.002
6	0.862	0.653	0.449	0.103
7		0.392	0.186	0.011
8			0.335	0.134
9				0.237

Note: The entries in the table are the prob-values of a two-sample t test with unequal variances of H_0: Difference in mean export quality $= 0$ vs. H_a: Difference in mean export quality > 0 where sample 1 refers to the firms in the decile of the productivity distribution listed in the first column of the table and sample 2 refers to the firms in the decile of the productivity distribution listed in the first row of the table. A prob-value of 0.05 (or smaller) indicates that the mean export quality in enterprises from the lower decile of the productivity distribution is larger than the mean export quality in enterprises from the higher decile of the productivity distribution at an error level of five percent (or smaller). For a definition of export quality and productivity see note to Table 1.

mean export quality between sample 1 and sample 2 $= 0$ vs. H_a: Difference in mean export quality between sample 1 and sample 2 > 0, where sample 1 refers to the firms in the decile of the productivity distribution listed in the first column of the Tables 3 and 4 and sample 2 refers to the firms in the decile of the productivity distribution listed in the first row of the table. A prob-value of 0.05 (or smaller) indicates that the mean export quality in enterprises from the lower decile of the productivity distribution is larger than the mean export quality in enterprises from the higher decile of the

Table 4: Test of equality of means of the export quality between the deciles of the productivity distribution, West German manufacturing enterprises, 2010.

Decile of productivity distribution	2	3	4	5	6
1	0.418	0.091	0.044	0.090	0.0001
2		0.147	0.087	0.145	0.001
3			0.406	0.487	0.050
4				0.578	0.064
5					0.061

	7	8	9	10
1	0.000	0.0001	0.000	0.000
2	0.0001	0.0007	0.000	0.000
3	0.007	0.031	0.0006	0.0002
4	0.008	0.039	0.0005	0.0001
5	0.011	0.039	0.001	0.0003
6	0.093	0.319	0.004	0.003
7		0.745	0.072	0.015
8			0.032	0.008
9				0.265

Note: The entries in the table are the prob-values of a two-sample t test with unequal variances of H_0: Difference in mean export quality = 0 vs. H_a: Difference in mean export quality > 0 where sample 1 refers to the firms in the decile of the productivity distribution listed in the first column of the table and sample 2 refers to the firms in the decile of the productivity distribution listed in the first row of the table. A prob-value of 0.05 (or smaller) indicates that the mean export quality in enterprises from the lower decile of the productivity distribution is larger than the mean export quality in enterprises from the higher decile of the productivity distribution at an error level of five percent (or smaller). For a definition of export quality and productivity see note to Table 1.

productivity distribution at an error level of five percent (or smaller). While the t test does not indicate that all differences in means of the export quality between firms from the deciles of the productivity distribution are statistically significantly different from zero and in favor of the export quality of firms from the lower decile of the productivity distribution, this pecking order is found when low-productive exporters from the first three deciles are compared to high-productive exports from the last three deciles.

In a third step of the empirical investigation the focus is not on the difference in the mean values of export quality between firms from various

Table 5: Test for stochastic dominance of the distribution of export quality between the deciles of the productivity distribution, West German manufacturing enterprises, 2009.

Decile of productivity distribution	2	3	4	5	6
1	0.161	0.004	0.001	0.000	0.000
2		0.198	0.056	0.016	0.000
3			0.041	0.082	0.000
4				0.374	0.010
5					0.009

	7	8	9	10
1	0.000	0.000	0.000	0.000
2	0.000	0.000	0.000	0.000
3	0.000	0.000	0.000	0.000
4	0.000	0.000	0.000	0.000
5	0.000	0.000	0.000	0.000
6	0.504	0.061	0.000	0.000
7		0.187	0.000	0.000
8			0.008	0.000
9				0.170

Note: The entries in the table refer to a Kolmogorov–Smirnov-Test of first-order stochastic dominance of the distribution of export quality for firms from the decile of the productivity distribution listed in the first column of the table over the distribution of export quality for firms from the decile of the productivity distribution listed in the first row of the table. If a reported prob-value is 0.05 (or smaller) this indicates that the distribution of export quality of the less productive firms stochastically dominates the distribution of export quality of the more productive firms at an error level of five percent (or smaller). For a definition of export quality and productivity see note to Table 1.

deciles of the productivity distribution but on the difference between the distributions of the export quality as a whole when firms from two deciles of the productivity distribution are compared. Tables 5 and 6 report results of a Kolmogorov–Smirnov-test of first-order stochastic dominance of the distribution of export quality for firms from the decile of the productivity distribution listed in the first column of the table over the distribution of export quality for firms from the decile of the productivity distribution listed in the first row of the table. If a reported prob-value is 0.05 (or smaller) this indicates that the distribution of export quality of

Table 6: Test for stochastic dominance of the distribution of export quality between the deciles of the productivity distribution, West German manufacturing enterprises, 2010.

Decile of productivity distribution	2	3	4	5	6
1	0.011	0.000	0.000	0.000	0.000
2		0.050	0.066	0.020	0.002
3			0.525	0.600	0.529
4				0.571	0.282
5					0.370

	7	8	9	10
1	0.000	0.000	0.000	0.000
2	0.000	0.000	0.000	0.000
3	0.000	0.000	0.000	0.000
4	0.000	0.000	0.000	0.000
5	0.000	0.000	0.000	0.000
6	0.000	0.000	0.000	0.000
7		0.247	0.012	0.000
8			0.113	0.002
9				0.037

Note: The entries in the table refer to a Kolmogorov–Smirnov-test of first-order stochastic dominance of the distribution of export quality for firms from the decile of the productivity distribution listed in the first column of the table over the distribution of export quality for firms from the decile of the productivity distribution listed in the first row of the table. If a reported prob-value is 0.05 (or smaller) this indicates that the distribution of export quality of the less productive firms stochastically dominates the distribution of export quality of the more productive firms at an error level of five percent (or smaller). For a definition of export quality and productivity see note to Table 1.

the less productive firms stochastically dominates the distribution of export quality of the more productive firms at an error level of five percent (or smaller). While not all results point to such a pattern of stochastic dominance, the picture is crystal clear for a comparison of low-productive exporters from the first three deciles compared to high-productive exports from the last three deciles of the productivity distribution — low-productive exporters have a higher export quality than high-productive exporters over the whole distribution of export quality.

Results for West German manufacturing firms can be summarizes as follows. Low-productive exporters have a higher export quality than high-productive exporters not only at the mean but over the whole distribution of export quality. These differences are both statistically highly significant and large from an economic point of view — the export quality values are about twice as high, both at the mean and at the median, in the exporting firms from the lowest decile of the productivity distribution than in the firms from the highest decile (see Tables 1 and 2).

The big picture reported in detail for West Germany here is identical for East Germany; results are available on request.

3. Concluding Remarks

The bottom line, then, is that in German manufacturing industries low-productive exporters (which are not marginal exporters defined according to the share of exports in total sales, or export participation over time, or the number of goods exported, or the number of countries exported to) tend to export high-quality goods. This indicates that comparably low productive firms can make a profit from serving a foreign market after paying the extra costs of exporting if they produce high-quality goods.

References

Bartelsman, Erik and Mark Doms (2000). Understanding productivity. Lessons from longitudinal micro data. *Journal of Economic Literature* 38 (3), 569–594.

Bernard, Andrew, J. Bradford Jensen, Stephen J. Redding and Peter K. Schott (2012). The empirics of firm heterogeneity and international trade. *Annual Review of Economics* 4 (1), 283–313.

Bundesministerium für Wirtschaft und Technologie (2011). *Jahreswirtschaftsbericht 2011. Deutschland im Aufschwung — Den Wohlstand von Morgen sichern.* Berlin: BMWi.

Foster, Lucia, John Haltiwanger and Chad Syverson (2008). Reallocation, firm turnover, and efficiency: Selection on productivity or profitability? *American Economic Review* 98 (1), 394–425.

Greenaway, David and Richard Kneller (2007). Firm heterogeneity, exporting and foreign direct investment. *Economic Journal* 117 (517), F134–F161.

Hallak, Juan Carlos and Jagadeesh Sivadasan (2013). Firms' exporting behavior under quality constraints. *Journal of International Economics* 91 (1), 53–67.

Malchin, Anja and Ramona Voshage (2009). Official firm data for Germany. *Schmollers Jahrbuch/Journal of Applied Social Science Studies* 129 (3), 501–513.

Melitz, Marc. (2003). The impact of trade on intra-industry reallocations and aggregate industry productivity. *Econometrica* 71 (6), 1695–1725.

Melitz, Marc J. and Stephen J. Redding (2014). Heterogeneous firms and trade. In: Gita Gopinath, Elhanan Helpman and Kenneth Rogoff (Eds.). *Handbook of International Economics*. Amsterdam: Elsevier, Vol. 4, pp. 1–54.

Statistisches Bundesamt (2012). Statistisches Jahrbuch 2012. *Wiesbaden: Statistisches Bundesamt.*

Syverson, Chad (2011). What determines productivity? *Journal of Economic Literature* 49 (2), 326–365.

Wagner, Joachim (2007). Exports and productivity: A survey of the evidence from firm level data. *The World Economy* 30 (1), 60–82.

Wagner, Joachim (2008). A note why more West than East German firms export. *International Economics and Economic Policy* 5 (4), 363–370.

Wagner, Joachim (2012). International trade and firm performance: A survey of empirical studies since 2006. *Review of World Economics* 148 (2), 235–267.

Wagner, Joachim (2013). Are low-productive exporters marginal exporters? Evidence from Germany. *Economics Bulletin* 33 (1), 467–481.

Chapter 12

What Makes a High-quality Exporter? Evidence from Germany*

Abstract

This chapter uses a tailor-made newly available data set to investigate for the first time the links between the quality of input factors and the quality of exports in enterprises from manufacturing industries in Germany, one of the leading actors on the world market for goods. The chapter demonstrates that in German manufacturing industries exporters of high-quality goods tend to use high-quality inputs, while the firm size is not related at all to export quality.

Keywords: Exports, export quality, Germany.

---

* Originally Published in *Economics Bulletin* (2014), 34 (2), 865–874.

All computations were done at the Research Data Centre of the Statistical Office of Berlin-Brandenburg in Berlin. The firm-level data used are strictly confidential but not exclusive; see http://www.forschungsdatenzentrum.de/datenzugang.asp for information on how to access the data. To facilitate replications the Stata do-file used is available from the author on request.

1. Motivation

High product quality is often regarded as a decisive characteristic of goods exported by German manufacturing firms. In a recent annual report published by the German Ministry of Economics and Technology it is argued that 40 percent of German exports are investment goods, and that for many of these goods quality is the most important factor, while demand is comparably price-inelastic (see Bundesministerium für Wirtschaft und Technologie, 2011, p. 16). High-quality investment goods that are highly attractive for customers in foreign countries are sold for a high price. The same holds for durable consumer goods like cars or kitchens.

Given this high importance of the quality of goods for German exports it comes as a surprise that the characteristics of high-quality exporters have not been investigated econometrically in the literature.[1] Bastos and Silva (2010, p. 99) call the quality of exports and its drivers "a relatively unexplored dimension of firms' cross-border activities". While a large number of studies use firm-level data to look at the link between firm characteristics and exports of German firms in general,[2] none of these papers deals with the quality of the goods exported. This paper intends to fill this gap.

A comprehensive theoretical model of a firm that maximizes profits by choosing an optimal mix of inputs of different quality to produce outputs of an optimal quality which can be used to derive a set of hypotheses for an econometric investigation of the characteristics of high-quality exporters is lacking. Therefore, the empirical models used in this study are based on hypotheses that are of a somewhat *ad hoc* character

---

[1] To the best of my knowledge there are no such econometric studies for other countries besides Germany, too. Bastos and Silva (2010) use Portuguese firm-level data on exports by product and destination market to demonstrate that export quality increases systematically with distance, and tends to be higher in shipments to richer nations. These authors do not investigate the role of firm characteristics like input quality or firm size for export quality.
[2] See Wagner (2011a) for a survey of 51 empirical studies on exports and firm characteristics based on German firm level data that were published between 1991 and 2011 and Wagner (2011b) for an econometric investigation based on new comprehensive longitudinal firm level data.

and that make use of knowledge of the export performance of German manufacturing firms.

First of all, we expect that there is a positive link between the quality of inputs used in a firm and the quality of its products — "garbage in, garbage out". Here, the quality of the workforce, research and development activities by a firm that aim to improve the products, and the quality of inputs bought from other firms are expected to play a decisive role.

Another characteristic of a firm besides the quality of the inputs used that might be expected to be linked to the quality of exports is firm size. It is a stylized fact that firm size and exports are positively related. This positive link between exports and firm size is due to fixed costs of exporting and efficiency advantages of larger firms due to scale economies, advantages of specialization in management and better conditions on the markets for inputs. Large firms can be expected to have cost advantages on credit markets while small firms often face higher restrictions on the capital market leading to a higher risk of insolvency and illiquidity. Furthermore, there might be disadvantages of small firms in the competition for highly qualified employees. While these considerations point to an advantage of larger firms when it comes to the production and export of high-quality goods anecdotal evidence of German firms of small to medium size that are so-called "hidden champions" on the world market for high-quality goods abounds. The role of firm size in making a high-quality exporter, therefore, is a topic to be investigated empirically.

This chapter uses a tailor-made newly available data set (described in detail in Section 2) to investigate for the first time the links between the quality of input factors and firm size on the one hand and the quality of exports on the other hand. To anticipate the most important finding, the chapter demonstrates that in German manufacturing industries exporters of high-quality goods tend to use high-quality inputs, while firm size is not related at all to export quality.

2. Data and Measurement Issues

The lack of empirical studies on the characteristics of high-quality exporters is due to the fact that until most recently suitable data at the level of the firm that could be used in an econometric investigation were not available. The empirical investigation here uses a tailor-made data set that combines for the first time high quality firm-level data from three official sources.

The first source is the regular survey of establishments from manufacturing industries performed by the Statistical Offices of the German federal states. The survey covers all establishments from manufacturing industries that employ at least twenty persons in the local production unit or in the company that owns the unit. Participation of firms in the survey is mandated in official statistics (see Malchin and Voshage, 2009 for details). For this study establishment data were aggregated to the enterprise level to match the unit of observation in the other data sources (described below). From this survey information on the number of employees in the firm, the sum of wages paid, and detailed industry affiliation is taken.

The second source of data is the cost structure survey for enterprises in the manufacturing sector. This survey is carried out annually as a representative random sample survey. The sample is stratified according to the number of employees and the industries; all firms with 500 and more employees are covered by the cost structure survey (see Fritsch *et al.*, 2004). This survey is the source for information on the sum of total sales and on the amount of spending for research and development (R&D) activities by a firm.

Information on the goods traded internationally is available from the statistic on foreign trade (*Außenhandelsstatistik*). This statistic is based on two sources. One source is the reports by German firms on transactions with firms from countries that are members of the European Union (EU); these reports are used to compile the so-called *Intrahandelsstatistik* on intra-EU trade. The other source is transaction-level data collected by the customs on trade with countries outside the EU (the so-called *Extrahandelsstatistik*).[3]

Data in the statistic of foreign trade are transaction-level data, i.e., they relate to one transaction of a German firm with a firm located outside

---

[3] Note that firms with a value of exports to EU-countries that does not exceed 400,000 Euro in 2009 do not have to report to the statistic on intra-EU trade. For trade with firms from non-member countries all transactions that exceed 1,000 Euro are registered. For details see Statistisches Bundesamt, Qualitätsbericht Außenhandel, January 2011.

Germany at a time. For the reporting years 2009 and 2010 these transaction-level data have been aggregated at the level of the exporting firm for the first time. Using the firms' registration number for turnover tax statistics these data were matched with the enterprise register system (*Unternehmensregister-System*) and with the enterprise level data from the two other sources discussed above. For each exporting or importing firm that reported either to the statistic on intra-EU trade, or to the statistic on trade with countries outside the EU, we know from the data the value and the volume of exports and imports for the ten most important exported goods.

With these data it is possible to investigate the relationship between the quality of goods exported and the quality of the inputs used in the production of goods inside the firm.

The quality of exported goods is defined as the unit value of exports and computed as value of exports (measured in Euro) over quantity of exports (measured in tons). In the data set used here we have information on the value of exports and the quantity of exports for the 10 most important products (measured by the value of exports) exported by a firm. For firms that exported more than one good the unit value of exports is the weighted sum of the unit values of the (up to 10) different goods exported, and the weights are the shares of the value of exports of a good in the total exports of the firm of these (up to 10) goods. The unit value of exports is expressed in percentage of the mean value of unit values in the 4-digit industry to take care of differences across industries due to the nature of the products (e.g., mobile phones and cement). This is the *index of the quality of exported goods* used in the empirical analysis.

The quality of inputs used by a firm is measured by three variables:

Human capital intensity is measured by the wage per employee paid by the firm (in Euro). Unfortunately, there is no information on the qualification of the employees (e.g., the share of employees with a university degree, or the share of employees that successfully passed the exams following an apprenticeship) of the firms in the data used. However, Wagner (2012a) uses a unique different data set to demonstrate that in German manufacturing firms the average wage is a useful proxy variable for the qualification of the employees.

R&D intensity is measured by expenditures on research and development over total turnover (in percent). This variable is used as a measure of the innovation orientation of a firm.

The *quality of imports* is measured in the same way as the quality of exported goods. This index is used as a measure for the quality of imported inputs.[4]

The empirical models include the *number of employees* (also included in squares to take care of non-linearity) to control for any relationship between firm size and the quality of exported goods. Furthermore, a complete set of 4-digit level *industry dummy variables* is included to control for the role of industry-specific factors related to the link between input quality and quality of exported goods.

Given that the East German economy still differs in many respects from the West German economy, especially with regard to exporting (see Wagner, 2008), and that the number of exporting firms is small in East Germany this study looks at West German manufacturing enterprises only.

All computations are performed for two years, 2009 and 2010. In 2009, the value of German exports of goods declined by 18.4 percent compared to 2008. This was followed by an increase in exports by 18.5 percent in 2010 (Statistisches Bundesamt, 2012, p. 414). Therefore, a look at these two very different years can be considered as a robustness check to make sure that the results reported are not specific for a crises or recovery period.

3. Empirical Findings

Descriptive statistics for the enterprise characteristics considered in this study are reported in the Table A.1.[5] Evidently, firms are rather heterogeneous.

---

[4] Note that the data set at hand does not contain information about intermediate goods purchased from German firms and on the quality of these inputs.

[5] Note that minimum and maximum values cannot be reported because they refer to a single enterprise and, therefore, are confidential. The correlation matrices for the two years that are reported in Table A.2 do not reveal any high positive or negative values for the variables used as independent variables in the empirical models used here.

Table 1: Quality of exported goods and enterprise characteristics: West Germany.

Enterprise characteristic		1	2	3	4	5
2009						
Number of employees	ß	0.0031				−0.0089
	p	0.389				0.177
Number of employees (Squared)	ß	−3.03e–8				7.20e–8
	p	0.346				0.209
R&D expenditures/ total sales (%)	ß			7.706		6.164
	p		0.000		0.000	
Human capital (wage per employee; Euro)	ß			0.0013		0.00085
	p			0.003		0.032
Quality of imported input(index)	ß				0.338	0.336
	p				0.000	0.000
Constant	ß	99.155	89.090	53.230	66.195	29.989
	p	0.000	0.000	0.000	0.000	0.055
4-digit industry controls		yes	yes	yes	yes	yes
No. of enterprises		5,933	5,933	5,933	5,933	5,933
2010						
Number of employees	ß	0.0064				−0.00127
	p	0.272				0.860
Number of employees (Squared)	ß	−5.97e–8				4.15e–9
	p	0.245				0.947
R&D expenditures/ total sales (%)	ß		6.725			5.214
	p	0.000			0.000	
Human capital (wage per employee; Euro)	ß			0.0013		0.00073
	p			0.001		0.073
Quality of imported inputs (index)	ß				0.273	0.270
	p				0.000	0.000
Constant	ß	98.295	91.051	54.292	72.684	39.656
	p	0.000	0.000	0.000	0.000	0.008
4-digit industry controls		yes	yes	yes	yes	yes
No. of enterprises		6,072	6,072	6,072	6,072	6,072

Note: OLS regressions; dependent variable: Index of quality of exported goods (see Section 2 for definition). ß is the estimated regression coefficient, p is the prob-value (based on heteroscedasticity-consistent standard errors). For a detailed definition of the variables see text.

This is not surprising at all for the number of employees (where the values for the percentiles reported range from just above the cut-off point of 20 employees applied in the survey the data are taken from to more than 2,600 employees), the wage per employee (that is some four times the value of the first percentile in the 99th percentile), the R&D intensity (where the majority of firms does not report any R&D spending at all) and the index of the quality of imported inputs (where some firms report no imports at all,[6] and the importers report imported inputs that vary widely in their quality). However, it might come as a surprise that many exporters from manufacturing industries in Germany do export low quality goods — the median value of export quality of the firms is only half of the mean value in both years.[7]

What makes an exporter of high quality goods, and how is the quality of inputs used in a firm related to the quality of exported outputs? To investigate this question empirical models are estimated with the index of the quality of exported goods as the dependent variable and the firm characteristics discussed above (firm size, R&D intensity, human capital intensity, and quality of imported inputs) as the independent variables, controlling for industry affiliation by including a full set of 4-digit industry dummy variables. Five variants of the empirical model are estimated — the first four variants each include one enterprise characteristic only, while model 5 includes all characteristics to see the ceteris paribus relationship of each characteristic with the quality of exported goods.

Results reported in Table 1 for Models 1–4 reveal that, considered separately, the three input quality measures (R&D intensity, human capital intensity, and quality of imported inputs) are positively and statistically highly significantly related to quality of exported goods (controlling for detailed industry affiliation of the enterprise at the 4-digit industry level). Firm size (that is measured by the number of employees, and that is also

---

[6] This holds for nine percent of the enterprises in the sample in 2009 and for eight percent in 2010.

[7] Note that by construction only exporting firms are in the sample of firms used in this investigation.

included as a squared term to control for a non-linear relationship) is not related with export quality — this is in line with anecdotal evidence that some successful exporters of high-quality goods are rather small "hidden champions". Results for Model 5 show that all these results hold ceteris paribus, too, in both years irrespective of the totally different macroeconomic situation on the export market. Controlling for firm size and industry affiliation a higher quality of inputs is positively related with a higher quality of inputs used in production.

The discussion of the results from the empirical models so far only considered the statistical significance of the links between input and output quality. Evidently, statistically highly significant links can be irrelevant from an economic point of view if a ceteris paribus change of considerable size in a firm characteristic leads to a tiny change in the (estimated) quality of exported goods only. To see whether the statistically significant links are relevant from an economic point of view, too, the estimated change in export quality that is caused by a ceteris paribus increase by one standard deviation of the respective firm characteristic is computed based on the estimated regression coefficients from Model 5. For 2009, an increase by one standard deviation is linked to an increase in the index of export quality by 20 for R&D intensity, by nine for human capital intensity and by 99 for import quality. For 2010, the respective figures are 17 (for R&D intensity), eight (for human capital intensity) and 76 (for import quality). Given the mean value of 100 and the median value of about 50 for the index of the quality of exported goods these estimated changes are large from an economic point of view. Input quality does matter for export quality.

4. Discussion

The bottom line, then, is that according to the empirical results presented in this study the exporters of high-quality goods in German manufacturing industries tend to use high-quality inputs, and that firm size is not related at all to export quality.

This link between input quality and output quality documents a correlation and should not be interpreted as a causal link from input quality to output quality. The huge and emerging literature on the links between international activities of heterogeneous firms and firm performance[8] has demonstrated that one can observe both self-selection of "better" firms on international markets and improvement of firms due to international activities. With the cross-section data at hand it is impossible to investigate whether the exporters of high-quality goods used high-quality inputs to produce high-quality products for the national market already before they started to export, or whether the export activity induced the firms to upgrade their inputs and their products (or whether both is the case).

Another open question that has not been dealt with in this paper is the potential role played by unobserved inputs like management quality for the quality of exports. If these unobserved firm characteristics are correlated with the observed characteristics that are included in the empirical model used to investigate the links between input quality and export quality, the estimated regression coefficients are biased and any conclusions based on the estimates have to take this potentially large bias into account. A standard solution to take at least those unobserved factors into account that do not change over the period under investigation is the addition of fixed firm effect to an empirical model that is estimated for panel data that covers all years from these period. This, however, is no feasible strategy here. As of today, the data used to construct the index of the quality of export goods are available for the years 2009 and 2010 only. Furthermore, both the export quality and the quality of inputs tend to be highly persistent at the level of the enterprise. Estimates from fixed effects panel data models that are based on the variation of variables over time inside a firm only, therefore, are no panacea here.

That said, the reported statistically significant and economically important correlation between the quality of observed inputs and the quality of exported goods should be regarded as an interesting new fact that might motivate further investigations of the causes and consequences of quality differences of internationally traded goods.

---

[8] For surveys of this literature see Bernard *et al.* (2012), Melitz and Redding (2014) and Wagner (2012b).

Table A.1: Descriptive statistics — enterprise characteristics, West Germany.

Enterprise characteristic	Mean	SD	p1	p50	p99
2009					
No. of enterprises: 5,933					
Quality of exported goods (index)	100.00	234.03	0.353	47.40	992.82
Number of employees	343.26	2,683.88	22	110.33	2,699.3
R&D expenditures/total sales	1.416	3.271	0	0	15.358
Human capital (wage/employee)	35,343	10,447	14,915	34.577	64,128
Quality of imported inputs (index)	100	292.99	0	29.34	1,193.5
2010					
No. of enterprises: 6,072					
Quality of exported goods (index)	100.00	237.15	0.650	47.72	833.16
Number of employees	319.49	2,313.16	23	106.54	2,626.3
R&D expenditures/total sales	1.331	3.261	0	0	14.455
Human capital (wage/employee)	36,563	10,618	15,132	35,966	65,492
Quality of imported inputs (index)	100	281,71	0	28.82	1,123.4

Note: For a detailed definition of the enterprise characteristics see text. p1, p50 and p99 refer to the 1st, 50th and 99th percentile of the distribution of the characteristic (minima and maxima cannot be reported due to violation of privacy).

Table A.2: Correlation matrix — enterprise characteristics, West Germany.

	Number of employees	R&D expenditure/ total sales	Human capital (wage/employee)
2009			
R&D expenditures/total sales	0.105 (0.000)		
Human capital (wage/employee)	0.093 (0.000)	0.255 (0.000)	
Quality of imported inputs (index)	0.018 (0.154)	0.039 (0.003)	0.018 (0.167)
2010			
R&D expenditures/total sales	0.086 (0.000)		
Human capital (wage/employee)	0.097 (0.000)	0.264 (0.000)	
Quality of imported inputs (index)	0.015 (0.234)	0.039 (0.003)	0.022 (0.083)

Note: For a detailed definition of the enterprise characteristics see text. Significance level (p-value) in brackets.

References

Bastos, Paulo and Joana Silva (2010). The quality of a firm's exports: Where you export to matters. *Journal of International Economics* 82 (2), 99–111.

Bernard, Andrew, J. Bradford Jensen, Stephen J. Redding and Peter K. Schott (2012). The empirics of firm heterogeneity and international trade. *Annual Review of Economics* 4, 283–313.

Bundesministerium für Wirtschaft und Technologie (2011). *Jahreswirtschaftsbericht 2011. Deutschland im Aufschwung — Den Wohlstand von Morgen sichern.* Berlin: BMWi.

Fritsch, Michael, Bernd Görzig, Ottmar Hennchen and Andreas Stephan (2004). Cost structure surveys for Germany. *Journal of Applied Social Science Studies* 124 (4), 557–566.

Malchin, Anja and Ramona Voshage (2009). Official firm data for Germany. *Schmollers Jahrbuch/Journal of Applied Social Science Studies* 129 (3), 501–513.

Melitz, Marc and Stephen Redding (2014). Heterogeneous firms and trade. *Handbook of International Economics* 4, 1–54.

Statistisches Bundesamt (2012). *Statistisches Jahrbuch 2012. Wiesbaden: Statistisches Bundesamt.*

Wagner, Joachim (2008). A note why more West than East German firms export. *International Economics and Economic Policy* 5 (4), 363–370.

Wagner, Joachim (2011a). Exports and firm characteristics in Germany: A survey of empirical studies (1991 to 2011). *Applied Economics Quarterly* 57 (2), 145–160.

Wagner, Joachim (2011b). Exports and firm characteristics in German manufacturing industries: New evidence from representative panel data. *Applied Economics Quarterly* 57 (2), 107–143.

Wagner, Joachim (2012a). Average wage, qualification of the workforce and export performance if German enterprises: Evidence from *KombiFiD* data. *Journal of Labour Market Research* 45 (2), 161–170.

Wagner, Joachim (2012b). International trade and firm performance: A survey of empirical studies since 2006. *Review of World Economics* 148 (2), 235–267.

Part 5

Firm Age and the Extensive Margins of Trade

Introduction

Transaction level data are used to investigate the link between firm age — a firm characteristic that tends to be neglected in empirical studies on exports and imports — and the margins in international trade. Chapters 13 and 14(originally published in Wagner, 2015a, 2015b show that in Germany older firms are more often exporters and importers, and they export and import more different goods to and from more different countries compared to younger firms from the same industry. In line with these findings Chapter 2 reports that older firms serve more markets in exports and source from more markets in imports, where a market is defined as a combination of a country and a good (classified at the HS6-level).

References

Wagner, Joachim (2015a). A note on firm age and the margins of exports: First evidence from Germany. *The International Trade Journal* 29 (2), 93–102.
Wagner, Joachim (2015b). A note on firm age and the margins of imports: First evidence from Germany. *Applied Economics Letters* 22 (9), 679–682.

Chapter 13

A Note on Firm Age and the Margins of Exports: First Evidence from Germany*

Abstract

This paper uses a new tailor-made data set to investigate the link between firm age and the extensive and intensive margins of exports empirically for the first time for Germany. Results turn out to be fully in line with the theoretical considerations. Older firms are more often exporters, export more and more different goods to more different destination countries, and export to more distant destination markets.

Keywords: Exports, firm age, export margins, Germany.

1. Motivation

Empirical models for the export participation of firms, or for the share of exports in total sales of firms, usually include variables that measure a

* Originally Published in *The International Trade Journal* (2015), 29 (2), 93–102.
All computations were done at the Research Data Centre of the Statistical Office of Berlin-Brandenburg in Berlin. The firm-level data used are strictly confidential but not exclusive; see http://www.forschungsdatenzentrum.de/datenzugang.asp for information on how to access the data. To facilitate replication the Stata do-file used is available from the author on request.

large number of firm characteristics, e.g., firm size, human capital, fixed capital, technology, research and development spending, innovations, patents, characteristics of the work force, foreign ownership, branch-plant status, number of products, and industry affiliation. One firm characteristic that is missing in nearly all of these models is firm age, and this holds for more recent empirical models that look at extensive margins of exports (number of goods exported, number of countries traded with), too.

Germany, one of the leading actors on the world market for goods,[1] is a case in point. Wagner (2011) summarizes 51 empirical studies published between 1991 and 2011 that use micro-data for German firms to investigate the determinants of exports. The role of firm age is only touched upon in one of these papers (see Wagner, 1996).

This neglect of the role of firm age in empirical models of firms' exports comes as a surprise because we can expect that firm age and the margins of export tend to be closely related. Audretsch (1998, p. 137) points out that "firms are typically created as an experiment to pursue a new idea. If that idea succeeds the firm will tend to grow and create jobs. If that idea is not viable the firm will tend to stagnate and ultimately exit". Although some of these new firms are "born global" firms that head for international markets from the start, typically it takes years before firms eventually export to one foreign market, and then enter other markets progressively. Firms gain expertise in entering new foreign markets from experience and this lowers the fixed costs of entry to any further new market over the next years (see Sheard, 2014, p. 536). A similar argument can be made with regard to the number of products exported. If a firm successfully exported one good and learned how to adopt it to the wants of customers or the legal regulations in a foreign market, how to prepare a user manual in a foreign language, how to set up a distribution network etc., this lowers the fixed costs of exporting any other goods, and the firm will start to export more goods in the years to come. Often firms will start

---

[1] According to the World Trade Organization's World Trade Report 2012 Germany hold rank three among the exporters of goods in 2011 with a share of 8.1 percent; see World Trade Organization (2012, p. 30).

to export to a foreign country that is close to their home country and that has low distance costs (including language barriers, differences in legal systems, or cultural differences), and export to more and more distant destinations after several years of experience only.

At any point in time, therefore, firm age and the margins of exports can be expected to be closely linked. The probability of exporting, the share of exports in total sales, the number of destination countries and the number of goods exported will be higher for older firms. Furthermore, older firms can be expected to export to more distant markets, too.

This paper uses a new tailor-made data set to investigate the link between firm age and the extensive and intensive margins of exports empirically for the first time for Germany. Results turn out to be fully in line with the theoretical considerations. Older firms are more often exporters, export more and more different goods to more different destination countries, and export to more distant destination markets.

The rest of the paper is organized as follows. Section 2 discusses the data and measurement issues. Section 3 presents the results of the empirical investigation. Section 4 concludes.

2. Data and Measurement Issues

The lack of empirical studies for Germany on the link between firm age and the margins of exports is due to the fact that until most recently suitable data at the level of the firm that could be used in an econometric investigation were not available. The empirical investigation here uses a tailor-made data set that combines for the first time high quality firm-level data from two official sources with data on the distance between Germany and destination countries of exports.

Information on the goods traded internationally is available from the statistic on foreign trade (*Außenhandelsstatistik*). This statistic is based on two sources. One source is the reports by German firms on transactions with firms from countries that are members of the European Union (EU); these reports are used to compile the so-called *Intrahandelsstatistik* on intra-EU trade. The other source is transaction-level data collected by the customs on trade with countries outside the EU (the so-called

Extrahandelsstatistik).[2] Data in the statistic of foreign trade are transaction-level data, i.e., they relate to one transaction of a German firm with a firm located outside Germany at a time.

For the reporting year 2010 these transaction-level data have been aggregated at the level of the exporting firm for the first time. Using the firms' registration number for turnover tax statistics these data were matched with the enterprise register system (*Unternehmensregister-System*). For each exporting firm that reported either to the statistic on intra-EU trade, or to the statistic on trade with countries outside the EU, we know from the data the number of goods exported and the number of countries exported to. Furthermore, this data has information about the ten most important destination countries of exports and the value of exports to these countries. Combined with information on the distance between Germany and each of the destination countries it is used to compute an index of the distance of exports of a firm. Details on the construction of this index are given below.

The second source of firm level information is the regular survey of establishments from manufacturing industries by the Statistical Offices of the German federal states. The survey covers all establishments from manufacturing industries that employ at least twenty persons in the local production unit or in the company that owns the unit. Participation of firms in the survey is mandated in official statistics (see Malchin and Voshage, 2009 for details). For this study establishment data were aggregated to the enterprise level to match the unit of observation in the other data sources (described below). From this survey information is used on the age of a firm, its total amount of exports, and its detailed industry affiliation.

Data on distance between Germany and the destination countries of exports are taken from the CEPII's *GeoDist* database (Mayer and Zignago, 2011). The "distw" — measure is used that calculates the distance between two countries based on bilateral distances between the biggest cities of

---

[2] Note that firms with a value of exports to EU-countries that does not exceed 400,000 Euro in 2009 do not have to report to the statistic on intra-EU trade. For trade with firms from non-member countries all transactions that exceed 1,000 Euro are registered. For details see Statistisches Bundesamt, Qualitätsbericht Außenhandel, January 2011.

those two countries, those inter-city distances being weighted by the share of the city in the overall country's population (see Mayer and Zignango, 2011, p. 11 for details).

With these data it is possible to investigate the relationship between the age of a firm, the extensive and intensive margins of the firm's exports, and characteristics of the destination countries of a firms export.

Information on the age of a firm is not included in the data used here. However, it is possible to distinguish firms that existed already in 1995 (the first year covered by the survey from official statistics) and firms that entered the data set in later years. Using this information three age cohorts of firms are identified. Cohort 1 is made of all firms that existed already in 1995. Cohort 2 includes all firms that entered the data set between 1996 and 2002. Cohort 3 covers all firms that entered the data set between 2003 and 2009. Note that this definition of age cohorts might be fuzzy because a firm that entered the data set in, say, 2003 has not necessarily been founded in 2003 — it might be the case that the firm existed for some years before but that the number of employees was below the threshold value of 20 and, therefore, the firm was not obliged to report to the survey.

The three extensive margins of exports by a firm in 2010 are measured by an exporter dummy variable that takes on the value one if the firm was an exporter (and the value zero otherwise), by the number of goods[3] exported, and by the number of destination countries of exports. The intensive margin of exports is measured by the share of exports in total sales of a firm.

Distance to export destination is measured by the distw-index between Germany and the destination country provided in the CEPII database (that is discussed above). For firms that exported to more than one country distance is computed as the weighted sum of the distance to (up to 10) destination countries, and the weights are the shares of the value of exports to a country in the total exports of the firm to these (up to 10) countries.

Furthermore, a complete set of 4-digit level industry dummy variables is included to control for the role of industry-specific factors.

---

[3]A good is an 8-digit number from the official nomenclature for the statistics of foreign trade.

Given that the East German economy still differs in many respects from the West German economy, especially with regard to exporting (see Wagner, 2008), and that the number of exporting firms is small in East Germany this study looks at West German manufacturing enterprises only.

3. Results

The empirical investigation uses information on 29,459 enterprises from manufacturing industries in West Germany in 2010. About half of these firms existed already in 1995 and form cohort 1. Cohort 2 (made of firms that entered the sample between 1996 and 2002) and cohort 3 (including firms that entered between 2003 and 2009) are approximately of same size and cover a quarter of all firms each. Table 1 shows that the share of exporters is larger in cohort 1 compared to the younger cohorts, while the share of exporters is the same in cohorts 2 and 3.

Results for empirical models that test for differences in the intensive and extensive margins of exports between firms from the three age cohorts are reported in Table 2. Note that these models are not used to empirically explain a margin, they are just vehicles to estimate the margin premium of a cohort (controlling for detailed industry affiliation by a complete set of 4-digit industry dummy variables).

The results for Model 1 clearly indicate that the probability of participation in exports (the first extensive margin) is lower in both cohorts 2 and 3 compared to cohort 1 (the reference category in all empirical models). The estimated average marginal effect for firms from cohorts 1 and 2 is −9.6 percent and −10.4 percent, respectively, and of the same order of magnitude.

Table 1: Firm age and export participation: Descriptive statistics.

Cohort	Description	No. of firms	Share of exporters in 2010
1	Firm existed in 1995	15,232	79.52
2	Firm entered between 1996 and 2002	6,892	65.74
3	Firm entered between 2003 and 2009	7,335	65.06

Table 2: Firm age and margins of export in 2010: Regression results.

Model		1	2	3	4
Endogenous variable		Exporter (Dummy; 1 = yes)	Log of share of exports in total sales	Log of number of goods exported	Log of number of destination countries of exports
Method		Probit	OLS	OLS	OLS
Cohort 2	ß	−0.096	−0.1757	−0.091	−0.183
(Dummy; 1 = yes)	p	(0.000)	(0.000)	(0.008)	(0.000)
Cohort 3	ß	−0.104	−0.184	−0.227	−0.336
(Dummy; 1 = yes)	p	(0.000)	(0.000)	(0.000)	(0.000)
Industry controls		yes	yes	yes	yes
No. of firms		29,459	21,415	11,725	11,725

Note: For a definition of cohorts see Table 1. Firms from cohort 1 are the reference category. The reported results for Model 1 are estimated average marginal effects; the prob-values reported are based on robust standard errors. For Models 2, 3 and 4, ß is the estimated regression coefficient and p is the prob-value based on heteroscedasticity-robust standard errors. Industry controls are dummy-variables for 2-digit industries in Model 1 and for 4-digit industries in Models 2, 3 and 4. All models include a constant term.

These differences are present at the intensive margin of exports (measured by the share of exports in total sales of a firm), too. On average, and controlling for industry affiliation, compared to the "old" firms from cohort 1 the export to sales ratio is 19.2 percent smaller in cohort 2 and 20.2 percent smaller in cohort 3.[4] Again, both estimated margin premia of cohorts 2 and 3 are of the same order of magnitude.

Results for model 3 show that the number of exported goods (the second extensive margin) tends to increase with firm age. Compared to firms from cohort 1, firms from cohort 2 export 9.5 percent less different goods, and the difference for firms from cohort 3 is 25.5 percent. Results for the number of destination countries (the third extensive margin) show a similar picture. Compared to firms from cohort 1, firms from cohort 2

---

[4] The percentage difference between the cohorts are computed from the estimated regression coefficient ß of the dummy variable in the semi-log empirical model by the formula $(e^{ß}-1) * 100$.

export to 20 percent less destination countries, and the difference for firms from cohort 3 is 39.9 percent.

The results discussed so far consider differences in the means of the margins of exports between age cohorts of firms (conditional on industry affiliation). This might not tell the whole story because firms are highly heterogeneous within the age cohorts, too. An empirical study of hetero-geneous firms should look at differences in the whole distribution of the variable under investigation between groups of firms, not only at differences at the mean. The empirical strategy used here, therefore, applies a non-parametric test for first order stochastic dominance of one distribution over another that was introduced into the empirical literature on international trade activities of firms by Delgado *et al.* (2002). Let F and G denote the cumulative distribution functions of an export margin for two age cohorts of firms. Fist order stochastic dominance of F relative to G is given if $F(z) - G(z)$ is less or equal zero for all z with strict inequality for some z. Given two independent random samples of firms from each group, the hypothesis that F is to the right of G can be tested by the Kolmogorov–Smirnov-test based on the empirical distribution functions for F and G in the samples. Note that this tests not only for differences in the mean value of the margin of both groups but for differences in all moments of the distribution.

Results for pair-wise Kolmogorov–Smirnov-tests for the three age cohorts of firms and for the extensive margin and the second and third intensive margin (i.e., the number of goods exported and the number of destination countries) are reported in Table 3. Note that all values of the margins are expressed as percentage values of the 4-digit industry mean value to control for detailed industry affiliation of the enterprises. Results are fully in line with the conclusions based on the results from the regression models in Table 2. The distribution of the share of exports in total sales for cohort 1 dominates both distributions of cohorts 2 and 3, while there is no difference between cohorts 2 and 3. For the number of goods exported and the number of destination countries we find evidence for a clear hierarchy. Each distribution for a younger cohort is dominated by the distribution for the older cohort. Both extensive margins increase with firm age.[5]

---

[5] The empirical evidence for the lack of absence of difference in the share of exports in total sales (the intensive margin) between the second and the third cohort and the evidence for

Table 3: Firm age and margins of export in 2010: Kolmogorov–Smirnov-tests.

Hypothesis (*p*-values)	Log of share of of exports in total sales	Log of number of goods exported	Log of number of destination countries of exports
	Margins of export		
Smaller values in cohort 1 compared to cohort 2	0.980	1.000	0.987
Smaller values in cohort 2 compared to cohort 1	0.000	0.013	0.000
Distributions differ between cohorts 1 and 2	0.000	0.023	0.000
Smaller values in cohort 1 compared to cohort 3	0.687	0.998	0.945
Smaller values in cohort 3 compared to cohort 1	0.000	0.000	0.000
Distributions differ between cohorts 1 and 3	0.000	0.000	0.000
Smaller values in cohort 2 compared to cohort 3	0.328	0.971	0.873
Smaller values in cohort 3 compared to cohort 2	0.511	0.003	0.000
Distributions differ between cohorts 2 and 3	0.622	0.005	0.000

Note: For a definition of cohorts see Table 1. All variables are expressed as percentage values of the 4-digit industry mean value to control for industry affiliation of enterprises.

As the next step we look at results for an empirical model that tests for differences in the distance to destination countries of exports between firms from the three age cohorts. To repeat, the model is not used to

---

differences between the two age cohorts in the extensive margins "no. of goods exported" and "no. of countries exported to" indicate that the older firms (from cohort 2) tend to spread a similar share of their total sales over a larger group of destination countries and exported goods — they are more diversified in their exports. But given that there is no information in the data about which goods are exported to which countries by which firm and that the samples used to estimate the margin premium are different due to the different sources of data used (as discussed in Section 2) this issue cannot be discussed further here.

Table 4: Firm age and distance to destination countries: Regression results.

Endogenous variable		Log of distance to destination countries
Method		OLS
Cohort 2	ß	−0,094
(Dummy; 1 = yes)	p	(0.001)
Cohort 3	ß	−0.072
(Dummy; 1 = yes)	p	(0.012)
Industry controls		yes
No. of firms		11,441

Note: For a definition of the distance to destination countries see text. For a definition of cohorts see Table 1. Firms from cohort 1 are the reference category. ß is the estimated regression coefficient and p is the prob-value based on heteroscedasticity-robust standard errors. Industry controls are dummy-variables for 4-digit industries. The model includes a constant term.

empirically explain this distance, it is just a vehicle to estimate the margin premium of a cohort (controlling for detailed industry affiliation by a complete set of 4-digit industry dummy variables).

Results reported in Table 4 show that the distance to destination countries is larger for firms from cohort 1 than for firms from the younger cohorts. The difference compared to firms from cohort 1 is −9.9 percent for firms from cohort 2 and −7.5 percent for firms from cohort 3.

Results for pair-wise Kolmogorov–Smirnov-tests for the three age cohorts of firms and for the distance to destination countries are reported in Table 5. Values of the distance to destination countries of the firms are expressed as percentage values of the 4-digit industry mean value to control for detailed industry affiliation of the enterprises. Results are in line with the conclusions based on the results from the regression model in Table 4. The distribution of the distance to destination countries for cohort 1 dominates both distributions of cohorts 2 and 3, while there is no difference between cohorts 2 and 3.

Table 5: Firm age and distance to destination countries: Kolmogorov–Smirnov-tests.

Hypothesis (*p*-values)	Log of distance to destination countries
Smaller values in cohort 1 compared to cohort 2	0.994
Smaller values in cohort 2 compared to cohort 1	0.004
Distributions differ between cohorts 1 and 2	0.007
Smaller values in cohort 1 compared to cohort 3	0.398
Smaller values in cohort 3 compared to cohort 1	0.001
Distributions differ between cohorts 1 and 3	0.002
Smaller values in cohort 2 compared to cohort 3	0.061
Smaller values in cohort 3 compared to cohort 2	0.513
Distributions differ between cohorts 2 and 3	0.114

Note: For a definition of cohorts see Table 1. For a definition of the distance to destination countries see text. Distance to destination countries is expressed as the percentage value of the 4-digit industry mean value to control for industry affiliation of enterprises.

4. Discussion

The empirical investigation demonstrate that, controlling for detailed industry affiliation, the export participation and the share of exports in total sales are both larger in old firms from cohort 1 than in younger firms from cohorts 2 and 3, while there are no differences in these export margins between firms from the two younger cohorts. Both the number of goods exported and the number of destination countries tend to increase with firm age. Furthermore, the weighted average distance to destination countries is larger for firms from cohort 1 than for firms from the younger cohorts.[6]

These results are in line with theoretical considerations. Furthermore, a positive link between firm age and export revenue, number of destination countries, and number of products exported has also been found by Bastos and Dias (2013) in an empirical investigation using Portuguese data. Future empirical research on the determinants of the margins of exports, therefore, should investigate these links further, ideally using longitudinal data that cover a large time span (and that are not yet available for Germany, unfortunately).

References

Audretsch, David B. (1998). New firms and creating employment. In: John T. Addison and Paul J. J. Welfens (Eds.), *Labour Markets and Social Security*. Berlin: Springer, pp. 129–165.

Bastos, Paulo and Daniel A. Dias (2013). The life cycle of exporting firms. Draft.

Delgado, Miguel A., Jose C. Farinas and Sonia Ruano (2002). Firm productivity and export markets: A non-parametric approach. *Journal on International Economics* 57 (2), 397–422.

Malchin, Anja and Ramona Voshage (2009). Official firm data for Germany. *Schmollers Jahrbuch/Journal of Applied Social Science Studies* 129 (3), 501–513.

Mayer, Thierry and Soledad Zignago (2011). Notes on CEPII's distance measures: The GeoDist database. CEPII Document de Travail, No 2011–2025.

Sheard, Nicholas (2014). Learning to export and the timing of entry to export markets. *Review of International Economics* 22 (3), 536–560.

---

[6] The reported results might be driven by the (arbitrary) choice of the cut-off point between the groups of entrants. As a robustness check all computations were done with a different definition of starter cohorts, namely defining four starter cohorts (instead of two) by using the cut-off points 1996–1998, 1999–2002, 2003–2005 and 2006–2009. Results are qualitatively similar to results from the estimations that use two starter cohorts.

Wagner, Joachim (1996). Export performance, human capital, and product innovation in Germany: A micro view. *Jahrbuch für Wirtschaftswissenschaften/ Review of Economics* 47 (1), 40–45.

Wagner, Joachim (2008). A note why more West than East German firms export. *International Economics and Economic Policy* 5 (4), 363–370.

Wagner, Joachim (2011). Exports and firm characteristics in Germany: A survey of empirical studies (1991 to 2011). *Applied Economics Quarterly* 57 (2), 145–160.

World Trade Organization (2012). World Trade Report 2012. (Geneva: WTO Publications).

Chapter 14

A Note on Firm Age
and the Margins of Imports:
First Evidence from Germany*

Abstract

This chapter uses a new tailor-made data set to investigate the link between firm age and the extensive margins of imports empirically for the first time for Germany. Results turn out to be fully in line with the theoretical considerations. Older firms are more often importers, import more different goods, and import from more different countries of origin.

Keywords: Imports, firm age, import margins, Germany.

1. Motivation

In their comprehensive empirical study of firms in the US that trade goods Bernard *et al.* (2005, p. 5) noted that "there is virtually no research documenting and analyzing importing firms". Ten years later, this is no longer

---

*Originally Published in *Applied Economics Letters* (2015), 22 (9), 679–682.

All computations were done at the Research Data Centre of the Statistical Office of Berlin-Brandenburg in Berlin. The firm-level data used are strictly confidential but not exclusive; see http://www.forschungsdatenzentrum.de/datenzugang.asp for information on how to access the data. To facilitate replications the Stata do-file used is available from the author on request.

the case. For more and more countries data (usually based on transactions recorded by customs) on the imports of firms become available that are used to describe the patterns of imports and to investigate empirically the links between various dimensions of firm performance (e.g., survival, productivity, profitability) and the margins of imports (participation in imports, number of imported goods, number of countries of origin).[1]

To the best of my knowledge, the role of firm age for the margins of imports is not discussed in this literature. This comes as a surprise because we can expect that firm age and the margins of import tend to be closely related. Although some new firms are "born global" firms that start to source on international markets from the start, typically it takes years before firms eventually import from one foreign market, and then enter other markets progressively. Firms gain expertise in entering new foreign markets from experience and this lowers the fixed costs of entry to any further new market over the next years (see Sheard 2014, p. 536 with regards to exports). A similar argument can be made with regard to the number of products imported.

At any point in time, therefore, firm age and the margins of imports can be expected to be closely linked. This chapter tests this hypothesis, using unique newly available data for Germany.[2]

2. Data and Measurement Issues

The empirical investigation here uses a tailor-made data set that combines for the first time high quality firm-level data from three official sources. The first source of firm level information is the regular survey of establishments from manufacturing industries by the Statistical Offices of the German federal states. The survey covers all establishments from manufacturing industries that employ at least 20 persons in the local production unit or in the company that owns the unit. Participation of firms in the survey is mandated in official statistics (see Malchin and Voshage, 2009 for details). For this study establishment data were aggregated to the enterprise level to match the unit of observation in the other

---

[1] See Wagner (2012) for a review of this literature.
[2] See Wagner (2014) for a study on the links between firm age and the margins of exports.

data sources (described below). From this survey information is used on the age of a firm and its detailed industry affiliation.

The second source of data is the German Turnover Tax Statistics Panel (described in detail in Vogel and Dittrich, 2008). This data set is based on the yearly turnover tax; all enterprises with a turnover that exceeds the rather low threshold of 17,500 Euro are covered in the data. This data set can be used to identify firms that were importers in a year. Details aside, this is due to two reasons. First, firms that imported from non-EU member countries had to pay an import turnover tax charged by the customs authorities that is deductible as input tax and therefore reported in the data set. Second, imports from EU-member countries are reported under the item of "intra Community acquisitions".

Information on the goods traded internationally is available from the statistic on foreign trade (*Außenhandelsstatistik*). This statistic is based on two sources. One source is the reports by German firms on transactions with firms from countries that are members of the EU; these reports are used to compile the so-called *Intrahandelsstatistik* on intra-EU trade. The other source is transaction-level data collected by the customs on trade with countries outside the EU (the so-called *Extrahandelsstatistik*).[3] Data in the statistic of foreign trade are transaction-level data, i.e., they relate to one transaction of a German firm with a firm located outside Germany at a time.

For the reporting year 2010 these transaction-level data have been aggregated at the level of the importing firm. These data were matched with the enterprise register system (*Unternehmensregister-System*) and with the enterprise level data from the two other sources discussed above. For each importing firm that reported either to the statistic on intra-EU trade, or to the statistic on trade with countries outside the EU, we know from the data the number of goods imported and the number of countries imported from.

---

[3] Note that firms with a value of imports from EU-countries that does not exceed 400,000 Euro do not have to report to the statistic on intra-EU trade. For trade with firms from non-member countries all transactions that exceed 1,000 Euro are registered. For details see Statistisches Bundesamt, Qualitätsbericht Außenhandel, January 2011.

With these data it is possible to investigate the relationship between the age of a firm and the extensive margins of the firm's exports. Information on the age of a firm is not included in the data used here. However, it is possible to distinguish firms that existed already in 1995 (the first year covered by the regular survey of establishments from manufacturing industries described above) and firms that entered the data set in later years. Using this information three age cohorts of firms are identified. Cohort 1 is made of all firms that existed already in 1995. Cohort 2 includes all firms that entered the data set between 1996 and 2002. Cohort 3 covers all firms that entered the data set between 2003 and 2009. Note that this definition of age cohorts might be fuzzy because a firm that entered the data set in, say, 2003 has not necessarily been founded in 2003 — it might be the case that the firm existed for some years before but that the number of employees was below the threshold value of 20 and, therefore, the firm was not obliged to report to the survey.

The three extensive margins of imports by a firm in 2010 are measured by an importer dummy variable that takes on the value one if the firm was an importer (and the value zero otherwise), by the number of goods[4] imported, and by the number of countries of origin of imports.

3. Results

The empirical investigation uses information on 29,459 enterprises from manufacturing industries in West Germany in 2010. About half of these firms existed already in 1995 and form cohort 1. Cohort 2 (made of firms that entered the sample between 1996 and 2002) and cohort 3 (including firms that entered between 2003 and 2009) are approximately of same size and cover a quarter of all firms each. Table 1 shows that the share of importers is larger in cohort 1 compared to the younger cohorts, while the share of importers is about the same in cohort 2 and cohort 3.

Results for empirical models that test for differences in the margins of imports between firms from the three age cohorts are reported in Table 2. Note that these models are not used to empirically explain a margin; they

---

[4]A good is an 8-digit number from the official nomenclature for the statistics of foreign trade.

Table 1: Firm age and import participation: Descriptive statistics.

Cohort	Description	No. of firms	Share of importers in 2010
1	Firm existed in 1995	15,232	56.64
2	Firm entered between 1996 and 2002	6,892	46.56
3	Firm entered between 2003 and 2009	7,335	45.40

Table 2: Firm age and margins of import in 2010: Regression results.

Model		1	2	3
Endogenous variable		Exporter (Dummy; 1 = yes)	Log of number of goods imported	Log of number of countries of origin of imports
Method		Probit	OLS	OLS
Cohort 2	ß	−0.079	−0.041	−0.059
(Dummy; 1 = yes)	p	(0.000)	(0.178)	(0.011)
Cohort 3	ß	−0.091	−0.137	−0.137
(Dummy; 1 = yes)	p	(0.000)	(0.000)	(0.000)
Industry controls		yes	yes	yes
No. of firms		29,459	11,828	11,828

Note: For a definition of cohorts see Table 1. Firms from cohort 1 are the reference category. The reported results for Model 1 are estimated average marginal effects; the prob-values reported are based on robust standard errors. For Models 2 and 3, ß is the estimated regression coefficient and p is the prob-value based on heteroscedasticity-robust standard errors. Industry controls are dummy-variables for 2-digit industries in Model 1 and for 4-digit industries in Models 2 and 3. All models include a constant term.

are just vehicles to estimate the margin premium of a cohort (controlling for industry affiliation).

The results for Model 1 clearly indicate that the probability of participation in imports is lower in both cohort 2 and cohort 3 compared to cohort 1 (the reference category in all empirical models). The estimated average marginal effect for firms from cohort 2 and cohort 3 is −7.9 percent and −9.1 percent, respectively.

Results for Model 2 show that the number of imported goods tends to increase with firm age. Compared to firms from cohort 1, firms from cohort 3 import 13.7 percent less different goods (while the point estimate is much lower and not statistically different from zero for firms from cohort 2). Results for the number of countries of origin show a similar picture. Compared to firms from cohort 1, firms from cohort 2 import from six percent less destination countries, and the difference for firms from cohort 3 is 13.7 percent.[5]

4. Concluding Remarks

The empirical investigation demonstrates that, controlling for industry affiliation, the import participation is larger in old firms from cohort 1. Furthermore, the number of goods imported and the number of countries of origin tend to increase with firm age. Future empirical research on the determinants of the margins of imports, therefore, should investigate these links further, ideally using longitudinal data that cover a large time span (and that are not yet available for Germany, unfortunately).

References

Bernard, Andrew, Bradford Jensen and Peter K. Schott (2005). Importers, exporters, and multinationals: A portrait of firms in the U.S. That trade goods'. *NBER Working Paper Series* 11404, June.

Malchin, Anja and Ramona Voshage (2009). Official firm data for Germany. *Schmollers Jahrbuch/Journal of Applied Social Science Studies* 129 (3), 501–513.

Sheard, Nicholas (2014). Learning to export and the timing of entry to export markets. *Review of International Economics* 22 (3), 536–560.

Vogel, Alexander and Stefan Dittrich (2008). The German turnover tax statistics panel. *Journal of Applied Social Science Studies* 128(4), 661–670.

---

[5] Results for pair-wise Kolmogorov–Smirnow-tests for the three age cohorts of firms and for both the number of goods imported and the number of countries of origin of imports are fully in line with the results reported in Table 2.

Wagner, Joachim (2012). International trade and firm performance: A survey of empirical studies since 2006. *Review of World Economics* 148 (2), 235–267.

Wagner, Joachim (2014). A note on firm age and the margins of exports: First evidence from Germany. *Working Paper Series in Economics*, No. 303, University of Lüneburg, Institute of Economics.

Part 6

Innovation Activities

Introduction

It is well documented in the literature that innovative firms are more likely to export. Germany is a case in point. Wagner (2011b) uses a large representative panel data set for German manufacturing firms to demonstrate that both the share of expenditures in research and development (R&D) in total sales and the share of employees in R&D are positively related to the probability that a firm exports and to the share of exports in total sales. These links are statistically highly significant after controlling for a number of firm characteristics that are related to exports. Similar results were found in other studies with different German firm level data sets (see Wagner, 2011a for a survey).

That said, innovative firms cannot only be expected to outperform non-innovative firms with respect to export participation and the share of exports in total sales. More innovative firms can be expected to serve more foreign markets because their advantage compared to local producers of competing similar goods can be expected to be not limited to only one foreign market (or a small number of markets). Furthermore, they can be expected to export more different goods because innovation activities are often not concentrated on the development of one single good only, but spread over several lines of production. In line with this Chapter 15 (originally published in Wagner, 2017) finds that more innovative firms outperform less innovative firms at both extensive margins of exports — they export more goods and they export to a larger number of countries. All these differences are statistically highly significant and large from an economic point of view after controlling for a number of firm characteristics that are related to exporting. Similarly Chapter 2 reports that more innovative firms serve more markets in exports and source from more markets in imports, where a market is defined as a combination of a country and a good (classified at the HS6-level).

References

Wagner, Joachim (2011a). Exports and firm characteristics in Germany: A survey of empirical studies (1991 to 2011). *Applied Economics Quarterly* 57 (2), 145–160.

Wagner, Joachim (2011b). Exports and firm characteristics in German manufacturing industries: New evidence from representative panel data. *Applied Economics Quarterly* 57 (2), 107–143.

Wagner, Joachim (2017). R&D activities and extensive margins of exports in manufacturing enterprises: First evidence for Germany. *The International Trade Journal* 31 (3), 232–244.

Chapter 15

R&D Activities and Extensive Margins of Exports in Manufacturing Enterprises: First Evidence for Germany*

Abstract

This chapter uses a new tailor-made data set to investigate for the first time the links between innovation activities (measured by employees active in research and development) and the extensive margins of exports (number of destination countries; number of goods exported) for manufacturing enterprises in Germany, the third largest exporter of goods on the world market. It documents that more innovative firms outperform less innovative firms at both margins of exports — they export more goods and they export to a larger number of

* Originally Published in *The International Trade Journal* (2017), 31 (3), 232–244.
I thank two anonymous referees for comments that helped to improve an earlier version of the paper. All computations were done at the Research Data Centre of the Statistical Office of Berlin-Brandenburg in Berlin. The firm-level data used are strictly confidential but not exclusive; see http://www.forschungsdatenzentrum.de/datenzugang.asp for information on how to access the data. To facilitate replications the Stata do-file used is available from the author on request.

countries. All these differences are statistically highly significant and large from an economic point of view.

Keywords: Extensive margins of exports, Germany, innovation, research and development.

1. Motivation

Firms with innovative products and innovative production processes can be expected to have an advantage compared to their competitors not only on their home market but on foreign markets, too. A large number of empirical studies document this positive link between innovation activities and exports of firms. A recent example is the study by Altomonte *et al.* (2013) that uses a representative and cross-country comparable sample of manufacturing firms from seven European countries (Austria, France, Germany, Hungary, Italy, Spain, United Kingdom). The authors report a positive correlation between exports and innovation. This is in line with the findings of a large number of studies for other countries.[1]

Germany, the third-largest exporter of goods in the world market (according to the World Trade Organization (2014, p. 34)), is a case in point. Wagner (2011b) uses a large representative panel data set for German manufacturing firms to demonstrate that both the share of expenditures in research and development (R&D) in total sales and the share of employees in R&D are positively related to the probability that a firm exports and to the share of exports in total sales. These links are statistically highly significant after controlling for a number of firm characteristics that are related to exports. Similar results were found in other studies with different German firm level data sets (see Wagner, 2011a for a survey).

That said, innovative firms cannot only be expected to outperform non-innovative firms with respect to export participation and the share of exports in total sales. More innovative firms can be expected to serve more foreign markets because their advantage compared to local producers of competing similar goods can be expected to be not limited to only one

---

[1] A survey of this large literature is far beyond the scope of this note. Unterlass (2013, p. 3) list several studies that confirm this positive link between exports and innovation and presents new evidence on it for firm level data from 22 countries based on the European Community Innovation Survey (CIS 3) for 1998–2000.

market (or a small number of markets). Furthermore, they can be expected to export more different goods because innovation activities are often not concentrated on the development of one single good only, but spread over several lines of production.

However, while a positive link between innovation and both the participation in exports and the share of exports in total sales can be seen as a stylized fact that has been found in many studies for a large number of countries, evidence on the link between a firm's innovation activities and the extensive margins of exports — the number of countries exported to and the number of goods exported — is scarce. This comes as a surprise because information on these extensive margins is widely available from transaction level data on exports (that are usually collected by the customs of a country), and this kind of data has been used in a large number of empirical studies for many countries to investigate the links between various firm characteristics (like productivity, size, or age) and these margins (see Wagner, 2016a for a survey). To the best of my knowledge, however, in this literature only Halpern and Muraközy (2012) look at innovation and the extensive margins of exports. Using data for Hungarian firms they document that innovative firms export more products to more countries.

This chapter contributes to the literature by investigating for the first time the links between German firms' innovation activities and the extensive margins of exports. To anticipate the most important result, it is found that more innovative firms outperform less innovative firms at both extensive margins of exports — they export more goods and they export to a larger number of countries. All these differences are statistically highly significant and large from an economic point of view after controlling for a number of firm characteristics that are related to exporting.

The rest of the chapter is organized as follows. Section 2 introduces the new data set used, details the definition of variables included in the empirical models and reports some descriptive statistics. Section 3 discusses the results of the econometric investigation. Section 4 concludes.

2. Data, Definition of Variables and Descriptive Statistics

The empirical investigation uses a tailor-made data set that combines high quality firm-level data from four official sources. The first source of firm level information is the regular survey of establishments from manufacturing industries by the Statistical Offices of the German federal states. The survey (known as the *Monatsbericht,* or monthly report) covers all establishments from manufacturing industries that employ at least twenty persons in the local production unit or in the company that owns the unit. Participation of firms in the survey is mandated in official statistics (see Malchin and Voshage, 2009 for details). For this study the monthly establishment data were aggregated to annual data and at the enterprise level to match the unit of observation in the other data sources (described below).[2] The use of the enterprise (the legal unit) instead of the establishment (the local production unit) as the unit of analysis is mandated by the use of the enterprise as the unit of observation in the other data sources used in this study. It seems appropriate here because decisions about export activities are taken at the enterprise level, taking the characteristics of all establishments in a multi-establishment enterprise into account.

The second source of data is the cost structure survey for enterprises in the manufacturing sector. This survey is carried out annually as a representative random sample survey in about 15,000 firms. The sample is stratified according to the number of employees and the industries; all firms with 500 and more employees are covered by the cost structure survey (see Fritsch *et al.*, 2004).

Information on the goods traded internationally is available from the statistic on foreign trade (*Außenhandelsstatistik*). This data set is based on two sources. One source is the reports by German firms on transactions with firms from countries that are members of the European Union (EU); these reports are used to compile the so-called *Intrahandelsstatistik* on intra-EU trade. The other source is transaction-level data collected by the customs on trade with countries outside the EU (the so-called *Extrahandelsstatistik*).[3] Data in the statistics of foreign trade are transaction-level data, i.e., they

---

[2] Note that beginning with reporting year 2007 firms with more than 20 but less than 50 persons no longer have to report to the *Monatsbericht*. However, these firms have to report information on total sales, exports, number of employees and the sum of wages and salaries paid in the so-called *Jahresbericht* (the annual report), and this information is added to the data set used here.

[3] Note that firms with a value of exports to EU-countries that does not exceed 400,000 Euro do not have to report to the statistic on intra-EU trade. For trade with firms from

relate to one transaction of a German firm with a firm located outside Germany at a time. For the reporting year 2010 these transaction-level data have been aggregated at the level of the exporting firm (see Wagner, 2014). This dataset is the third source of data used in this study.

These data were matched with the enterprise register system (*Unternehmensregister-System*) and with the enterprise level data from the two other sources discussed above. The enterprise register system is used as the fourth source of data. With these linked four data sets it is possible to investigate the margins of exports in manufacturing firms from Germany.

The study looks at two extensive margins of exports. The first is the *Number of exported goods,*where a good is defined as an 8-digit number from the official nomenclature for the statistics of foreign trade. The second extensive margin of exports investigated is the *Number of export destination countries.* Information on the number of exported goods and the number of export destination countries is taken from the third source of data (the statistics on foreign trade). This information is available for each year starting in 2009; the most recent year the data were available when the computations for this chapter were performed is 2010. Note that by construction this information is only available for exporting firms covered by the statistics on foreign trade.

In the empirical investigation cross-section data for the year 2010 for 7,216 enterprises from manufacturing industries are used. On average, these firms exported 36.18 different goods to 24.54 different countries in 2010 (see the descriptive statistics reported in Table 1). Many firms exported only a small number of goods and to a small number of countries with the median number being much smaller than the mean. Note that the maximum number of goods and countries is confidential (because these numbers refer to single firms), but from the values for the 99th percentile we see that some firms export a large number of goods and to a large number of countries.

Innovation is measured by a firm's activities in research and development (R&D) that are closely related to product and process innovations.

---

non-member countries all transactions that exceed 1,000 Euro are registered. For details see Statistisches Bundesamt, Qualitätsbericht Außenhandel, January 2011.

Table 1: Descriptive statistics: German manufacturing enterprises, 2010.

	Mean	SD	p1	p50	p99
No. of destination countries	24.54	22.41	1	19	98
No. of goods exported	36.18	84.98	1	10	391
R&D activity (Dummy; 1 = yes)	0.43	0.50			
R&D intensity (Share of employees)	0.031	0.063	0.000	0.000	0.305
Control variables					
West Germany (Dummy; 1 = yes)	0.86	0.35			
Firm size (No. of employees)	306.15	2253	23	104	2469
Labor productivity (Values added/employees)	62,232	46,019	12,500	55,481	191,570
Human capital (Wage per employee)	35,239	11,111	14,207	34,649	65,307
Old firm (Dummy) (1 = founded < 1996)	0.58	0.49			
Foreign owned firm (Dummy; 1 = yes)	0.16	0.37			
No. of firms	7216				

Note: SD is the standard deviation; p1, p50 and p99 are the 1st, 50th, and 99th percentile, respectively. The minimum and maximum values of all variables are confidential.

These activities are known to be positively linked to firms' participation in exports and to export intensity in German firms (see Wagner, 2011a; 2011b). R&D activity is measured here either as a dummy variable that takes on the value of one if a firms employs at least one person that is active in R&D (and zero otherwise), or by the share of employees that are active in R&D in all employees in a firm. This intensity measure is also included in squares in the empirical model to take care of any non-linearity in the link between R&D activities and the extensive margins of exports. Information on R&D employees and total employees are taken from the second data source (the cost structure survey).

The share of firms with R&D activities in all firms in the sample used here is 43 percent. This is a rather large share, but it should be kept in mind that by construction only exporting firms are included in the sample, and that R&D activities and participation in exports is positively related. The overall average share of employees in R&D is 3.1 percent in the firms in the sample (see Table 1). Some firms are rather intensively engaged in R&D activities. Again, information on the maximum of the variable is confidential, but note that the firm at the 99th percentile of the distribution has 30.5 percent of its employees working in R&D.

In the empirical investigation of the extensive margins of exports a number of firm characteristics are included as control variables. The relation of these variables to export activities and the definition of variables is discussed in detail below.

West Germany: It is well known that there are large differences in export activities between firms located in West Germany and those located in the former communist East Germany even 20 years after the unification of both parts of Germany. West German firms outperform East German firms in all margins of exports (Wagner, 2016b). A dummy variable that takes on the value of one if a firm is from West Germany (and zero otherwise) is included in the empirical models to control for the location of the firm. 86 percent of all firms in the sample come from West Germany (see Table 1).

Firm size: A positive link between firm size and margins of exports qualifies as a stylized fact. This positive link is due to fixed costs of exporting and efficiency advantages of larger firms due to scale economies, advantages of specialization in management and better conditions on the markets for inputs. Large firms can be expected to have cost advantages on credit markets while small firms often face higher restrictions on the capital market leading to a higher risk of insolvency and illiquidity. Furthermore, there might be disadvantages of small firms in the competition for highly qualified employees. There are limits to the advantage of size, because coordination costs mount as the scale of operations increases, and at some point any further expansion might cease to be profitable. Therefore, a positive relationship between firm size and exports, at least up to a point, is expected. For Germany empirical evidence in line with this is reported in a number of studies (see Wagner, 2011a for a survey). Firm size is measured here by the number of employees in a firm (also included in squares to take care of non-linearity). The source is the first data set (the monthly report).

On average, the firms in the sample have 306 employees, which is quite large. Note, however, that by construction the data set used is limited to exporting firms, and these exporters tend to be considerably larger on average than non-exporting firms.

Labor productivity: The positive link between exports and productivity qualifies as a stylized fact that has been documented in hundreds of studies for countries from all over the world (see Wagner,2007 for a survey). According to findings from this literature an important reason for the positive productivity differential between exporters and non-exporters is self-selection of more productive plants on export markets. Furthermore, there is evidence for a market driven selection process in which exporters that have low productivity fail as a successful exporter, while only those that are more productive continue to export. The reason for this is that there exist additional costs of selling goods in foreign countries. The range of extra costs include transportation costs, distribution or marketing costs, or production costs in modifying current domestic products for foreign consumption. This implies that firms that export to a larger number of foreign markets and a larger number of different goods have to be more productive, because at least some of the extra costs mentioned (e.g., preparing a user's manual in another language, or checking the relevant national laws) recur for each foreign market served and for each good exported. Empirical evidence for Germany reported in Wagner (2012b) is fully in line with this.

Labor productivity is measured here by value added per employee; the information on sales and costs used in the computation of this productivity variable are taken from the cost structure survey.[4]

Human capital intensity: Given that Germany is relatively rich in human capital, firms that use human capital intensively can be expected to have a comparative advantage on international markets. Empirical studies find that the qualification of the workforce is an important factor for the

---

[4] Note that the data used has no information on the capital stock of the firms, so more elaborate measures of productivity like total factor productivity cannot be computed.

international competitiveness of German firms (Wagner, 2011b). Human capital intensity is measured here by the average wage per employee. Direct information on the qualification of the employees in a firm is not available in the data used in this study, but Wagner (2012a) demonstrates that the average wage is indeed a good proxy variable for the qualification of the workforce in German manufacturing firms. The source for information on the amount of wages paid and the number of employees is the first data set (the monthly report).

Firm age: Although some newly founded firms are "born globals" that export from the start, typically it takes years before firms eventually export to one foreign market, and then enter further markets progressively. Firms gain expertise in entering new foreign markets from experience, and this lowers the fixed costs of entry to any further new market. A similar argument can be made with regard to the number of products exported. At any point in time, therefore, firm age and the margins of exports can be expected to be closely linked. Germany is a case in point. Wagner (2015) reports that older firms are more often exporters, export more and more different goods to more different destination countries. Information on firm age is not available from the data used in this study. However, we know whether a firm was already active in 1995 (the first year data from the monthly report are available for). Firms that were active in 1995, and that were founded before 1996 accordingly, are classified as old firms (based on information from the first data source, the monthly report).

Foreign owned firm: Firms that are subsidiaries of a multinational enterprise that has its headquarter in a foreign country are termed foreign owned firms. Foreign ownership is known to have a positive impact on the margins of exports, because these firms can use the international networks and trade contacts of their parent companies and are involved in international supply chains (see Raff and Wagner, 2014 for a discussion of the literature, a theoretical model, and empirical evidence for Germany). A firm is considered to be foreign owned if more than 50 percent of the voting rights of the owners or more than 50 percent of the shares are controlled (directly or indirectly) by a firm or a person/institution located outside Germany. Information on foreign ownership status of an enterprise is taken from the fourth source of data, the enterprise register system.

Industry: Dummy variables for 2-digit-industries are included in the empirical models to control for industry specific effects like competitive pressure, policy measures, demand shocks etc. The source is the first data set (the monthly report).

3. Econometric Investigation

The link between R&D activity of a firm and each of the two extensive margins of the firm's exports — the number of destination countries and the number of different goods exported is investigated with a set of six differently specified econometric reduced-form models that are estimated with cross-section data for 2010. Formally these empirical models are specified as follows:

$[1]$ $\text{Exp-Marg}_i = \text{ß}_0 + \text{ß}_1 * \text{R\&Dact}_i + e_i$

$[2]$ $\text{Exp-Marg}_i = \text{ß}_0 + \text{ß}_1 * \text{R\&Dact}_i + \text{ß}_2 * \text{West}_i + \text{ß}_3 * \text{Fsize}_i + \text{ß}_4 * \text{Fsizesq}_i$ $+ \text{ß}_5 * \text{HC}_i + \text{ß}_6 * \text{Old}_i + \text{ß}_7 * \text{Foreign}_i + \text{ß}_8 * \text{Lprod}_i + e_i$

$[3]$ $\text{Exp-Marg}_i = \text{ß}_0 + \text{ß}_1 * \text{R\&Dint}_i + e_i$

$[4]$ $\text{Exp-Marg}_i = \text{ß}_0 + \text{ß}_1 * \text{R\&Dint}_i + \text{ß}_2 * \text{R\&Dintsq}_i + e_i$

$[5]$ $\text{Exp-Marg}_i = \text{ß}_0 + \text{ß}_1 * \text{R\&Dint}_i + \text{ß}_2 * \text{West}_i + \text{ß}_3 * \text{Fsize}_i + \text{ß}_4 * \text{Fsizesq}_i$ $+ \text{ß}_5 * \text{HC}_i + \text{ß}_6 * \text{Old}_i + \text{ß}_7 * \text{Foreign}_i + \text{ß}_8 * \text{Lprod}_i + e_i$

$[6]$ $\text{Exp-Marg}_i = \text{ß}_0 + \text{ß}_1 * \text{R\&Dint}_i + \text{ß}_2 * \text{R\&Dintsq}_i + \text{ß}_3 * \text{West}_i + \text{ß}_4 * \text{Fsize}_i + \text{ß}_5 * \text{Fsizesq}_i + \text{ß}_6 * \text{HC}_i + \text{ß}_7 * \text{Old}_i + \text{ß}_8 * \text{Foreign}_i + \text{ß}_9 * \text{Lprod}_i + e_i$

where the index i refers to firm i and *Exp-Marg* is an extensive margin of exports (either the number of goods exported or the number of countries exported to); *R&Dact* is a dummy-variable that takes on the value 1 if a firm is active in R&D; *R&Dint* is the share of employees in a firm that are active in R&D and *R&Dintsq* is the squared value of this share; *West* is a dummy-variable that takes on the value one if a firm is located in West-Germany; *Fsize* is firm size (measured by the number of employees in the firm) and *Fsizesq* is the squared value of this number; *HC* is human capital (measured by the wage per employee); *Old* is a dummy variable that takes on the value one if the firm is an old firm that was founded before 1996; *Foreign* is dummy variable that takes on the value one if a firm is a foreign-owned firm; *Lprod* is labor productivity (measured by value added per employee); and e is an error term.

In Models (1) and (2) R&D activity is measured by a dummy variable that indicates whether a firm is engaged in R&D or not; Models (3) and (5) include the R&D intensity, measured by the share of employees working in R&D; Models (4) and (6) include both the R&D intensity and its squared value to take care of a non-linear form of the relationship between R&D activity and the export margins. Here, Models (1), (3) and (4) only include the respective R&D variable(s) plus a constant, while Models (2), (5) and (6) include the full set of control variables (discussed in Section 2) too.[5]

Note that the results of the empirical models cannot reveal any causal relationship between R&D activity and the extensive margins of exports. The cross-section data at hand are not rich enough to estimate a structural model for the interrelationships between innovation and exports. However, given the scarcity of information on the links between, on the one hand, the number of countries exported to and the number of goods exported, and on the engagement of firms in R&D on the other hand, it seems interesting and important to report descriptive evidence on this topic for Germany, the third largest actor on the world market for goods.

Results for R&D and the number of destination countries are reported in Table 2.[6] The estimation results show that, irrespective of the way R&D is measured and whether control variables are included or not, the link between the number of destination countries and R&D is positive Models (4) and (6) both show a hump-shaped relationship between R&D intensity

---

[5] Although the dependent variable in the empirical models is a count variable that can only take positive integer values equal to or larger to one (because by construction only firms that export to at least one country and one good are included in the sample) all models are estimated by OLS. Both the number of destination countries and the number of goods exported are distributed over a broad range (see Table 1). This justifies the use of OLS in estimating the empirical models.

[6] Given the focus of this study the estimation results for the control variables will not be discussed here.

Table 2: R&D and the number of destination countries of exports in enterprises from manufacturing industries in Germany 2010.

Model		1	2	3	4	5	6
R&D activity	ß	17.14**	11.48**				
(Dummy, 1 = yes)	p	0.000	0.000				
R&D intensity	ß			81.77**	221.28**	31.19**	136.72**
(Share of employees)	p			0.000	0.000	0.000	0.000
R&D intensity (Squared)	ß				−501.05**		−363.89**
	p				0.000		0.000
Control variables							
West Germany	ß		4.82**			4.27**	4.38**
(Dummy; 1 = yes)	p		0.000			0.000	0.000
Firm size	ß		0.007**			0.008**	0.007**
(No. of employees)	p		0.000			0.000	0.000
Firm size (Squared)	ß		−5.31e–8**			−5.73e–8**	−5.51e–8**
	p		0.000			0.000	0.000
Human capital	ß		3.63e–4**			4.63e–4**	4.34e–4**
(Wage per employee)	p		0.000			0.000	0.000
Old firm (Dummy)	ß		3.46**			3.57**	3.39**
(1 = founded < 1996)	p		0.000			0.000	0.000
Foreign owned firm	ß		1.91**			2.13**	1.97**
(Dummy; 1 = yes)	p		0.005			0.003	0.005
Labor productivity	ß		3.45e–5**			3.01e–5**	3.14e–5**
(Value added/empl.)	p		0.000			0.001	0.000
Constant	ß	17.16**	5.69	22.02**	20.17**	5.55	5.57
	p	0.000	0.433	0.000	0.000	0.446	0.452
Industry controls		no	yes	no	no	yes	yes
R^2		0.143	0.350	0.052	0.102	0.302	0.325
No. of firms		7.216	7.216	7.216	7.216	7.216	7.216

Note: All models are estimated by OLS. ß is the estimated regression coefficient and p is the prob-value. Standard errors are based on heteroscedasticity-robust estimates.**/* indicate statistical significance at the 1/5 percent level.

and the number of destination countries. The estimated maximum of this relationship, which is 0.19 in the complete Model (6), is high compared to the mean of the R&D intensity of 0.03 in the sample, and to the 90th percentile of the R&D intensity distribution which is 0.10. Only a small number of observations lay to the right of the estimated maximum of the hump-shaped relationship. Therefore, the results should be interpreted to point to a nonlinear increase of the number of destination countries in the R&D intensity at a decreasing rate.

This positive link is statistically highly significant, and it is large from an economic point of view. Model (2) indicates that, ceteris paribus, a firm which is active in R&D exports on average to 11.5 more countries than a firm that does no R&D at all. This difference is large compared to both the average number and to the median number of destination countries.[7]

The big picture is identical for the link between R&D and the number of different goods exported. The estimation results reported in Table 3 show that, irrespective of the way R&D is measured and whether control variables are included or not, the link between the number of goods exported and R&D is positive. Models (4) and (6) both show a hump-shaped relationship between R&D intensity and the number of exported goods. The estimated maximum of this relationship, which is 0.21 in the complete Model (6), is high compared to the mean of the R&D intensity of 0.03 in the sample, and to the 90th percentile of the R&D intensity distribution which is 0.10. Only a small number of observations lay to the right of the estimated maximum of the hump-shaped relationship. Therefore, the results should be interpreted to point to a nonlinear increase of the number of exported goods in the R&D intensity at a decreasing rate.

This positive link is statistically highly significant, and it is large from an economic point of view. Model (2) indicates that, ceteris paribus, a firm which is active in R&D exports on average 18 more goods than a firm that does no R&D at all. This difference is large compared to both the average number and to the median number of goods exported.[8]

---

[7] Note that the estimated increase in the number of destination countries is considerably smaller in Model (2) compared to Model (1) that does not include any control variables.

[8] Note that the estimated increase in the number of exported goods is considerably smaller in Model (2) compared to Model (1) that does not include any control variables.

Table 3: R&D and the number of exported goods in enterprises from manufacturing industries in Germany 2010.

Model		1	2	3	4	5	6
R&D activity	ß	38.82**	18.04**				
(Dummy, 1 = yes)	p	0.000	0.000				
R&D intensity	ß			279.15**	664.79**	116.59**	359.25**
(Share of employees)	p			0.000	0.000	0.000	0.000
R&D intensity	ß				−1385.02**		−836.72**
(Squared)	p				0.000		0.000
Control variables:							
West Germany	ß		9.92**			10.20**	10.47**
(Dummy; 1 = yes)	p		0.000			0.000	0.000
Firm size	ß		0.047**			0.048**	0.047**
(No. of employees)	p		0.000			0.000	0.000
Firm size (Squared)	ß		−2.87e−7**			−2.89e−7**	−2.84e−7**
	p		0.000			0.000	0.000
Human capital	ß		8.07e−4**			8.37e−4**	8.17e−4**
(Wage per employee)	p		0.000			0.000	0.000
Old firm (Dummy)	ß		1.05			1.55	1.13
(1 = founded < 1996)	p		0.466			0.287	0.436
Foreign owned firm	ß		−1.72			−0.97	−1.35
(Dummy; 1 = yes)	p		0.471			0.685	0.570
Labor productivity	ß		1.14e−5			4.92e−6	7.93e−6
(Value added/empl.)	p		0.449			0.748	0.590
Constant	ß		−20.97*	27.60**	22.49**	−19.83*	−19.90*
	p		0.021	0.000	0.000	0.016	0.020
Industry controls		no	yes	no	no	yes	yes
R^2		0.051	0.494	0.042	0.069	0.490	0.499
No. of firms		7.216	7.216	7.216	7.216	7.216	7.216

Note: All models are estimated by OLS. ß is the estimated regression coefficient and p is the prob-value. Standard errors are based on heteroscedasticity-robust estimates. **/* indicate statistical significance at the 1/5 percent level.

4. Concluding Remarks

This chapter documents that more innovative firms from manufacturing industries in Germany outperform less innovative firms at both extensive margins of exports — they export more goods and they export to a larger number of countries. All these differences are statistically highly significant and large from an economic point of view after controlling for a number of firm characteristics that are related to exporting.

When putting these findings into perspective a number of limitations of this study should be kept in mind. First of all, the results are correlations only, and they do not indicate any causal relationship that runs (solely) from innovation activities of firms to the extensive margins of exports. Altomonte *et al.* (2013, p. 680) argue that there is a growing consensus that both innovation and exporting are the result of the endogenous choices of firms. They are inextricably linked. Firms may invest in R&D to foster innovation because they plan to start to export; they may start to export to collect rents related to new products on larger markets outside the home country; they may be induced or even forced to innovate to stay competitive on export market; or they may learn from customers and competitors in export market how to produce new products using new production processes. The data at hand here, however, are not rich enough to estimate a dynamic structural model of these complex interrelationships between R&D activities and exports of firms like in Aw *et al.* (2011).

Second, the data used are cross-section data for one year only. Therefore, it is not possible to control for the role of (time-invariant) unobserved firm characteristics that might be correlated with both R&D activities and the extensive margins of exports, like the quality of the management of a firm, by including firm fixed effects. However, experience with panel data for German manufacturing firms reveals that the within variation of firm characteristics over time tends to be very small compared to the between variation (see Wagner, 2011b). Therefore, panel data are far from being a panacea in an exercise like the one performed here.

Third, R&D activities are related to innovation activities at the firm level, but they are a rather indirect measure of innovativeness of the firm. More direct measures like the number of newly introduced products over a period of time or the share of sales of new products in total sales, are available for samples of firms from innovation surveys. However, firm level data from these surveys cannot be linked to the detailed data on extensive margins of exports investigated in this study.

Nevertheless, the results documented here reveal some interesting and hitherto not known facts on the links between innovation activities and extensive margins of exports in German manufacturing firms.

References

Altomonte, Carlo, Tommaso Aquilante, Gábor Nékés and Gianmarco I. P. Ottaviano (2013). Internationalization and innovation of firms: Evidence and policy. *Economic Policy* 28 (76), 663–700.

Aw, Bee Yan, Mark J. Roberts and Daniel Yi Xu (2011). R&D investment, exporting, and productivity dynamics. *American Economic Review* 101 (4), 1312–1344.

Fritsch, Michael, Bernd Görzig, Ottmar Hennchen and Andreas Stephan (2004). Cost structure surveys for Germany. *Schmollers Jahrbuch/Journal of Applied Social Science Studies* 124 (4), 557–566.

Malchin, Anja and Ramona Voshage (2009). Official firm data for Germany. *Schmollers Jahrbuch/Journal of Applied Social Science Studies* 129 (3), 501–513.

Halpern, László and Balázs Muraközy (2012). Innovation, productivity and exports: The case of Hungary. *Economics of Innovation and New Technology* 21 (2), 151–173.

Raff, Horst and Joachim Wagner (2014). Foreign ownership and the extensive margins of exports: Evidence for manufacturing enterprises in Germany. *The World Economy* 37 (5), 579–591.

Unterlass, Fabian (2013). The nexus of innovation, exports and economic performance of firms — revisiting self-selection and learning-by-exporting. Paper prepared for the EcoMod conference in Prague, July 1–3, 2013. Vienna: Austrian Institute of Economic Research (WIFO).

Wagner, Joachim (2007). Exports and productivity: A survey of the evidence from firm-level data. *The World Economy* 30 (1), 60–82.

Wagner, Joachim (2011a). Exports and firm characteristics in Germany: A survey of empirical studies (1991 to 2011). *Applied Economics Quarterly* 57 (2), 145–160.

Wagner, Joachim (2011b). Exports and firm characteristics in German manufacturing industries: New evidence from representative panel data. *Applied Economics Quarterly* 57 (2), 107–143.

Wagner, Joachim (2012a). Average wage, qualification of the workforce and export performance in German enterprises: Evidence from *KombiFiD* data. *Journal of Labour Market Research* 45 (2), 161–170.

Wagner, Joachim (2012b). Trading many goods with many countries: Exporters and importers from German manufacturing industries. *Jahrbuch für Wirtschaftswissenschaften/Review of Economics* 63 (2), 170–186.

Wagner, Joachim (2014). New data from official statistics for imports and exports of goods by German enterprises. *Schmollers Jahrbuch/Journal of Applied Social Science Studies* 134 (3), 371–378.

Wagner, Joachim (2015). A note on firm age and the margins of exports: First evidence from Germany. *The International Trade Journal* 29 (2), 93–102.

Wagner, Joachim (2016a). A survey of empirical studies using transaction level data on exports and imports. *Review of World Economics* 152 (1), 215–225.

Wagner, Joachim (2016b). Still different after all these years. Extensive and intensive margins of exports in East and West German manufacturing enterprises. *Jahrbücher für Nationalökonomie und Statistik/Journal of Economics and Statistics* 236 (2), 297–322.

World Trade Organization (2014). World Trade Report 2014. Trade and development: recent trends and the role of the WTO. (Geneva: WTO Publications).

Part 7

International Trade
and Profits

Introduction

Firm profitability is an important dimension of firm performance. In general, the links between profitability and the margins of international trade qualify as an under-researched area. This comes as a surprise because profit maximization can be regarded as a central aim of a firm. The number of studies on trade and profits, however, is still small and the number of countries covered is even smaller. As regards the links between the extensive margins of trade (number of countries traded with, number of goods traded) and firm profitability empirical evidence is even scarcer.

From a theoretical point of view the sign of this link is ambitious. On the one hand, there are extra costs (that are often fixed costs) that come with every extra country served in exports or sourced in imports, and with every extra good traded internationally. On the other hand, every international extra deal a firm engages in voluntarily is (at least, potentially) profitable. And it might well be the case that only more productive firms self-select on more foreign markets because only these better firms are able to cover the extra costs caused by these extra extensive margins of trade. It is an open question whether the extra costs that come with extra international markets eat up any extra profits and any productivity advantages.

The chapters in this part of the volume look at the links between firm profits and either the number of countries traded with, or the number of goods traded. Results differ for imports and exports. As regards exports

Chapter 16 (originally published as Wagner, 2014a) finds that profits tend to be larger in firms with less diversified export sales over goods and in firms with more diversified export sales over destination countries. Chapter 17 (originally published in Wagner, 2014b) demonstrates that exporters of high-quality goods tend to be more profitable. For imports Chapter 18 (originally published in Wagner, 2014c) reports that profits are not higher in firms that import more goods and from more countries. Here, productivity advantages of importers with larger extensive margins are eaten up by extra costs related to buying more goods in more countries.

References

Wagner, Joachim (2014a). Is export diversification good for profitability? First evidence for manufacturing enterprises in Germany. *Applied Economics* 46 (33), 4083–4090.

Wagner, Joachim (2014b). Exports and firm profitability: Quality matters! *Economics Bulletin* 34 (3), 1644–1652.

Wagner, Joachim (2014c). Extensive margins of imports, productivity and profitability: First evidence for manufacturing enterprises in Germany. *Economics Bulletin* 34 (3), 1669–1678.

Chapter 16

Is Export Diversification Good for Profitability? First Evidence for Manufacturing Enterprises in Germany*

Abstract

This paper uses a tailor-made newly available data set for enterprises from manufacturing industries in Germany to investigate for the first time the links between export diversification over destination countries and goods on the one hand and the profitability of the exporting firms on the other hand. We find that profits tend to be larger in firms with less diversified export sales over goods and in firms with more diversified export sales over destination countries.

Keywords: Exports, diversification, profitability, Germany.

* Originally Published in *Applied Economics* (2014), 46 (33), 4083–4090.
I thank two anonymous reviewers for helpful comments on an earlier version of this paper. All computations were done at the Research Data Centre of the Statistical Office of Berlin-Brandenburg in Berlin. The firm-level data used are strictly confidential but not exclusive; see http://www.forschungsdatenzentrum.de/datenzugang.asp for information on how to access the data. To facilitate replications the Stata do-file used is available from the author on request.

1. Motivation

Over the past twenty years a huge literature emerged that uses micro-data at the firm level to investigate econometrically the links between different forms of international firm activities (exports, imports, offshoring, foreign direct investment) and various dimensions of firm performance (including firm size, productivity, wages, innovation and survival).[1] A central focus of this empirical literature is on the existence and size of an *exporter premium* in a performance dimension. A typical research question is whether firms that export are more productive than firms that do not even within narrowly defined industries and after controlling for firm size, and if so, whether this premium existed before the firm started to export (pointing to self-selection of more productive firms into exporting) or whether it is caused by exporting (pointing to learning-by-exporting). Firm performance premia of this type for the extensive and intensive margins of exports or imports, and for other international firm activities, have been estimated in hundreds of empirical studies for countries from all over the world. Germany, one of the leading actors on the world market for goods and services, is a case in point, and the existence and size of performance premia of internationally active firms are documented in a number of empirical studies.[2]

---

[1] The literature started with two seminal papers by Bernard and Jensen (1995; 1999) that used firm level data from the US to document differences between exporting and non-exporting firms even within narrowly defined industries and controlling for firm size. Further empirical research looked at the determinants of firms' entry into export markets (Bernard and Jensen, 2004). In a next step transaction-level data on firms and trade were used to investigate the margins of exports and imports, i.e., the number of goods traded and the number of countries traded with (Bernard *et al.*, 2007). Furthermore, links between other forms of international firm activities besides trade and various dimensions of firm performance were investigated. For recent surveys of this empirical literature see Bernard *et al.* (2012) and Wagner (2012a).

[2] See Bernard and Wagner (1997) on exporter premia; Bernard and Wagner (2001) on export entry and exit; Wagner (2002) on causal effects of exports on firm size and productivity; Wagner (2006) on productivity differences between non-exporters, exporters, and firms with foreign direct investments; Schank *et al.* (2007; 2010) on exporter wage premia; Wagner (2007) on productivity and size of the export market; Wagner (2008a) on export entry, export exit and productivity; Fryges and Wagner (2008) on exports and productivity

One performance dimension that has been investigated only in a very small number of studies from this literature is profitability. This comes as a surprise because profit maximization can be regarded as a central aim of a firm. The number of studies on trade and profits, however, is still small and the number of countries covered (all of which are member states of the EU) is even smaller. Wagner (2012b) surveys the evidence for five countries from six studies. Results differ widely across the studies — from positive to no to negative profitability differences between exporters and non-exporters; from evidence for self-selection of more or less profitable firms into exporting to no evidence for self-selection at all; from no positive effects of exports on profits to positive effects.

A dimension of the export performance of firms that has to the best of my knowledge not been investigated at all empirically with a look at its link to firm profitability is the diversification of export activities of firms. It is now well known that not all exporting firm do export only one good to one country of destination — many firms diversify their exports by trading many different goods with customers that are located in many different destination countries. Wagner (2012c) documents that Germany, one of the leading actors on the world market for goods, is a case in point.

How is the extent of diversification of exports in product space and country space linked to firm profitability? Should a firm diversify their exports, i.e., should it export more than one good and spread export activities across markets when it goes for a better performance? In the literature, a related question has been discussed widely with regard to the link between firm profitability and diversification on the local or national market without viewing exports as another option for diversification. Braakmann and Wagner (2011, p. 326f.) summarize this discussion as follows.

---

growth; Vogel and Wagner (2010a) on imports and productivity; Fryges and Wagner (2010) on exports and profitability in manufacturing and Vogel and Wagner (2010b) on exports and profitability in services; Wagner (2011) on offshoring and firm performance; Wagner (2012c; 2012d) on performance premia of multiple-product and multiple-destination exporters; Wagner (2012b) on exports, imports and profitability; Wagner (2013) on exports, imports and firm survival.

According to the resource view (Montgomery 1994, p. 167f.) firms that have an excess capacity in productive factors — for example, special knowledge the firm has accumulated through time, and that can be used in other markets without reducing the use in the market the firm is already active in — can reap economies of scope by expanding into different product markets. Alternatively, the firm may sell this specific asset to another firm active in this market. However, it is reasonable to expect that market failure does exist when it comes to trade in intangible assets like knowledge, and this is an incentive to internalize the use of the assets. Furthermore, productive factors of this type are often closely linked to persons who cannot simultaneously work for several firms producing different products. If a firm owns intangible assets of this type that make it successful in one market, and if these assets can be used in other markets, too, one would expect diversification into other product markets to be positive for firm performance. However, there are extra costs to be considered, too, because producing for a new market usually is connected to costs for developing and introducing the new product, including costs for market research and marketing.

A second line of reasoning points to the reduction of risk and uncertainty that can be reached by diversification across product markets (Lipczynski and Wilson, 2001, p. 324f.). Demand shocks or new competitors may have a negative impact on sales and profits in a product market in an unpredictable manner. A single-product firm, therefore, is highly vulnerable to adverse shocks that hit their market. A multi-product firm can substantially reduce this vulnerability, especially if the risks on the various product markets are randomly distributed or negatively correlated (for a formal model see Hirsch and Lev, 1971). Risk reduction will lead to more stable profits. More stable profits may be positively related to growth because they can secure the funds for investment at lower costs, and this may have a positive influence on the level of profits. Again, there are extra costs associated with the serving of different product markets that have to be considered, too.

Whether product diversification is good or bad for firm performance, and to which extent, therefore, is an empirical question. Results so far are mixed. Hall (1995, p. 26) summarizes the findings of a number of studies as follows: "The relationship between diversification and organizational performance has been the subject of numerous studies over the years …, with results suggesting: negative relationships …, positive relationships …, and lack of relationship …. Regardless of how diversification is measured …, the corporate diversification literature has failed to reach consensus about the relationship between firm diversification and performance". Similarly, Montgomery (1994, p. 172) argues that the literature surveyed by her "clearly shows that diversification is not a guaranteed route to success".

The theoretical arguments pro and contra diversification as a strategy for a firm to improve its profits discussed above hold for the diversification of exports, too. That said, the link between firm profitability on the one hand and *export* diversification in product space and country space on the other hand has not been investigated econometrically before. This paper intends to fill this gap. It uses a tailor-made newly available data set (described in detail in Section 2) to investigate this link for enterprises from manufacturing industries in Germany, one of the leading actors on the world market for goods. To anticipate the most important finding, the paper demonstrates that profits tend to be larger in firms with less diversified export sales over goods and in firms with more diversified export sales over destination countries.

2. Data and Measurement Issues

The lack of empirical studies on the link between profitability and export diversification is due to the fact that until most recently suitable data at the level of the firm that could be used in an econometric investigation were not available. The empirical investigation here uses a tailor-mad data set that combines for the first time high quality firm-level data from three official sources.

The first source is the regular survey of establishments from manufacturing industries by the Statistical Offices of the German federal states. The survey covers all establishments from manufacturing industries that employ at least 20 persons in the local production unit or in the company that owns the unit. Participation of firms in the survey is mandated in official statistics (see Malchin and Voshage, 2009 for details). For this study establishment data were aggregated to the enterprise level to match the unit of observation in the other data sources (described below). From this survey information is used on the number of employees in the firm and detailed industry affiliation.

The second source of data is the cost structure survey for enterprises in the manufacturing sector. This survey is carried out annually as a representative random sample survey. The sample is stratified according to the number of employees and the industries; all firms with 500 and more employees are covered by the cost structure survey (see Fritsch *et al.*, 2004). This survey is the source for information on the profitability of a firm.

Information on the goods traded internationally is available from the statistic on foreign trade (*Außenhandelsstatistik*). This statistic is based on two sources. One source is the reports by German firms on transactions with firms from countries that are members of the European Union (EU); these reports are used to compile the so-called *Intrahandelsstatistik* on intra-EU trade. The other source is transaction-level data collected by the customs on trade with countries outside the EU (the so-called *Extrahandelsstatistik*).[3] Data in the statistic of foreign trade are transaction-level data, i.e., they relate to one transaction of a German firm with a firm located outside Germany at a time.

For the reporting years 2009 and 2010 these transaction-level data have been aggregated at the level of the exporting firm for the first time. Using the firms' registration number for turnover tax statistics these data were matched with the enterprise register system (*Unternehmensregister-System*) and with the enterprise level data from the two other sources discussed above. For each exporting or importing firm that reported either to the statistic on intra-EU trade, or to the statistic on trade with countries outside the EU, we know from the data the value and the volume of exports and imports for the 10 most important exported goods. This information is used to compute indicators for the diversification of exports.

---

[3] Note that firms with a value of exports to EU-countries that does not exceed 400,000 Euro in 2009 do not have to report to the statistic on intra-EU trade. For trade with firms from non-member countries all transactions that exceed 1,000 Euro are registered. For details see Statistisches Bundesamt, Qualitätsbericht Außenhandel, January 2011.

With these data it is possible to investigate the relationship between export diversification and the profitability of the firm.

Diversification of exports is measured along two dimension, traded goods and partners in trade. Three indicators are used to measure the *degree of diversification of goods exported by a firm*. The first indicator is the *number of different goods exported* by a firm, were a good refers to an 8-digit number from the official nomenclature for the statistics of foreign trade. A higher number of different exported goods indicates a higher degree of diversification. While this indicator treats each exported good alike, the second and the third indicator take care of the importance of the various products for the firm. The second indicator is defined as the *share of the most important product of a firm in total exports* of the firm, where importance is measured by the share of sales due to this good in total export sales. Analogously, the third indicator is defined as the *share of the three most important products* in total exports. A higher value of both indicators two and three points to a lower degree of export diversification of a firm.

The *degree of diversification of countries exported to by a firm* is measured in a similar way as the degree of diversification of goods exported. The first indicator is the *number of different destination countries of exports* by a firm. A higher number of different destination countries indicates a higher degree of diversification. While this indicator treats each destination country good alike, the second and the third indicator take care of the importance of the various trading partner countries for the firm. The second indicator is defined as the *share of the most important destination country of a firm in total exports* of that firm, where importance is measured by the share of sales to this country in total export sales. Analogously, the third indicator is defined as the *share of the three most important destination countries* in total exports. A higher value of both indicators two and three points to a lower degree of export diversification of a firm.[4]

---

[4] The data set used in this study has only information on the sales generated by the 10 most important goods exported. Therefore, it is not possible to compute concentration measures that use the information on the share of each product exported in total sales for firms with more than 10 different exported goods like the Berry index (that is defined as one minus the sum of the squared shares of all products in total exports). The same holds for information on export sales to different countries.

The *rate of profit of a firm* is computed as a rate of return, defined as gross firm surplus (computed in line with the definition of the European Commission (1998) as gross value added at factor costs minus gross wages and salaries minus costs for social insurance paid by the firm) divided by total sales (net of VAT) minus net change of inventories[5]:

$$\text{Rate of profit} = \frac{\text{gross value added} - \text{gross wages} - \text{costs for social insurance}}{\text{total sales} - \text{net change of inventories}}$$

(1)

This profit measure is a measure for the price-cost margin which, under competitive conditions, should on average equal the required rental on assets employed per money unit of sales (see Schmalensee, 1989, p. 960f.). Differences in profitability between firms, therefore, can follow from productivity differences, but also from different mark-ups of prices over costs and from differences in the capital intensity.[6]

Furthermore, the empirical model includes the *number of employees* (also included in squares to take care of non-linearity) to control for any relationship between firm size and firm profitability and a complete set of 4-digit level *industry dummy variables* to control for the role of industry-specific factors.

Given that the East German economy still differs in many respects from the West German economy, especially with regard to exporting (see Wagner, 2008b), and that the number of exporting firms is small in East Germany this study looks at West German manufacturing enterprises only.

All computations are performed for two years, 2009 and 2010. In 2009, the value of German exports of goods declined by 18.4 percent compared to 2008. This was followed by an increase in exports by 18.5 percent in 2010 (Statistisches Bundesamt, 2012, p. 414). Therefore, a look at these two very different years can be considered as a robustness check to make sure that the results reported are not specific for a crises or recovery period.

---

[5] Note that the data set does not have any information on the capital stock, or the sum of assets or equity, of the firm, so that it is not possible to construct profit indicators based thereon like return on assets or return on equity.

[6] Given that the data set does not have information on the capital stock employed by the firms in the econometric investigations in the following sections differences in the capital intensity are controlled for by including detailed industry dummy variables at the 4-digit level.

3. Empirical Findings

Descriptive statistics for profitability and the six measures for export diversification of the enterprises are reported in Table 1.[7] Note that firms are rather heterogeneous with regard to all characteristics looked at here. Both the rate of profitability and the extent of export diversification vary widely among the firms in the sample. Note further that profitability improved to a large degree from the export crisis in 2009 to the export boom in 2010.

How is the profitability of an exporting firm linked to the degree of export diversification? Are more diversified exporters more profitable? To investigate this question empirical models are estimated with the rate of profit of a firm as the dependent variable and one of the six indicators of diversification of exports as the independent variable, controlling for firm size and a full set of detailed industry dummy variables measured at the 4-digit industry level. These estimated regression equations are not meant to be empirical models to explain profitability differences at the firm level; the data set at hand is not rich enough for such an exercise. The regression equations are just a vehicle to test for, and estimate the size of, diversification premia controlling for firm size and industry affiliation. This is a standard approach used in a huge number of empirical papers from the emerging literature on the links between international activities of heterogeneous firms and firm performance.[8]

Results for the estimated profitability premia from the six different empirical models and the two years are reported in Table 2. While the number of goods exported per se is unrelated to the rate of profit earned by a firm according to the statistically insignificant regression coefficients from Model 1 in both years there is a profitability premium for firms with a higher share of the most important good or the most important three goods in total exports (see Model 2 and Model 3, respectively). The estimated size of the premium is remarkably similar in the export crisis in 2009 and the export boom in 2010. Results differ when it comes to diversification of exports over space. In both years a higher number of

---

[7] Note that minimum and maximum values cannot be reported because they refer to a single enterprise and, therefore, are confidential.

[8] For recent surveys of this literature see Bernard *et al.* (2012), Melitz and Redding (2014) and Wagner (2012a).

Table 1: Descriptive statistics — enterprise characteristics, West Germany.

Enterprise characteristic	Mean	SD	p1	p50	p99
2009					
No. of enterprises: 5,993					
Profitability (%)	4.79	11.48	−31.87	5.29	29.48
No. of exported products	36.84	89.18	1	11	383
Share of most important product in total exports (%)	66.47	24.95	16.29	66.64	100
Share of three most important products in total exports (%)	88.97	14.80	37.99	95.82	100
No. of destination countries in exports	24.57	21.46	1	19	95
Share of most important country in total exports (%)	71.71	22.92	18.70	77.23	100
Share of three most important countries in total exports (%)	89.37	12.53	46.02	94.05	100
No. of employees	343.26	2,683.88	22	110.33	2,699.3
2010					
No. of enterprises: 6,067					
Profitability (%)	7.61	10.10	−18.96	7.41	31.04
No. of exported products	39.92	88.97	1	12	408
Share of most important product in total exports (%)	66.45	24.82	16.65	66.75	100
Share of three most important products in total exports (%)	88.86	14.90	38.12	95.58	100
No. of destination countries in exports	26.24	22.82	1	20	99
Share of most important country in total exports (%)	41.62	24.74	10.13	34.33	100
Share of three most important countries in total exports (%)	68.05	22.60	26.47	67.09	100
No. of employees	319.69	2,314.10	23	106.67	2,626.3

Note: For a detailed definition of the enterprise characteristics see text. p1, p50 and p99 refer to the 1st, 50th and 99th percentile of the distribution of the characteristic (minima and maxima cannot be reported due to violation of privacy).

destination countries of exports leads to a profitability premium (that is similar in both years), and at least in the boom year 2010 a higher concentration of exports on a small number of foreign markets goes hand in hand with lower profits. The big picture that emerges from the premia regressions reported in Table 2, therefore, can be summarized as follows: While it pays for the firms to concentrate exports on a smaller number of goods it pays to export to a larger number of countries.

The discussion of the results from the empirical models so far only considered the statistical significance of the links between profitability and various indicators of export diversification. Evidently, statistically highly significant links can be irrelevant from an economic point of view if a ceteris paribus change of considerable size in export diversification goes hand in hand with tiny change in the (estimated) rate of profit only. To see whether the statistically significant links are relevant from an economic point of view, too, the estimated change in profits that is linked to a ceteris paribus increase by one standard deviation of the measure of export diversification is computed based on the estimated regression coefficients reported in Table 2.

To start with the diversification over goods exported an increase in the share of the most important product (or the three most important products) in total exports by one standard deviation leads to an estimated increase in the rate of profit by about 0.6 percentage points in both years. With a look at the average rate of profit of 4.8 percent in 2009 and 7.6 percent in 2010 this is a non-negligible effect from an economic point of view. Concentration of export sales on a small number of goods does matter for profitability.

Next, we look at export diversification over space. An increase of the number of destination countries by one standard deviation leads to an estimated increase in the rate of profit by 0.6 percentage points in 2009 and by 0.7 percentage points in 2010. This is the same order of magnitude as in the case of an increase in the share of the most important product(s) by one standard deviation discussed above, and, therefore, it should be considered as non-negligible, too. However, a change by one standard deviation of the distribution of the number of destination countries means adding or dropping more than twenty countries (see Table 1), and

Table 2: Profitability and diversification of exports: West Germany.

Enterprise characteristic		1	2	3	4	5	6
2009							
Number of exported products	β	−0.0013					
	p	0.603					
Share of most important product in total exports	β		0.024				
	p		0.000				
Share of three most important products in total exports	β			0.043			
	p			0.000			
Number of destination countries in exports	β				0.028		
	p				0.001		
Share of most important country in total exports	β					0.0012	
	p					0.865	
Share of three most import. countries in total exports	β						−0.00030
	p						0.981
No. of employees	β	−0.00027	−0.00021	−0.00015	**−0.00061**	**−0.00034**	**−0.00034**
	p	0.179	0.215	0.380	0.003	0.050	0.052
No. of employees (Squared)	β	2.06e−9	1.41e−9	9.99e−10	**4.57e−9**	2.51e−9	2.46e−9
	p	0.232	0.369	0.535	0.019	0.129	0.133
Constant	β	**4.91**	**3.23**	**0.99**	**4.27**	**4.80**	**4.91**
	p	0.000	0.000	0.329	0.000	0.000	0.000
4-digit industry controls		yes	yes	yes	yes	yes	yes
No. of enterprises		5,993	5,993	5,933	5,933	5,933	5,933

2010

		(1)	(2)	(3)	(4)	(5)	(6)
No. of exported products	ß	−0.0030					
	p	0.201					
Share of most important product in total exports	ß		**0.027**				
	p		0.000				
Share of three most important products in total exports	ß			**0.043**			
	p			0.000			
No. of destination countries in exports	ß				**0.031**		
	p				0.000		
Share of most important country in total exports	ß					**−0.012**	
	p					0.026	
Share of three most import. countries in total exports	ß						**−0.021**
	p						0.001
No. of employees	ß	−0.00003	−0.00005	−0.00002	**−0.00050**	−0.00025	−0.00031
	p	0.900	0.763	0.929	0.011	0.157	0.088
No. of employees (Squared)	ß	5.88e−10	1.58e−9	2.45e−10	**3.99e−9**	2.14e−9	2.61e−9
	p	0.720	0.739	0.880	0.020	0.173	0.103
Constant	ß	**7.74**	**5.83**	**3.81**	**6.94**	**8.19**	**9.12**
	p	0.000	0.000	0.000	0.000	0.000	0.000
4-digit industry controls		yes	yes	yes	yes	yes	yes
No. of enterprises		6,067	6,067	6,067	6,067	6,067	6,067

Note: OLS regressions; dependent variable: Profitability (percent). ß is the estimated regression coefficient; p is the prob-value (based on heteroscedasticity-consistent standard errors). To facilitate interpretation of the results, coefficient estimates with a p-value of 0.05 or less (rounded to two digits) are now reported in bold to indicate statistical significance at the usual error level of five percent. The note to the table has been augmented accordingly. For a detailed definition of the variables see text.

this is really a large change. A decrease in the share of the most important country (or the three most important countries) in total exports has a statistically significant effect on profits in the boom year 2010 only.[9] Here a change by one standard deviation is linked to an estimated increase in the rate of profit by 0.3 and 0.5 percentage points, respectively. These changes can be considered as non-negligible from an economic point of view. Therefore, we have some evidence that diversification of exports over space does matter for profitability.

4. Discussion

The discussion of theoretical considerations in Section 1 pointed out that whether diversification of exports is good or bad for profitability is an empirical question. According to the empirical results presented in this study profitability in enterprises from German manufacturing industries is positively related to a higher degree of concentration of exports with regard to the share of the most important products in total sales on the one hand and to a higher degree of diversification of exports with regard to the number of destination countries on the other hand.

This link between export diversification and profitability documents a correlation and should not be interpreted as a causal link from different dimensions of export diversification to profitability. With the cross-section data at hand it is impossible to investigate whether firms with a higher degree of diversification of exports with regard to the number and share of destination countries in total exports made higher profits on the national market already before they started to export, or whether a larger degree of export markets diversification lead to higher profits (or whether both is the case).

Another open question that has not been dealt with in this paper is the potential role played by unobserved firm characteristics like management quality for the profitability of firms. If these unobserved firm characteristics

---

[9] Interestingly, this link between profitability and export diversification is different during the export crisis of 2009 and during the export boom in 2010. However, evidence for more years is needed before any relation between macroeconomic conditions and the profitability — export diversification link can be investigated in more detail.

are correlated with the measures of export diversification that are included in the empirical model used to investigate the diversification premium, the estimated regression coefficients are biased and any conclusions based on the estimates have to take this potentially large bias into account. A standard solution to take at least those unobserved factors into account that do not change over the period under investigation is the addition of fixed firm effect to an empirical model that is estimated for panel data that cover all years from these period. This, however, is no feasible strategy here. As of today, the data used to construct the measures of export diversification are available for the years 2009 and 2010 only. Furthermore, these diversification indicators tend to be highly persistent at the level of the enterprise. Estimates from fixed effects panel data models that are based on the variation of variables over time inside a firm only, therefore, are no panacea here.

That said, the reported statistically significant and economically non-negligible correlation between the profitability of a firm and the diversification over exported goods and destination countries of exports should be regarded as an interesting new finding that might motivate further investigations of the causes and consequences of differences in the diversification of exports in manufacturing firms.

References

Bernard, Andrew and Bradford Jensen (1995). Exporters, jobs, and wages in U.S. manufacturing: 1976–1987. *Brookings Papers on Economic Activity, Microeconomics* 26 (1995), 67–119.

Bernard, Andrew and Joachim Wagner (1997). Exports and success in German manufacturing. *Weltwirtschaftliches Archiv/Review of World Economics* 133 (1), 134–157.

Bernard, Andrew and Bradford Jensen (1999). Exceptional exporter performance: Cause, effect, or both? *Journal of International Economics* 47 (1), 1–25.

Bernard, Andrew and Joachim Wagner (2001). Export entry and exit by German firms. *Weltwirtschaftliches Archiv/Review of World Economics* 137 (1), 105–1123.

Bernard, Andrew and Bradford Jensen (2004). Why some firms export. *Review of Economics and Statistics* 86 (2), 561–569.

Bernard, Andrew, Bradford Jensen, Stephen J. Redding and Peter K. Schott (2007). Firms in international trade. *Journal of Economic Perspectives* 21 (3), 105–130.

Bernard, Andrew, Bradford Jensen, Stephen J. Redding and Peter K. Schott (2012). The empirics of firm heterogeneity and international trade. *Annual Review of Economics* 4, 283–313.

Braakmann, Nils and Joachim Wagner (2011). Product diversification and profitability in German manufacturing firms. *Journal of Economics and Statistics/ Jahrbücher für Nationalökonomie und Statistik* 231 (3), 326–335.

European Commission (1998). Commission Regulation (EC) No. 2700/98 concerning the definitions of characteristics for structural business statistics, Brussels. *Official Journal of the European Communities* L344, 18/12/1998, 49–80.

Fritsch, Michael, Bernd Görzig, Ottmar Hennchen and Andreas Stephan (2004). Cost structure surveys for Germany. *Journal of Applied Social Science Studies* 124 (4), 557–566.

Fryges, Helmut and Joachim Wagner (2008). Exports and productivity growth: First evidence from a continuous treatment approach. *Review of World Economics* 144 (4), 695–722.

Fryges, Helmut and Joachim Wagner (2010). Exports and profitability: First evidence for German manufacturing firms. *The World Economy* 33 (3), 399–423.

Hall, Ernest (1995). Corporate diversification and performance: An investigation of causality. *Australian Journal of Management* 20 (1), 25–42.

Hirsch, Seev and Baruch Lev (1971). Sales stabilization through export diversification. *Review of Economics and Statistics* 53 (3), 270–277.

Lipczynski, John and John Wilson (2001). Industrial organisation. An analysis of competitive markets. (Harlow, Prentice Hall: Financial Times).

Malchin, Anja and Ramona Voshage (2009). Official firm data for Germany. *Schmollers Jahrbuch/Journal of Applied Social Science Studies* 129 (3), 501–513.

Melitz, Marc and Stephen Redding (2014). Heterogeneous firms and trade. *Handbook of International Economics*, 4, 1–54.

Montgomery, Cynthia (1994). Corporate diversification. *Journal of Economic Perspectives* 8 (3), 163–178.Schank, Thorsten, Claus Schnabel and Joachim Wagner (2007). Do exporters really pay higher wages? First evidence from German linked employer–employee data. *Journal of International Economics* 72 (1), 52–74.

Schank, Thorsten, Claus Schnabel and Joachim Wagner (2010). Higher wages in exporting firms: Self-selection, export effect, or both? First evidence from German linked employer–employee data. *Review of World Economics* 146 (2), 303–322.

Schmalensee, Richard (1989). Inter-industry studies of structure and performance. In: Schmalensee, R./Willig, R.D. (Ed.), *Handbook of Industrial Organization*, Vol. 2, Amsterdam, North-Holland: Elsevier, 951–1009.

Statistisches Bundesamt (2012). Statistisches Jahrbuch 2012. Wiesbaden: Statistisches Bundesamt.

Vogel, Alexander and Joachim Wagner (2010a). Higher productivity in importing German manufacturing firms: Self-selection, learning from importing, or both? *Review of World Economics* 145 (4), 641–665.

Vogel, Alexander and Joachim Wagner (2010b). Exports and profitability — First evidence for German business services enterprises. *Applied Economics Quarterly* 56 (1), 7–30.

Wagner, Joachim (2002). The causal effects of exports on firm size and labor productivity: First evidence from a matching approach. *Economics Letters* 77 (2), 287–292.

Wagner, Joachim (2006). Exports, foreign direct investment, and productivity: Evidence from German firm level data. *Applied Economics Letters* 13 (6), 347–349.

Wagner, Joachim (2007). Productivity and size of the export market: Evidence for West and East German plants, 2004. *Journal of Economics and Statistics/ Jahrbücher für Nationalökonomie und Statistik* 227 (4), 403–408.

Wagner, Joachim (2008a). Export entry, export exit and productivity in German manufacturing industries. *International Journal of the Economics of Business* 15 (2), 169–180.

Wagner, Joachim (2008b). A note why more West than East German firms export. *International Economics and Economic Policy* 5 (4), 363–370.

Wagner, Joachim (2011). Off shoring and firm performance: Self-selection, effects on performance, or both? *Review of World Economics* 147 (2), 217–247.

Wagner, Joachim (2012a). International trade and firm performance: A survey of empirical studies since 2006. *Review of World Economics* 148 (2), 235–267.

Wagner, Joachim (2012b). Exports, imports and profitability: First evidence for manufacturing enterprises. *Open Economies Review* 23 (5), 747–765.

Wagner, Joachim (2012c). Trading many goods with many countries: Exporters and importers from German manufacturing industries. *Review of Economics* 63 (2), 170–186.

Wagner, Joachim (2012d). German multiple-product, multiple-destination exporters: Bernard-Redding-Schott under test. *Economics Bulletin* 32 (2), 1708–1714.

Wagner, Joachim (2013). Exports, imports and firm survival: First evidence for manufacturing enterprises in Germany. *Review of World Economics* 149 (1), 113–130.

Chapter 17

Exports and Firm Profitability: Quality Matters!*

Abstract

This paper uses a tailor-made newly available data set to investigate for the first time the links between profitability and the quality of exports in enterprises from manufacturing industries in Germany, one of the leading actors on the world market for goods. The paper demonstrates that exporters of high-quality goods tend to be more profitable.

Keywords: Exports, export quality, profitability, Germany.

1. Motivation

Over the past 20 years a huge literature emerged that investigates the links between various forms of international firm activities and various dimensions of firm performance (see Wagner, 2012a for a recent survey). From

*Originally Published in *Economics Bulletin* (2014), 34 (3), 1644–1652.

All computations were done at the Research Data Centre of the Statistical Office of Berlin-Brandenburg in Berlin. The firm-level data used are strictly confidential but not exclusive; see http://www.forschungsdatenzentrum.de/datenzugang.asp for information on how to access the data. To facilitate replications the Stata do-file used is available from the author on request.

this micro-econometric literature two conclusions emerge than can be regarded as uncontroversial. First, exporters are more productive than firms that do not trade internationally. Second, firms engaged in exports have to bear extra costs. Exporting firms have to pay for, among others, market research in foreign countries, adaptation of products to local regulations there, or transport costs. Furthermore, exporting firms tend to pay higher wages than non-exporting firms. These extra costs are the reason for self-selection of more productive firms on international markets — only firms with a productivity that is high enough can be profitable when extra costs have to be covered.

A question that has been investigated in the literature on the micro-econometrics of international trade only recently is whether the productivity advantage of exporting firms does lead to a profitability advantage of firms that engage in exports compared to otherwise identical non-trading firms even when exporters are facing extra costs. This apparent gap in the literature on the micro-econometrics of international trade comes as a surprise because maximization of profits (and not of productivity) is usually considered as a central goal for firms. Furthermore, looking at profitability instead of productivity is more appropriate from a theoretical point of view, too. Even if productivity and profitability are positively correlated (which tends to be the case) productivity is, as was recently pointed out by Foster *et al.* (2008, p. 395), only one of several possible idiosyncratic factors that determine profits. Success of firms in general, and especially survival, depends on profitability. Often profitability is viewed both in theoretical models of market selection and in empirical studies on firm entry and exit as a positive monotonic function of productivity, and selection on profits then is equivalent to selection on productivity.

In empirical studies the use of productivity instead of profitability is usually due to the fact that productivity is easily observed in the data sets at hand while profitability is not. Fortunately, there are data sets that are rich enough to allow to measure profitability. The number of studies on trade and profits, however, is still small and the number of countries covered (all of which are member states of the European Union (EU)) is even smaller. Wagner (2012b) surveys the evidence for five countries from six studies. Results differ widely across the studies — from positive to no to negative profitability differences between exporters and non-exporters; from evidence for self-selection of more or less profitable firms into exporting to no evidence for self-selection at all; from no positive effects of exports on profits to positive effects.

One reason for the absence of a clear-cut result for the link of exports and profits at the firm level might be due to the fact that in all of these studies exports of goods from an industry[1] are treated as homogeneous in the sense that exports of, say, low-budget cars and Porsches are treated alike as exports of cars. Although one should expect that the link between exports and profitability should be (more) positive for high-quality exports than for standardized low-quality products, none of these studies looks at the link between the quality of exports and firm profitability.

This paper intends to fill this gap. It uses a tailor-made newly available data set (described in detail in Section 2) to investigate for the first time the links between profitability and the quality of exports in enterprises from manufacturing industries in Germany, one of the leading actors on the world market for goods. To anticipate the most important finding, the paper demonstrates that in German manufacturing industries exporters of high-quality goods tend to be more profitable.

2. Data and Measurement Issues

The lack of empirical studies on the link between profitability and quality of exported goods is due to the fact that until most recently suitable data at the level of the firm that could be used in an econometric investigation were not available. The empirical investigation here uses a tailor-made data set that combines for the first time high quality firm-level data from three official sources.

The first source is the regular survey of establishments from manufacturing industries by the Statistical Offices of the German federal states. The survey covers all establishments from manufacturing industries that employ at least twenty persons in the local production unit or in the

---

[1] The empirical models used to investigate the link between exports and profitability usually include a full set of industry dummies to control for the industry affiliation of the firms.

company that owns the unit. Participation of firms in the survey is mandated in official statistics (see Malchin and Voshage, 2009 for details). For
this study establishment data were aggregated to the enterprise level to
match the unit of observation in the other data sources (described below).
From this survey information is used on the number of employees in the
firm, the sum of wages paid, and detailed industry affiliation.

The second source of data is the cost structure survey for enterprises
in the manufacturing sector. This survey is carried out annually as a representative random sample survey. The sample is stratified according to
the number of employees and the industries; all firms with 500 and more
employees are covered by the cost structure survey (see Fritsch *et al.*,
2004). This survey is the source for information on the profitability of
a firm.

Information on the goods traded internationally is available from the
statistic on foreign trade (*Außenhandelsstatistik*). This statistic is based on
two sources. One source is the reports by German firms on transactions
with firms from countries that are members of the EU; these reports are
used to compile the so-called *Intrahandelsstatistik* on intra-EU trade. The
other source is transaction-level data collected by the customs on trade
with countries outside the EU (the so-called *Extrahandelsstatistik*).[2] Data
in the statistic of foreign trade are transaction-level data, i.e., they relate to
one transaction of a German firm with a firm located outside Germany at
a time.

For the reporting years 2009 and 2010 these transaction-level data
have been aggregated at the level of the exporting firm for the first time.
Using the firms' registration number for turnover tax statistics these data
were matched with the enterprise register system (*Unternehmensregister-
System*) and with the enterprise level data from the two other sources
discussed above. For each exporting or importing firm that reported either
to the statistic on intra-EU trade, or to the statistic on trade with countries
outside the EU, we know from the data the value and the volume of

---

[2] Note that firms with a value of exports to EU-countries that does not exceed 400,000 Euro
in 2009 do not have to report to the statistic on intra-EU trade. For trade with firms from
non-member countries all transactions that exceed 1,000 Euro are registered. For details
see Statistisches Bundesamt, Qualitätsbericht Außenhandel, January 2011.

exports and imports for the 10 most important exported goods. This information is used to compute an index for the quality of exports.

With these data it is possible to investigate the relationship between the quality of goods exported and the profitability of the firm.

The *rate of profit of a firm* is computed as a rate of return, defined as gross firm surplus (computed in line with the definition of the European Commission (1998) as gross value added at factor costs minus gross wages and salaries minus costs for social insurance paid by the firm) divided by total sales (net of VAT) minus net change of inventories[3]:

$$\text{Rate of profit} = \frac{\text{gross value added} - \text{gross wages} - \text{costs for social insurance}}{\text{total sales} - \text{net change of inventories}}$$

$$(1)$$

This profit measure is a measure for the price-cost margin which, under competitive conditions, should on average equal the required rental on assets employed per money unit of sales (see Schmalensee, 1989, p. 960f.). Differences in profitability between firms, therefore, can follow from productivity differences, but also from different mark-ups of prices over costs and from differences in the capital intensity.[4]

The *quality of exported goods* is defined as the unit value of exports and computed as value of exports (measured in Euro) over quantity of exports (measured in tons). In the data set used here we have information on the value of exports and the quantity of exports for the 10 most important products (measured by the value of exports) exported by a firm. For firms that exported more than one good the unit value of exports is the weighted sum of the unit values of the (up to 10) different goods exported, and the weights are the shares of the value of exports of a good in the total exports

---

[3] Note that the data set does not have any information on the capital stock, or the sum of assets or equity, of the firm, so that it is not possible to construct profit indicators based thereon like return on assets or return on equity.

[4] Given that the data set does not have information on the capital stock employed by the firms in the econometric investigations in the following sections differences in the capital intensity are controlled for by including detailed industry dummy variables at the 4-digit level.

of the firm of these (up to 10) goods. The unit value of exports is expressed in percentage of the mean value of unit values in the 4-digit industry to take care of differences across industries due to the nature of the products (e.g., mobile phones and cement).

The empirical model includes a number of control variables. The *number of employees* (also included in squares to take care of non-linearity) is included to control for any relationship between firm size and firm profitability. The *sum of wages per employee* is used as a proxy variable for human capital intensity which might be expected to be positively correlated with the profitability of an exporting firm from one of the most highly developed industrial countries of the world.[5] Furthermore, a complete set of 4-digit level *industry dummy variables* is included to control for the role of industry-specific factors related to the link between profitability and quality of exported goods.

Given that the East German economy still differs in many respects from the West German economy, especially with regard to exporting (see Wagner, 2008), and that the number of exporting firms is small in East Germany this study looks at West German manufacturing enterprises only.

All computations are performed for two years, 2009 and 2010. In 2009, the value of German exports of goods declined by 18.4 percent compared to 2008. This was followed by an increase in exports by 18.5 percent in 2010 (Statistisches Bundesamt 2012, p. 414). Therefore, a look at these two very different years can be considered as a robustness check to make sure that the results reported are not specific for a crises or recovery period.

3. Empirical Findings

Descriptive statistics for the enterprise characteristics considered in this study are reported in Table 1.[6] Note that firms are rather heterogeneous

---

[5] Unfortunately, there is no information on the qualification of the employees (e.g., the share of employees with a university degree, or the share of employees that successfully passed the exams following an apprenticeship) of the firm in the data used. However, Wagner (2012c) uses a unique different data set to demonstrate that in German manufacturing firms the average wage is a useful proxy variable for the qualification of the employees.

[6] Note that minimum and maximum values cannot be reported because they refer to a single enterprise and, therefore, are confidential.

Table 1: Descriptive statistics — enterprise characteristics, West Germany.

Enterprise characteristic	Mean	SD	p1	p50	p99
2009					
No. of enterprises: 5,993					
Profitability (%)	4.79	11.48	−31.87	5.29	29.48
Quality of exported goods (Index)	100.00	234.03	0.353	47.40	992.82
No. of employees	343.26	2,683.88	22	110.33	2,699.3
Wage/employee (Euro)	35,343	10,447	14,915	34,577	64,128
2010					
No. of enterprises: 6,072					
Profitability (%)	7.61	10.11	−19.11	7.42	31.04
Quality of exported goods (Index)	100.00	237.15	0.65	47.72	833.16
No. of employees	319.49	2,313.16	23	106.54	2,626.33
Wage/employee (Euro)	36,563	10,618	15,132	35,966	65,492

Note: For a detailed definition of the enterprise characteristics see text. p1, p50 and p99 refer to the 1st, 50th and 99th percentile of the distribution of the characteristic (minima and maxima cannot be reported due to violation of privacy).

with regard to all characteristics looked at here. Both the rate of profitability and the quality of exported goods vary widely among the firms in the sample. Note further that profitability improved to a large degree from the export crisis in 2009 to the export boom in 2010.

How is the profitability of an exporting firm linked to the quality of goods exported? Are exporters of high-quality goods really more profitable than exporters of goods with a lower quality? To investigate this question empirical models are estimated with the rate of profit of a firm as the dependent variable and index of the quality of exports as the independent variable, controlling for firm size, human capital intensity and a full set of detailed industry dummy variables measured at the 4-digit industry level. Results are reported in Table 2.

Three variants of the empirical model with different independent variables are estimated — the first includes only the index of export quality (plus the detailed industry controls), the second adds firm size (measured by the number of employees that is also included in squares to take care of a non-linear relationship) and the third adds the wage per employee, too.

Table 2: **Profitability and quality of exported goods: West Germany.**

Enterprise characteristic		1	2	3
2009				
Quality of exported goods (Index)	ß	0.0016	0.0016	0.0016
	p	0.032	0.030	0.030
No. of employees	ß		−0.00035	−0.00035
	p		0.045	0.048
No. of employees (Squared)	ß		2.54e–9	2.55e–9
	p		0.120	0.123
Wage per employee(Euro)	ß			7.00e–8
	p			0.997
Constant	ß	4.63	4.73	4.73
	p	0.000	0.000	0.000
4-digit industry controls		yes	yes	yes
No. of enterprises		5,993	5,993	5,933
2010				
Quality of exported goods (Index)	ß	0.0012	0.0012	0.0012
	p	0.081	0.079	0.072
No. of employees	ß		−0.00020	−0.00017
	p		0.240	0.322
No. of employees (Squared)	ß		1.75e–9	1.52e–9
	p		0.254	0.331
Wage per employee (Euro)	ß			−0.000014
	p			0.448
Constant	ß	7.49	7.55	8.06
	p	0.000	0.000	0.000
4-digit industry controls		yes	yes	yes
No. of enterprises		6,072	6,072	6,072

Note: OLS regressions; dependent variable: Profitability (percent). ß is the estimated regression coefficient, p is the prob-value (based on heteroscedasticity-consistent standard errors). For a detailed definition of the variables see text.

The point estimates and the level of statistical significance of the quality of exported goods are stable over the estimated variants of the empirical model. Results reveal that the quality of exported goods is positively related to the rate of profit in a firm. This link is statistically significant at an error level of three percent for 2009, while the level of statistical significance is somewhat smaller in 2010.[7]

The discussion of the results from the empirical models so far only considered the statistical significance of the links between input and output quality. Evidently, statistically highly significant links can be irrelevant from an economic point of view if a ceteris paribus change of considerable size in export quality leads to a tiny change in the (estimated) rate of profit only. To see whether the statistically significant links are relevant from an economic point of view, too, the estimated change in profits that is caused by a ceteris paribus increase by one standard deviation of the quality of exports is computed based on the estimated regression coefficients from Model 3. For 2009, an increase by one standard deviation is linked to an increase in the rate of profit by 0.37 percentage points. For 2010, the respective figure is 0.28 percentage points. Given the mean value for the rate of profit of 4.8 percent in 2009 and 7.6 percent in 2010 these estimated changes are non-negligible from an economic point of view. Export quality does matter for profitability.

Interestingly, the link between profitability and export quality is stronger (both statistically and economically) during the export crisis of 2009 than during the export boom in 2010. However, evidence for more years is needed before any relation between macroeconomic conditions and the profitability — export quality link can be investigated in more detail.

4. Discussion

The bottom line, then, is that according to the empirical results presented in this study the quality of exported goods in German manufacturing industries is positively related to the rate of profit of the exporting firms.

This link between export quality and profitability documents a correlation and should not be interpreted as a causal link from export quality

---

[7] Given that the inclusion of control variables for firm size and human capital intensity does not change the results for the link between profits and export quality we do not discuss the estimation results for these variables in detail here.

to profitability. The huge and emerging literature on the links between international activities of heterogeneous firms and firm performance[8] has demonstrated that one can observe both self-selection of "better" firms on international markets and improvement of firms due to international activities. With the cross-section data at hand it is impossible to investigate whether the exporters of high-quality goods made higher profits on the national market already from selling high-quality goods before they started to export, or whether the higher challenges on the export markets induced improvement in the products of the firm that eventually lead to higher profits (or whether both is the case).

Another open question that has not been dealt with in this paper is the potential role played by unobserved inputs like management quality for the profitability of firms. If these unobserved firm characteristics are correlated with the observed characteristics that are included in the empirical model used to investigate the links between export quality and profitability, the estimated regression coefficients are biased and any conclusions based on the estimates have to take this potentially large bias into account. A standard solution to take at least those unobserved factors into account that do not change over the period under investigation is the addition of fixed firm effect to an empirical model that is estimated for panel data that cover all years from these period. This, however, is no feasible strategy here. As of today, the data used to construct the index of the quality of export goods are available for the years 2009 and 2010 only. Furthermore, both the export quality and the control variables include tend to be highly persistent at the level of the enterprise. Estimates from fixed effects panel data models that are based on the variation of variables over time inside a firm only, therefore, are no panacea here.

That said, the reported statistically significant and economically important correlation between the profitability of a firm and the quality of its exported goods should be regarded as an interesting new fact that might motivate further investigations of the causes and consequences of quality differences of internationally traded goods.

---

[8] For surveys of this literature see Bernard *et al.* (2012), Melitz and Redding (2014) and Wagner (2012a).

References

Bernard, Andrew, Bradford Jensen, Stephen J. Redding and Peter K. Schott (2012). The Empirics of firm heterogeneity and international trade. *Annual Review of Economics* 4 (1), 283–313.

European Commission (1998). Commission Regulation (EC) No. 2700/98 concerning the definitions of characteristics for structural business statistics, Brussels. *Official Journal of the European Communities* L344, 18/12/1998, 49–80.

Foster, Lucia, John Haltiwanger and Chad Syverson (2008). Reallocation, firm turnover, and efficiency: Selection on productivity or profitability? *American Economic Review* 98 (1), 394–425.

Fritsch, Michael, Bernd Görzig, Ottmar Hennchen and Andreas Stephan (2004). Cost structure surveys for Germany. *Journal of Applied Social Science Studies* 124 (4), 557–566.

Malchin, Anja and Ramona Voshage (2009). Official firm data for Germany. *Schmollers Jahrbuch/Journal of Applied Social Science Studies* 129 (3), 501–513.

Melitz, Marc and Stephen Redding (2014). Heterogeneous firms and trade. *Handbook of International Economics*, 4, 1–54.

Schmalensee, Richard (1989). Inter-industry studies of structure and performance, In: Schmalensee, R./Willig, R.D. (Ed.), *Handbook of Industrial Organization*, Vol. 2, Amsterdam: North-Holland, 951–1009.

Statistisches Bundesamt (2012). Statistisches Jahrbuch 2012. Wiesbaden: Statistisches Bundesamt.

Wagner, Joachim (2008). A note why more West than East German firms export. *International Economics and Economic Policy* 5 (4), 363–370.

Wagner, Joachim (2012a). International trade and firm performance: A survey of empirical studies since 2006. *Review of World Economics* 148 (2), 235–267.

Wagner, Joachim (2012b). Exports, imports and profitability: First evidence for manufacturing enterprises. *Open Economies Review* 23 (5), 747–765.

Wagner, Joachim (2012c). Average wage, qualification of the workforce and export performance if German enterprises: Evidence from *KombiFiD* data. *Journal of Labour Market Research* 45 (2), 161–170.

Chapter 18

Extensive Margins of Imports, Productivity and Profitability: First Evidence for Manufacturing Enterprises in Germany*

Abstract

This chapter uses a tailor-made newly available data set for enterprises from manufacturing industries in Germany to investigate for the first time the links between the extensive margins of imports (the number of imported goods and the number of countries imported from) and two dimensions of firm performance, productivity and profitability. While both extensive margins are highly positively linked with firm productivity, profits are not higher in firms that import more goods and from more countries. This demonstrates that productivity advantages

*Originally Published in *Economics Bulletin* (2014), 34 (3), 1669–1678.

I thank an anonymous referee for helpful comments on an earlier version of the paper. All computations were done at the Research Data Centre of the Statistical Office of Berlin-Brandenburg in Berlin. The firm-level data used are strictly confidential but not exclusive; see http://www.forschungsdatenzentrum.de/datenzugang.asp for information on how to access the data. To facilitate replications the Stata do-file used is available from the author on request.

of importers are eaten up by extra costs related to buying more goods in more countries.

Keywords: Imports, intensive margins, profitability, Germany.

1. Motivation

Over the past 20 years a huge literature emerged that uses micro-data at the firm level to investigate econometrically the links between different forms of international firm activities (exports, imports, offshoring, foreign direct investment) and various dimensions of firm performance (including firm size, productivity, wages, innovation and survival).[1] One performance dimension that has been investigated only in a very small number of studies from this literature is profitability. This comes as a surprise because profit maximization can be regarded as a central aim of a firm. The number of studies on trade and profits, however, is still small and the number of countries covered (all of which are member states of the European Union (EU)) is even smaller. Wagner (2012b) surveys the evidence for five countries from six studies. Remarkably, all of these studies look at the link between exports and profitability only, and none of the studies investigates the role of imports for profitability. Results differ widely across the studies — from positive to no to negative profitability differences between exporters and non-exporters; from evidence for self-selection of more or less profitable firms into exporting to no evidence for self-selection at all; from no positive effects of exports on profits to positive effects.

To the best of my knowledge, the only study that investigates the link between imports and profitability is Wagner (2012b). This study looks at manufacturing firms from Germany. Descriptive statistics and regression analysis point to the absence of any statistically significant and economically large effects of imports on profits. This comes as a surprise because importing firms are known to be much more productive than comparable firms that do not import.[2] It seems that any productivity advantages of

---

[1] For a recent survey of this literature see Wagner (2012a).
[2] See Vogel and Wagner (2010) for a survey of the literature and for evidence for Germany.

trading firms are eaten up by extra costs related to buying on foreign markets.

One shortcoming of the study by Wagner (2012b) is that it looks at the link between the importer status of firm (i.e., being an importer or not) and profitability only, while the extensive margins of import activity — the number of imported goods and the number of countries imported from — are not considered due to missing information. This is a gap in the literature because it is known that these extensive margins of imports are positively related to productivity. Firms that import more goods and that import from more countries of origin are more productive (Wagner, 2012c). Are these productivity premia absorbed by higher costs related to sourcing more goods abroad and from more countries? Importing is associated with fixed costs that are sunk costs, because the import agreement is preceded by a search process for potential foreign suppliers, inspection of goods, negotiations, contract formulation etc. Furthermore, there are sunk costs of importing due to learning and acquisition of customs procedures. Many of these costs tend to occur again for each source country and for each imported good. It is argued that these extra costs are a reason for self-selection of more productive firms into imports, because only firms with a productivity that is high enough can be profitable when these extra costs have to be covered. However, it is an open question whether all the productivity advantages of multi-country/ multi-goods importers are needed to cover the extra costs caused by the extensive margins of imports, or whether the productivity advantage is mirrored in a profitability advantage.

This paper intends to fill this gap. It uses a tailor-made newly available data set (described in detail in Section 2) to investigate for the first time the links between the extensive margins of imports (the number of imported goods and the number of countries imported from) and two dimensions of firm performance, productivity and profitability in Germany, one of the leading actors on the world market for goods. To anticipate the most important result, we report that both extensive margins are highly positively linked with firm productivity, but that profits are not higher in firms that import more goods and from more countries. This demonstrates that productivity advantages of importers are indeed eaten up by extra costs related to import more goods and from more countries.

2. Data and Measurement Issues

The lack of empirical studies on the link between profitability and the extensive margins of imports is due to the fact that until most recently suitable data at the level of the firm that could be used in an econometric investigation were not available. The empirical investigation here uses a tailor-made data set that combines for the first time high quality firm-level data from three official sources.

The first source is the regular survey of establishments from manufacturing industries by the Statistical Offices of the German federal states. The survey covers all establishments from manufacturing industries that employ at least twenty persons in the local production unit or in the company that owns the unit. Participation of firms in the survey is mandated in official statistics (see Malchin and Voshage, 2009 for details). For this study establishment data were aggregated to the enterprise level to match the unit of observation in the other data sources (described below). From this survey information is used on total sales, the number of employees in the firm and detailed industry affiliation.

The second source of data is the cost structure survey for enterprises in the manufacturing sector. This survey is carried out annually as a representative random sample survey. The sample is stratified according to the number of employees and the industries; all firms with 500 and more employees are covered by the cost structure survey (see Fritsch *et al.*, 2004). This survey is the source for information on the profitability of a firm.

Information on the goods traded internationally is available from the statistic on foreign trade (*Außenhandelsstatistik*). This statistic is based on two sources. One source is the reports by German firms on transactions with firms from countries that are members of the EU; these reports are used to compile the so-called *Intrahandelsstatistik* on intra-EU trade. The other source is transaction-level data collected by the customs on trade with countries outside the EU (the so-called *Extrahandelsstatistik*).[3] Data in the statistic of foreign trade are transaction-level data, i.e., they relate to

---

[3] Note that firms with a value of imports from EU-countries that does not exceed 400,000 Euro in 2009 do not have to report to the statistic on intra-EU trade. For trade with firms from non-member countries all transactions that exceed 1,000 Euro are registered. For details see Statistisches Bundesamt, Qualitätsbericht Außenhandel, January 2011.

one transaction of a German firm with a firm located outside Germany at a time.

For the reporting years 2009 and 2010 these transaction-level data have been aggregated at the level of the importing firm for the first time. Using the firms' registration number for turnover tax statistics these data were matched with the enterprise register system (*Unternehmensregister-System*) and with the enterprise level data from the two other sources discussed above. For each importing firm that reported either to the statistic on intra-EU trade, or to the statistic on trade with countries outside the EU, we know from the data the number of goods imported and the number of countries imported from. This information is the source for information on the extensive margins of imports by a firm.

The *rate of profit of a firm* is computed as a rate of return, defined as gross firm surplus (computed in line with the definition of the European Commission (1998) as gross value added at factor costs minus gross wages and salaries minus costs for social insurance paid by the firm) divided by total sales (net of VAT) minus net change of inventories[4]:

$$\text{Rate of profit} = \frac{\text{gross value added} - \text{gross wages} - \text{cos ts for social insurance}}{\text{total sales} - \text{net change of inventories}}$$

$$(1)$$

This profit measure is a measure for the price-cost margin which, under competitive conditions, should on average equal the required rental on assets employed per money unit of sales (see Schmalensee, 1989, p. 960f.). Differences in profitability between firms, therefore, can follow from productivity differences, but also from different mark-ups of prices over costs and from differences in the capital intensity.[5]

---

[4] Note that the data set does not have any information on the capital stock, or the sum of assets or equity, of the firm, so that it is not possible to construct profit indicators based thereon like return on assets or return on equity.

[5] Given that the data set does not have information on the capital stock employed by the firms in the econometric investigations in the following sections differences in the capital intensity are controlled for by including detailed industry dummy variables at the 4-digit level.

Productivity is measured as labor productivity (defined as total turnover per employee) because information on the capital stock of a firm is not available, so more elaborate measures of total factor productivity cannot be used in this study. Bartelsman and Doms (2000, p. 575) point to the fact that heterogeneity in labor productivity has been found to be accompanied by similar heterogeneity in total factor productivity in the reviewed research where both concepts are measured. In a recent comprehensive survey Syverson (2011) argues that high-productivity producers will tend to look efficient regardless of the specific way that their productivity is measured. Furthermore, Foster *et al.* (2008) show that productivity measures that use sales (i.e., quantities multiplied by prices) and measures that use quantities only are highly positively correlated. Therefore, we argue that labor productivity is a suitable measure for productivity at the firm level.

Furthermore, the empirical models includes the *number of employees* (also included in squares to take care of non-linearity) to control for any relationship between firm size and firm productivity or profitability, and a complete set of 4-digit level *industry dummy variables* to control for the role of industry-specific factors.

Given that the East German economy still differs in many respects from the West German economy, especially with regard to foreign trade (see Wagner, 2008), this study looks at manufacturing enterprises from West Germany and East Germany separately.

With these data it is possible to investigate the relationship between the extensive margins of imports — the number of countries imported from and the number of different goods imported — on the one hand and the productivity or the profitability of the firm on the other hand.

All computations are performed for two years, 2009 and 2010. In 2009, the value of German imports of goods declined by 17.5 percent compared to 2008. This was followed by an increase in imports by 19.9 percent in 2010 (Statistisches Bundesamt, 2012, p. 414). Therefore, a look at these two very different years can be considered as a robustness check to make sure that the results reported are not specific for a crises or recovery period.

3. Empirical Findings

Among importing firms both the number of goods imported and the number of countries imported from differ widely. For the sample of firms used in this study the shares of firms from six groups for both extensive margins of imports in the two years 2009 and 2010 and in both parts of Germany are reported in Table 1.[6] While some firms import only one good or a small number of goods and from one country or a small number of countries only, others import many goods and from many countries. Firms from East Germany tend to have smaller values for both extensive margins of imports.

How are productivity and profitability of an importing firm linked to the extensive margins of imports? To investigate this question empirical models are estimated with the productivity or the rate of profit of a firm as the dependent variable and either the number of goods imported or the number of countries imported from as the independent variable, controlling for firm size and a full set of detailed industry dummy variables measured at the 4-digit industry level. In the empirical model the number of products and the number of countries is included either as the number itself or in form of five dummy variables for groups of firms with different numbers of products and countries (using the firms that import only one good or that import from one country only as the reference group).[7] These regression equations are not meant to be empirical models to explain productivity or profitability differences at the firm level; the data at hand are not rich enough for such an exercise. The regression equations are just a vehicle to test for, and estimate the size of, the difference in productivity

---

[6] For information on the share of countries of origin and the type of products imported in total imports see Statistisches Bundesamt (2012, p. 411ff). Note that in 2010, 68 percent of imports originated in Europe (56 percent in the EU), nine percent in America and 20.5 percent in Asia. The 10 most important countries of origin were China, The Netherlands, France, United States, Italy, United Kingdom, Austria, Belgium, Switzerland and Russia. As regards types of imported goods, the shares in 2010 were 31 percent for intermediate goods, 29.5 percent for capital goods, 15.7 percent for consumer non-durables, 11.5 percent for energy, and 3.7 percent for consumer durables.

[7] Note that by construction only importing firms are included in the data set.

Table 1: Extensive margins of imports in German manufacturing firms.

		Share of firms (%)			
		West Germany		East Germany	
		2009	2010	2009	2010
Group	Number of goods				
1	1	5.25	5.38	8.72	7.95
2	2–5	16.09	14.44	17.53	18.28
3	6–10	13.54	13.37	18.97	17.90
4	11–25	24.07	23.33	29.60	26.70
5	26–49	20.12	20.20	14.56	16.67
6	50+	20.94	23.28	10.63	12.50
No. of firms		6,004	6,060	1,044	1,056
Group	Number of goods				
1	1	8.49	9.09	12.45	12.78
2	2–5	22.58	22.00	26.05	26.14
3	6–10	23.92	22.01	29.69	25.76
4	11–25	33.78	35.00	27.78	30.11
5	26–49	10.14	11.02	3.64	4.55
6	50+	1.08	0.87	0.38	0.66
No. of firms		6,004	6,060	1,044	1,056

and profitability in firms with different values of the extensive margins of imports while controlling for firm size and industry affiliation. This is a standard approach used in a huge number of empirical papers from the emerging literature on the links between international activities of heterogeneous firms and firm performance.[8]

Results for the estimated productivity premia are reported in Table 2. The big picture is identical to the one reported in earlier investigations

---

[8] For recent surveys of this literature see Bernard *et al.* (2012), Melitz and Redding (2014) and Wagner (2012a).

Table 2: Extensive margins of imports and productivity in German manufacturing firms.

Model	Year		West Germany		East Germany	
			2009	2010	2009	2010
1	Number of products	ß	0.194	0.237	0.495	0.460
		p	0.000	0.000	0.000	0.000
2	2–5 products	ß	14.668	6.618	13.725	5.304
	(Dummy; 1 = yes)	p	0.000	0.041	0.034	0.419
	6–10 products	ß	22.389	15.750	33.452	27.664
	(Dummy; 1 = yes)	p	0.000	0.000	0.000	0.000
	11–25 products	ß	31.596	26.495	40.218	38.071
	(Dummy; 1 = yes)	p	0.000	0.000	0.000	0.000
	26–49 products	ß	36.321	36.234	48.086	49.892
	(Dummy; 1 = yes)	p	0.000	0.000	0.000	0.000
	50+ products	ß	47.398	48.267	72.688	74.922
	(Dummy; 1 = yes)	p	0.000	0.000	0.000	0.000
1	Number of countries	ß	1.557	1.898	3.181	3.298
		p	0.000	0.000	0.000	0.000
2	2–5 countries	ß	17.001	11.166	31.639	23.166
	(Dummy; 1 = yes)	p	0.000	0.000	0.000	0.000
	6–10 countries	ß	29.928	28.350	35.700	41.131
	(Dummy; 1 = yes)	p	0.000	0.000	0.000	0.000
	11–25 countries	ß	43.402	43.100	67.080	59.597
	(Dummy; 1 = yes)	p	0.000	0.000	0.000	0.000
	26–49 countries	ß	55.449	58.934	84.562	100.83
	(Dummy; 1 = yes)	p	0.000	0.000	0.000	0.000
	50+ countries	ß	84.068	103.50	223.88	171.50
	(Dummy; 1 = yes)	p	0.000	0.000	0.003	0.000

Note: Dependent variable is labor productivity. ß is the estimated regression coefficient, p is the prob-value (based on heteroscedasticity consistent standard error estimates). All empirical models include the number of employees (also included in squares), a complete set of 4-digit industry control variables, and a constant. Reference group in Model 2 is made of firms that import one good and from one country, respectively.

based on different samples of manufacturing firms from Germany. All estimated regression coefficients are positive and highly significant statistically (with larger coefficients for East Germany than for West Germany). Productivity increases with both margins of imports, and the estimated premia are large from an economic point of view. In West Germany in 2009 the (unconditional) average amount of sales per employee in all firms in our sample was 227,726 Euro. Compared to firms from the reference group that imported only one product, labor productivity was 14,668 Euro higher on average (controlling for firm size and industry) in firms that imported two to five products, and 47,398 Euro higher in firms that imported 50 or more products. These premia are large with regard to the overall average productivity. The same holds for the estimated productivity premia with regard to the number of countries imported from. The big picture for West Germany in 2010 is the same, and this holds for East Germany in both years and with regard to both extensive margins of imports, too.

In West Germany in 2009 the (unconditional) average rate of profit in all firms in our sample was 4.9 percent, with a value of −30.7 percent in first percentile and 29.0 percent in the 99th percentile. Results for 2010 and for East Germany are similar.[9] How are the large differences in productivity between importers with lower and higher values of the extensive margins of imports documented in Table 2 related to these differences in firm profitability? Results from profitability premia regressions that are specified identically compared to the empirical models used to estimate the productivity premia are reported in Table 3. The estimated regression coefficients are never statistically different from zero at an error level of five percent,[10] and the point estimates do not indicate a consistent pattern over both years and both parts of Germany. Firm profitability is not related to the extensive margins of imports.

---

[9] Details are available on request. Note that minimum and maximum values are confidential because they refer to a single (but unknown) firm.

[10] Note that the (negative!) coefficient from Model 1 for East Germany in 2010 for the number of products has a prob-value that comes close to the significance level of five percent. However, this seemingly negative link of the number of imported products and the rate of profit does not show up in the estimated coefficients of the group dummy variables that are not statistically different from zero at any conventional level.

Table 3: Extensive margins of imports and profitability in German manufacturing firms.

Model	Year		West Germany		East Germany	
			2009	2010	2009	2010
1	Number of products	ß	0.194	0.022	2.523	−1.069
		p	0.180	0.798	0.192	0.055
2	2–5 products	ß	−30.035	49.325	−67.776	111.96
	(Dummy; 1 = yes)	p	0.520	0.084	0.487	0.198
	6–10 products	ß	1.038	11.428	3.689	62.922
	(Dummy; 1 = yes)	p	0.977	0.709	0.959	0.461
	11–25 products	ß	7.411	21.207	−81.104	72.101
	(Dummy; 1 = yes)	p	0.836	0.505	0.322	0.393
	26–49 products	ß	22.865	21.512	−35.225	41.596
	(Dummy; 1 = yes)	p	0.500	0.465	0.725	0.595
	50+ products	ß	10.853	28.055	−53.323	29.302
	(Dummy; 1 = yes)	p	0.757	0.346	0.735	0.757
1	Number of countries	ß	1.156	0.110	8.909	−1.286
		p	0.328	0.806	0.218	0.497
2	2–5 countries	ß	36.631	−12.052	−87.706	33.649
	(Dummy; 1 = yes)	p	0.589	0.332	0.244	0.608
	6–10 countries	ß	37.389	−16.784	−82.381	21.740
	(Dummy; 1 = yes)	p	0.553	0.327	0.313	0.670
	11–25 countries	ß	53.197	−12.181	18.060	41.994
	(Dummy; 1 = yes)	p	0.446	0.283	0.841	0.456
	26–49 countries	ß	74.966	−2.800	349.49	−31.079
	(Dummy; 1 = yes)	p	0.357	0.852	0.225	0.726
	50+ countries	ß	47.905	7.467	117.75	21.358
	(Dummy; 1 = yes)	p	0.622	0.845	0.706	0.824

Note: Dependent variable is profitability. ß is the estimated regression coefficient, p is the prob-value (based on heteroscedasticity consistent standard error estimates). All empirical models include the number of employees (also included in squares), a complete set of 4-digit industry control variables, and a constant. Reference group in Model 2 is made of firms that import one good and from one country, respectively.

4. Discussion

This paper uses a tailor-made newly available data set for enterprises from manufacturing industries in Germany to investigate for the first time the links between the extensive margins of imports (the number of imported goods and the number of countries imported from) and two dimensions of firm performance, productivity and profitability. In line with results from earlier studies it is found that productivity increases with both margins of imports, and that the estimated premia are large from an economic point of view in West Germany and in East Germany, and in the import crisis year 2009 and the import boom year 2010. These large productivity premia of firms that import more goods and from more countries does not lead to a positive link between the extensive margins of imports and profitability. The evidence suggests that productivity advantages of firms with larger extensive margins of imports are eaten up by extra costs related to buying more goods in more countries.

An open question that has not been dealt with in this paper is the potential role played by unobserved firm characteristics like management quality for the links between productivity or profitability of firms on the one hand and the extensive margins of import on the other hand. If these unobserved firm characteristics are correlated with the extensive margins the estimated regression coefficients are biased and any conclusions based on the estimates have to take this potentially large bias into account. A standard solution to take at least those unobserved factors into account that do not change over the period under investigation is the addition of fixed firm effect to an empirical model that is estimated for panel data that cover all years from these period. This, however, is not a feasible strategy here. As of today, the data for the extensive margins of imports are available for the years 2009 and 2010 only. Furthermore, these extensive margins tend to be highly persistent at the level of the enterprise. Estimates from fixed effects panel data models that are based on the variation of variables over time inside a firm only, therefore, are no panacea here.

That said, the reported statistically significant and economically non-negligible correlation between the productivity of a firm and the extensive margins of imports that goes hand in hand with no correlation at all between the profitability of a firm and these extensive margins should be regarded as an interesting new finding. This finding might motivate further investigations of the causes and consequences of differences in the diversification of imports over space and products in manufacturing firms.

References

Bartelsman, Eric and Mark Doms (2000). Understanding productivity: Lessons from longitudinal microdata. *Journal of Economic Literature* 38 (3), 569–594.

Bernard, Andrew, Bradford Jensen, Stephen J. Redding and Peter K. Schott (2012). The empirics of irm heterogeneity and international trade. *Annual Review of Economics* 4, 283–313.

European Commission (1998). Commission Regulation (EC) No. 2700/98 concerning the definitions of characteristics for structural business statistics, Brussels. *Official Journal of the European Communities* L344, 18/12/1998, 49–80.

Foster, Lucia, John Haltiwanger and Chad Syverson (2008). Reallocation, firm turnover, and efficiency: Selection on productivity or profitability? *American Economic Review* 98 (1), 394–425.

Fritsch, Michael, Bernd Görzig, Ottmar Hennchen and Andreas Stephan (2004). Cost structure surveys for Germany. *Journal of Applied Social Science Studies* 124 (4), 557–566.

Malchin, Anja and Ramona Voshage (2009). Official firm data for Germany. *Schmollers Jahrbuch/Journal of Applied Social Science Studies* 129 (3), 501–513.

Melitz, Marc and Stephen Redding (2014). Heterogeneous firms and trade. *Handbook of International Economics* 4, 1–54.

Schmalensee, Richard (1989). Inter-industry studies of structure and performance, In. Schmalensee, R./Willig, R.D. (Ed.), *Handbook of Industrial Organization*, Vol. 2, Amsterdam, North-Holland: Elsevier, 951–1009.

Statistisches Bundesamt (2012). Statistisches Jahrbuch 2012. *Wiesbaden: Statistisches Bundesamt.*

Syverson, Chad (2011). What determines productivity? *Journal of Economic Literature* 49 (2), 326–365.

Vogel, Alexander and Joachim Wagner (2010). Higher productivity in importing German manufacturing firms: Self-selection, learning from importing, or both? *Review of World Economics* 145 (4), 641–665.

Wagner, Joachim (2008). A note why more West than East German firms export. *International Economics and Economic Policy* 5 (4), 363–370.

Wagner, Joachim (2012a). International trade and firm performance: A survey of empirical studies since 2006. *Review of World Economics* 148 (2), 235–267.

Wagner, Joachim (2012b). Exports, imports and profitability: First evidence for manufacturing enterprises. *Open Economies Review* 23 (5), 747–765.

Wagner, Joachim (2012c). Productivity and the extensive margins of trade in German manufacturing firms: Evidence from a non-parametric test. *Economics Bulletin* 32 (4), 3061–3070.

Part 8

Distance and International Trade

Introduction

Transaction data at the firm-product-country of destination (origin) level have been used to estimate gravity-type equations to investigate empirically the role of distance for the quantity of good traded. Chapters 19 and 21 (originally published in Wagner, 2016a and 2017) report that, in line with stylized facts based on aggregate data, the quantity of exports and imports declines significantly with distance within a firm for a given product.

Chapters 20 and 22 (originally published as Wagner, 2016b and 2016c) look at the relation between the distance to countries of destination of exports and countries of origin of imports on the one hand and the quality of the goods traded on the other hand. It turns out that both export quality and import quality increase with distance after controlling for firm-product fixed effects. Distance-related trade costs lead to within-firm selection of product quality across countries of destination and countries of origin.

References

Wagner, Joachim (2016a). Distance-sensitivity of German imports: First evidence from firm-product level data. *Economics Bulletin* 36 (3),1275–1279.

Wagner, Joachim (2016b). Quality of firms' exports and distance to destination countries: First evidence from Germany. *Open Economies Review* 27 (4), 811–818.

Wagner, Joachim (2016c). Quality of firms' imports and distance to countries of origin: First evidence from Germany. *Economics Bulletin* 36 (1), 515–521.

Wagner, Joachim (2017). Distance-sensitivity of German exports: First evidence from firm-product level data. *Applied Economics Letters* 24 (3), 140–142.

Chapter 19

Distance-sensitivity of German Exports: First Evidence from Firm-product Level Data*

Abstract

This paper uses a tailor-made new data set of 7,580,251 observations for German exports at the firm-product-destination level to estimate a gravity equation and to investigate the link between the amount of firms' exports and the distance to destination countries. It is shown that, in line with stylized facts based on aggregate data, the quantity of exports declines significantly with distance within a firm for a given product.

Keywords: Exports, distance, gravity equation, Germany.

---

* Originally Published in *Applied Economics Letters* (2017), 24 (3), 140–142.
All computations were done at the Research Data Centre of the Federal Statistical Office in Wiesbaden. I thank Melanie Scheller for preparing the transaction level data for exports and for checking the output of my do-files for the violation of privacy. The micro data used are strictly confidential but not exclusive; see http://www.forschungsdatenzentrum.de/datenzugang.asp for information on how to access the data. To facilitate replications the Stata do-file used is available from the author on request.

1. Motivation

The negative effect of distance on international trade qualifies as a stylized fact that is presented to students at the very beginning of introductory textbooks on the subject; a one percent in distance between two countries is said to be typically associated with a fall of 0.7 to one percent in trade between those countries (Krugman *et al.*, 2015, p. 46). This distance effect is due to trade costs that tend to increase with the distance between the country of origin and the country of destination, including transportation costs (freight costs and time costs), information costs, language barriers, different currencies, legal and regulatory costs, and cultural distance.

Empirical estimates of the distance-sensitivity of trade usually are based on estimated gravity equations[1] that regress the (log of) trade between two countries on the (log of) distance between them plus a number of other variables that control for the size of the countries, the level of per capita income, whether a country is landlocked, and whether the countries share a common language or a common border, among others. Gravity equations are usually estimated with aggregate data at the country or sectoral level. Trade costs, however, that are behind the negative distance effect, can be expected to vary to a large amount between heterogeneous firms engaged in trade. For example, firms differ with regard to intercultural competence of their managers, knowledge of foreign languages of employees and experience of doing business with various destination countries. Furthermore, as Anderson and van Wincorp (2004, p. 747) point out, trade costs also vary widely across products lines. Therefore, trade costs related to distance can be expected to vary not only between a country of origin and different destination countries, but also between the different products traded between two countries and between firms engaged in these transactions. Estimates of the distance-sensitivity of exports, therefore, should control for these firm specific and product specific effects by including firm-product fixed

---

[1] A discussion of the gravity model and its relation to theoretical models of trade is far beyond the scope of this letter; see Head and Mayer (2014) for a comprehensive treatment. For a meta-analysis of 1,467 distance effects estimated in 103 papers; see Disdier and Head (2008).

effects. Identification of the regression coefficient of the distance variable then comes from the within-firm-product variation of export values across countries.

Estimates of the distance-sensitivity of exports that use transaction-level data at the firm-product-destination level and that control for firm-product fixed effects, however, are rare. To the best of my knowledge, the only exception is Bastos and Silva (2010) who report results for Portugal that show that export quantities decrease with distance when identification comes from the within-firm-product variation of export quantities across destination. This paper contributes to the literature by reporting comparable estimates for Germany, one of the most important actors on the world market for goods.

The rest of the paper is organized as follows. Section 2 discusses the data and measurement issues. Section 3 presents the results of the empirical investigation. Section 4 concludes.

2. Data and Measurement Issues

The empirical investigation uses a new tailor-made data set that combines high quality export data from official statistics with data on the distance between Germany and destination countries of exports plus other information for characteristics of the destination countries.

Data on exports are based on either the reports by German firms on transactions with firms from countries that are members of the European Union (EU) or on transaction-level data collected by the customs on trade with countries outside the EU. The raw data relate to one transaction of a German firm with a firm located outside Germany at a time. For a given year, the sum over all export transactions is identical to the figures published by the Federal Statistical Office for total exports of Germany.

The record of the transaction usually includes a firm identifier (tax registration number) of the trading firm. Using this identifier information at the transaction level can be aggregated at the level of the trading firm to generate year-firm-product-value-country data. These data show who trades how much of which good with customers from which country in a given year. Products are distinguished here according to the Harmonized System at 6-digit level (HS6).This paper uses data for the reporting year 2011.

The dependent variable in the empirical models is the value of exports of a (HS6) good by a firm to a destination country. The export value is regressed on the distance to the destination country and on a set of control variables.

Data on *distance to export destination* between Germany and the destination countries of exports are taken from the CEPII's *GeoDist* database (Mayer and Zignago, 2011). The "distw" — measure is used that calculates the distance between two countries based on bilateral distances between the biggest cities of those two countries, those inter-city distances being weighted by the share of the city in the overall country's population (see Mayer and Zignago, 2011, p. 11 for details).

The empirical models include a number of standard gravity variables as control variables (see Bustos and Silva, 2010):

Market size is proxied by the Gross Domestic Product (GDP) of the country of destination, measured in Millions of US Dollar in current prices. Information is taken from the World Bank World Development Indicators database (see http://data.worldbank.org/indicator/NY.GDP.MKTP.CD).

GDP per capita is measured in current prices and US Dollars. Data are from the International Monetary Fund's World Economic Outlook Data Base, April 2012 edition (see https://www.imf.org/external/pubs/ft/weo/2012/01/weodata/index.aspx).

Landlocked is a dummy-variables that takes the value 1 if a country has no direct access to the sea. Information is taken from the CEPII's *GeoDist* database (Mayer and Zignago, 2011).

Furthermore, two groups of trade partner countries are distinguished, namely countries that are *members of the* EU and non-EU countries. This controls for the different level of policy-made trade barriers that are absent for intra-EU trade.

3. Results

The empirical investigation uses 7,580,251 observations for the value of exports at the firm-product-destination level for the reporting year 2011.

These data cover 93.2 percent of total German exports of goods recorded in the official statistics.

For trade with the 26 EU-countries the number of observations is 4,148,699 that cover 59.5 percent of all exports included in this study. Data are from 46,880 firms that exported 4,949 products (recorded at the HS6-level) in 907,937 firm-product combinations. Data for exports to non-EU countries are for 3,431,552 observations from 106,096 firms that traded 4,900 different goods in 1,173,304 firm-product combinations with firms in 148 countries. A table with descriptive statistics for all variables is available on request.

To investigate the link between export quantity and the distance to destination countries separate regression models are estimated for observations on exports to firms from other EU-countries and to firms from non-EU countries with the log of export quantity as the endogenous variable and the log of distance to the destination country as exogenous variable. Following Bustos and Silva (2010), the model includes a set of control variables for further characteristics of the destination country (described in detail above), namely the log of GDP, the log of GDP per capita, and a dummy variable indicating whether the country is landlocked. To control for the role of firm and goods specific factors fixed effects at the firm-good level are included in the empirical models, too. Here, identification of the regression coefficient of the distance variable comes from the within-firm-product variation of export values across destination countries. Results are reported in Table 1.

The regression coefficient of log(distance) is an estimate of the elasticity of the quantity of firms' export with respect to distance to destination countries. According to the results, therefore, an increase in distance by one percent leads to a decrease of export quantity by 0.424 percent in intra-EU trade and by 0.248 percent in extra-EU trade, controlling for the size (measured by GDP) and the wealth (measured by GDP per capita) of the destination country and for the status of a landlocked country.[2] This means that doubling the distance is related to a

---

[2] Given that the control variables serve as controls only in the empirical models we do not comment on the results for the estimated regression coefficients.

Table 1: Quantity of firms' exports and characteristics of destination countries: Regression results.

		Dependent variable: log(quantity of exports)	
Destination country characteristic		EU-countries	Non-EU countries
log(distance)	ß	−0.424	−0.248
	p	0.000	0.000
log(GDP)	ß	0.486	0.380
	p	0.000	0.000
log(GDP per capita)	ß	−0.022	0.047
	p	0.064	0.000
Landlocked (Dummy variable)	ß	0.482	0.190
	p	0.000	0.000
Constant	ß	−9.861	−9.766
	p	0.000	0.000
Fixed effects: Firms * Goods		yes	yes
R^2		0.739	0.735
Number of observations		4,148,699	3,431,552

Note: OLS regressions. ß is the estimated regression coefficient, p is the prob-value (based on hetero-scedasticity-consistent standard errors clustered at the level of the exporting firm). For a detailed definition of the variables see text.

decrease in exports by some 40 percent inside the EU and by some 25 percent outside the EU.

4. Concluding Remarks

The bottom line, then, is that the link between the quantity of exports and the distance to destination countries is negative within firm-product export flows from Germany. This new evidence is in line with stylized facts based on aggregate data and with evidence reported for Portugal based on firm-product-destination data by Bastos and Silva (2010). Distance is not dead at all when it comes to exports of goods.

References

Anderson, James and Eric van Wincoop (2004). Trade Costs. *Journal of Economic Literature* 42 (3), 691–751.

Bastos, Paulo and Joana Silva (2010). The quality of a firm's exports: Where you export to matters. *Journal of International Economics* 82 (2), 99–111.

Disdier, Anne-Célia and Keith Head (2008). The puzzling persistence of the distance effect on bilateral trade. *Review of Economics and Statistics* 90 (1), 37–48.

Head, Keith and Thierry Mayer (2014). Gravity equations: Workhorse, toolkit, and cookbook. *Handbook of International Economics* 4, 131–195.

Krugman, Paul, Maurice Obstfeld and Marc J. Melitz (2015). *International Economics: Theory and Policy*, Tenth Edition. Boston: Pearson.

Mayer, Thierry and Soledad Zignago (2011). Notes on CEPII's distance measures: The GeoDist database. *CEPII Document de Travail No* 2011–25, December.

Chapter 20

Quality of Firms' Exports and Distance to Destination Countries: First Evidence from Germany*

Abstract

This paper uses a tailor-made new data set of 7,112,614 observations for export quality (measured by the unit value of exports) at the firm-product-destination level for German and the reporting year 2011. Data are from 119,280 firms that exported 4,986 products (recorded at the HS6-level) in 1,632,731 firm-product combinations to 174 countries. The paper investigates for the first time the link between the quality of firms' exports and the distance to destination countries for

*Originally Published in *Open Economies Reviews* (2016), 27 (4), 811–818.

This is a completely revised version of a working paper published in July 2014 (see Wagner, 2014a). I thank an anonymous referee for helpful comments. All computations were done at the Research Data Centre of the Federal Statistical Office in Wiesbaden. I thank Melanie Scheller for preparing the transaction level data for exports and for checking the output of my do-files for the violation of privacy. The micro data used are strictly confidential but not exclusive; see http://www.forschungsdatenzentrum.de/datenzugang.asp for information on how to access the data. To facilitate replications the Stata do-file used is available from the author on request.

Germany. It is shown that, in line with theory, the quality of exported goods and distance to destination countries are statistically positively correlated.

Keywords: Exports, export quality, distance, Germany.

1. Motivation

In a recently published paper Feenstra and Romalis (2014) present a theoretical model where firms, in addition to choosing the price, simultaneously choose quality subject to non-homothetic demand in an extended monopolistic competition framework. They show that in this model of endogenous quality choice by firms goods of higher quality are shipped over longer distances. This positive relationship between quality of exports and distance to destination countries follows from the first-order condition of firms for optimal quality choice (see Feenstra and Ronalis, 2014 for details). Bastos and Silva, 2010, p. 100 discuss other recent theoretical models that relate the quality of exported products to the distance of destination countries and argue that the systematic increase of unit values (used as proxy variables for the quality of goods) with distance is linked to self-selection of heterogeneous firms across destinations, with only higher quality producers entering more distant markets.

Empirical evidence on the relationship between quality of exports and distance to destination countries is scarce. Bastos and Silva (2010, p. 99) termed the quality of exports and its drivers "a relatively unexplored dimension of firms' cross-border activities". Using Portuguese firm-level data on exports by product and destination market from 2005, they find that export unit values (used as the proxy-variable for export quality) increase systematically with distance.

As yet, comparable evidence for Germany has not been reported in the literature. This can be considered as an important gap in knowledge for at least two reasons. First of all, Germany is one of the most important actors on the world market for goods.[1] Empirical evidence on the relation between export quality and distance to destination countries for this large

---

[1] According to the World Trade Organization's World Trade Report 2012 Germany hold rank 3 among the exporters of goods in 2011 with a share of 8.1 percent; see World Trade Organization (2012, p. 30).

"global player", therefore, is interesting in itself. Second, Germany is a high-wage economy, and the international competitiveness of goods produced in Germany is widely considered to depend on non-price factors, especially on product quality.[2] Further evidence on the role of quality of exported goods in shaping the spatial distribution of German exports, therefore, adds to our knowledge with regard to an important aspect of international competitiveness of German manufacturing firms.[3]

This paper uses a tailor-made new data set to investigate for the first time the link between the quality of a firm's exports and the distance to destination countries for Germany. To anticipate the most important result, in line with both the implications of the theoretical model by Feenstra and Romalis (2014) and other recent models, and with the empirical results reported for Portuguese firms by Bastos and Silva (2010), it is shown that the quality of exported goods and the distance to destination countries are statistically positively correlated.

The rest of the paper is organized as follows. Section 2 discusses the data and measurement issues. Section 3 presents the results of the empirical investigation. Section 4 concludes.

2. Data and Measurement Issues

The lack of empirical studies for Germany on the link between the distance to destination countries and the quality of exported goods is due to the fact that until most recently suitable data on exports at the firm-product-destination level that could be used in an econometric investigation were not available. The empirical investigation here uses a tailor-made data set that combines for the first time high quality export data from official statistics with data on the distance between Germany

---

[2] See the recent report by the Federal Ministry of Economics and Energy (Bundesministerium für Wirtschaft und Energie, 2014).

[3] Other aspects of the quality of exports by German firms discussed in recent papers are the role of high-quality goods for the international competitiveness of low-productive exporters (Wagner, 2014b), the relation between high-quality inputs and high-quality exports (Wagner, 2014c) and the links between firm profitability and quality of exports (Wagner, 2014d).

and destination countries of exports, plus other information for characteristics of the destination countries.

In Germany information on the goods exported and on the countries to which these goods are exported[4] is available from the statistic on foreign trade (*Außenhandelsstatistik*). This statistic is based on two sources. One source is the reports by German firms on transactions with firms from countries that are members of the European Union (EU); these reports are used to compile the so-called *Intrahandelsstatistik* on intra-EU trade. The other source is transaction-level data collected by the customs on trade with countries outside the EU (the so-called *Extrahandelsstatistik*).[5] The raw data that are used to build the statistic on foreign trade are transaction level data, i.e., they relate to one transaction of a German firm with a firm located outside Germany at a time. Published data from this statistic report exports aggregated at the level of goods traded and by country of destination.

The data used in this paper are based on the raw data at the transaction level. The unit of observation in these data is a single transaction between economic agents located in two countries, e.g., the export of X kilogram of *good A* with a value of Y Euro from Germany to China.[6] For a given year, the sum over all export transactions is identical to the figures published by the Federal Statistical Office for total exports of Germany.

The record of the transaction usually[7] includes a firm identifier (tax registration number) of the exporting firm. Using this identifier

---

[4] Note that in Germany information on international trade in services is compiled by the German Central Bank (*Deutsche Bundesbank*) to build the balance of services trade (*Dienstleistungsbilanz*).

[5] Note that firms with a value of exports to and imports from EU-countries that did not exceed 400,000 Euro in the previous year or in the current year do not have to report to the statistic on intra-EU trade. For trade with firms from non-member countries all transactions that exceed 1,000 Euro (or have a weight that exceeds 1,000 kilogram) are registered. For details see Statistisches Bundesamt, Qualitätsbericht Außenhandel, January 2011.

[6] Transaction level data of this type have been used in numerous empirical studies on international trade for many countries in recent years; see Wagner (2016) for a survey.

[7] Note that this identifier is missing for several transactions for various reasons including traders that do not have a (German) tax identification number; further details were not revealed to me.

information at the transaction level can be aggregated at the level of the trading firm to generate year-firm-product-value-weight-destination data. These data show who trades how much of which good with customers from which country in a given year. Products are distinguished according to very detailed classifications. In the data used for this paper, the Harmonized System at 6-digit level (HS6) is used as the product classification system.

For the reporting year 2011 the transaction level data at the firm-product-destination level were used to compute the *quality of exported goods* that is defined as the unit value of exports and that is computed as value of exports (measured in Euro) over quantity of exports (measured in kilogram). This measure of quality is widely used in the empirical literature. While it is far from perfect, it can be considered as a suitable proxy-variable, because the "unit values of internationally traded goods are heavily influenced by quality" (Feenstra and Romalis, 2014, p. 477).

Data on *distance to export destination* between Germany and the destination countries of exports are taken from the CEPII's *GeoDist* database (Mayer and Zignago, 2011). The "distw" — measure is used that calculates the distance between two countries based on bilateral distances between the biggest cities of those two countries, those inter-city distances being weighted by the share of the city in the overall country's population (see Mayer and Zignago, 2011, p. 11 for details).

The empirical models that link the quality of firms' exports to the distance to destination countries are estimated with a number of standard gravity variables as control variables, too (see Bustos and Silva, 2010):

Market size is proxied by the Gross Domestic Product (GDP) of the country of destination, measured in Millions of US-Dollar in current prices. Information is taken from the World Bank World Development Indicators database (see http://data.worldbank.org/indicator/NY.GDP.MKTP.CD).

GDP per capita is measured in current prices and U. S. dollars. Data are from the International Monetary Fund's World Economic Outlook Data Base, April 2012 edition (see https://www.imf.org/external/pubs/ft/weo/2012/01/weodata/index.aspx).

Landlocked is a dummy-variables that takes the value one if a country has no direct access to the sea. Information is taken from the CEPII's *GeoDist* database (Mayer and Zignago, 2011).

Furthermore, two groups of trade partner countries are distinguished, namely countries that are *members of the European Union* (EU) and Non-EU countries. This dummy variable takes on the value of one for EU-member countries, and it controls for the cut-off-point used when exports to EU-members are recorded (see footnote 5).

3. Results

The empirical investigation uses 7,112,614 observations for export quality (measured by the unit value of exports) at the firm-product-destination level for the reporting year 2011. Data are from 119,280 firms that exported 4,986 products (recorded at the HS6-level) in 1,632,731 firm-product combinations to 174 countries. The total export value covered by the transaction included in the estimation sample amounts to 507,396 Million Euro, 92.7 percent of the total German exports of goods recorded in the official statistics.[8]

Descriptive statistics for the variables are reported in Table 1. The distance index varies between 378 kilometers (which refers to exports to Luxembourg) and 18,220 kilometers (which refers to exports to New Zealand).[9] The index of export quality varies widely between less than one Euro per kilogram and more than 1,645 Euro per kilogram. Note, however, that these are unconditional descriptive statistics that do not control for the goods exported. Therefore, the large range between the top and the bottom of the value-to-weight ratio are no surprise — think, for example, of mobile phones and cement.

To investigate the link between export quality and the distance to destination countries a regression model is estimated based on 7,112,614

---

[8] Transactions without a firm identifier (see footnote 7) and with a weight below 0.5 kilogram (that is reported as zero in the original data, and for which a unit value could not be calculated) are excluded. Furthermore, information on some of the country characteristics is missing for some destination countries.

[9] Descriptive statistics are reported in logs (except for the dummy variables) because the variables enter the empirical models in logs, following the usual specification of gravity-models. Note that the minimum and maximum values of the variables cannot be reported because they (may) refer to a single firm and, therefore, this information is confidential. For the distance to destination countries, however, these values are known.

Table 1: Descriptive statistics.

	Mean	Std. Dev.	p1	p50	p99
log(export quality)	−10.557	1.734	−14.585	−10.585	−6.410
log(distance to destination)	7.336	1.084	5.935	6.944	9.676
log(GDP destination county)	13.051	1.550	9.224	13.170	16.558
log(GDP per capita dest. country)	10.054	1.057	7.091	10.385	11.640
Destination EU member (1 = yes)	0.548	0.500	0.000	1.000	1.000
Destination landlocked (1 = yes)	0.224	0.417	0.000	0.000	1.000
Number of observations	7,112,614				

Note: For a detailed definition of the variables see text. p1, p50 and p99 refer to the 1st, 50th and 99th percentile of the distribution of the variable (minima and maxima cannot be reported due to violation of privacy).

observations of export quality at the firm-product-destination level with the log of export quality as the endogenous variable and the log of distance to the destination country as exogenous variable. Following Bustos and Silva (2010), the model includes a set of control variables for further characteristics of the destination country (described in detail above), namely the log of GDP, the log of GDP per capita, a dummy variable indicating whether the country is a member of the EU, and a dummy variable indicating whether the country is landlocked. Four variants of the empirical model are estimated: without any fixed effects, with fixed effects for 4,986 goods (measured at the HS6-level), with fixed effects for 119,280 firms, and with 1,632,731 fixed effects at the firm-good level. Results are reported in Table 2.

The regression coefficient of log(distance) is an estimate of the elasticity of the quality of firms' export with respect to distance to destination countries. According to the results for Model 1, therefore, an increase in distance by one percent leads to an increase of export quality by 0.22 percent. This means that doubling the distance is related to an increase in quality by 22 percent.

Note that these figures are based on the results for Model 1 that does not control for the goods exported and for the exporting firms. Controlling

Table 2: Quality of firms' exports and distance to destination countries: Regression results.

Destination country characteristic		Dependent variable: log(quality of exports)			
		Model 1	Model 2	Model 3	Model 4
log(distance)	ß	0.2214	0.0831	0.0492	0.0118
	p	0.000	0.000	0.000	0.000
log(GDP)	ß	0.0509	0.0322	−0.0039	0.0016
	p	0.000	0.000	0.000	0.129
log(GDP per capita)	ß	0.0774	0.0490	0.0309	0.0188
	p	0.000	0.000	0.000	0.000
EU-member (Dummy variable)	ß	−0.0769	−0.1065	−0.0456	−0.0627
	p	0.000	0.000	0.000	0.000
Landlocked (Dummy variable)	ß	−0.0208	0.0151	−0.0075	0.0024
	p	0.000	0.000	0.000	0.250
Constant	ß	−13.5769	−12.0241	−11.1518	−10.8196
	p	0.000	0.000	0.000	0.000
Fixed effects: Goods ($N = 4,986$)		no	yes	no	no
Fixed effects: Firms ($N = 119,280$)		no	no	yes	no
Fixed effects: Firms * Goods ($N = 1,632,731$)		no	no	no	yes
R^2		0.0249	0.5728	0.4441	0.8579
Number of observations		7,112,614	7,112,614	7,112,614	7,112,614

Note: OLS regressions. ß is the estimated regression coefficient, p is the prob-value (based on heteroscedasticity-consistent standard errors clustered at the level of the exporting firm). For a detailed definition of the variables see text.

for goods by adding 4,986 fixed goods effects in Model 2 reduces the estimated positive effect of distance on export unit values considerably to less than a half. The regression coefficient of the distance variable here is solely identified from the within-goods variation of export quality between exporting firms. This points to sorting of heterogeneous firms across destination markets — firms with higher quality variants of the same good tend to serve more distant markets.

To test whether a positive effect of distance on export unit values also occurs within each firm (irrespective of the goods exported), Model 3 includes 119,280 firm fixed effects (but no goods fixed effects). The regression coefficient of the distance variable here is solely identified from the within-firm variation of export quality across destination countries. Results show that distance has also a positive effect on within-firm unit values of exports.

It is known that many German firms export more than one good and to more than one destination (see Wagner, 2012). Therefore, unit values are often not directly comparable within a firm across destinations. To control for this, Model 4 includes 1,632,731 firm-product fixed effects. Here, identification of the regression coefficient of the distance variable comes from the within-firm-product variation of unit values across destination countries (see Bustos and Silva, 2010). The results for Model 4 show that the effect of distance on export quality is positive, although the estimated elasticity is considerably smaller than in Models 2 and 3.

To put the results of the four empirical models into perspective, consider the following argument. When quality is measured by means of unit values, product level fixed effects need to be included. Otherwise, one would compare "quality" across different products whose unit values are hardly comparable. To illustrate this, think of sand. It is obvious that something with high weight and low value like sand will be subject to high transportation costs and, thus, will not be sent very far. This has nothing to do with quality. It is simply a matter of transportation costs for bulky items relative to the value of the item. Including product fixed effects in the empirical model takes care of this. Consider again Model 4 which includes firm-product fixed effects. The *within-firm-product variation of unit values across destination countries* identifies the regression coefficient of the distance variable. A positive regression coefficient, therefore, indicates a positive link between the quality of one specific product exported by one specific firm and the distance to the various destination countries where the firm exports this product to.

The bottom line, then, is that the link between the quality of exports and the distance to destination countries is positive — overall, within goods across firms, within firms across goods, and within firm-product export

354 International Trade in Goods: Evidence from Transaction Data

flows.[10] In line with results reported for Portugal by Bastos and Silva (2010), the positive effect of distance on export quality in Germany is not only due to sorting of firms across markets, but also a consequence of the within-firm-product variation of export unit-values across destination countries.

4. Concluding Remarks

Feenstra and Romalis (2014) present a theoretical model where firms, in addition to choosing the price, simultaneously choose quality subject to non-homothetic demand in an extended monopolistic competition framework. They show that in this model of endogenous quality choice by firms goods of higher quality are shipped over longer distances. Results of the empirical investigation presented in Section 3 are fully in line with the implication of the theoretical model by Feenstra and Romalis (2014) or other recent models that discuss the link between the quality of exported goods and the distance to destination countries, and with the empirical results reported for Portuguese firms by Bastos and Silva (2010). Following Bastos and Silva (2010, p. 105) this might indicate that trade costs — which are related to distance — lead to within-firm selection of product quality across destinations. Firms that produce multiple vertically-differentiated varieties of a product ship only higher quality varieties to more distant markets.

References

Bastos, Paulo and Joana Silva (2010). The quality of a firm's exports: Where you export to matters. *Journal of International Economics* 82 (2), 99–111.

Bundesministerium für Wirtschaft und Energie (2014). *Schlaglichter der Wirtschaftspolitik, Monatsbericht Mai 2014, Hintergründe zum deutschen Leistungsbilanzüberschuss*, pp. 19–23.

Feenstra, Robert and John Romalis (2014). International prices and endogeneous quality. *Quarterly Journal of Economics* 129 (2), 477–527.

---

[10] This holds in models without the control variables, too, where the estimated regression coefficients for the distance-variable are of the same size in Models 1, 2 and 3 from Table 2, while the coefficient in Model 4 is 0.0226 (which is about double the size of the model with controls). Given that the control variables serve as controls only in the empirical models we do not comment on the results for the estimated regression coefficients.

Mayer, Thierry and Soledad Zignago (2011). Notes on CEPII's distance measures: The GeoDist database. *CEPII Document de Travail No* 2011–25, December.

Wagner, Joachim (2012). Trading many goods with many countries: Exporters and importers from German manufacturing industries. *Review of Economics* 63 (2), 170–186.

Wagner, Joachim (2014a). A note on the quality of a firm's exports and distance to destination countries: First evidence from Germany. *Working Paper Series in Economics* 302, University of Lüneburg, Institute of Economics.

Wagner, Joachim (2014b). Low-productive exporters are high-quality exporters. Evidence from Germany. *Economics Bulletin* 34 (2), 745–756.

Wagner, Joachim (2014c). What makes a high-quality exporter? Evidence from Germany. *Economics Bulletin* 34 (2), 865–874.

Wagner, Joachim (2014d), Exports and firm profitability: Quality matters! *Economics Bulletin* 34 (3), 1644–1652.

Wagner, Joachim (2016). A survey of empirical studies using transaction level data on exports and imports. *Review of World Economics/Weltwirtschaftliches Archiv* 152 (1), 215–225.

World Trade Organization (2012). World Trade Report 2012. (Geneva: WTO Publications).

Chapter 21

Distance-sensitivity of German Imports: First Evidence from Firm-product Level Data*

Abstract

This paper uses a tailor-made new data set of 3,376,598 observations for German imports at the firm-product-country of origin level to estimate a gravity equation and to investigate the link between the amount of firms' imports and the distance to countries of origin. It is shown that, in line with stylized facts based on aggregate data, the quantity of imports declines significantly with distance within a firm for a given product.

Keywords: Imports, distance, gravity equation, Germany.

*Originally Published in *Economics Bulletin* (2016), 36 (3), 1275–1279.
I thank an anonymous referee for helpful comments. All computations were done at the Research Data Centre of the Federal Statistical Office in Wiesbaden. I thank Melanie Scheller for preparing the transaction level data for imports and for checking the output of my do-files for the violation of privacy. The micro data used are strictly confidential but not exclusive; see http://www.forschungsdatenzentrum.de/datenzugang.asp for information on how to access the data. To facilitate replications the Stata do-file used is available from the author on request.

1. Motivation

The negative effect of distance on international trade qualifies as a stylized fact. As Leamer (2007, p. 110) put it, "(t)here is very little that we economists fully understand about global trade but there is one thing that we know — commerce declines dramatically with distance". This distance effect is due to trade costs that tend to increase with the distance between the country of origin and the country of destination, including transportation costs (freight costs and time costs), information costs, language barriers, different currencies, legal and regulatory costs, and cultural distance.

Empirical estimates of the distance-sensitivity of trade usually are based on estimated gravity equations[1] that regress the (log of) trade between two countries on the (log of) distance between them plus a number of other variables that control for the size of the countries, the level of per capita income, whether a country is landlocked, and whether the countries share a common language or a common border, among others. Gravity equations are usually estimated with aggregate data at the country or sectoral level. Trade costs, however, that are behind the negative distance effect, can be expected to vary to a large amount between heterogeneous firms engaged in trade. For example, firms differ with regard to intercultural competence of their managers, knowledge of foreign languages of employees and experience of doing business with various countries. Furthermore, as Anderson and van Wincorp (2004, p. 747) point out, trade costs also vary widely across products lines. Therefore, trade costs related to distance can be expected to vary not only between an importing country and different countries of origin, but also between the different products traded between two countries and between firms engaged in these transactions. Estimates of the distance-sensitivity of imports, therefore, should control for these firm specific and product specific effects by including firm-product fixed effects. Identification of the

---

[1] A discussion of the gravity model and its relation to theoretical models of trade is far beyond the scope of this letter; see Head and Mayer (2014) for a comprehensive treatment. For a meta-analysis of 1,467 distance effects estimated in 103 papers; see Disdier and Head (2008).

regression coefficient of the distance variable then comes from the within-firm-product variation of import values across countries of origin.

For exports, there are two studies that apply this empirical strategy. Bastos and Silva (2010) report results for Portugal that show that export quantities decrease with distance when identification comes from the within-firm-product variation of export quantities across destination. Wagner (2017) shows that this is the case for exports by German firms, too. To the best of my knowledge, comparable estimates of the distance-sensitivity of imports are missing. This paper contributes to the literature by reporting such estimates for Germany, one of the most important actors on the world market for goods.

The rest of the paper is organized as follows. Section 2 discusses the data and measurement issues. Section 3 presents the results of the empirical investigation. Section 4 concludes.

2. Data and Measurement Issues

The empirical investigation uses a new tailor-made data set that combines high quality import data from official statistics with data on the distance between Germany and countries of origin of imports plus other information for characteristics of these countries.

Data on imports are based on either the reports by German firms on transactions with firms from countries that are members of the European Union (EU) or on transaction-level data collected by the customs on trade with countries outside the EU. The raw data relate to one transaction of a German firm with a firm located outside Germany at a time. For a given year, the sum over all import transactions is identical to the figures published by the Federal Statistical Office for total imports of Germany.

The record of the transaction usually includes a firm identifier (tax registration number) of the trading firm. Using this identifier information at the transaction level can be aggregated at the level of the trading firm to generate year-firm-product-value-country data. These data show who trades how much of which good with customers from which country in a given year. Products are distinguished here according to the Harmonized System at 6-digit level (HS6). This paper uses data for the reporting year 2011.

The dependent variable in the empirical models is the value of imports of a (HS6) good by a firm from a country of origin. The import value is regressed on the distance to the country of origin and on a set of control variables.

Data on *distance to import origin* between Germany and the countries of origin of imports are taken from the CEPII's *GeoDist* database (Mayer and Zignago, 2011). The "distw" — measure is used that calculates the distance between two countries based on bilateral distances between the biggest cities of those two countries, those inter-city distances being weighted by the share of the city in the overall country's population (see Mayer and Zignago, 2011, p. 11 for details).

The empirical models include a number of standard gravity variables as control variables (see Bustos and Silva, 2010, and Wagner, 2016):

Market size is proxied by the Gross Domestic Product (GDP) of the country of origin, measured in Millions of US Dollar in current prices. Information is taken from the World Bank World Development Indicators database (see http://data.worldbank.org/indicator/NY.GDP.MKTP.CD).

GDP per capita is measured in current prices and US Dollars. Data are from the International Monetary Fund's World Economic Outlook Data Base, April 2012 edition (see https://www.imf.org/external/pubs/ft/weo/2012/01/weodata/index.aspx).

Landlocked is a dummy-variables that takes the value 1 if a country has no direct access to the sea. Information is taken from the CEPII's *GeoDist* database (Mayer and Zignago, 2011).

Furthermore, two groups of trade partner countries are distinguished, namely countries that are *members of the* EU and non-EU countries. This controls for the different level of policy-made trade barriers that are absent for intra-EU trade.

3. Results

The empirical investigation uses 3,376,598 observations for the value of imports at the firm-product-country of origin level for the reporting year

2011. For trade with the EU-countries the number of observations is 1,332,507. Data are from 48,121 firms that imported 4,909 products (recorded at the HS6-level) in 795,228 firm-product combinations. Data for imports from non-EU countries are for 2,044,091 observations from 123,852 firms that traded 4,908 different goods in 1,432,235 firm-product combinations. A table with descriptive statistics for all variables is available on request.

To investigate the link between import quantity and the distance to the countries of origin separate regression models are estimated for observations on imports from other EU-countries and from non-EU countries with the log of import quantity as the endogenous variable and the log of distance to the country of origin as exogenous variable. Following Bustos and Silva (2010) and Wagner (2017), the model includes a set of control variables for further characteristics of the country of origin (described in detail above), namely the log of GDP, the log of GDP per capita, and a dummy variable indicating whether the country is landlocked. To control for the role of firm and goods specific factors fixed effects at the firm-good level are included in the empirical models, too. Here, identification of the regression coefficient of the distance variable comes from the within-firm-product variation of import values across countries of origin. Results are reported in Table 1.

The regression coefficient of log(distance) is an estimate of the elasticity of the quantity of firms' import with respect to distance to countries of origin. According to the results, therefore, an increase in distance by one percent leads to a decrease of import quantity by 0.271 percent in intra-EU trade and by 0.081 percent in extra-EU trade, controlling for the size (measured by GDP) and the wealth (measured by GDP per capita) of the country of origin and for the status of a landlocked country.[2] This means that doubling the distance is related to a decrease in imports by 27 percent inside the EU and by eight percent outside the EU. Note that these estimates are considerably smaller than comparable estimates for the distance-sensitivity of exports reported in Wagner (2017), where the respective figures are 42 percent for exports inside the EU and 25 percent for extra-EU exports.

---

[2] Given that the control variables serve as controls only in the empirical models we do not comment on the results for the estimated regression coefficients.

Table 1: Quantity of firms' imports and characteristics of countries of origin: Regression results.

Characteristics of country of origin		Dependent variable: log(quantity of imports)	
		EU-countries	Non-EU countries
log(distance)	ß	−0.271	−0.081
	p	0.000	0.003
log(GDP)	ß	0.249	0.325
	p	0.000	0.000
log(GDP per capita)	ß	−0.219	−0.077
	p	0.000	0.000
Landlocked (Dummy variable)	ß	0.134	0.705
	p	0.002	0.000
Constant	ß	−4.541	−10.015
	p	0.000	0.000
Fixed effects: Firms * Goods		yes	yes
R^2		0.432	0.802
Number of observations		1,332,507	2,044,091

Note: OLS regressions. ß is the estimated regression coefficient, p is the prob-value (based on heteroscedasticity-consistent standard errors clustered at the level of the importing firm). For a detailed definition of the variables see text.

4. Concluding Remarks

The bottom line, then, is that the link between the quantity of imports and the distance to countries of origin is negative within firm-product import flows to Germany. This empirical result is based on a gravity-type empirical model. As Anderson and van Wincoop (2003) point out in their seminal paper on gravity models, after controlling for size, trade between two countries is decreasing in their bilateral trade barrier relative to the *average* barrier of the two countries with all their trade partners. They refer to the theoretically appropriate average trade barrier as *multilateral resistance* (MR). Neglecting this issue leads to biased estimates of the coefficients of the variables in the gravity equation. Given that MR is unobserved, usually importer and exporter country — year fixed effects are included in the estimated equations as proxy variables for MR in order to obtain unbiased estimates (see e.g., Behar and Nelson, 2014, p. 543). With the cross section firm level data from Germany used in my study this approach is not feasible.

It might be the case that firms from more remote foreign countries supply less of a given good to German importers because these foreign firms are closer to other potential markets. The reason for the decline of the quantity of imports with distance within a firm for a given product then is not only the larger distance between Germany and the country of origin, but the smaller distance between the country of origin and other potential markets, too. The central result of the paper, however, that the quantity of imports declines significantly with distance within a firm for a given product is still valid.

This new evidence is in line with stylized facts based on aggregate data and with evidence for exports based on firm-product-destination data by Bastos and Silva (2010) for Portugal and by Wagner (2017) for Germany. Distance is not dead at all when it comes to international trade in goods.

References

Anderson, James E. and Eric van Wincoop (2003). Gravity with gravitas: A solution to the border puzzle. *American Economic Review* 93 (1), 170–192.

Anderson, James E. and Eric van Wincoop (2004). Trade costs. *Journal of Economic Literature* 42 (3), 691–751.

Bastos, Paulo and Joana Silva (2010). The quality of a firm's exports: Where you export to matters. *Journal of International Economics* 82 (2), 99–111.

Behar, Alberto and Benjamin D. Nelson (2014). Trade flows, multilateral resistance, and firm heterogeneity. *Review of Economics and Statistics* 96 (3), 538–549.

Disdier, Anne-Célia and Keith Head (2008). The puzzling persistence of the distance effect on bilateral trade. *Review of Economics and Statistics* 90 (1), 37–48.

Head, Keith and Thierry Mayer (2014). Gravity equations: Workhorse, toolkit, and cookbook. *Handbook of International Economics* 4, 131–195.

Leamer, Edward (2007). A flat world, a level playing field, a small world after all, or none of the above? A review of Thomas L. Friedman's The World is Flat. *Journal of Economic Literature* 45 (1), 83–126.

Mayer, Thierry and Soledad Zignago (2011). Notes on CEPII's distance measures: The GeoDist database. *CEPII Document de Travail No* 2011–25, December.

Wagner, Joachim (2017). Distance-sensitivity of German exports: First evidence from firm-product level data. *Applied Economics Letters* 24 (3), 140–142.

Chapter 22

Quality of Firms' Imports and Distance to Countries of Origin: First Evidence from Germany*

Abstract

This paper documents a new fact: The quality of goods imported by German firms increases with distance to the countries of origin. This holds after controlling for fixed effects for goods, for firms, and for firm-product combinations. The empirical investigation uses a tailor-made new data set of 3,204,851 observations for import quality (measured by the unit value of imports) at the firm-product-origin level for the reporting year 2011. Data are from 138,688 firms that imported 4,986 products (recorded at the HS6-level) in 1,938,602 firm-product combinations from 175 countries. Trade costs — which are related to distance — lead to

*Originally Published in *Economics Bulletin* (2016), 36 (1), 515–521.

Many thanks to two anonymous reviewers for helpful comments on an earlier version. All computations were done at the Research Data Centre of the Federal Statistical Office in Wiesbaden. I thank Melanie Scheller for preparing the transaction level data for imports and for checking the output of my do-files for the violation of privacy. The micro data used are strictly confidential but not exclusive; see http://www.forschungsdatenzentrum.de/ datenzugang.asp for information on how to access the data. To facilitate replications the Stata do-file used is available from the author on request.

within-firm selection of product quality across countries of origin. Firms that import multiple vertically-differentiated varieties of a product source higher quality varieties on more distant markets.

Keywords: Imports, import quality, distance, Germany.

1. Motivation

The quality of internationally traded goods can be considered as a key characteristic of exports and imports. Empirical evidence on this dimension of trade, however, tends to be scarce. The quality of traded goods and its drivers are a relatively unexplored dimension of firms' cross-border activities. While we have some evidence that export unit values (used as the proxy-variable for export quality) increase systematically with distance to destination countries from studies using data for Portugal (Bastos and Silva, 2010) and Germany (Wagner, 2016a), to the best of my knowledge comparable evidence for imports has not been reported in the literature.

This can be considered as an important gap in knowledge. For exports, the positive effect of distance on export quality reported for Portugal and Germany is not only due to sorting of firms across markets, but also a consequence of the within-firm-product variation of export unit-values across countries of destination. Trade costs — which are related to distance — lead to within-firm selection of product quality across countries of destination. Firms that export multiple vertically-differentiated varieties of a product sell higher quality varieties on more distant markets. Does the same hold for imports? Do firms that import multiple vertically-differentiated varieties of a product buy varieties of a higher quality on more distant markets? Empirical evidence on this might contribute to our understanding of the structure of trade in goods and of the geographical structure of this trade. The case of Germany is especially interesting here because Germany is one of the most important actors on the world market for goods.[1] Empirical evidence on the relation between import quality and distance to countries of origin for this large "global player", therefore, is

---

[1] According to the World Trade Organization's World Trade Report 2014 Germany hold rank three among the importers of goods in 2013 with a share of 6.3 percent; see World Trade Organization (2014, p. 34).

interesting in itself. Furthermore, facts that are revealed on this topic might be useful as a benchmark for the formulation of the assumptions used in theoretical models of models for firms trade variants of goods as importers and exporters on different markets.

This paper contributes to the literature by documenting a new fact: The quality of goods imported by German firms increases with distance to the countries of origin. This holds after controlling for fixed effects for goods and for firm-product combinations. Trade costs — which are related to distance — lead to within-firm selection of product quality across countries of origin. Firms that import multiple vertically-differentiated varieties of a product buy higher quality varieties on more distant markets.

The rest of the paper is organized as follows. Section 2 discusses the data used. Section 3 presents the results of the empirical investigation. Section 4 concludes.

2. Data and Measurement Issues

The lack of empirical studies for Germany on the link between the distance to countries of origin and the quality of imported goods is due to the fact that until most recently suitable data on imports at the firm-product-origin level that could be used in an econometric investigation were not available. The empirical investigation here uses a tailor-made data set that combines for the first time high quality import data from official statistics with data on the distance between Germany and countries of origin of imports, plus other information for characteristics of the countries of origin.

In Germany information on the goods imported and on the countries from which these goods are imported[2] is available from the statistic on foreign trade (*Außenhandelsstatistik*). This statistic is based on two sources. One source is the reports by German firms on transactions with firms from countries that are members of the European Union (EU); these reports are

---

[2] Note that in Germany information on international trade in services is compiled by the German Central Bank (*Deutsche Bundesbank*) to build the balance of services trade (*Dienstleistungsbilanz*).

used to compile the so-called *Intrahandelsstatistik* on intra-EU trade. The other source is transaction-level data collected by the customs on trade with countries outside the EU (the so-called *Extrahandelsstatistik*).[3] The raw data that are used to build the statistic on foreign trade are transaction level data, i.e., they relate to one transaction of a German firm with a firm located outside Germany at a time. Published data from this statistic report imports aggregated at the level of goods traded and by country of origin.

The data used in this paper are based on the raw data at the transaction level. The unit of observation in these data is a single transaction between economic agents located in two countries, e.g., the import of X kilogram of *good A* with a value of Y Euro from China to Germany.[4] For a given year, the sum over all import transactions is identical to the figures published by the Federal Statistical Office for total imports of Germany.

The record of the transaction usually includes a firm identifier (tax registration number) of the importing firm.[5] Using this identifier information at the transaction level can be aggregated at the level of the trading firm to generate year-firm-product-value-weight-origin data. These data show who trades how much of which good with suppliers from which country in a given year. Products are distinguished according to very detailed classifications. In the data used for this paper, the Harmonized System at 6-digit level (HS6) is used as the product classification system.

For the reporting year 2011 the transaction level data at the firm-product-origin level were used to compute the *quality of imported goods* that is defined as the unit value of imports and that is computed as value of imports (measured in Euro) over quantity of imports (measured in kilogram). This measure of quality is widely used in the empirical

---

[3] Note that firms with a value of imports to and imports from EU-countries that did not exceed 400,000 Euro in the previous year or in the current year do not have to report to the statistic on intra-EU trade. For trade with firms from non-member countries all transactions that exceed 1,000 Euro (or have a weight that exceeds 1,000 kilogram) are registered. For details see Statistisches Bundesamt, Qualitätsbericht Außenhandel, January 2011.

[4] Transaction level data of this type have been used in numerous empirical studies on international trade for many countries in recent years; see Wagner (2016b) for a survey.

[5] Note that this identifier is missing for several transactions for various reasons including traders that do not have a (German) tax identification number; further details were not revealed to me.

literature. While it is far from perfect, it can be considered as a suitable proxy-variable, because the "unit values of internationally traded goods are heavily influenced by quality" (Feenstra and Romalis, 2014, p. 477).

Note that the import values are the so-called "statistical values" which is the value of an imported good at the German border without any tariffs, taxes and other duties. Transport costs like shipping charges, therefore, are included. This could be a problem here, but according to managers active in international trade direct transport costs tend to be minimal due to the low per-item transport costs, especially when imports are shipped in containers. The most important dimension of transport costs for import tends to be the time that it takes to transport goods from a country of origin to Germany. This kind of transport cost is not included in import values.

Data on *distance to countries of origin* between Germany and the countries of origin of imports are taken from the CEPII's *GeoDist* database (Mayer and Zignago, 2011). The "distw" — measure is used that calculates the distance between two countries based on bilateral distances between the biggest cities of those two countries, those inter-city distances being weighted by the share of the city in the overall country's population (see Mayer and Zignago, 2011, p. 11 for details).

The empirical models that link the quality of firms' imports to the distance to countries of origin are estimated with a number of standard gravity variables as control variables (see Bustos and Silva, 2010):

Market size is proxied by the Gross Domestic Product (GDP) of the country of origin, measured in Millions of US Dollar in current prices. Information is taken from the World Bank World Development Indicators database (see http://data.worldbank.org/indicator/NY.GDP.MKTP.CD).

GDP per capita is measured in current prices and US Dollars. Data are from the International Monetary Fund's World Economic Outlook Data Base, April 2012 edition (see https://www.imf.org/external/pubs/ft/weo/2012/01/weodata/index.aspx).

Landlocked is a dummy-variables that takes the value 1 if a country has no direct access to the sea. Information is taken from the CEPII's *GeoDist* database (Mayer and Zignago, 2011).

Furthermore, two groups of trade partner countries are distinguished, namely countries that are members of the EU and non-EU countries.

This dummy variable takes on the value of one for EU-member countries, and it controls for the cut-off-point used when imports to EU-members are recorded.

3. Results

The empirical investigation uses 3,204,815 observations for import quality (measured by the unit value of imports) at the firm-product-origin level for the reporting year 2011. Data are from 138,688 firms that imported 4,986 products (recorded at the HS6-level) in 1,938,602 firm-product combinations from 175 countries. The total import value covered by the transaction included in the estimation sample amounts to 416,265 Million Euro, 86.4 percent of the total German imports of goods recorded in the official statistics.[6]

Descriptive statistics for the variables are reported in Table 1. The distance varies between 378 kilometers (which refers to imports from Luxembourg) and 18,220 kilometers (which refers to imports from New Zealand).[7] The index of import quality varies widely between less than one Euro per kilogram and more than 1,865 Euro per kilogram. Note, however, that these are unconditional descriptive statistics that do not control for the goods imported. Therefore, the large range between the top and the bottom of the value-to-weight ratio are no surprise — think, for example, of mobile phones and cement.

To investigate the link between import quality and the distance to countries of origin a regression model is estimated based on 3,204,805 observations of import quality at the firm-product-origin level with the log of import quality as the endogenous variable and the log of distance to the country of origin as exogenous variable. Following Bastos and Silva

---

[6] Transactions without a firm identifier (see footnote 5) and with a weight below 0.5 kilogram (that is reported as zero in the original data, and for which a unit value could not be calculated) are excluded. Furthermore, information on some of the country characteristics is missing for some countries of origin.

[7] Descriptive statistics are reported in logs (except for the dummy variables) because the variables enter the empirical models in logs, following the usual specification of gravity-models. Note that the minimum and maximum values of the variables cannot be reported because they (may) refer to a single firm and, therefore, this information is confidential. For the distance to countries of origin, however, these values are known.

Table 1: Descriptive statistics.

	Mean	Std. Dev.	p1	p50	p99
log(import quality)	−10.829	1.856	−14.914	−10.874	−6.284
log(distance to origin)	7.671	1.252	5.938	7.394	9.308
log(GDP county of origin)	14.224	1.509	10.599	14.143	16.558
log(GDP per capita country of origin)	10.073	1.100	7.225	10.561	11.304
Origin EU member (1 = yes)	0.406	0.491	0.000	0.000	1.000
Origin landlocked (1 = yes)	0.174	0.379	0.000	0.000	1.000
Number of observations	3,204,815				

Note: For a detailed definition of the variables see text. p1, p50 and p99 refer to the 1st, 50th and 99th percentile of the distribution of the variable (minima and maxima cannot be reported due to violation of privacy).

(2010), the model includes a set of control variables for further characteristics of the country of origin (described in detail above), namely the log of GDP, the log of GDP per capita, a dummy variable indicating whether the country is a member of the EU, and a dummy variable indicating whether the country is landlocked. Two variants of the empirical model are estimated: Model 1 includes fixed effects for 4,986 goods (measured at the HS6-level), and Model 2 includes 1,938,602 fixed effects at the firm-good level. Results are reported in Table 2.

The regression coefficient of log(distance) is an estimate of the elasticity of the quality of firms' imports with respect to distance to countries of origin. According to the results for Model 1, therefore, an increase in distance by one percent leads to an increase of import quality by 0.1 percent. This means that doubling the distance is related to an increase in quality by 10 percent. The regression coefficient of the distance variable here is solely identified from the within-goods variation of import quality between importing firms. This points to sorting of heterogeneous firms across markets of origin — firms that import higher quality variants of the same good tend to buy from more distant markets.

Table 2: Quality of firms' imports and distance to countries of origin: Regression results.

Characteristics of country of origin		Dependent variable: log(quality of imports)	
		Model 1	Model 2
log(distance)	ß	0.104	0.038
	p	0.000	0.000
log(GDP)	ß	0.005	0.001
	p	0.021	0.493
log(GDP per capita)	ß	0.277	0.126
	p	0.000	0.000
EU-member (Dummy variable)	ß	0.040	0.052
	p	0.000	0.000
Landlocked (Dummy variable)	ß	0.095	0.048
	p	0.000	0.000
Constant	ß	−14.516	−12.439
	p	0.000	0.000
Fixed effects: Goods ($N = 4{,}986$)		yes	no
Fixed effects: Firms ∗ Goods ($N = 1{,}938{,}602$)		no	yes
R^2		0.559	0.890
Number of observations		3,204,815	3,204,815

Note: OLS regressions. ß is the estimated regression coefficient, p is the prob-value (based on heteroscedasticity-consistent standard errors clustered at the level of the importing firm). For a detailed definition of the variables see text.

It is known that many German firms import more than one good and from more than one country of origin (see Wagner, 2012). Therefore, unit values are often not directly comparable within a firm across origins. To control for this, Model 2 includes 1,938,602 firm-product fixed effects. Here, identification of the regression coefficient of the distance variable comes from the within-firm-product variation of unit values across countries of origin. The results for Model 2 show that the effect of distance on import quality is positive, although the estimated elasticity is considerably smaller than in Model 1.

4. Concluding Remarks

The bottom line, then, is that the link between the quality of imports and the distance to countries of origin is positive — within goods across firms and within firm-product import flows. In line with results reported for exports for Portugal by Bastos and Silva (2010) and for Germany by Wagner (2016a), this positive effect of distance on import quality is not only due to sorting of firms across markets, but also a consequence of the within-firm-product variation of import unit-values across countries of origin. This might indicate that trade costs — which are related to distance — lead to within-firm selection of product quality across countries of origin. Firms that import multiple vertically-differentiated varieties of a product source higher quality varieties on more distant markets.

References

Bastos, Paulo and Joana Silva (2010). The quality of a firm's exports: Where you export to matters. *Journal of International Economics* 82 (2), 99–111.

Feenstra, Robert and John Romalis (2014). International prices and endogeneous quality. *Quarterly Journal of Economics* 129 (2), 477–527.

Mayer, Thierry and Soledad Zignago (2011). Notes on CEPII's distance measures: The GeoDist database. *CEPII Document de Travail No* 2011–25, December.

Wagner, Joachim (2012). Trading many goods with many countries: Exporters and importers from German manufacturing industries. *Review of Economics* 63 (2), 170–186.

Wagner, Joachim (2016a). Quality of firms' exports and distance to destination countries: First evidence from Germany. *Open Economics Review* 27 (4), 811–818.

Wagner, Joachim (2016b). A survey of empirical studies using transaction level data on exports and imports. *Review of World Economics/Weltwirtschaftliches Archiv* 152 (1), 215–225.

World Trade Organization (2014). World Trade Report 2014. (Geneva: WTO Publications).

Part 9

The Lumpiness
of International Trade

Introduction

In Chapter 23 (originally published as Wagner, 2016) transaction level data are used to look at a hitherto neglected extensive margin of international trade by investigating for the first time the frequency at which German exporters and importers trade a given good with a given country. Imports and exports show a high degree of lumpiness. In a given year about half of all firm-good-country combinations are recorded only once or twice for trade with EU-countries, and this is the case for more than 60 percent of all firm-good-country combinations in trade with non-EU countries. The frequency of recorded transactions tends to decline with an increase in the number of transactions per year. This is in accordance with the presence of per-shipment fixed costs that provide an incentive for trading firms to engage in cross-border transactions infrequently. Empirical models show that for Germany the frequency of transactions at the firm-good-country level tends to decrease with an increase in per-shipment costs when unobserved firm and goods characteristics are controlled for.

In a companion paper reprinted in Chapter 24 (that was originally published as Wagner, 2017) a difference-in-differences approach is applied to test the hypothesis that the increase in the per-shipment costs of imports from Japan due to the Fukushima disaster in 2011 lead to an increase in the lumpiness of imports from Japan. Using China and the USA as control groups it is found that the Fukushima trade cost shock reduced the average number of import transactions per year at the firm-good level and, therefore, increased the degree of lumpiness of imports from Japan.

References

Wagner, Joachim (2016). The lumpiness of German exports and imports of goods. *Economics — The Open-Access Open-Assesment E-Journal* 10, 2016–21.

Wagner, Joachim (2017). Trade costs shocks and lumpiness of imports: Evidence from the Fukushima disaster. *Economics Bulletin* 37 (1), 149–155

Chapter 23

The Lumpiness of German Exports and Imports of Goods*

Abstract

This paper looks at a hitherto neglected extensive margin of international trade by investigating for the first time the frequency at which German exporters and importers trade a given good with a given country. Imports and exports show a high degree of lumpiness. In a given year about half of all firm-good-country combinations are recorded only once or twice for trade with EU-countries, and this is the case for more than 60 percent of all firm-good-country combinations in trade with non-EU countries. The frequency of recorded transactions tends to decline with an increase in the number of transactions per year. This is in accordance with the presence of per-shipment fixed costs that provide an incentive for trading

*Originally Published in *Economics — The Open-Access Open-Assesment E-Journal* 10 (2016), 2016–2021.

I thank Horst Raff for introducing me to the concept of lumpiness of trade and two anonymous referees for suggesting changes that helped to improve an earlier version of the paper. All computations were done at the Research Data Centre of the Federal Statistical Office in Wiesbaden. I thank Melanie Scheller for preparing the transaction level data and for checking the output of my do-files for the violation of privacy. The micro data used are strictly confidential but not exclusive; see http://www.forschungsdatenzentrum.de/datenzugang.asp for information on how to access the data. To facilitate replications the Stata do-files used are available from the author on request.

firms to engage in cross-border transactions infrequently. Empirical models show that for Germany the frequency of transactions at the firm-good-country level tends to decrease with an increase in per-shipment costs when unobserved firm and goods characteristics are controlled for.

Keywords: Lumpiness of trade, imports, exports, Germany.

1. Motivation

International trade is costly. While tariff-type trade restrictions tend to play a diminishing role only today, other barriers to trade still matter. Hornok and Koren (2015a) argue that some of these trade costs are not proportional to the value of the transaction. Hence, the assumption of iceberg-type trade costs used in most models of international trade is not appropriate here. There are fixed costs that come with every shipment across borders. These costs include paper work (filling in customs declarations and other forms) and the time and monetary costs related to having the cargo inspected. These fixed costs lead to a trade-off between per-shipment trade costs and shipping frequency. On the one hand, firms engaged in international trade would like to economize on these per-shipment costs by sending fewer and larger shipments. On the other hand, this comes at a cost due to time-lags related to waiting to fill a larger shipment and because of the need to keep costly inventories between shipment arrivals. At the firm level, shipping frequency can be considered as an additional margin of trade besides the intensive margin (the volume of trade) and the extensive margins made of the number of goods traded and the number of countries traded with (see Békés *et al.*, 2011).

That said, per-shipment costs may make it optimal for traders to engage in cross-border transactions infrequently. If this is the case, trade flows at the microeconomic level — imports by one firm of one good from one country of origin, or exports by one firm of one good to one country of destination — are lumpy. Empirical evidence on the lumpiness of international trade has been reported in a small number of studies. Alessandria *et al.* (2010) use monthly data on the universe of US exports for goods in narrowly defined categories to six destination countries from January 1990 to April 2005 and find that goods are traded infrequently over the course of a year. Exports are lumpy, trade is highly concentrated in a few months. Békés *et al.* (2015) explore transaction level data for exports from France in 2007 at the firm-product-destination level and approximate the number of shipments by the number of months within a year in which a transaction is recorded for a given firm-product-destination. A large number of firms ship their products only in a few months. The authors report a high degree of lumpiness in exports — almost 45 percent of firms ship a given product to a given destination only once a year to EU markets and more that 60 percent do so to extra-EU markets. Hornok and Koren (2015a) examine disaggregated data on exports of the United States and Spain in 2009 and look at the lumpiness of trade transactions by documenting how frequently the same good is exported to the same destination country within a year. Trade transactions for a given product to a given destination show strong signs of lumpiness. Kropf and Sauré (2014) look at transaction level data for Swiss exports from 2007, a subset of which contains a firm identifier so that export data are at the firm-product-destination level. Exports are lumpy; the mean value of shipments per year is 3.5.

Hornok and Koren (2015a) investigate how the frequency and the size of shipments vary with the level of per-shipment costs. They estimate a number of gravity-like regressions (that include variables for GDP and GDP per capita of destination countries, and distance to destination countries of exports, among others, as control variables) for exports of the US and Spain at the product-country level and find that the number of shipments decrease ceteris paribus when the time costs or the monetary costs per shipment increase.

Up to now, we have no evidence on the degree of lumpiness of international trade in goods by German firms and its relation to per-shipment costs. Given that Germany is one of the leading actors on the world market for goods (according to the WTO's World Trade Report, it was number three in both exports and imports in 2013; see World Trade Organization (2014, p. 34), empirical evidence here is interesting in itself. This paper contributes to the literature by providing such evidence based on transaction data for complete German exports and imports at the firm-good-country level for the years 2009 to 2012.

To anticipate the most import results I document that imports and exports show a high degree of lumpiness. In a given year about half of all firm-good-country combinations are recorded only once or twice for trade with EU-countries, and this is the case for more than 60 percent of all firm-good-country combinations in trade with non-EU countries. Empirical models show that the frequency of transactions at the firm-good-country level tends to decrease with an increase in per-shipment costs when unobserved firm and goods characteristics are controlled for.

The rest of the paper is organized as follows. Section 2 introduces the data used and discusses measurement issues. Section 3 reports descriptive results for the lumpiness of German exports and imports of goods. Section 4 presents results from regressions of the number of shipments on per-shipment costs. Section 5 concludes.

2. Data and Measurement Issues

The empirical investigation uses a tailor-made data set that combines high quality transaction level data on Germany's exports and imports of goods from official statistics with data on per-shipment costs in international trade plus other information for characteristics of the countries traded with.

In Germany information on goods[1] traded across borders and on the countries traded with is available from the statistic on foreign trade (*Außenhandelsstatistik*). This statistic is based on two sources. One source is the reports by German firms on transactions with firms from countries that are members of the EU; these reports are used to compile the so-called *Intrahandelsstatistik* on intra-EU trade. The other source is transaction-level data collected by the customs on trade with countries outside the EU (the so-called *Extrahandelsstatistik*).[2] The raw data that are

---

[1] Note that in Germany information on international trade in services is compiled by the German Central Bank (*Deutsche Bundesbank*) to build the balance of services trade (*Dienstleistungsbilanz*).

[2] Note that firms with a value of trade with EU-countries that did not exceed 400,000 Euro in the previous year or in the current year per direction of trade do not have to report to the statistic on intra-EU trade. For trade with firms from non-member countries all transactions that exceed 1,000 Euro (or have a weight that exceeds 1,000 kilogram) are registered. For details see Statistisches Bundesamt, Qualitätsbericht Außenhandel, January 2011.

used to build the statistic on foreign trade are transaction level data, i.e., they relate to one transaction of a German firm with a firm located outside Germany at a time. Published data from this statistic report exports and imports aggregated at the level of goods traded and by country of origin.

The data used in this paper are based on the raw data at the transaction level. The unit of observation in these raw data is a single transaction between economic agents located in two countries, e.g., the import of X kilogram of *good A* with a value of Y Euro from China to Germany.[3] For a given year, the sum over all transactions is identical to the figures published by the Federal Statistical Office for total exports or imports of Germany.

The record of the transaction usually includes a firm identifier (tax registration number) of the trading German firm.[4] Using this identifier information at the transaction level can be aggregated at the level of the trading firm. These data show which firm trades how much of which good with firms from which country in a given month. Products are distinguished according to very detailed classifications. In the data used for this paper, the Harmonized System at 6-digit level (HS6) is used as the product classification system.

For the reporting years 2009 to 2012 the transaction level data at the month- firm-product-country level were used to compute a proxy-variable for the frequency of export or import transactions by one firm for one HS6-good and one country in a year. This proxy-variable is given by the number of months in a year in which transactions of this firm-good-country combination are recorded. Note that within a month all exports or imports of a specific HS6-good to a specific country by a firm are aggregated and reported as one data point only. Therefore, the proxy for trade frequency used here may be biased for high frequency traders which trade the same good with the same country in (nearly) every month several times. For low frequency traders, however, the number of months with

---

[3] Transaction level data of this type have been used in numerous empirical studies on international trade for many countries in recent years; see Wagner (2016) for a survey.

[4] Note that this identifier is missing for several transactions for various reasons including traders that do not have a (German) tax identification number; further details were not revealed to me.

recorded transactions is a reliable approximation (see the discussion in Békés *et al.*, 2015).

The transaction level data at the firm-good-country level were matched to country-specific information that is taken from two sources.

Information on two types of *per-shipment trade costs* is taken from the World Bank's Doing Business Data Base (see www.doingbusiness.org). *Doing Business* measures the time and cost (excluding tariffs) necessary to complete every official procedure that is needed for exporting and importing a standardized cargo of goods by ocean transport. Time is recorded in calendar days, costs are in US Dollars; for details see Appendix.[5]

Note that the time and cost of ocean transport are not included in the cost indicators from the Doing Business data base. The time dimension of transport can be considered as another per-shipment cost — it takes *X* days to ship a container from Germany to *country Y*, irrespective of the amount of goods in this container. Time for transport is closely linked to distance between countries. Therefore, distance is included as another trade cost variable. Data on *distance* between Germany and the countries of origin of imports, and the countries of destination of exports, are taken from the CEPII's *GeoDist* database (Mayer and Zignago, 2011). The "distw" — measure is used that calculates the distance between two countries based on bilateral distances between the biggest cities of those two countries, those inter-city distances being weighted by the share of the city in the overall country's population (see Mayer and Zignago, 2011, p. 11 for details).

The empirical models that link the number of international trade transactions at the firm-good-country level to per-shipment costs of trade include two control variables that are standard in gravity models of trade, namely *Gross National Income* and *per capita Gross National Income* (see Hornok and Koren, 2015a for a similar approach). Gross National Income per capita (measured in current US Dollar) is taken from the Doing Business database directly, Gross National Income is

---

[5] Data from the World Bank's Doing Business database have been used in the literature on the lumpiness of international trade before; see Alessandria *et al.* (2010) and Hornok and Koren (2015a; 2015b).

calculated from the per capita values and the size of the population reported in the data base.[6]

In the empirical study two groups of trade partner countries are distinguished, namely countries that are members of the EU and non-EU countries. This controls for the cutoff-point used when imports from and exports to EU-members are recorded. Furthermore, information on per-shipment costs is not relevant for intra-EU trade.

3. The Lumpiness of German Exports and Imports: Descriptive Evidence

The degree of lumpiness of trade is measured by the number of import or export transactions at the firm-product-country level. In the German trade data used here trade frequency is measured by the number of months in a year in which transactions of this firm-good-country combination are recorded. Note that within a month all exports or imports of a specific HS6-good to or from a specific country by one single firm are aggregated and reported as one data point only. Therefore, the proxy for trade frequency used here may be biased for high frequency traders which trade the same good with the same country in (nearly) every month several times. For low frequency traders, however, the number of months with recorded transactions is a reliable approximation (see the discussion in Békés *et al.*, 2015).

That said, information on the lumpiness of German trade in goods is reported in Tables 1 to 8. All data are for the reporting year 2012.[7] Information is provided for trade with EU-countries and non-EU countries separately.

To begin with imports, Table 1 shows a high degree of lumpiness. About half of all firm-good-country combinations are recorded only

---

[6] Note that information whether a country is landlocked or not (that is available from CEPII's GeoDist database described in Mayer and Zignago (2011) and that has been used in the literature on the lumpiness of trade) is not used here because this country characteristic is closely related to the time and monetary costs of exports and imports.

[7] The detailed picture is identical for the years 2009 to 2011, so we focus on information for the most recent year 2012.

Table 1: Number of import transactions per year by firm-good-country of origin in 2012.

No. of transactions per year	EU-countries		Non-EU countries	
	Frequency	Share (%)	Frequency	Share (%)
1	475,589	35.46	1,135,184	55.95
2	190,471	14.20	286,341	14.11
3	117,854	8.79	144,043	7.10
4	86,268	6.43	91,788	4.52
5	69,206	5.16	66,050	3.26
6	58,412	4.36	51,017	2.51
7	53,006	3.95	41,885	2.06
8	52,214	3.89	36,207	1.78
9	51,163	3.81	33,181	1.64
10	50,252	3.75	31,752	1.56
11	54,671	4.08	33,863	1.67
12	82,096	6.12	77,578	3.82
Average number of transactions	4.168		2.783	

Note: Number of transactions refers to months with recorded import transactions at the firm-product-country of origin level; goods refer to categories at the HS6 level.

once or twice for imports from EU-countries, and this is the case for 70 percent of all firm-good-country combinations in imports from non-EU-countries. The frequency of recorded transactions tends to decline with an increase in the number of transactions per year. This is in accordance with the presence of per-shipment fixed costs that provide an incentive for importers in engage in cross-border transactions infrequently. However, there is a remarkable increase in the frequency of the number of transactions when it comes to twelve transactions per year. This might be due to the fact (mentioned above) that within a month all imports of a specific HS6-good from a specific country by one single firm are aggregated and reported as one data point only. Therefore, the proxy for trade frequency used here may be biased for high frequency traders which trade the same good with the same country in (nearly) every month several times.

Tables 2 and 3 report more detailed information by looking at four of the most important countries of origin for German imports of goods, namely the Netherlands and France from the EU, and the US and China from outside the EU. The big picture is highly similar if results for these countries are compared to results reported for the EU as a whole, or for all non-EU countries, in Table 1. Table A.1 reports the average number of import transactions per year by firm-good-country of origin for countries of origin with more than 5,000 recorded import transactions in 2012. The degree of lumpiness varies widely over the countries. Within the EU, the average number of transactions is 3.31 for Luxembourg and

Table 2: Number of import transactions per year by firm-good-country of origin in 2012 for imports from the Netherlands and France.

No. of transactions per year	Netherlands		France	
	Frequency	Share (%)	Frequency	Share (%)
1	71,647	34.07	49,291	34.14
2	29,803	14.17	20,223	14.01
3	18,324	8.71	13,018	9.02
4	13,515	6,43	9,408	6.52
5	10,996	5.23	7,475	5.18
6	9,555	4.54	6,474	4.48
7	8,642	4.11	5,776	4.00
8	8,765	4.17	5,700	3.95
9	8,811	4.19	5,591	3,87
10	8,753	4.16	5,735	3.97
11	9,073	4.32	6,031	4.18
12	12,482	5.89	9,659	6.69
Average number of transactions	4.273		4.284	

Note: Number of transactions refers to months with recorded import transactions at the firm-product-country of origin level; goods refer to categories at the HS6 level.

Table 3: Number of import transactions per year by firm-good-country of origin in 2012 for imports from the United States and China.

No. of transactions per year	United States		China	
	Frequency	Share (%)	Frequency	Share (%)
1	203,598	57.38	261,148	51.69
2	49,297	13.89	74,316	14.71
3	24,133	6.80	39,135	7.75
4	15,456	4.36	25,794	5.11
5	10,866	3.06	18,754	3.71
6	8,463	2.38	14,459	2.86
7	6,914	1.95	12,008	2.38
8	5,981	1.69	10,362	2.05
9	5,495	1.55	9,770	1.93
10	5,333	1.50	9,086	1.80
11	5,890	1.66	9,578	1.90
12	13,427	3.78	20,765	4.11
Average number of transactions	2.724		2.991	

Note: Number of transactions refers to months with recorded import transactions at the firm-product-country of origin level; goods refer to categories at the HS6 level.

4.63 for the Czech Republic. Outside the EU, imports from the United Arab Emirates (1.82), Hong Kong (1.98) and Australia (2.04) show a high degree of lumpiness compared to countries like Bangladesh (3.79), Tunisia (3.45) or Vietnam (3.27). The role of EU-membership is nicely illustrated by comparing the neighbor countries Austria (4.00) and Switzerland (2.67), or Sweden (3.98) and Norway (2.16).

Table 4 illustrates that the degree of lumpiness of imports differs between goods (classified by section at the HS2 level) when EU-membership is controlled for. For example, live animals and animal products (HS2-Section 1) have the lowest degree of lumpiness in imports for both EU-members and non-members. This does not come as a surprise — it is obvious that an importer will only rarely trade all the beef he intends to

Table 4: Average number of import transactions per year by firm-good-country of origin for HS2-sections of goods in 2012.

HS2-section	Description	EU-countries Average number of transactions	Non-EU countries Average number of transactions
1	Live animals; animal products	5.02	3.44
2	Vegetable products	4.39	3.01
3	Animal or vegetable fats and oils etc.	4.50	2.70
4	Prepared foodstuffs; beverages; tobacco	5.00	3.02
5	Mineral products	4.75	2.79
6	Products of chemical or allied industries	4.20	2.99
7	Plastics, rubber and articles thereof	4.31	2.77
8	Leather, furskins and articles thereof	3.83	2.74
9	Wood, cork and articles thereof	4.49	2.71
10	Pulp, paper, paperboard and articles thereof	4.18	2.15
11	Textiles and textile articles	3.63	3.05
12	Footwear, headgear, umbrellas	4.02	3.09
13	Articles of stone, ceramic products, glass	4.06	2.63
14	Pearls, precious stones or metals	3.94	2.72
15	Base metals and articles of base metals	4.16	2.81
16	Machinery, electrical equipment	4.04	2.72
17	Vehicles, aircraft, vessels, transport equipment	4.60	3.14
18	Optical etc. instruments; clocks; musical instruments	3.89	2.74
19	Arms and ammunition	4.37	3.03

(*Continued*)

Table 4: (*Continued*)

HS2-section	Description	EU-countries Average number of transactions	Non-EU countries Average number of transactions
20	Miscellaneous manufactures articles	4.42	2.83
21	Works of art, collectors' pieces and antiques	3.84	2.08

Note: Number of transactions refers to months with recorded import transactions at the firm-product-country of origin level. For a detailed description of the HS2 classification by section see the web at: http://unstats.un.org/unsd/tradekb/Knowledgebase/HS-Classification-by-Section.

import over the year from Poland or Brazil in one deal. Other figures in the table are more difficult to understand — for example, why is the extra-EU trade with "Pulp, paper, paperboard and articles thereof" (HS2-Section 10) so lumpy? Is this due to trade costs related to the countries of origin? This will be investigated empirically in the next section of the paper. But before this, we will look at exports.

Table 5 shows that the big picture for exports is very much the same as the one for imports (documented in Table 1) — exports are lumpy, the degree of lumpiness is much larger for trade with non-EU countries than for trade with EU-countries, and there is a remarkable increase in the frequency of the number of transactions when it comes to twelve transactions per year. Compared to imports, exports tend to be less lumpy, but the difference is small.

Tables 6 and 7 report more detailed information by looking at four of the most important destination countries for German exports of goods, namely the Netherlands and France from the EU, and the US and China from outside the EU. The big picture is highly similar if results for these countries are compared to results reported for the EU as a whole, or for all non-EU countries, in Table 5. Table A.2 reports the average number of export transactions per year by firm-good-destination country for destination countries with more than 5,000 recorded export transactions in 2012. The degree of lumpiness varies widely over the countries. Within the

Table 5: Number of export transactions per year by firm-good-destination country in 2012.

No. of transactions per year	EU-countries		Non-EU countries	
	Frequency	Share (%)	Frequency	Share (%)
1	1,241,816	31.45	1,708,600	48.46
2	558,044	14.13	552,527	15.67
3	352,014	8.91	294,976	8.37
4	258,440	6.54	190,405	5.40
5	208,554	5.28	139,314	3.95
6	176,977	4.48	107,841	3.06
7	156,478	3.96	87,384	2.48
8	152,904	3.87	74,160	2.10
9	150,814	3.82	66,545	1.89
10	156,217	3.96	64,440	1.83
11	187,298	4.74	68,936	1.96
12	349,211	8.84	170,687	4.48
Average number of transactions	4,569		3.136	

Note: Number of transactions refers to months with recorded export transactions at the firm-product-destination country level; goods refer to categories at the HS6 level.

EU, the average number of transactions is 5.29 for Austria and 2.85 for Malta. Outside the EU, imports from the Syria (1.67), Ethiopia (1.71) and Libya (1.78) show a high degree of lumpiness compared to countries like the United States (3.84) or Switzerland (3.90). Like in the case of imports the role of EU-membership is nicely illustrated by comparing the neighbor countries Austria (5.29) and Switzerland (3.90), or Sweden (4.60) and Norway (3.53).

Table 8 illustrates that the degree of lumpiness of exports differs between goods (classified by section at the HS2 level) when EU-membership is controlled for. Similar to the case of imports discussed above, some of these differences are easily explained by the characteristics of the goods traded (e.g., the low degree of lumpiness in exports of "Live animals; animal

Table 6: Number of export transactions per year by firm-good-destination country in 2012 for exports to the Netherlands and France.

No. of transactions per year	Netherlands		France	
	Frequency	Share (%)	Frequency	Share (%)
1	84,931	28.38	86,775	27.31
2	39,141	13.08	40,536	12.76
3	25,461	8.51	26,266	8.27
4	19,297	6.45	19,851	6.25
5	16,116	5.38	16,585	5.22
6	13,717	4.58	14,864	4.68
7	12,367	4.13	13,336	4.20
8	12,742	4.26	13,436	4.23
9	12,939	4.32	13,558	4.27
10	13,433	4.49	15,117	4.76
11	17,006	5.68	18,629	5.86
12	32,144	10,74	38,784	12.21
Average number of transactions	4.984		5,169	

Note: Number of transactions refers to months with recorded export transactions at the firm-product-destination country level; goods refer to categories at the HS6 level.

products" — HS2-Section 1 — and in exports of "Prepared foodstuffs; beverages; tobacco" — HS2-Section 4) while others are not (e.g., the high degree of lumpiness in exports of "Footwear, headgear, umbrellas" – HS2-Section 12-in trade with non-EU members).

The big picture on the lumpiness of trade reported for Germany is in line with the empirical evidence (summarized in Section 1 above) for exports from the US, France, Spain and Switzerland. The role of differences in trade costs between the destination countries of exports or the countries of origin of imports for an explanation of differences in the degree of lumpiness of exports or imports will be investigated in the next section.

Table 7: Number of export transactions per year by firm-good-destination country in 2012 for exports to the United States and China.

No. of transactions per year	United States		China	
	Frequency	Share (%)	Frequency	Share (%)
1	85,713	41.95	68,031	45.23
2	29,365	14.37	22,151	14.73
3	16,934	8.29	12,173	8.09
4	11,363	5.56.	8,173	5.43
5	8,894	4.35	6,283	4.18
6	7,256	3.55	4,977	3.31
7	5,907	2.89	4,377	2.91
8	5,345	2.62	3,628	2.41
9	4,940	2.42	3,406	2.26
10	5,151	2.52	3,359	2.23
11	5,811	2.84	3,738	2.49
12	17,651	8.64	10,113	6.72
Average number of transactions	3.839		3.518	

Note: Number of transactions refers to months with recorded export transactions at the firm-product-destination country level; goods refer to categories at the HS6 level.

4. Per-shipment Costs and the Lumpiness of German Exports and Imports: Econometric Results

One empirical fact documented in Section 3 is the large difference in the degree of lumpiness of imports and of exports in trade with EU-members on the one hand and with non-EU countries on the other hand. This might be due to the much lower per-shipment costs in trade with EU-countries, because there are no costs related to customs' procedures in intra-EU trade. However, this might be due to different concepts used to record the trade with EU-countries and non-EU countries (see footnote 2), too. Given that information on per-shipment costs (detailed below) is

Table 8: Average number of export transactions per year by firm-good-destination country for HS2-sections of goods in 2012.

		EU-countries	Non-EU countries
HS2-section	Description	Average number of transactions	Average number of transactions
1	Live animals; animal products	5.53	3.49
2	Vegetable products	4.63	3.18
3	Animal or vegetable fats and oils etc.	4.74	3.09
4	Prepared foodstuffs; beverages; tobacco	5.59	3.56
5	Mineral products	4.65	3.38
6	Products of chemical or allied industries	4.88	3.64
7	Plastics, rubber and articles thereof	4.73	3.37
8	Leather, furskins and articles thereof	4.31	2.83
9	Wood, cork and articles thereof	4.54	3.07
10	Pulp, paper, paperboard and articles thereof	4.29	2.71
11	Textiles and textile articles	4.43	3.14
12	Footwear, headgear, umbrellas	4.67	2.88
13	Articles of stone, ceramic products, glass	4.60	3.10
14	Pearls, precious stones or metals	4.39	3.03
15	Base metals and articles of base metals	4.61	3.20
16	Machinery, electrical equipment	4.42	3.09
17	Vehicles, aircraft, vessels, transport equipment	4.26	2.62
18	Optical etc. instruments; clocks; musical instruments	4.43	3.07
19	Arms and ammunition	4.45	2.73
20	Miscellaneous manufactures articles	4.63	2.95
21	Works of art, collectors' pieces and antiques	4.07	2.82

Note: Number of transactions refers to months with recorded export transactions at the firm-product-destination country level. For a detailed description of the HS2 classification by section see the web at: http://unstats.un.org/unsd/tradekb/Knowledgebase/HS-Classification-by-Section.

relevant for extra-EU trade only we will focus on trade with countries outside the EU for the rest of this section.

4.1 Empirical strategy

Information on two indicators of *per-shipment trade costs* is taken from the World Bank's Doing Business Data Base (see www.doingbusiness.org). *Doing Business* measures the time and cost (excluding tariffs) necessary to complete every official procedure that is needed for exporting and importing a standardized cargo of goods by ocean transport. Time is recorded in calendar days, costs are in US Dollars. The data used here (that are discussed in detail in the Appendix) are taken from the report for 2013 and refer to June 2012.[8]

Note that the time and cost of ocean transport are not included in the cost indicators from the Doing Business data base. The time dimension of transport can be considered as another per-shipment cost — it takes *X* days to ship a container from Germany to *country Y*, irrespective of the amount of goods in this container. Time for transport is closely linked to distance between countries. Therefore, distance is included as another trade cost variable (for details, see Section 2 above).

The value of an indicator of per-shipment costs varies widely between countries. The figures for the 151 non-EU countries included in the econometric investigation are reported in Appendix Table 3. The time necessary to complete every official procedure that is needed for exporting and importing a standardized cargo of goods by ocean transport is between 5 days (Hong Kong) and 81 days (Kazakhstan) for exports, and between 4 days (Singapore) and 101 days (Chad) for imports. Cost (excluding tariffs) necessary for this is between 435 US Dollar (Malaysia) and 8,450 US Dollar (Tajikistan) for exports, and between 420 US Dollar (Malaysia) and 9,800 US Dollar (Tajikistan) for imports. Distance between Germany

---

[8] This information on trade costs is available for a number of years, including the years 2009 to 2012 for which the transaction level data for German exports and imports of goods are available. A look at these cost data reveals a high degree of stability over time — the coefficient of correlation for the value of a cost measure between two years usually is much larger than +0.9. Given this lack of variance in trade costs measures over time we focus data for 2012, the year used in the descriptive analysis in Section 3.

and the country of origin of imports or the destination country of exports varies between 543 kilometers (Switzerland) and 18,220 kilometers (New Zealand).

To see how these per-shipment costs are related to the degree of lumpiness of imports and exports in German trade with goods with non-EU countries in 2012, empirical models are estimated with the number of transactions for firm-HS6-good-country combinations as the endogenous variable and trade-cost variables measured at the level of the country of origin (for imports) or destination country (for exports) plus data on other characteristics of the country. Some of the empirical models include fixed effects for the firms engaged in international trade and the goods traded (discussed in detail below).

In the econometric investigation six variants of empirical models are estimated that include different sets of exogenous variables. Models 1, 3 and 5 include the time to export (for imports to Germany) or the time to import (for exports from Germany), Models 2, 4 and 6 include the costs of exports (for imports to Germany) or the costs of imports (for exports from Germany). Note that both indicators of per-shipment costs of trade are highly positively correlated with a correlation coefficient of +0.79 for export costs and +0.77 for import costs; therefore, the two indicators are included in the empirical models alternatively.

All models include the distance to the country of origin (for imports to Germany) or the distance to the destination country (for exports from Germany). Distance is closely related to the time necessary to transport a good from the country of origin or to the country of destination, and to the costs of transport. For the countries included in the empirical investigation distance is negatively correlated with the time and cost indicators, but the correlation is small (−0.17 for time to export and −0.18 for time to import; −0.24 for cost to export or import).

Furthermore, all models include two standard variables from gravity models of trade, Gross National Income and per capital Gross National Income, as control variables.[9]

---

[9] Gross National Income per capita (measured in current US Dollar) is taken from the Doing Business database directly, Gross National Income is calculated from the per capita

The indicators for trade costs and the control variables are included in Models 1 and 2 (where Model 1 includes the time to trade, and Model 2 includes the costs of trade from the Doing Business Database detailed above). All these variables are constant for a given country of destination (for exports) or origin (for imports). Descriptive evidence reported in Tables 3 and 7 (for import and export transactions with the United States and China) demonstrates that the number of transactions per year by firm-good-country is not constant. For a given country of destination or origin with given values for trade costs (and control variables) the number of transactions varies widely between one and 12.

This illustrates that for some firms trading some goods with a specific country the same measured trade costs lead to a high degree of lumpiness in trade, and for others they lead to a low degree of lumpiness. This might be caused by differences between firms with respect to productivity, size, or other characteristics. Unfortunately, the data available have no information on the trading German firm (besides the firm identifier). To control for unobserved firm characteristics in the link between trade costs and lumpiness of trade Models 3 and 4 include firm fixed effects. Identification of the role of trade costs for the number of transactions per year by firm-good-country here comes from the within-firm variation over goods and countries.

Descriptive evidence reported in Table 4 (for imports) and Table 8 (for exports) shows that the average number of transactions per year by firm-good-country differs between different groups of goods. This variation is expected to be related to the differences in the fixed costs of trade with the different countries of destination or origin of these goods, but it might as well be related to the characteristics of the goods itself (irrespective of the countries traded with). To control for these unobserved characteristics of goods in the link between trade costs and lumpiness of trade, and to take care of the role of unobserved firm characteristics discussed above, Models 5 and 6 include fixed effects at the firm-good level. Identification of the role of trade costs for the number of

---

values and the size of the population reported in the data base. Information for 2012 used here is taken from the 2014 edition.

transactions per year by firm-good-country here comes from the within-firm within-good variation over countries.

Following the literature on the lumpiness of trade all variables are included in logs. The regression coefficients, therefore, are estimates for the elasticity of the number of trade transactions per year by firm-good-country with respect to an indicator of trade costs (or a control variable).[10]

If higher per-shipment costs make it optimal for traders to engage in cross-border transactions more infrequently and if the degree of lumpiness is positively related to fixed costs of trade this means that the number of transactions per year at the firm-good-country level decreases with an increase in trade costs. In the empirical models this implies a negative sign of the estimated elasticity of the number of transactions with respect to a variable that measures trade costs.

4.2 Imports

Results for the empirical models for the lumpiness of imports are reported in Table 9.[11] Here Models 5 and 6 are the preferred models because the unobserved characteristics of both firms and goods are controlled for by including fixed effects at the firm-good level.

From Model 6 we see that the costs of exports in the country of origin and the distance between Germany and the country of origin are negatively related to the number of transaction per year at the firm-good-country level. Both variables can be regarded as indicators of per-shipment trade costs (see the discussion in Section 4.1). These results, therefore, are in line with the expectations regarding the link between per-shipment costs and the degree of the lumpiness of trade, because fixed costs lead to a trade-off between per-shipment trade costs and shipping frequency. On the one hand, firms engaged in international trade would like to economize on these per-shipment costs by sending fewer and larger shipments. On the other hand, this comes at a cost due to time-lags related to waiting to fill a

---

[10] The big picture is identical when all variables enter the empirical models in levels; details are available on request.

[11] Note that all p-values are based on estimated standard errors that are clustered at the level of the firm.

Table 9: Determinants of lumpiness of German imports of goods from non-EU countries 2012.

Exogenous variables	Model	1	2	3	4	5	6
		Endogenous variable: Log of (number of transactions for firm-HS6-good-country of origin combination)					
Log(time to export) (days)	ß	C.045		0.028		0.053	
	p	C.000		0.002		0.133	
Log (costs of export) (US Dollar)	ß		−0.036		−0.057		−0.153
	p		0.000		0.000		0.000
Log (distance to country of origin) (kilometer)	ß	−0.014	−0.027	−0.044	−0.058	−0.109	−0.145
	p	0.000	0.000	0.000	0.000	0.000	0.000
Log (Gross National Income of country of origin)	ß	0.019	0.021	0.045	0.047	0.135	0.141
	p	0.000	0.000	0.000	0.000	0.000	0.000
Log (per capita Gross National Income of country of origin)	ß	−0.026	−0.042	−0.014	−0.022	−0.0062	−0.020
	p	0.000	0.000	0.000	0.000	0.616	0.000
Constant	ß	0.610	1.189	0.407	1.022	−0.473	1.052
	p	0.000	0.000	0.000	0.000	0.002	0.000
Firm fixed effects (N = 121,581)		no	no	yes	yes	no	no
Firm-HS6 fixed effects (N = 1,397,566)		no	no	no	no	yes	yes
R^2		0.2044	0.0044	0.213	0.213	0.726	0.727
No. of observations		2,016,846	2,016,846	2,016,846	2,016,846	2,016,846	2,016,846

Note: For a definition of exogenous variables see text. ß is the estimated regression coefficient, p is the prob-value of this estimate (based on estimated standard errors that are clustered at the level of the firm).

larger shipment and because of the need to keep costly inventories between shipment arrivals.

A negative impact of costs of exports in the countries of origin and of distance to Germany is found in all other models listed in Table 9 (including models without fixed effects,[12] and with firm fixed-effects only), too. The exception is the time to export in the country of origin. The estimated regression coefficient of this indicator of per-shipment costs is statistically insignificant at a conventional level in the preferred Model 5 (and positive and significant in Models 1 and 3).[13]

Regarding the estimated size of the elasticities of the number of transactions with respect to trade costs, from Model 6 we see that a one hundred percent increase in the cost of export in the country of origin leads to a reduction in the number of import transactions by 15.3 percent. Doubling the distance between Germany and the country of origin reduces the number of transactions by 11 percent according to Model 5 and by 14.5 percent according to Model 6. As is documented in Table A.3 trade costs vary considerably between the countries of origin; therefore, the estimated elasticities can be considered to be significant from an economic point of view (and not only from a statistical point of view), too.

It was pointed out in Section 3 that within a month all imports of a specific HS6-good from a specific country by one single firm are aggregated and reported as one data point only. Therefore, the proxy for trade frequency used here may be biased for high frequency traders which trade the same good with the same country in (nearly) every month several times. The large increase in the frequency of the number of import transactions per year from 11 to 12 reported in Tables 1 to 3 illustrates this. As a robustness check, therefore, all empirical models were estimated using a restricted sample that excludes cases with a calculated number of 12 transactions (see the discussion in Békés *et al.* 2015).

---

[12] As suggested by a referee, the models without fixed effects were estimated using the sample that is used to identify the estimated coefficients in the models with firm-HS6 fixed effects, too, i.e., after dropping 1,100,883 singletons in firm-good groups from the estimation sample. Results did not change qualitatively; details are available on request.

[13] Note that both GNI and GNI per capita in the country of origin are included as control variables in the empirical models only. Therefore, we do not discuss the results for the estimated coefficients of these variables here and in the next section.

The big picture from this robustness check is identical to the one reported in Table 9; details are available on request.

4.3 Exports

Results for the empirical models for the lumpiness of exports are reported in Table 10. From Models 5 and 6, which are again the preferred models because the unobserved characteristics of both firms and goods are controlled for, we see that all three indicators of trade costs are negatively related to the number of transaction per year at the firm-good-country level. As in the case of imports these results are in line with the expectations regarding the link between per-shipment costs and the degree of the lumpiness of trade, and this holds for results reported for the other models (without fixed effects,[14] and with firm fixed-effects only), too.

Regarding the estimated size of the elasticities of the number of transactions with respect to trade costs, from Model 5 we see that a one hundred percent increase in the time to import in the country of destination leads to a reduction in the number of import transactions by 6.7 percent. According to Model 6, doubling the costs of imports in the destination country reduces the number of export transactions by 2.4 percent. This estimated elasticity is considerable smaller than the value for import transactions. Doubling the distance between Germany and the destination country reduces the number of transactions by ca. 18 percent according to Model 5 and Model 6. As is documented in Appendix Table 3 trade costs vary considerably between the countries of destination; therefore, the estimated elasticities can be considered to be significant from an economic point of view (and not only from a statistical point of view), too.

Like in the case of import transactions, as a robustness check all empirical models were estimated using a restricted sample that excludes cases with a calculated number of 12 transactions. Again, the big picture from this robustness check is identical to the one reported in Table 10; details are available on request.

---

[14] As suggested by a referee, the models without fixed effects were estimated using the sample that is used to identify the estimated coefficients in the models with firm-HS6 fixed effects, too, i.e., after dropping 750,615 singletons in firm-good groups from the estimation sample. Results did not change qualitatively; details are available on request.

Table 10: **Determinants of lumpiness of German exports of goods to non-EU countries 2012.**

Exogenous variables	Model	Endogenous variable: Log of (No. of transactions for firm-HS6-good-country of destination combination)					
		1	2	3	4	5	6
Log (time to import) (days)	ß	-0.051		-0.039		-0.067	
	p	0.000		0.000		0.000	
Log (costs of import) (US Dollar)	ß		-0.027		-0.011		-0.024
	p		0.000		0.002		0.001
Log (distance to country of destination) (kilometer)	ß	-0.059	-0.056	-0.107	-0.103	-0.181	-0.176
	p	0.000	0.000	0.000	0.000	0.000	0.000
Log (Gross National Income of country of destination)	ß	0.054	0.053	0.084	0.083	0.155	0.154
	p	0.000	0.000	0.000	0.000	0.000	0.000
Log (per capita Gross National Income of country of destination)	ß	0.010	0.028	0.018	0.032	0.028	0.051
	p	0.000	0.000	0.000	0.000	0.000	0.000
Constant	ß	0.567	0.441	0.458	0.284	0.144	-0.134
	p	0.000	0.000	0.000	0.000	0.053	0.025
Firm fixed effects ($N = 106{,}550$)		no	no	yes	yes	no	no
Firm-HS6 fixed effects ($N = 1{,}168{,}442$)		no	no	no	no	yes	yes
R^2		0.024	0.023	0.218	0.218	0.564	0.563
No. of observations		3,388,205	3,388,205	3,388,205	3,388,205	3,388,205	3,388,205

Note: For a definition of exogenous variables see text. ß is the estimated regression coefficient, p is the prob-value of this estimate (based on estimated standard errors that are clustered at the level of the firm).

5. Concluding Remarks

This paper looks at a hitherto neglected extensive margin of international trade by investigating for the first time the frequency at which German exporters and importers trade a given good with a given country over a year. Imports and exports show a high degree of lumpiness. In a given year about half of all firm-good-country combinations are recorded only once or twice for trade with EU countries, and this is the case for more than 60 percent of all firm-good-country combinations in trade with non-EU countries.

The frequency of recorded transactions tends to decline with an increase in the number of transactions per year. This is in accordance with the presence of per-shipment fixed costs that provide an incentive for trading firms to engage in cross-border transactions infrequently. Empirical models show that for Germany the frequency of transactions at the firm-good-country level tends to decrease with an increase in per-shipment costs when unobserved firm and goods characteristics are controlled for.

To put the findings for Germany reported in this paper into perspective we compare them to results reported in empirical studies on the lumpiness of trade for other countries. This, however, is not an easy task because these studies differ in details in the empirical approach used and as regards the type of data that are analyzed. That said, a high degree of lumpiness in exports is reported for the US (in trade with six destination countries) by Alessandria *et al.* (2010), for France by Békés *et al.* (2015), for the US and Spain by Hornok and Koren (2015a), and by Kropf and Sauré (2014) for Switzerland. The findings for the lumpiness of German exports, therefore, are in line with the big picture from empirical studies for exports from the US, France, Spain and Switzerland. Note that none of the studies on the lumpiness of trade for other countries looks at the degree of lumpiness of imports.

The finding that for Germany the frequency of export transactions at the firm-good-country level tends to decrease with an increase in per-shipment costs when unobserved firm and goods characteristics are controlled for is in line with results reported by Hornok and Koren (2015a) for exports of the US and Spain at the product-country level (without control for the exporting firms). Again, comparable results for imports are not available for other countries.

The bottom line, then, is that according to the empirical results presented in this paper for Germany and with a view on the results for other countries summarized above a reduction of per-shipment costs can be expected to lead to a decrease in the degree of lumpiness of trade and to a reduction of costly inventories. This will foster international trade by pushing a hitherto neglected extensive margin of international trade of firms — the number of transactions at the firm-good-country level.

Appendix: The Measurement of Trade Costs in the *Doing Business* Reports

[From *Doing Business 2012* available at *http://www.doingbusiness.org/reports/global-reports/doing-business-2012*, pp. 55–56]

Doing Business measures the time and cost (excluding tariffs) associated with exporting and importing a standardized cargo of goods by ocean transport. The time and cost necessary to complete every official procedure for exporting and importing the goods — from the contractual agreement between the two parties to the delivery of goods — are recorded. All documents needed by the trader to export or import the goods across the border are also recorded. For exporting goods, procedures range from packing the goods into the container at the warehouse to their departure from the port of exit. For importing goods, procedures range from the vessel's arrival at the port of entry to the cargo's delivery at the warehouse. The time and cost for ocean transport are not included. Payment is made by letter of credit, and the time, cost and documents required for the issuance or advising of a letter of credit are taken into account. Local freight forwarders, shipping lines, customs brokers, port officials and banks provide information on required documents and cost as well as the time to complete each procedure. To make the data comparable across economies, several assumptions about the business and the traded goods are used.

Assumptions about the business

The business:

- Has at least 60 employees.
- Is located in the economy's largest business city.
- Is a private, limited liability company. It does not operate in an export processing zone or an industrial estate with special export or import privileges.
- Is domestically owned with no foreign ownership.
- Exports more than 10 percent of its sales.

Assumptions about the traded goods

The traded product travels in a dry-cargo, 20-foot, full container load. It weighs 10 tons and is valued at $20,000. The product:

- Is not hazardous nor does it include military items.
- Does not require refrigeration or any other special environment.
- Does not require any special phytosanitary or environmental safety standards other than accepted international standards.
- Is one of the economy's leading export or import products.

Documents

All documents required per shipment to export and import the goods are recorded.

It is assumed that the contract has already been agreed upon and signed by both parties. Documents required for clearance by government ministries, customs authorities, port and container terminal authorities, health and technical control agencies, and banks are taken into account. Since payment is by letter of credit, all documents required by banks for the issuance or securing of a letter of credit are also taken into account. Documents that are renewed annually and that do not require renewal per shipment (for example, an annual tax clearance certificate) are not included.

Time

The time for exporting and importing is recorded in calendar days. The time calculation for a procedure starts from the moment it is initiated and runs until it is completed. If a procedure can be accelerated for an additional cost and is available to all trading companies, the fastest legal procedure is chosen. Fast-track procedures applying to firms located in an export processing zone are not taken into account because they are not available to all trading companies. Ocean transport time is not included. It is assumed that neither the exporter nor the importer wastes time and that each commits to completing each remaining procedure without delay. Procedures that can be completed in parallel are measured as simultaneous. The waiting time between procedures — for example, during unloading of the cargo — is included in the measure.

Cost

Cost measures the fees levied on a 20-foot container in US Dollars. All the fees associated with completing the procedures to export or import the goods are included. These include costs for documents, administrative fees for customs clearance and technical control, customs broker fees, terminal handling charges and inland transport. The cost does not include customs tariffs and duties or costs related to ocean transport. Only official costs are recorded.

Table A.1: Average number of import transactions per year by firm-good-country of origin for selected countries of origin in 2012.

Country	Average number of import transactions	No. of total import transactions
Argentina	2.42	5,110
Australia	2.04	14,614
Austria	4.00	154,996
Bangladesh	3.79	8,281
Belgium	4.26	93,742
Bosnia Herzegovina	4.15	5,106
Brazil	2.82	17,969
Bulgaria	3.71	8,416
Canada	2.30	31,891
China	2.99	505,175
Croatia	2.68	9,105
Czech Republic	4.63	55,445
Denmark	4.03	55,234
Egypt Arab Republic	2.43	6,176
Finland	3.75	14,193
France	4.28	144,381
Greece	3.59	8,388
Hong Kong	1.98	47,839
Hungary	4.43	26,325
India	2.84	69,065
Indonesia	2.85	20,388
Ireland	4.09	11,447
Israel	2.40	21,616
Italy	4.21	207,884
Japan	3.20	99,257
Korea Republic	2.67	43,730
Lithuania	3.58	5,036
Luxembourg	3.31	12,017
Malaysia	2.88	24,893

(Continued)

Table A.1: (*Continued*)

Country	Average number of import transactions	No. of total import transactions
Mexico	2.79	23,214
Morocco	3.14	5,920
Netherlands	4.27	210,266
Norway	2.16	20,595
Pakistan	2.80	14,106
Philippines	2.93	10,177
Poland	4.53	63,449
Portugal	3.88	16,446
Romania	4.15	15,077
Russian Federation	2.38	14,031
Singapore	2.38	18,496
Slovak Republic	4.42	15,956
Slovenia	4.25	13,567
South Africa	2.52	13,950
Spain	3.94	62,551
Sweden	3.98	36,236
Switzerland	2.67	279,411
Taiwan China	2.83	90,017
Thailand	2.95	32,147
Tunisia	3.45	5,691
Turkey	2.70	97,903
Ukraine	2.96	7,141
United Arab Emirates	1.82	8,790
United Kingdom	3.94	102,918
United States	2.72	354,853
Vietnam	3.27	18,344

Note: Number of transactions refers to months with recorded import transactions at the firm-product-country of origin level. Countries of origin with more than 5,000 recorded import transactions are included in the table.

Table A.2: Average number of export transactions per year by firm-good-destination country for selected destination countries in 2012.

Country	Average number of export transactions	No. of total export transactions
Afghanistan	2.10	6,068
Albania	2.27	9,557
Algeria	2.07	13,204
Angola	1.84	5,571
Argentina	3.14	23,330
Armenia	2.05	9,766
Australia	3.44	75,705
Austria	5.29	408,875
Azerbaijan	2.09	20,000
Bahrein	2.19	12,200
Bangladesh	2.30	6,645
Belarus	2.77	41,084
Belgium	4.73	234,168
Bolivia	1.97	5,852
Bosnia Herzegovina	3.04	30,790
Brazil	3.55	65,121
Bulgaria	3.58	68,289
Cameroon	2.17	5,640
Canada	3.18	58,022
Chile	2.92	34,272
China	3.52	150,409
Colombia	3.00	21,893
Costa Rica	2.53	8,034
Cote D'Ivoire	2.06	5,415
Croatia	3.47	71,531
Cyprus	2.76	27,312
Czech Republic	4.73	217,071
Denmark	4.47	154,696
Dominican Republic	2.51	6,438

(Continued)

Table A.2: (*Continued*)

Country	Average number of export transactions	No. of total export transactions
Ecuador	2.42	11,495
Egypt Arab Republic	2.44	41,162
Estonia	3.63	55,689
Ethiopia	1.71	5,463
Finland	4.15	113,999
France	5.17	317,737
Georgia	2.28	18,147
Ghana	2.06	12,132
Greece	3.70	87,598
Guatemala	2.54	7,170
Hong Kong	3.06	55,894
Hungary	4.41	154,500
Iceland	2.88	24,740
India	3.25	80,580
Indonesia	2.87	28,163
Iran Islamic Republic	1.95	26,741
Iraq	1.86	13,057
Ireland	3.72	61,386
Israel	3.09	54,268
Italy	4.77	250,195
Japan	3.51	81,998
Jordan	2.17	19,624
Kazakhstan	2.49	43,487
Kenya	2.23	10,250
Korea Republic	3.23	64,477
Kuwait	2.33	20,621
Kyrgyz Republic	1.81	5,453
Latvia	3.52	57,823
Lebanon	2.27	25,643
Libya	1.78	12,123

(*Continued*)

Table A.2: (*Continued*)

Country	Average number of export transactions	No. of total export transactions
Liechtenstein	2.59	10,514
Lithuania	3.65	66,230
Luxembourg	4.22	125,158
Macedonia FYR	3.15	21,626
Malaysia	2.95	39,291
Malta	2.85	22,221
Mauritius	2.28	7,024
Mexico	3.42	51,643
Moldova	2.42	18,757
Mongolia	1.89	8,355
Montenegro	2.48	6,265
Morocco	2.63	25,425
Netherlands	4.98	299,294
New Zealand	2.99	25,005
Nigeria	2.31	22,909
Norway	3.53	105,112
Oman	2.37	13,822
Pakistan	2.48	15,487
Panama	2.36	7,971
Paraguay	2.25	6,509
Peru	2.79	18,350
Philippines	2.53	18,910
Poland	4.58	247,609
Portugal	3.90	90,222
Qatar	2.37	19,826
Romania	4.00	120,169
Russian Federation	3.41	218,922
Saudi Arabia	2.77	52,843
Singapore	3.29	64,283
Slovak Republic	4.19	105,368

(*Continued*)

Table A.2: (*Continued*)

Country	Average number of export transactions	No. of total export transactions
Slovenia	4.08	101,438
South Africa	3.41	68,383
Spain	4.66	198,416
Sri Lanka	2.31	8,914
Sweden	4.60	151,848
Switzerland	3.90	463,713
Syrian Arab Republic	1.67	6,632
Taiwan China	2.97	44,556
Tanzania	2.04	5,397
Thailand	3.09	44,929
Tunisia	2.99	28,350
Turkey	3.33	118,634
Turkmenistan	1.89	5,131
Ukraine	3.17	84,334
United Arab Emirates	2.81	73,974
United Kingdom	4.80	211,467
United States	3.84	204,330
Uruguay	2.48	9,756
Uzbekistan	1.83	6,994
Venezuela	2.28	13,380
Vietnam	2.52	20,899

Note: Number of transactions refers to months with recorded export transactions at the firm-product-country of origin level. Destination countries with more than 5,000 recorded export transactions are included in the table.

Table A.3: Trade cost data for 2012.

Country	Time to export (Days)	Cost of export (US$)	Time to import (Days)	Cost of import (US$)	Dist. to Germany (km)
Afghanistan	74	3545	77	3830	4946
Albania	19	745	18	730	1384
Angola	48	1850	45	2690	6826
Antigua Barbados	16	1440	23	1870	7278
Argentina	13	1650	30	2260	11646
Armenia	13	1815	18	2195	2934
Australia	9	1100	8	1120	15935
Azerbaijan	38	3430	38	3490	3218
Bahamas	19	930	13	1405	7666
Bahrein	11	955	15	995	4423
Bangladesh	25	1025	34	1430	7348
Belarus	15	1510	30	2315	1262
Belize	19	1355	20	1600	9065
Benin	29	1079	30	1549	4912
Bhutan	38	2230	38	2330	7014
Bolivia	19	1425	23	1747	10576
Bosnia Herzegovina	15	1240	13	1200	1020
Botswana	27	2945	37	3445	8473
Brazil	13	2215	17	2275	9396
Brunei Daressalam	19	680	15	745	10614
Burkina Faso	41	2412	47	4030	4503
Burundi	32	2965	46	5005	6374
Cambodia	22	755	26	900	9311
Cameroon	23	1379	25	2167	5072
Canada	7	1610	11	1660	6542
Capa Verde	19	1200	18	1000	4979
Central Africa	54	5491	62	5554	5231
Chad	75	5902	101	8525	4511
Chile	15	980	12	965	12267

(*Continued*)

Table A.3: (*Continued*)

Country	Time to export (Days)	Cost of export (US$)	Time to import (Days)	Cost of import (US$)	Dist. to Germany (km)
China	21	580	24	615	8032
Colombia	14	2255	13	2830	9137
Comoros	31	1295	26	1295	7765
Congo Dem Rep	44	3155	63	3435	6393
Congo Republic	50	3818	62	7709	6192
Costa Rica	13	1030	14	1020	9425
Cote D'Ivoire	25	1999	34	2710	5223
Croatia	20	1300	16	1180	853
Djibouti	18	836	18	911	5357
Dominica	13	1340	14	1350	7388
Dominican Rep	8	1040	10	1150	7710
Ecuador	20	1535	25	1530	10096
Egypt Arab Republic	12	625	13	755	2957
El Salvador	14	980	10	980	9440
Equatorial Guinea	29	1390	44	1600	5422
Eritrea	50	1460	59	1600	4826
Ethiopia	42	2160	44	2660	5379
Fiji	22	655	23	635	16158
Gabon	20	1945	22	1955	5731
Gambia	23	1180	21	885	4839
Georgia	9	1355	10	1595	2771
Ghana	19	815	34	1315	5105
Grenada	9	1300	9	2235	7687
Guatemala	17	1307	17	1425	9459
Guinea	35	855	32	1391	5072
Guinea Bissau	23	1448	22	2006	4960
Guyana	19	730	22	745	7928
Haiti	33	1185	31	1545	7873
Honduras	12	1342	16	1510	9221

(*Continued*)

Table A.3: (*Continued*)

Country	Time to export (Days)	Cost of export (US$)	Time to import (Days)	Cost of import (US$)	Dist. to Germany (km)
Hong Kong	5	575	5	565	9026
Iceland	19	1465	14	1620	2317
India	16	1120	20	1200	6566
Indonesia	17	644	23	660	11030
Iran Islamic Republic	25	1470	32	2100	3811
Iraq	80	3550	82	3650	3449
Israel	10	620	10	565	2972
Jamaica	20	1500	17	1560	8244
Japan	10	880	11	970	9086
Jordan	13	825	15	1335	3037
Kazakhstan	81	4685	69	4665	4333
Kenya	26	2255	26	2350	6410
Kiribati	21	1120	21	1120	13979
Korea Republic	7	665	7	695	8505
Kuwait	15	1775	15	1810	3999
Kyrgyz Republic	63	4160	75	4700	4849
Lao PDR	26	2140	26	2120	8725
Lebanon	22	1080	30	1365	2849
Liberia	15	1220	28	1320	5355
Macedonia FYR	12	1376	11	1380	1404
Madagascar	21	1197	24	1555	8666
Malawi	34	2175	43	2870	7701
Malaysia	11	435	8	420	9987
Maldives	21	1550	22	1526	7886
Mali	26	2202	31	3067	4526
Marshall Islands	21	945	25	970	13191
Mauretania	34	1520	38	1523	4293
Mauritius	10	660	10	695	9224
Mexico	12	1450	12	1780	9476

(*Continued*)

Table A.3: (*Continued*)

Country	Time to export (Days)	Cost of export (US$)	Time to import (Days)	Cost of import (US$)	Dist. to Germany (km)
Micrones Fed	30	1295	30	1295	12591
Moldova	32	1545	35	1870	1463
Mongolia	49	2555	50	2710	6409
Morocco	11	577	16	950	2405
Mozambique	23	1100	28	1545	8426
Namibia	25	1800	20	1905	8196
Nepal	41	1975	38	2095	6636
New Zealand	10	870	9	825	18220
Nicaragua	21	1140	20	1245	9364
Niger	59	3676	64	3711	4182
Nigeria	24	1380	39	1540	4847
Norway	7	1125	7	1100	1039
Oman	10	745	9	680	5139
Pakistan	21	660	18	705	5551
Palau	29	970	33	930	11639
Panama	9	615	9	965	9247
Papua New Guinea	23	949	32	1130	13779
Paraguay	33	1440	33	1750	10734
Peru	12	890	17	880	10747
Philippines	15	585	14	660	10309
Puerto Rico	15	1300	15	1350	7477
Qatar	17	885	17	1033	4554
Russian Federation	21	2820	36	2920	2655
Rwanda	29	3245	31	4990	6238
Samoa	25	690	28	775	15845
Sao Tome Principe	26	690	28	577	5689
Saudi Arabia	13	935	17	1054	4211
Senegal	11	1098	14	1740	4746
Seychelles	16	876	17	876	7589

(*Continued*)

Table A.3: (*Continued*)

Country	Time to export (Days)	Cost of export (US$)	Time to import (Days)	Cost of import (US$)	Dist. to Germany (km)
Sierra Leone	24	1385	27	1780	5205
Singapore	5	456	4	439	10181
Solomon Islands	24	1070	20	1037	14596
South Africa	16	1620	23	1940	9111
Sri Lanka	20	720	19	775	8004
St Kitts Nevis	11	805	12	2635	7274
St Lucia	14	1375	17	2675	7480
St Vinct Grenadines	12	935	13	1575	7566
Sudan	32	2050	46	2900	4552
Suriname	23	1000	21	1165	7793
Swaziland	18	1880	27	2085	8916
Switzerland	8	1435	9	1440	543
Syrian Arab Rep	15	1190	21	1625	2843
Taiwan China	10	655	10	720	9275
Tajikistan	71	8450	72	9800	4724
Tanzania	18	1040	31	1565	6900
Thailand	14	585	13	750	8878
Timor-Leste	25	750	26	755	12548
Togo	24	940	28	1109	4983
Tonga	22	755	26	740	16597
Trinidad Tobago	11	843	14	1260	7813
Tunisia	13	773	17	858	1729
Turkey	13	990	14	1235	2168
Uganda	33	3050	33	3215	6039
Ukraine	30	1865	33	2155	1696
United Arab Emirates	7	630	7	590	4824
United States	6	1090	5	1315	7595
Uruguay	16	1125	18	1440	11496
Uzbekistan	80	4585	99	4750	4539

(*Continued*)

Table A.3: (*Continued*)

Country	Time to export (Days)	Cost of export (US$)	Time to import (Days)	Cost of import (US$)	Dist. to Germany (km)
Vanuatu	21	1690	20	1690	15745
Venezuela	49	2590	71	2868	8290
Vietnam	21	610	21	600	9259
Yemen	29	995	25	1490	5136
Zambia	44	2765	56	3560	7517
Zimbabwe	53	3280	73	5200	8044
N	151	151	151	151	151
mean	23.93	1565	27.04	1876	7072
SD	15.79	1134	18.49	1449	3530
min	5	435	4	420	543
max	81	8450	101	9800	18220
p1	5	456	5	439	853
p50	20	1240	22	1510	7014
p99	80	5902	99	8525	16597

Note: For description and source of data, see text.

References

Alessandria, George, Joseph P. Kaborski, and Virgiliu Midrigan (2010). Inventories, lumpy trade, and large devaluations. *American Economic Review* 100 (5), 2304–2339.

Békés, Gábor, Lionel Fontagné, Balázs Murakösy, and Vincent Vicard (2011). Frequency of export: An additional margin of trade. Extended abstract, December 9.

Békés, Gábor, Lionel Fontagné, Balázs Murakösy, and Vincent Vicard (2015). Shipment frequency of exporters and demand uncertainty: An inventory management approach. *Centre for Economic Policy Research CEPR Discussion Paper* 11013, December.

Hornok, Cecília and Miklós Koren (2015a). Per-shipment costs and the lumpiness of international trade. *Review of Economics and Statistics* 97 (2), 525–530.

Hornok, Cecília and Miklós Koren (2015b). Administrative barriers to trade. *Journal of International Economics* 96, Supplement 1, S110–S122.

Kropf, Andreas and Philip Sauré (2014). Fixed costs per shipment. *Journal of International Economics* 92 (1), 166–184.

Mayer, Thierry and Soledad Zignago (2011). Notes on CEPII's distance measures: The GeoDist database. *CEPII Document de Travail*, No 2011–25, December.

Wagner, Joachim (2016). A survey of empirical studies using transaction level data on exports and imports. *Review of World Economics* 152 (1), 215–225.

World Trade Organization (2014). World Trade Report 2014. Trade and public policies: A closer look at non-tariff measures in the 21st century. Geneva: WTO.

Chapter 24

Trade Costs Shocks and Lumpiness of Imports: Evidence from the Fukushima Disaster*

Abstract

This paper uses a difference-in-differences approach to test the hypothesis that the increase in the per-shipment costs of imports from Japan due to the Fukushima disaster in 2011 lead to an increase in the lumpiness of imports from Japan. Using China and the USA as control groups it is found that the Fukushima trade cost shock reduced the average number of import transactions per year at the firm-good level and, therefore, increased the degree of lumpiness of imports from Japan.

Keywords: Fukushima disaster, trade shock, imports, Germany.

*Originally Published in *Economics Bulletin* (2017), 37 (1), 149–155.
All computations were done at the Research Data Centre of the Federal Statistical Office in Wiesbaden. I thank Melanie Scheller for preparing the transaction level data and for checking the output of my do-files for the violation of privacy. The micro data used are strictly confidential but not exclusive; see http://www.forschungsdatenzentrum.de/ datenzugang.asp for information on how to access the data. To facilitate replications the Stata do-files used are available from the author on request.

1. Motivation

Transaction level data on exports and imports of firms from many countries have been used in a large number of empirical studies to investigate the margins of foreign trade. These data typically have information on the goods traded by a firm (at a detailed classification level), the countries these goods are traded with, the value of each export and import transaction and the weight of the goods traded. Empirical studies look at the number of goods traded by a firm and the number of countries traded with and its relation with firm characteristics (like size, age or productivity) and with dimensions of firm performance (like growth and profits). These empirical studies shed new light on many topics related to international trade activities of firms (see Wagner, 2016b for a review of this literature).

At the firm level, shipping frequency — the number of times a specific good is traded by one firm with a firm in a specific foreign country during a time period — can be considered as an additional margin of trade besides the intensive margin (the volume of trade) and the extensive margins made of the number of goods traded and the number of countries traded with (see Békés *et al.*, 2011). This shipping frequency is related to trade costs. International trade is costly, and these trade costs are in part not proportional to the value of the international transaction. There are fixed costs that come with every shipment including paper work (filling in customs declarations and other forms) and the time and monetary costs related to having the cargo inspected. These fixed costs lead to a trade-off between per-shipment trade costs and shipping frequency. On the one hand, firms would like to economize on per-shipment costs by sending fewer and larger shipments. On the other hand, this comes at a cost due to time-lags related to waiting to fill a larger shipment and because of the need to keep costly inventories between shipment arrivals (see Hornok and Koren, 2015).

Therefore, per-shipment costs may make it optimal for traders to engage in cross-border transactions infrequently, and trade flows at the level of the firm — imports (exports) by a firm of a specific good from (to) a specific country — are lumpy. That said, a reduction of per-shipment costs can be expected to lead to a decrease in the degree of lumpiness of trade and to foster international trade. Evidence on the link between trade costs and lumpiness of trade, therefore, is important to understand the size of these effects.

While a high degree of lumpiness of trade has been documented for a number of countries, empirical evidence for the role of trade costs in shaping this lumpiness is scarce. Furthermore, this evidence is based on cross-section regressions only. The reason for this shortcoming is that the indicators used to measure per-shipment trade costs are either constant (like distance to the country of origin or destination) or highly stable (like the time that it takes to have a container inspected by the customs, or the costs related to exporting a container) over time for a single country of destination or origin, and do vary only between countries (see Wagner, 2016a).

This paper contributes to the literature by using an exogenous shock that lead to an increase in the per-shipment costs of imports from one country of origin to Germany to identify the effect of per-shipment costs on the degree of lumpiness of imports. On 11 March 2011, in Japan a tsunami disabled the power supply and cooling of three Fukushima Daiichi reactors, causing a disastrous nuclear accident. As a consequence, imports from Japan were inspected carefully by the customs to detect any radioactivity that might have contaminated the cargo. This lead to an increase of per-shipment costs for imports from Japan due to a delay in time of delivery caused by this inspection.[1] Per-shipment costs for imports from other countries of origin did not change due to the Fukushima disaster.

In this paper we use a difference-in-differences approach (discussed in detail in Section 3) to test the hypothesis that the increase in the per-shipment costs of imports from Japan between 2010 and 2011due to the Fukushima disaster lead to an increase in the lumpiness of imports from Japan. In doing so, China and the USA, the most important countries of

---

[1] See contemporaneous newspaper articles, e.g., http://www.focus.de/wissen/natur/ katastrophen/tid-21835/atomkatastrophe-strahlende-importe_aid_613820.html, http:// www.handelsblatt.com/-panorama/aus-aller-welt/fukushima-verseuchung-des-meeres- weitet-sich-aus/4016560.html, http://www.n-tv.de/wirtschaft/Europas-Haefen-ruesten- sich-article2976226.html.

origin for German imports outside the EU in 2011, are used as control groups.

To anticipate the most important result, we find that the increase in the per-shipment costs due to the Fukushima disaster reduced the average number of transactions per year and, therefore, increased the degree of lumpiness of imports from Japan.

The rest of the paper is organized as follows. Section 2 introduces the data used, Section 3 presents the empirical investigation, Section 4 concludes.

2. Data

This paper uses transaction-level data for German imports from Japan, China and the USA. In Germany information on goods traded across borders and on the countries traded with is available from the statistic on foreign trade (*Außenhandelsstatistik*). For trade with non-EU countries the source of information is data collected by the customs (the so-called *Extrahandelsstatistik*). The data used in this paper are based on these raw data at the transaction level. The unit of observation in these raw data is a single transaction between economic agents located in two countries, e.g., the import of X kilogram of *good A* with a value of Y Euro from Japan to Germany. For a given year, the sum over all transactions is identical to the figures published by the Federal Statistical Office for total imports of Germany.

The record of the transaction usually includes a firm identifier (tax registration number) of the trading German firm.[2] Using this identifier information at the transaction level can be aggregated at the level of the trading firm. These data show which firm trades how much of which good with firms from which country in a given month. Products are distinguished according to very detailed classifications. In the data used for this paper, the Harmonized System at 6-digit level (HS6) is used as the product classification system.

---

[2] Note that this identifier is missing for several transactions for various reasons including traders that do not have a (German) tax identification number; further details were not revealed to me.

3. Empirical Investigation

The degree of lumpiness of imports is measured by the number of import transactions at the firm-product-country level. In the German data used here trade frequency is measured by the number of months in a year in which transactions of this firm-good-country combination are recorded. Note that within a month all imports of a specific HS6-good from a specific country by one single firm are aggregated and reported as one data point only. Therefore, the proxy for trade frequency used here may be biased for high frequency traders which import the same good from the same country in (nearly) every month several times. For low frequency traders, however, the number of months with recorded transactions is a reliable approximation (see the discussion in Békés *et al.*, 2015).

That said, information on the lumpiness of German imports from Japan (the country where the Fukushima disaster happened), China and the USA (the countries that are used as control group) in 2010 (the year before the disaster) and 2011 (when on 11 March the nuclear catastrophe happened) is reported in Table 1.

In line with results reported for other countries and for Germany before Table 1 shows a high degree of lumpiness of imports for all three countries in both years. About two thirds of all firm-good-country combinations are recorded only once or twice. The frequency of recorded transactions tends to decline with an increase in the number of transactions per year. This is in accordance with the presence of per-shipment fixed costs that provide an incentive for importers to engage in cross-border transactions infrequently. However, there is a remarkable increase in the frequency of the number of transactions when it comes to 12 transactions per year. This might be due to the fact (mentioned above) that within a month all imports of a specific HS6-good from a specific country by one single firm are aggregated and reported as one data point only. Therefore, the proxy for trade frequency used here may be biased for high frequency traders which trade the same good with the same country in (nearly) every month several times.

The big picture is remarkably similar for the three countries considered. The average number of transactions — a summary measure of the degree of lumpiness of imports in trade with a country — does not differ

Table 1: German import transactions per year by firm-good-country of origin.

Country	Japan		China		USA	
year	2010 (Share; %)	2011 (Share; %)	2010 (Share; %)	2011 (Share; %)	2010 (Share; %)	2011 (Share; %)
Number of transactions per year						
1	51.87	52.12	51.76	52.05	55.89	57.24
2	13.36	13.47	14.76	14.84	14.10	13.98
3	7.05	6.92	7.80	7.77	7.02	6.80
4	4.45	4.57	5.13	5.02	4.48	4.33
5	3.40	3.39	3.68	3.67	3.19	3.08
6	2.72	2.65	2.91	2.82	2.45	2.36
7	2.33	2.26	2.38	2.33	2.05	1.88
8	2.02	1.99	2.02	2.02	1.75	1.68
9	2.04	1.96	1.81	1.78	1.64	1.55
10	2.12	2.10	1.78	1.77	1.66	1.50
11	2.26	2.23	1.90	1.86	1.75	1.61
12	6.39	6.36	4.07	4.06	4.02	3.99
Average number of transactions	3.24	3.22	2.98	2.96	2.81	2.74

Note: Number of transactions refers to months with recorded import transactions at the firm-product-country of origin level; goods refer to categories at the HS6 level.

much between the countries, and it is stable over time though it decreased slightly in all three countries from 2010 to 2011 (pointing to a small increase in the degree of lumpiness of imports).

From the results reported in Table 1 one might conclude that the trade cost shock caused by the Fukushima disaster did not have any impact on the degree of lumpiness of imports from Japan. This conclusion, however, might be precipitate. It has been documented for a number of countries that many firm-product-country combinations in international trade are recorded in one year only and do not survive over a longer period (see Wagner, 2016b, Section 3.3, for a survey of these studies). Given that the link between per-shipment trade costs and the degree of lumpiness of imports tends to be different for different goods and

Table 2: Number of firm-HS6 good-country of origin observations in German imports.

	2010 only (Share; %)	2011 only (Share; %)	2010 and 2011 (Share; %)
Japan	47,667	53,723	98,544
	(23.84)	(26.87)	(49.29)
China	217,217	270,234	429,598
	(23.69)	(29.47)	(46.85)
USA	167,067	211,630	309,500
	(24.28)	(30.75)	(44.97)

different firms (see Wagner, 2016a) changes in the degree of lumpiness should be investigated for firm-product-country combinations that took place in both years only.

Table 2 documents that this point might be highly relevant for an analysis of German imports from Japan, China and the USA in 2010–2011. Only about half of all firm-good-country observations in German imports in this period are observed in both years. The econometric investigation uses only these survivor cases.

To test for the presence of an impact of the Fukushima trade cost shock on the degree of lumpiness of German imports from Japan, and to estimate the size of this effect, a difference-in-differences approach is applied.[3] Informally stated, for all firm-good combinations in imports from Japan that were observed in 2010 and in 2011 the difference in the number of transactions that took place in 2010 and 2011 is computed, and this difference is compared to the respective difference in the number of transactions in imports from either China or the USA. Formally, the following empirical model is estimated (by OLS)[4]

[1] $transactions_i = \text{ß}0 + \text{ß}_1 \times year_i + \text{ß}_2 \times Japan_i + \text{ß}_3 \times year_i \times Japan_i + e_i$

Here, transactions is the number of import transactions by firm i (the outcome variable), $year_i$ is a dummy variable that has either the value 0

---

[3] A discussion of any details of this method is beyond the scope of this paper; see Angrist and Pischke (2015), Ch. 5, for a textbook treatment.
[4] Computations used the Stata command diff (Villa, 2016).

Table 3: Effect of Fukushima disaster on lumpiness
of German imports from Japan.

Control group	China	USA
Estimated effect	−0.060	−0.063
Robust standard errors	0.028	0.029

Note: The estimated effect is the regression coefficient of
the interaction term between a dummy variable indicating
whether a transaction occurred with a firm in Japan (1) or
with a firm from the country in the control group (0) and
a dummy variable indicating whether the transaction took
place in 2010 (0) or in 2011 (1); see text.

(for 2010, the period before the disaster) or the value 1 (for 2011, the period in which the disaster happened), $Japan_i$ is a dummy variable that has either the value one (for imports from Japan, the treatment group) or the value zero (for imports from the country that serves as a control group, i.e., either China or the USA), and e_i is an error term. $ß_3$, the regression coefficient of the interaction term of the variable year and the variable Japan, is the difference-in-differences estimate of the treatment effect — the import costs shock due to the Fukushima disaster.

Results from the difference-in-differences analysis are reported in Table 3.[5] In line with the hypothesis stated in the introductory section the estimated treatment effect is negative (indicating an increase in the degree of lumpiness of imports due to the increase in per-shipment costs), statistically significant at a usual error level, and of the same size for firms from both control groups.

4. Concluding Remarks

This paper uses a difference-in-differences approach to test the hypothesis that the increase in the per-shipment costs of imports from Japan due to the Fukushima disaster in 2011 lead to an increase in the lumpiness of imports from Japan. Using China and the USA as control groups it is

---

[5] To economize on space, only the estimated treatment effects and its p-values are reported. The complete results for all coefficients and more statistics are available on request.

found that the Fukushima trade cost shock reduced the average number of import transactions per year at the firm-good level and, therefore, increased the degree of lumpiness of imports from Japan.

However, the size of the estimated effect of the Fukushima trade cost shock that points to a reduction of the average number of import transactions per year by 0.06 can be regarded as small compared to the average number of transactions reported in Table 1. This small size of the effect might be due to a small size of the increase in per-shipment costs. While I am not aware of any estimates of this increase in trade costs, anecdotal evidence points to an increase of the waiting time for the delivery of imported goods from Japan due to time-lags introduced by additional inspection of containers by the port authorities and customs as the source of increased costs. Maybe, a few days more until the goods can leave the port are considered as a small cost shocks that leads to a small change in import behavior of the firms only.

Furthermore, it should be kept in mind that the empirical study performed in this note is limited by the available data. Typically for an application of a difference-in-differences approach we require pre-treatment trends across the different countries to be the same. Given that here information on one pre-treatment year only is available this assumption cannot be tested. Also, it would have been interesting to see how long it takes for the effect to die out. However, due to the fact that data for the years after the shock are not (yet) available, this is not possible. These limitations of the study should be kept in mind when putting the reported results into perspective.

References

Angrist, Joshua D. and Jörn-Steffen Pischke (2015). Mastering 'metrics. The path from cause to effect. Princeton and Oxford: Princeton University Press.

Békés, Gábor, Lionel Fontagné, Balázs Muraközy, and Vincent Vicard (2011). Frequency of export: An additional margin of trade. Extended abstract, December 9.

Békés, Gábor, Lionel Fontagné, Balázs Muraközy, and Vincent Vicard (2015). Shipment frequency of exporters and demand uncertainty: An inventory management approach. *Centre for Economic Policy Research CEPR Discussion Paper* 11013, December.

Hornok, Cecília and Miklós Koren (2015). Per-shipment costs and the lumpiness of international trade. *Review of Economics and Statistics* 97 (2), 525–530.

Villa, Juan M. (2016). Diff: Simplifying the estimation of difference-in-differences treatment effects. *The Stata Journal* 16 (1), 52–71.

Wagner, Joachim (2016a). The lumpiness of German exports and imports of goods. *Economics — The Open-Access, Open-Assessment E-Journal* 10 (2016–21), 1–38.

Wagner, Joachim (2016b). A survey of empirical studies using transaction level data on exports and imports. *Review of World Economics* 152 (1), 215–225.